# Digital Speech Processing, Synthesis, and Recognition

## ELECTRICAL ENGINEERING AND ELECTRONICS

*A Series of Reference Books and Textbooks*

1. Rational Fault Analysis, *edited by Richard Saeks and S. R. Liberty*
2. Nonparametric Methods in Communications, *edited by P. Papantoni-Kazakos and Dimitri Kazakos*
3. Interactive Pattern Recognition, *Yi-tzuu Chien*
4. Solid-State Electronics, *Lawrence E. Murr*
5. Electronic, Magnetic, and Thermal Properties of Solid Materials, *Klaus Schröder*
6. Magnetic-Bubble Memory Technology, *Hsu Chang*
7. Transformer and Inductor Design Handbook, *Colonel Wm. T. McLyman*
8. Electromagnetics: Classical and Modern Theory and Applications, *Samuel Seely and Alexander D. Poularikas*
9. One-Dimensional Digital Signal Processing, *Chi-Tsong Chen*
10. Interconnected Dynamical Systems, *Raymond A. DeCarlo and Richard Saeks*
11. Modern Digital Control Systems, *Raymond G. Jacquot*
12. Hybrid Circuit Design and Manufacture, *Roydn D. Jones*
13. Magnetic Core Selection for Transformers and Inductors: A User's Guide to Practice and Specification, *Colonel Wm. T. McLyman*
14. Static and Rotating Electromagnetic Devices, *Richard H. Engelmann*
15. Energy-Efficient Electric Motors: Selection and Application, *John C. Andreas*
16. Electromagnetic Compossibility, *Heinz M. Schlicke*
17. Electronics: Models, Analysis, and Systems, *James G. Gottling*
18. Digital Filter Design Handbook, *Fred J. Taylor*
19. Multivariable Control: An Introduction, *P. K. Sinha*
20. Flexible Circuits: Design and Applications, *Steve Gurley, with contributions by Carl A. Edstrom, Jr., Ray D. Greenway, and William P. Kelly*
21. Circuit Interruption: Theory and Techniques, *Thomas E. Browne, Jr.*
22. Switch Mode Power Conversion: Basic Theory and Design, *K. Kit Sum*
23. Pattern Recognition: Applications to Large Data-Set Problems, *Sing-Tze Bow*
24. Custom-Specific Integrated Circuits: Design and Fabrication, *Stanley L. Hurst*
25. Digital Circuits: Logic and Design, *Ronald C. Emery*
26. Large-Scale Control Systems: Theories and Techniques, *Magdi S. Mahmoud, Mohamed F. Hassan, and Mohamed G. Darwish*
27. Microprocessor Software Project Management, *Eli T. Fathi and Cedric V. W. Armstrong (Sponsored by Ontario Centre for Microelectronics)*
28. Low Frequency Electromagnetic Design, *Michael P. Perry*
29. Multidimensional Systems: Techniques and Applications, *edited by Spyros G. Tzafestas*
30. AC Motors for High-Performance Applications: Analysis and Control, *Sakae Yamamura*

31. Ceramic Materials for Electronics: Processing, Properties, and Applications, *edited by Relva C. Buchanan*
32. Microcomputer Bus Structures and Bus Interface Design, *Arthur L. Dexter*
33. End User's Guide to Innovative Flexible Circuit Packaging, *Jay J. Miniet*
34. Reliability Engineering for Electronic Design, *Norman B. Fuqua*
35. Design Fundamentals for Low-Voltage Distribution and Control, *Frank W. Kussy and Jack L. Warren*
36. Encapsulation of Electronic Devices and Components, *Edward R. Salmon*
37. Protective Relaying: Principles and Applications, *J. Lewis Blackburn*
38. Testing Active and Passive Electronic Components, *Richard F. Powell*
39. Adaptive Control Systems: Techniques and Applications, *V. V. Chalam*
40. Computer-Aided Analysis of Power Electronic Systems, *Venkatachari Rajagopalan*
41. Integrated Circuit Quality and Reliability, *Eugene R. Hnatek*
42. Systolic Signal Processing Systems, *edited by Earl E. Swartzlander, Jr.*
43. Adaptive Digital Filters and Signal Analysis, *Maurice G. Bellanger*
44. Electronic Ceramics: Properties, Configuration, and Applications, *edited by Lionel M. Levinson*
45. Computer Systems Engineering Management, *Robert S. Alford*
46. Systems Modeling and Computer Simulation, *edited by Naim A. Kheir*
47. Rigid-Flex Printed Wiring Design for Production Readiness, *Walter S. Rigling*
48. Analog Methods for Computer-Aided Circuit Analysis and Diagnosis, *edited by Takao Ozawa*
49. Transformer and Inductor Design Handbook, Second Edition, Revised and Expanded, *Colonel Wm. T. McLyman*
50. Power System Grounding and Transients: An Introduction, *A. P. Sakis Meliopoulos*
51. Signal Processing Handbook, *edited by C. H. Chen*
52. Electronic Product Design for Automated Manufacturing, *H. Richard Stillwell*
53. Dynamic Models and Discrete Event Simulation, *William Delaney and Erminia Vaccari*
54. FET Technology and Application: An Introduction, *Edwin S. Oxner*
55. Digital Speech Processing, Synthesis, and Recognition, *Sadaoki Furui*
56. VLSI RISC Architecture and Organization, *Stephen B. Furber*
57. Surface Mount and Related Technologies, *Gerald Ginsberg*

*Additional Volumes in Preparation*

Uninterruptable Power Supplies, *David C. Griffith*
Polyphase Induction Motor Analysis, Design, and Application, *Paul L. Cochran*

**Electrical Engineering-Electronics Software**

1. Transformer and Inductor Design Software for the IBM PC, *Colonel Wm. T. McLyman*
2. Transformer and Inductor Design Software for the Macintosh, *Colonel Wm. T. McLyman*
3. Digital Filter Design Software for the IBM PC, *Fred J. Taylor and Thanos Stouraitis*

# Digital Speech Processing, Synthesis, and Recognition

**Sadaoki Furui**
NTT Human Interface Laboratories
Nippon Telegraph and Telephone Corporation
Musashino-Shi, Tokyo, Japan

MARCEL DEKKER, INC. New York and Basel

Library of Congress Cataloging-in-Publication Data

Furui, Sadaoki.
Digital speech processing, synthesis, and recognition.

(Electrical engineering and electronics ; 55)
Based on the author's Digital speech processing.
Tokyo : Tokai University Press, 1985.
Bibliography: p.
Includes index.
1. Speech processing systems. I. Furui, Sadaoki.
Dijitaru onsei shori. English. II. Title.
III. Series.
TK7882.S65F87 1989 621.39'9 88-33506
ISBN 0-8247-7965-7 (alk. paper)

This book is printed on acid-free paper.



MARCEL DEKKER, INC.
270 Madison Avenue, New York, New York 10016

Current printing (last digit):
10 9 8 7 6 5 4 3 2 1

PRINTED IN THE UNITED STATES OF AMERICA

# Preface

Research in speech processing has recently witnessed remarkable progress. Such progress has ensured the wide use of speech recognizers and synthesizers in a great many fields, such as banking services and data input during quality control inspections. Although the level and range of applications remain somewhat restricted, this technological progress has transpired through an efficient and effective combination of the long and continuing history of speech research with the latest remarkable advances in digital signal processing (DSP) technologies. In particular, these DSP technologies, including fast Fourier transform, linear predictive coding, and cepstrum representation, have been developed principally to solve several of the more complicated problems in speech processing. The aim of this book is, therefore, to introduce the reader to the most fundamental and important speech processing technologies derived from the level of technological progress reached in speech production, coding, analysis, synthesis, and recognition, as well as in speaker recognition.

Although the structure of this book is based on my book in Japanese entitled "Digital Speech Processing" (Tokai University Press, Tokyo, 1985), I have revised and updated almost all chapters in line with the latest progress. The present book also includes several important speech processing technologies developed in Japan, which, for the most part, are somewhat unfamiliar to researchers from western nations. Nevertheless, I have made every effort to remain as objective as possible in presenting the state of the art of speech processing.

This book has been designed primarily to serve as a text for an advanced undergraduate- or for a first-year graduate-level course. It has also been designed as a reference book with the speech researcher in mind. The reader is expected to have an introductory understanding of linear systems and digital signal processing.

Several people have had a significant impact, both directly and indirectly, on the material presented in this book. My biggest debt of gratitude goes to Drs. Shuzo Saito and Fumitada Itakura, both former heads of the Fourth Research Section of the Electrical Communications Laboratories (ECLs), Nippon Telegraph and Telephone Corporation (NTT). For many years they have provided me with invaluable insight into the conducting and reporting of my research. In addition, I had the priviledge of working as a visiting researcher from 1978 to 1979 in AT&T Bell Laboratories' Acoustics Research Department under Dr. James L. Flanagan. During that period, I profited immeasurably from his views and opinions. Doctors Saito, Itakura, and Flanagan have not only had a profound effect on my personal life and professional career but have also had a direct influence in many ways on the information presented in this book.

I also wish to thank the many members of NTT's ECLs for providing me with the necessary support and stimulating environment in which many of the ideas outlined in this book could be developed. Dr. Frank K. Soong of AT&T Bell Laboratories deserves a note of gratitude for his valuable comments and criticism on Chapter 6 during his stay at the ECLs as a visiting researcher. Additionally, I would like to extend my sincere thanks to Patrick Fulmer of Nexus International Corporation, Tokyo, for his careful technical review of the manuscript.

Finally, I would like to express my deep and endearing appreciation to my wife and family for their patience and for the time they sacrificed on my behalf throughout the book's preparation.

Sadaoki Furui

# Acknowledgments

I am grateful for permission from many organizations and authors to use their copyright material, in original or adapted form:

- Figure 2.5 contains material which is copyright © Lawrence Erlbaum Associates, 1986. Used with permission. All rights reserved.
- Figures 2.6 and 7.5 contain material which is copyright © Dr. H. Sato, 1975 and 1984. Reprinted with permission of copyright owner. All rights reserved.
- Figures 2.7, 3.8, 4.9, 7.1, 7.4, 7.6, and 7.7 contain material which is copyright © 1952, 1980, 1967, 1972, 1980, 1987, 1987 American Institute of Physics, respectively. Reproduced with permission. All rights reserved.
- Figures 2.8, 2.9, and 2.10 contain material which is copyright © Dr. H. Irii, 1987. Used with permission. All rights reserved.
- Figure 2.11 contains material which is copyright © Dr. S. Saito, 1958. Reprinted with permission of copyright owner. All rights rights reserved.
- Figure 3.5 contains material which is copyright © Dr. G. Fant, 1959. Reproduced with permission. All rights reserved.
- Figures 3.6, 3.7, 6.4, 6.18, 6.33, 7.8, and 8.9 contain material which is copyright © 1972, 1972, 1975, 1986, 1986, 1986, 1986 AT&T, respectively. Used with permission. All rights reserved.
- Figures 3.9 and 3.10 contain material which is copyright © Dr. K. Shirai, 1980. Reprinted with permission of copyright owner. All rights reserved.

- Figures 4.12, 4.14, 4.15, 6.10, 6.11, 6.17, 6.19, 6.23, 6.24, 6.25, 6.29, 6.30, 6.31, 6.32, 8.4, 8.11, 8.17, 8.18, 9.10, B.1, E.1, E.2 and E.3 contain material which is copyright © 1983, 1983, 1966, 1986, 1986, 1982, 1982, 1981, 1982, 1981, 1983, 1983, 1983, 1980, 1978, 1981, 1987, 1979, 1985, 1984, 1987, 1987, 1987, IEEE, respectively. Reproduced with permission. All rights reserved.

- Figures 5.2, 5.3, 5.9, 5.10, 5.11 and 5.22, as well as Tables 4.1, 4.3, 4.4 and 5.1 contain material which is copyright © Dr. F. Itakura, 1970, 1970, 1971, 1971, 1973, 1981, 1978, 1981, 1978 and 1981, respectively. Used with permission of copyright owner. All rights reserved.

- Figures 5.14, 5.15 and 5.16 contain material which is copyright © Dr. N. Kitawaki, 1978. Reprinted with permission of copyright owner. All rights reserved.

- Figure 5.19 contains material which is copyright © Dr. T. Nakajima, 1978. Reproduced with permission. All rights reserved.

- Figures 6.20 and 6.22 contain material which is copyright © Dr. T. Moriya, 1986. Used with permission of copyright owner. All rights reserved.

- Figures 6.34, 6.35 and C.1 contain material which is copyright © Mr. Y. Shiraki, 1986 and 1988. Reprinted with permission of copyright owner. All rights reserved.

- Figures 6.38, 6.39 and 6.40 contain material which is copyright © Mr. T. Watanabe, 1982. Reproduced with permission. All rights reserved.

- Figure 7.9 contains material which is copyright © Dr. D. B. Pisoni, 1979. Reprinted with permission. All rights reserved.

- Figure 8.15 contains material which is copyright © Media Dimensions, 1986. Reproduced with permission. All rights reserved.

- Figure 8.19 contains material which is copyright © Dr. T. Watanabe, 1981. Used with permission of copyright owner. All rights reserved.

- Table 8.4 contains material which is copyright © Dr. S. Nagakawa, 1983. Reprinted with permission. All rights reserved.

# Contents

# Digital Speech Processing, Synthesis, and Recognition

# 1

# Introduction

Speech communication is one of the basic and most essential capabilities possessed by human beings. Speech can be said to be the single most important method through which people can readily convey information without the need for any "carry-along" tool. Although we passively receive more stimuli from outside through the eyes than through the ears, mutually communicating visually is almost totally ineffective compared to what is possible through speech communication.

The speech wave itself conveys linguistic information, the speaker's tone, and the speaker's emotion. Information exchange by speech clearly plays a very significant role in our lives. The acoustical and linguistic structures of speech have been confirmed to be intricately related to our intellectual ability, and are, moreover, closely intertwined with our cultural and social development. Interestingly, the most culturally developed areas in the world correspond to those areas in which the telephone network is the most highly developed.

One evening in early 1875, Alexander Graham Bell was speaking with his assistant T.A. Watson (Fagen, 1975). He had just conceived the idea of a mechanism based on the structure of the human ear during the course of his research into fabricating a telegram machine for conveying music. He said, "Watson, I have another idea I haven't told you about that I think will surprise you. If I can get a mechanism which will make a current of electricity vary in its intensity as the air varies in density when a sound is passing through it, I can telegraph any sound, even the sound of speech." This, as we know, became the central concept coming to fruition as the telephone in the following year.

The invention of the telephone constitutes not only the most important epoch in the history of communications, but it also represents the first step in which speech began to be dealt with as an engineering target. The history of speech research actually started, however, long before the invention of the telephone. Initial speech research began with the development of mechanical speech synthesizers toward the end of the 18th century and into vocal vibration and hearing mechanisms in the mid-19th century. Before the invention of pulse code modulation (PCM) in 1938, however, the speech wave had been dealt with by analog processing techniques. The invention of PCM and the development of digital circuits and electronic computers have made possible the digital processing of speech and have brought about the remarkable progress in speech information processing, especially after 1960.

The two most important papers to appear since 1960 were presented at the 6th International Congress on Acoustics held in Tokyo, Japan, in 1968: the paper on a speech analysis-synthesis system based on the maximum likelihood method presented by NTT's Electrical Communications Laboratories, and the paper on predictive coding presented by Bell Laboratories. These papers essentially produced the greatest thrust to progress in speech information processing technology; in other words, they opened the way to digital speech processing technology. Specifically, both papers deal with the information compression technique using the linear prediction of speech waves and are based on mathematical techniques for stochastic processes. These techniques gave rise to linear predictive coding (LPC), which has led to the creation of a new academic field. Various other complementary digital speech processing techniques have also been developed. In combination, these techniques have facilitated the realization of a wide range of systems operating on the principles of speech coding, speech analysis-synthesis, speech synthesis, speech recognition, and speaker recognition.

Books on speech information processing have already been published, and each has its own special features (Flanagan, 1972; Markel and Gray 1976; Rabiner and Schafer, 1978; Saito and Nakata, 1985). The purpose of the present book is to explain the technologies essential to the speech researcher and to clarify and hopefully widen his or her understanding of speech by focusing on the most recent of the digital processing technologies. I hope that those readers planning to study and conduct research in the area of speech information processing will find this book useful as a reference or text. To those readers already extensively involved in speech research, I hope it will serve as a guidebook for sorting through the increasingly more sophisticated knowledge base forming around the technology and for gaining insight into expected future progress.

I have tried to cite wherever possible the most important aspects of the speech information processing field, including the precise development of equations, by omitting what is now considered classic information. In such instances, I have recommended well-known reference books. Since understanding the intricate relationships between various aspects of digital speech processing technology is essential to speech researchers, I have attempted to maintain a sense of descriptive unity and to sufficiently describe the mutual relationships between the techniques involved. I have also tried to refer to as many notable papers as permissible to further broaden the reader's perspective. Due to space restrictions, however, several important research areas, such as noise reduction and echo cancellation, unfortunately could not be included in this book.

Chapters 2, 3, and 4 explore the fundamental and principal elements of digital speech processing technology. Chapters 5 through 9 present the more important techniques as well as applications of LPC analysis, speech waveform coding, speech synthesis, speech recognition, and speaker recognition. The final chapter discusses future research problems. Several important concepts, terms, and mathematical relationships are precisely explained in the appendixes. Since the design of this book relates the digital speech processing techniques to each other in developmental and precise terms as mentioned, the reader is urged to read each chapter of this book in the order presented.

# 2

# Principal Characteristics of Speech

## 2.1 LINGUISTIC INFORMATION

The speech wave conveys several kinds of information, which consists principally of linguistic information that indicates the meaning the speaker wishes to impart, individual information representing who is speaking, and emotional information depicting the emotion of the speaker. Needless to say, the first informational type is the most important.

Undeniably, the ability to acquire and produce language and to actually make and use tools are the two principal features that distinguish humans from other animals. Furthermore, language and cultural development are inseparable. Although written language is effective for exchanging knowledge and lasts longer than spoken language if properly preserved, the amount of information exchanged by speech is considerably larger. In more simplified terms, books, magazines, and the like are effective as one-way information transmission media, but are wholly unsuited to two-way communication.

Human speech production begins with the initial conceptualization of an idea which the speaker wants to convey to a listener. The speaker subsequently converts that idea into a linguistic structure by selecting the appropriate words or phrases which distinctly represent it, and then ordering them according to loose or rigid grammatical rules depending upon the speaker-listener relationship. Following these processes, the human brain produces motor nerve commands which move the various muscles of the vocal organs. This process is essentially divisible into two subprocesses: the physiological process involving nerves and muscles, and the physical process through which the speech wave is produced and propagated. The speech characteristics as physical phenomena are continuous, although language conveyed by speech is essentially composed of discretely coded units.

A sentence is constructed using basic word units, with each word being composed of syllables, and each syllable being composed of phonemes, which, in turn, can be classified as vowels or consonants. Although the syllable itself is not well defined, one syllable is generally formed by the concatenation of one vowel and one to several consonants. The number of vowels and consonants vary, depending on the classification method and language involved. Roughly speaking, English has 12 vowels and 24 consonants, whereas Japanese has 5 vowels and 20 consonants. The number of phonemes in a language rarely exceeds 50. Since there are combination rules for building phonemes into syllables, the number of syllables in each language comprises only a fraction of all possible phoneme combinations.

In contrast with the phoneme, which is the smallest speech unit from the linguistic or phonemic point of view, the physical unit of actual speech is referred to as the phone. The phoneme and phone are respectively indicated by phonemic and phonetic symbols, such as /a/ and [a]. As another example, the phones [ɛ] and [e], which correspond to the phonemes /ɛ/ and /e/ in French, correspond to the same phoneme /e/ in Japanese.

Although the number of words in each language is very large and new words are constantly added, the total number is much smaller than all of the syllable or phoneme combinations possible. It has been claimed that the number of frequently used words is between 2000 and 3000, and that the number of words used by the average person lies between 5000 and 10,000.

Stress and intonation also play critical roles in indicating the location of important words, in making interrogative sentences, and in conveying the emotion of the speaker.

## 2.2 SPEECH AND HEARING

Speech is uttered for the purpose of being, and on the assumption that it actually is, received and understood by the intended listeners. This obviously means that speech production is intrinsically related to hearing ability.

The speech wave produced by the vocal organs is transmitted through the air to the ears of the listeners, as shown in Fig.

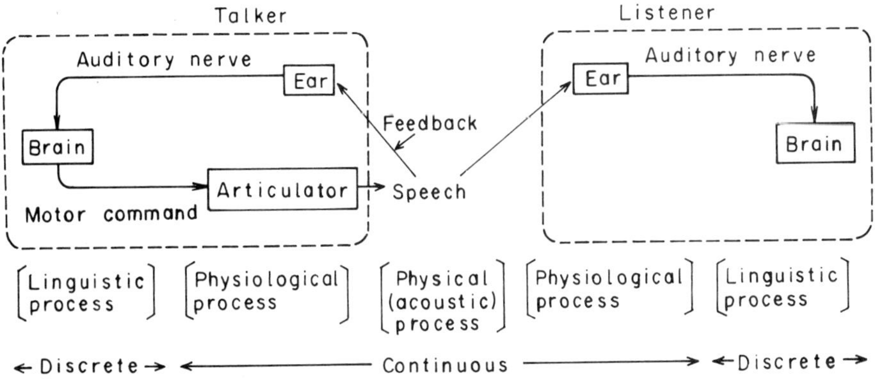


Fig. 2.1 Speech chain.

2.1. At the ear, it activates the hearing organs to produce nerve impulses which are transmitted to the listener's brain through the auditory nerve system. This permits the linguistic information which the speaker intends to convey to be readily understood by the listener. The same speech wave is naturally transmitted to the speaker's ears as well, allowing him to continuously control his vocal organs by receiving his own speech as feedback. The critical importance of this feedback mechanism is clearly apparent with people whose hearing has become disabled for more than a year or two. It is also evident in the fact that it is very hard to speak when our own speech is fed back to our ear with a certain amount of time delay (delayed feedback effect).

The intrinsic connection between speech production and hearing is called the speech chain (Denes and Pinson, 1963). In terms of production, the speech chain consists of the linguistic, physiological, and physical (acoustical) stages, the order of which is reversed for hearing.

The human hearing mechanism constitutes such a sophisticated capability that, at this point in time anyway, it cannot be closely imitated by artificial intelligence (AI) means. One advantage of this hearing capability is selective listening, which permits the listener to hear only one voice even when several people are speaking simultaneously, and even when the voice a person wants to hear is spoken indistinctly, with a strong dialectal accent, or with strong voice individuality.

On the other hand, the human hearing mechanism exhibits very low capability. One example of its inherent disadvantage is that the ear cannot separate two tones that are similar in frequency or that have a very short time interval between them. Another negative aspect is that when two tones exist at the same time, one cannot be heard since it is masked by the other.

The sophisticated hearing capability noted is supported by the complex language understanding mechanism controlled by the brain, which employs various context information in executing the mental processes concerned. The interrelationships between these mechanisms thus allows people to effectively communicate with each other. Although research into speech processing has thus far been undertaken without a detailed consideration of the concept of hearing, it is vital to connect any future speech research to the hearing mechanism inclusive of the realm of language perception.

## 2.3 SPEECH PRODUCTION MECHANISM

The speech production process involves three subprocesses: source generation, articulation, and radiation. The human vocal organ complex consists of the lungs, trachea, larynx, pharynx, and nasal and oral cavities. Together these form a connected tube as indicated in Fig. 2.2. The upper portion beginning with the larynx is called the vocal tract, which is changeable into various shapes by moving the jaw, tongue, lips, and other internal parts. The nasal cavity is separated from the pharynx and oral cavity by raising the velum or soft palate.

When the abdominal muscles force the diaphragm up, air is pushed up and out from the lungs, with the airflow passing through the trachea and glottis into the larynx. The glottis, or the gap between the left and right vocal cords, which is usually open during breathing, becomes narrower when the speaker intends to produce sound. The airflow through the glottis is then periodically interrupted by opening and closing the gap in accordance with the interaction between the airflow and the vocal cords. This intermittent flow, called the glottal source or the source of speech, can be simulated by asymmetrical triangular waves.

The mechanism of vocal vibration is actually very complicated. In principle, however, the Bernoulli effect associated with the airflow and the stability produced by the elasticity of the muscles draw the vocal cords toward each other. When the vocal cords

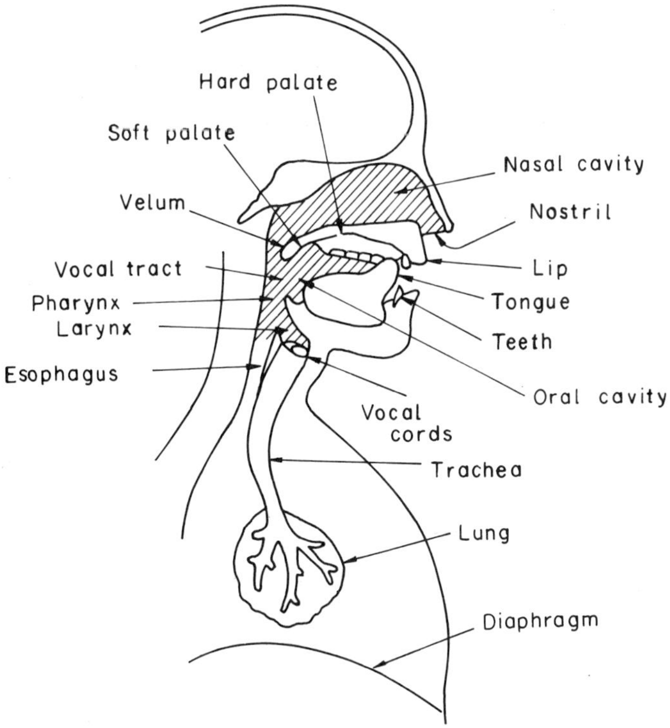


Fig. 2.2 Schematic diagram of the human vocal mechanism.

are strongly strained and the pressure of the air rising from the lungs (subglottal air pressure) is high, the open-and-close period (that is, the vocal cord vibration period) becomes short and the pitch of the sound source becomes high. Conversely, the low-air-pressure condition produces lower-pitched sound. This vocal cord vibration period is called the fundamental period, and its reciprocal is called the fundamental frequency. Accent and intonation result from temporal variation of the fundamental period. The sound source, consisting of fundamental and harmonic components, is modified by the vocal tract to produce tonal qualities, such as /a/ and /o/, in vowel production. During vowel production, the vocal tract is maintained in a relatively stable configuration throughout the utterance.

Two other mechanisms are responsible for changing the airflow from the lungs into speech sound. These are the mechanisms underlying the production of two kinds of consonants: fricatives and plosives. Fricatives, such as /s/, /f/, and /ʃ/, are noiselike sounds produced by turbulent flow which occurs when the airflow passes through a constriction in the vocal tract made by the tongue or lips. The tonal difference of each fricative corresponds to a fairly precisely located constriction and vocal tract shape. Plosives (stop consonants), such as /p/, /t/, and /k/, are impulsive sounds which occur with the sudden release of high-pressure air produced by checking the airflow in the vocal tract, again by using the tongue or lips. The tonal difference corresponds to the difference between the checking position and the vocal tract shape.

The production of these consonants is wholly independent of vocal cord vibration. Consonants which are accompanied by vocal cord vibration are known as voiced consonants, and those which are not accompanied by this vibration are called unvoiced consonants. The sounds emitted with vocal cord vibration are referred to as voiced sounds, and those without are named unvoiced sounds. Aspiration or whispering is produced when a turbulent flow is made at the glottis by slightly opening the vocal cords so that vocal cord vibration is not produced.

Semivowel, nasal, and affricate sounds are also included in the family of consonants. Semivowels are produced in a similar way as vowels, but their physical properties gradually change without a steady utterance period. Although semivowels are included in consonants, they are accompanied by neither turbulent airflow nor pulselike sound, since the vocal tract constriction is loose and vocal organ movement is relatively slow.

In the production of nasal sounds, the nasal cavity becomes an extended branch of the oral cavity, with the airflow being supplied to the nasal cavity by lowering the velum and arresting the airflow at some particular place in the oral cavity. When the nasal cavity forms a part of the vocal tract together with the oral cavity during vowel production, the vowel quality acquires nasalization and produces the nasalized vowel.

Affricates are produced by the succession of plosive and fricative sounds while maintaining a close constriction at the same position.

Adjusting the vocal tract shape to produce various linguistic sounds is called articulation, while the movement of each part in the vocal tract is known as articulatory movement. The parts of the vocal tract used for articulation are called articulatory organs, and those which can actively move, such as the tongue, lips, and velum, are named articulators.

The difference between articulatory methods for producing fricatives, plosives, nasals, and so on, is termed the manner of articulation. The constriction place in the vocal tract produced by articulatory movement is designated as the place of articulation. Various tone qualities are produced by varying the vocal tract shape which changes the transmission characteristics (that is, the resonance characteristics) of the vocal tract.

Speech sounds can be classified according to the combination of source and vocal tract (articulatory organ) resonance characteristics based on the production mechanism described above. The consonants and vowels of English are classified in Table 2.1 and Fig. 2.3, respectively. The horizontal lines in Fig. 2.3 indicate the approximate location of the vocal tract constriction in the representation: the more to the left it is, the closer to the front (near the lips) is the constriction. The vertical lines indicate the degree of constriction, which corresponds to the jaw opening position; the lowest line in the figure indicates maximum jaw opening.

These two conditions in conjunction with lip rounding represent the basic characteristics of vowel articulation. Each of the vowel pairs located side by side in the figure indicates a pair in which only the articulation of the lips is different: the left one

TABLE 2.1 Consonants

| Articulation place | | Labial | | Dental | | Alveolar | | Palatal | | Glottal | |
|---|---|---|---|---|---|---|---|---|---|---|---|
| Source | | V | UV | V | UV | V | UV | V | UV | V | UV |
| Articulation manner | Fricatives | v | f | ð | θ | z | s | ʒ | ʃ | | h |
| | Affricates | | | | | dz | ts | dʒ | tʃ | | |
| | Plosives | b | p | | | d | t | g | k | | |
| | Semivowels | w | | | | l | | j,r | | | |
| | Nasals | m | | | | n | | ŋ | | | |

V = voiced; UV = unvoiced

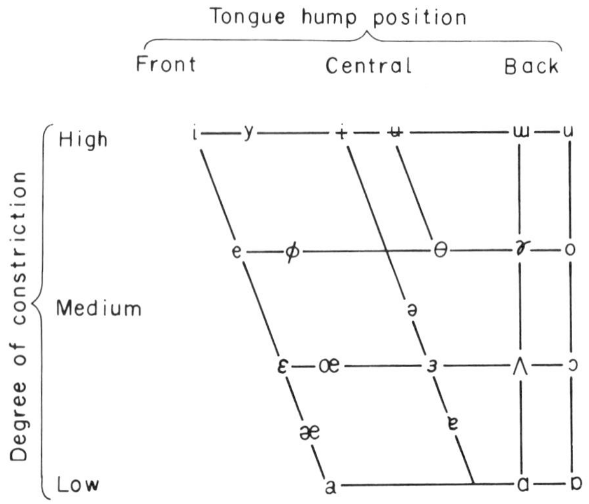


Fig. 2.3 Vowel classification from approximate vocal organ representation.

does not involve lip rounding, whereas the right one is produced by rounding the lips. This lip rounding rarely happens for vowels produced by extended jaw opening. The phoneme [ə] is called a neutral vowel, since the tongue and lips for producing this vowel are in the most neutral position; hence, the vocal tract shape is similar to a homogeneous tube having a constant cross section.

Relatively simple vowel structures, such as that of the Japanese language, are constructed of those vowels located along the exterior of the figure. These exterior vowels consist of [i, e, ε, a, ɑ, ɒ, ɔ, o, u, ɯ]. This means that the back tongue vowels tend to feature lip rounding while the front tongue vowels exhibit no such tendency.

Gliding monosyllabic speech sounds produced by varying the vocal tract smoothly between vowel or semivowel configurations are referred to as diphthongs. There are six diphthongs in American English, /ey/, /oɯ/, /ay/, /aɯ/, /oy/, and /ju/, but there are none in Japanese.

The articulated speech wave with linguistic information is radiated from the lips into the air and diffused. In nasalized sound, the speech wave is also radiated from the nostrils.

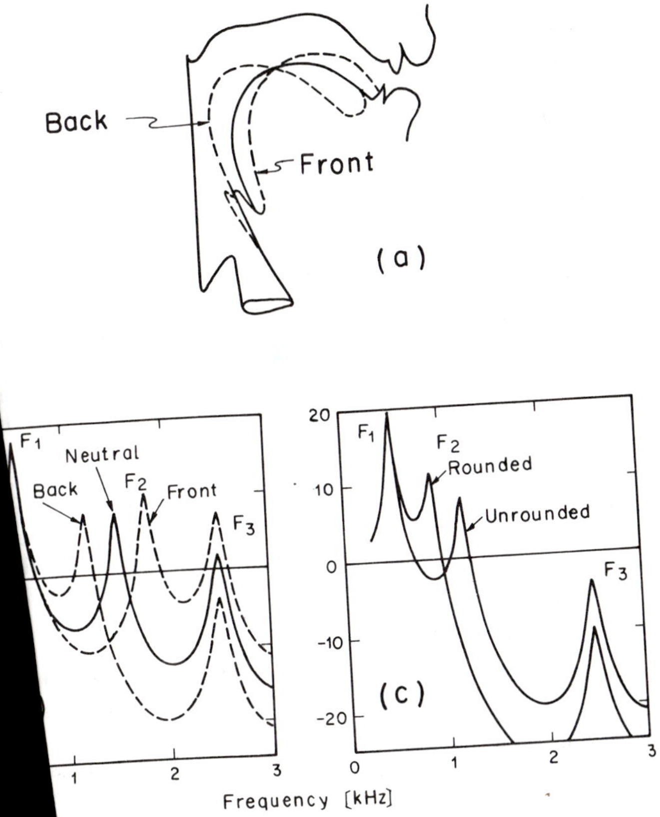


xamples of the relationship between vocal tract shapes
pectral envelopes: (a) schematization of mid-sagittal
ocal tract for a neutral vowel (solid contour), and
l front tongue-body positions; (b) idealized spectral
rresponding to the three tongue-body configurations
pproximate effect of lip rounding on the spectral
a back vowel.



## 2.4 ACOUSTIC CHARACTERISTICS OF SPEECH

Figure 2.4 represents the speech wave, short-time averaged energy, short-time spectral variation (Furui, 1986), fundamental frequency (modified correlation functions; see Sec. 5.4), and sound spectrogram for the Japanese phrase /tʃo:seN naNbuni/, or "in the southern part of Korea," uttered by a male speaker. The sound spectrogram, the details of which will be described in Sec. 4.2.4, visually presents the light and dark time pattern of the frequency spectrum. The dark parts indicate the spectral components having high energy, and the vertical stripes correspond to the fundamental period.

This figure shows that the speech wave and spectrum vary as nonstationary processes in periods of $\frac{1}{2}$ s or longer. In appropriately divided periods of 20–40 ms, however, the speech wave and spectrum can be regarded as having constant characteristics. The vertical lines in Fig. 2.4 indicate these boundaries. The segmentation was done automatically based on the amount of short-time spectral variation. During the periods of /tʃ/ or /s/ unvoiced consonant production, the speech waves show random waves with small amplitudes, and the spectra show random patterns. On the other hand, during the production periods of voiced sounds, such as those with /i/, /e/, /a/, /o/, /u/, /N/, the speech waves present periodic waves having large amplitudes, with the spectra indicating relatively global iterations of light and dark patterns. The dynamic range of the speech wave amplitude is so large that the amplitude difference between the unvoiced sounds having smaller amplitudes and the voiced sound having larger amplitudes sometimes exceeds 30 dB.

The dominant frequency components which characterize the phonemes correspond to the resonant frequency components of the vocal tract and are named formants. Voiced sounds, especially vowels, generally have three formants, which are called the first, second, and third formants, beginning with the lowest-frequency component. They are usually written as $F_1$, $F_2$, and $F_3$. Even for the same phoneme, however, these formant frequencies largely vary, depending on the speaker. Furthermore, the formant frequencies vary, depending on the adjacent phonemes in continuously spoken utterances, such as those emitted during conversation. This phenomenon, in other words, the occurrence of a transitional period in the middle of adjacent phonemes where the acoustic characteristics change continuously, is generally noted as coarticulation.

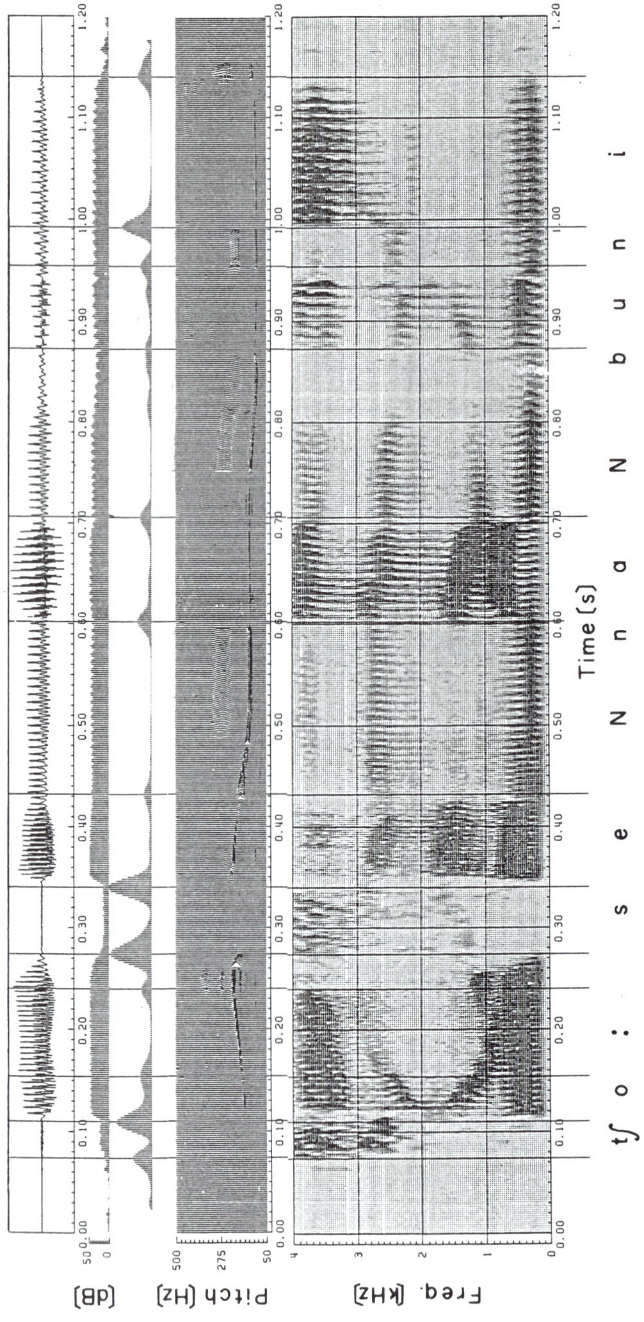


Fig. 2.4 Speech wave, short-time averaged energy, short-time spectral variation, fundamental frequency, and sound spectrogram (from top to bottom) for the Japanese sentence /tʃo:seN naNbuni/.





Examples of the relationship betwee vowel spectral envelopes are presented al., 1986). Fronting or backing of th taining approximately the same tongue or lowering of $F_2$, with the effect on accordingly produced as shown. As with $F_1$ for back vowels and with $F_3$ ther lowering of $F_2$ can be achieved lustrated in Fig. 2.5(c).

The basic acoustic characteristi characterized by $F_1$ and $F_2$. Figur formant frequencies of the isolated on the $F_1$-$F_2$ plane, the horizontal correspond to the first- and secor $F_2$, respectively (Sato, 1975). T butions for 30 male and 30 female and standard deviation values fo vowels are typically distributed in this figure, which is sometim comparative purposes, Fig. 2.7 formant frequencies of 10 Engl (33 adult males, 28 adult fema plane (Peterson and Barney,

The distribution of the v speech generally indicates an The variation owing to the s can be approximated by the quency plane, in other wor linear frequency, which ca comparison in Fig. 2.6. H vowels can be considerabl amined in three-dimension formant, which character higher-order formant ind the vowels uttered. Th peculiar value for each tract length.

Although difficult, attempted by many res from 30 to 120 Hz (me Hz) for $F_2$, and 40 tc in bandwidth has litt

Consonants are c unvoiced), frequenc

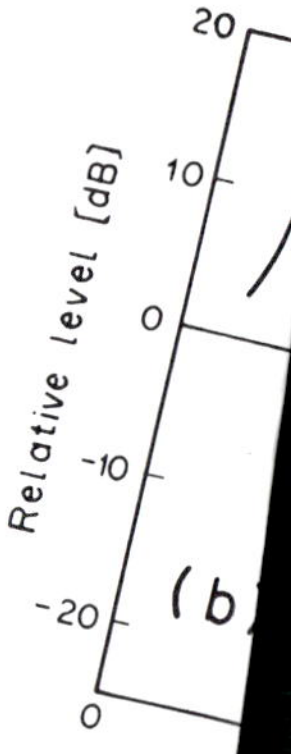


Fig. 2.5 E and vowel s section of v for back and envelopes co in (a); (c) a envelope for

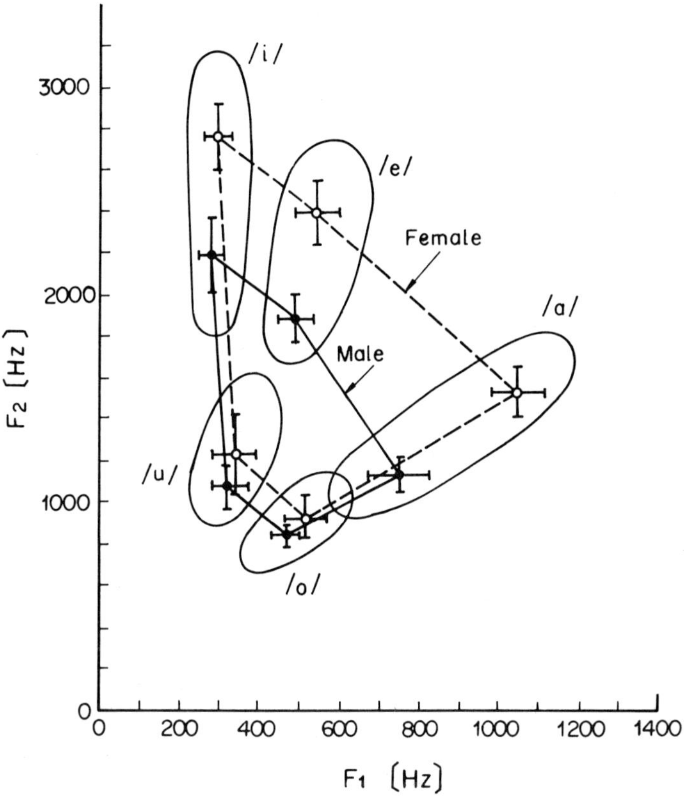


Fig. 2.6 Scatter diagram of formant frequencies of five Japanese vowels uttered by 60 speakers (30 males and 30 females) in the $F_1$-$F_2$ plane.

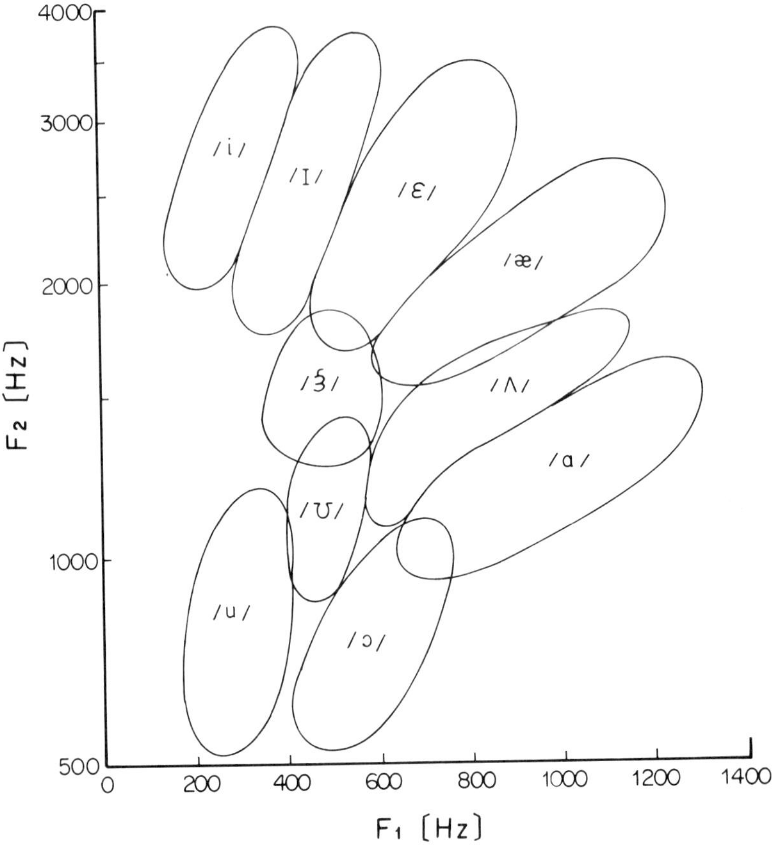


Fig. 2.7 Scatter diagram of formant frequencies of 10 English vowels uttered by 76 speakers (33 adult males, 28 adult females, and 15 children) in the $F_1$-$F_2$ plane.

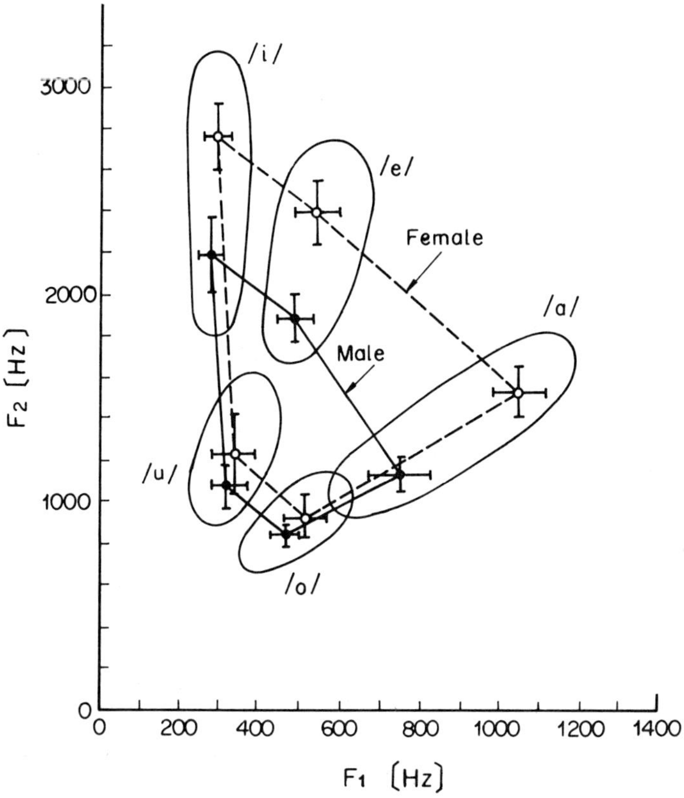


Fig. 2.6 Scatter diagram of formant frequencies of five Japanese vowels uttered by 60 speakers (30 males and 30 females) in the $F_1$-$F_2$ plane.

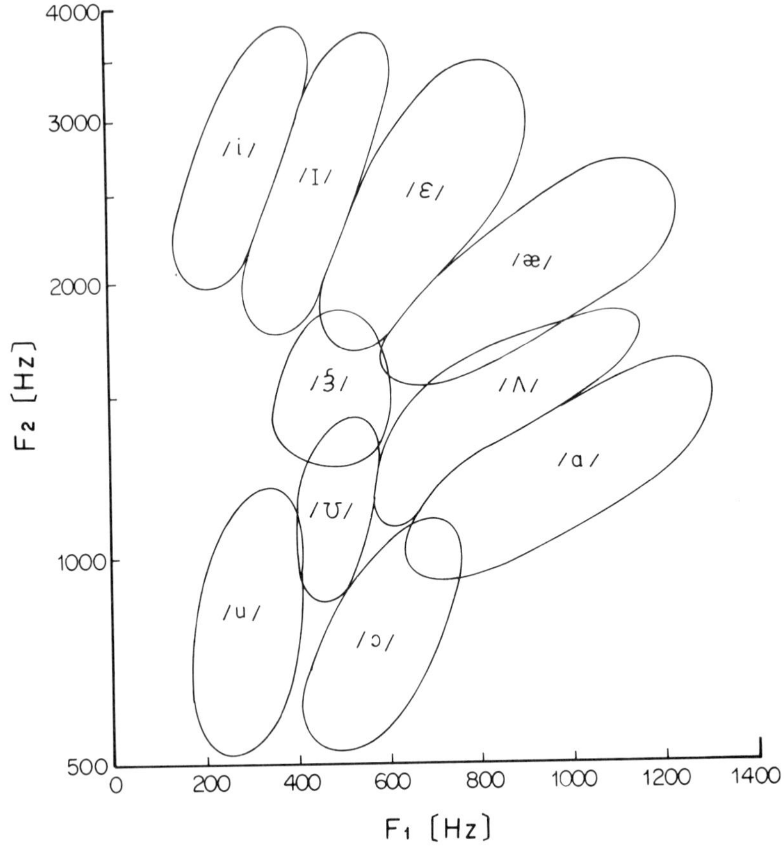


Fig. 2.7 Scatter diagram of formant frequencies of 10 English vowels uttered by 76 speakers (33 adult males, 28 adult females, and 15 children) in the $F_1$-$F_2$ plane.

## 2.4 ACOUSTIC CHARACTERISTICS OF SPEECH

Figure 2.4 represents the speech wave, short-time averaged energy, short-time spectral variation (Furui, 1986), fundamental frequency (modified correlation functions; see Sec. 5.4), and sound spectrogram for the Japanese phrase /tʃo:seN naNbuni/, or "in the southern part of Korea," uttered by a male speaker. The sound spectrogram, the details of which will be described in Sec. 4.2.4, visually presents the light and dark time pattern of the frequency spectrum. The dark parts indicate the spectral components having high energy, and the vertical stripes correspond to the fundamental period.

This figure shows that the speech wave and spectrum vary as nonstationary processes in periods of $\frac{1}{2}$ s or longer. In appropriately divided periods of 20–40 ms, however, the speech wave and spectrum can be regarded as having constant characteristics. The vertical lines in Fig. 2.4 indicate these boundaries. The segmentation was done automatically based on the amount of short-time spectral variation. During the periods of /tʃ/ or /s/ unvoiced consonant production, the speech waves show random waves with small amplitudes, and the spectra show random patterns. On the other hand, during the production periods of voiced sounds, such as those with /i/, /e/, /a/, /o/, /u/, /N/, the speech waves present periodic waves having large amplitudes, with the spectra indicating relatively global iterations of light and dark patterns. The dynamic range of the speech wave amplitude is so large that the amplitude difference between the unvoiced sounds having smaller amplitudes and the voiced sound having larger amplitudes sometimes exceeds 30 dB.

The dominant frequency components which characterize the phonemes correspond to the resonant frequency components of the vocal tract and are named formants. Voiced sounds, especially vowels, generally have three formants, which are called the first, second, and third formants, beginning with the lowest-frequency component. They are usually written as $F_1$, $F_2$, and $F_3$. Even for the same phoneme, however, these formant frequencies largely vary, depending on the speaker. Furthermore, the formant frequencies vary, depending on the adjacent phonemes in continuously spoken utterances, such as those emitted during conversation. This phenomenon, in other words, the occurrence of a transitional period in the middle of adjacent phonemes where the acoustic characteristics change continuously, is generally noted as coarticulation.

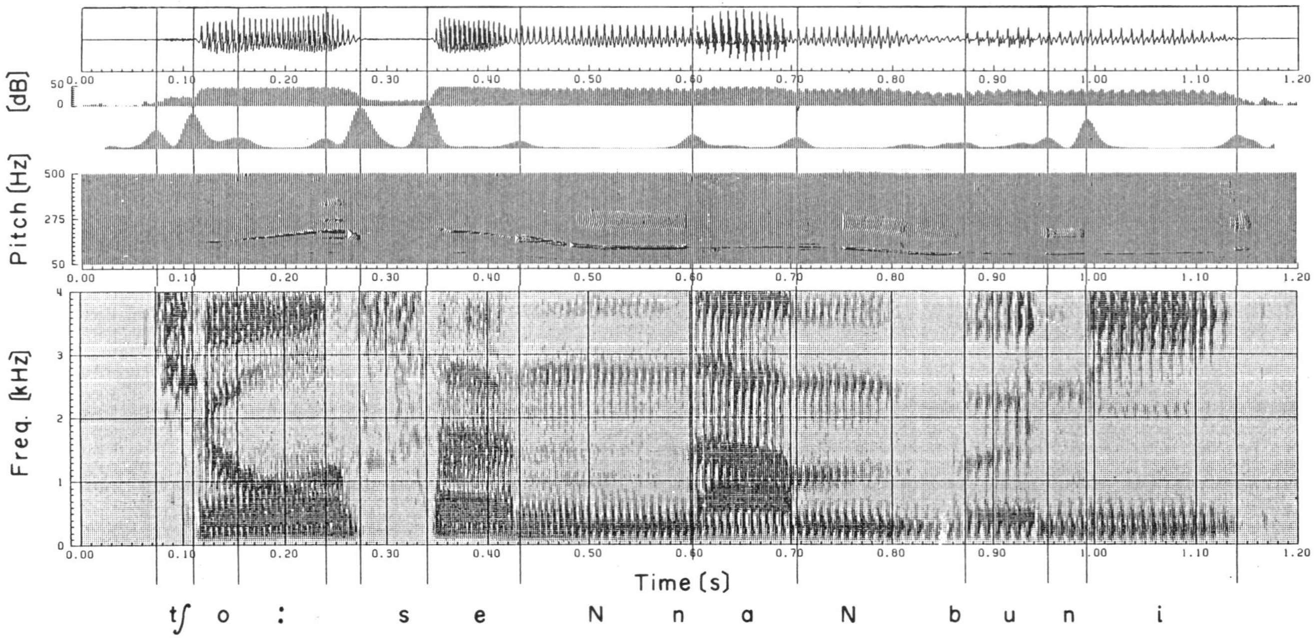


Fig. 2.4 Speech wave, short-time averaged energy, short-time spectral variation, fundamental frequency, and sound spectrogram (from top to bottom) for the Japanese sentence /tʃo:seN naNbuni/.

Examples of the relationship between vocal tract shapes and vowel spectral envelopes are presented in Fig. 2.5 (Stevens et al., 1986). Fronting or backing of the tongue body while maintaining approximately the same tongue height causes a raising or lowering of $F_2$, with the effect on the overall spectral shape accordingly produced as shown. As is clear, $F_2$ has an affinity with $F_1$ for back vowels and with $F_3$ for front vowels. A further lowering of $F_2$ can be achieved by rounding the lips as illustrated in Fig. 2.5(c).

The basic acoustic characteristics of vowel formants can be characterized by $F_1$ and $F_2$. Figure 2.6 is a scatter diagram of formant frequencies of the isolatedly spoken five Japanese vowels on the $F_1$-$F_2$ plane, the horizontal and vertical axes of which correspond to the first- and second-formant frequencies, $F_1$ and $F_2$, respectively (Sato, 1975). This figure indicates the distributions for 30 male and 30 female speakers as well as the mean and standard deviation values for these speakers. The five vowels are typically distributed in a triangular shape as shown in this figure, which is sometimes called the vowel triangle. For comparative purposes, Fig. 2.7 presents the scatter diagram of formant frequencies of 10 English vowels uttered by 76 speakers (33 adult males, 28 adult females, and 15 children) on the $F_1$-$F_2$ plane (Peterson and Barney, 1952).

The distribution of the vowels extracted from continuous speech generally indicates an overlap between different vowels. The variation owing to the speakers and their ages, however, can be approximated by the parallel shift in the logarithmic frequency plane, in other words, by the proportional change in the linear frequency, which can be seen in the male and female voice comparison in Fig. 2.6. Hence, this overlapping of different vowels can be considerably reduced when the distribution is examined in three-dimensional space formed from adding the third formant, which characterizes the individuality of voice. The higher-order formant indicates a smaller variation, depending on the vowels uttered. Therefore, the higher-order formant has a peculiar value for each speaker corresponding to his or her vocal tract length.

Although difficult, measuring formant bandwidths has been attempted by many researchers. The extracted values range from 30 to 120 Hz (mean 50 Hz) for $F_1$, 30 to 200 Hz (mean 60 Hz) for $F_2$, and 40 to 300 Hz (mean 115 Hz) for $F_3$. Variation in bandwidth has little influence on the quality of speech heard.

Consonants are classified by the periodicity of waves (voiced/unvoiced), frequency spectrum, duration, and temporal variation.

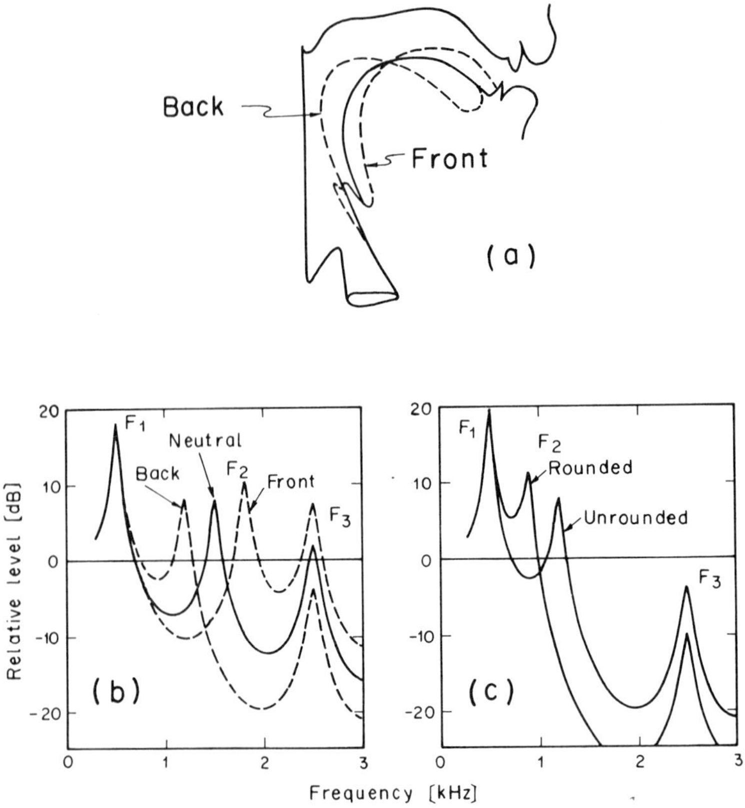


Fig. 2.5 Examples of the relationship between vocal tract shapes and vowel spectral envelopes: (a) schematization of mid-sagittal section of vocal tract for a neutral vowel (solid contour), and for back and front tongue-body positions; (b) idealized spectral envelopes corresponding to the three tongue-body configurations in (a); (c) approximate effect of lip rounding on the spectral envelope for a back vowel.

The acoustic characteristics of the consonants largely vary as the result of coarticulation with vowels since the consonants originally have no stable or steady-state period. Especially with rapid speech, articulation of the phoneme which follows, that is, tongue and lip movement toward the articulation place of the following phoneme, starts before completion of articulation of the phoneme being presently uttered.

Coarticulation sometimes affects phonemes located beyond adjacent phonemes. Furthermore, since various articulatory organs participate in actual speech production, and since each organ has its own time constant of movement, the acoustic phenomena resulting from these movements are highly complicated. Hence, it is very difficult to obtain one-to-one correspondence between phonemic symbols and acoustic characteristics.

Under these circumstances, the focus has been on examining ways to specify each phoneme by combining relatively simple features instead of on determining the specific acoustic features of each phoneme (Jakobson et al., 1963). These features thus far formalized, which are called distinctive features, consist of the binary representation of nine descriptive pairs: vocal/nonvocalic, consonantal/nonconsonantal, compact/diffuse, grave/acute, flat/plain, nasal/oral, tense/lax, continuant/interrupted, and strident/mellow. Since the selection of these features has been based mainly on auditory rather than articulatory characteristics, many of them are qualitative, having weak correspondence to physical characteristics. Therefore, considerable room still remains in their final clarification.

## 2.5 STATISTICAL CHARACTERISTICS OF SPEECH

### 2.5.1 Distribution of Amplitude Level

Figure 2.8 shows accumulated distributions of the speech amplitude level calculated for utterances by 80 speakers (4 speakers × 20 languages) having a duration of roughly 37 minutes (Irii et al., 1987). The horizontal axis, specifically the amplitude level, is normalized by the long-term effective value. The vertical axis indicates the frequency of amplitude accumulated from large values, in other words, the frequency of amplitude values larger than the indicated value. These results clearly confirm that the dynamic range of speech amplitude exceeds 50 dB.

The difference between the amplitude level, at which the accumulated value amounts to 1%, and the long-term effective value, or root mean square (rms) value, is called the peak factor

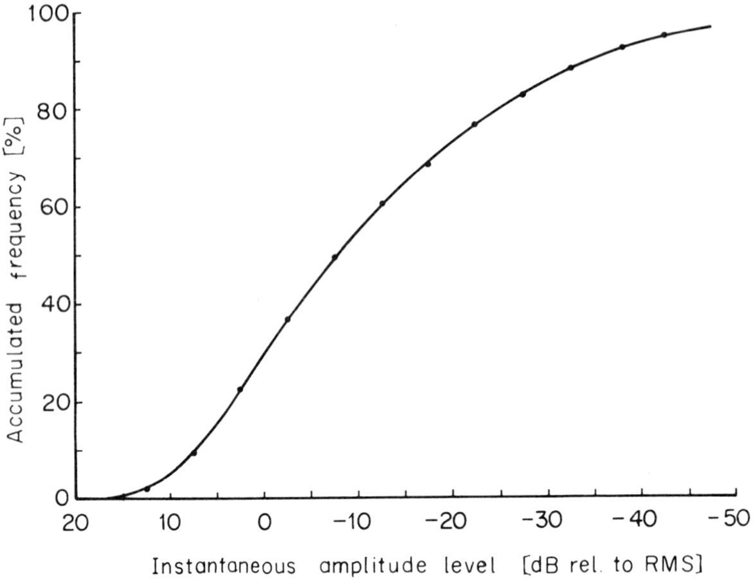


Fig. 2.8 Accumulated distribution of speech amplitude level calculated for utterances made by 80 speakers having a duration of roughly 37 min.

because it relates to the sharpness of the wave. The speech and sinusoidal wave peak factors are about 12 dB and 3 dB, respectively, indicating that the speech wave is much higher in sharpness.

The derivative of the accumulated distribution curve corresponds to the amplitude density distribution function. The results derived from Fig. 2.8 are presented in Fig. 2.9 (Irii et al., 1987). The distribution can be approximated by an exponential distribution:

$$p(x) = \frac{1}{\sqrt{2}\,\sigma} \exp\left(\frac{-\sqrt{2}\,|x|}{\sigma}\right) \tag{2.1}$$

Here, $\sigma$ is the effective value ($\sigma^2$ corresponds to the mean energy).

Distribution of the long-term effective speech level over many speakers is regarded as being the normal distribution for both

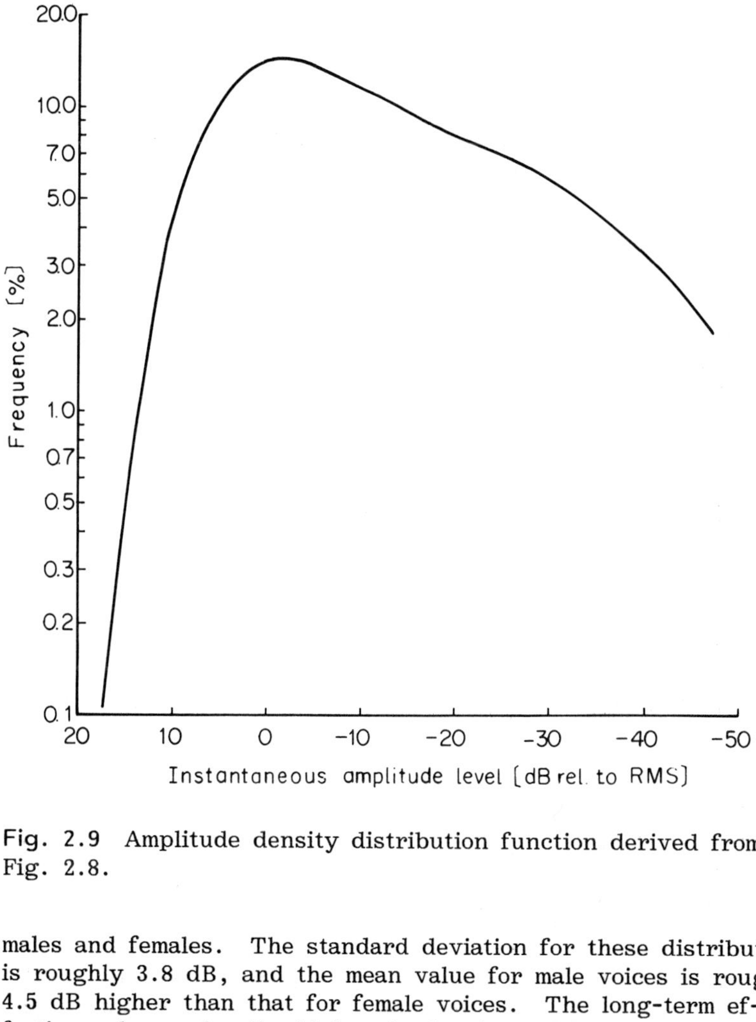


Fig. 2.9 Amplitude density distribution function derived from Fig. 2.8.

males and females. The standard deviation for these distributions is roughly 3.8 dB, and the mean value for male voices is roughly 4.5 dB higher than that for female voices. The long-term effective value under the high-noise-level condition is usually raised according to that noise level.

### 2.5.2 Long-Time Averaged Spectrum

Figure 2.10 shows the long-time averaged speech spectra extracted using 20 channels of one-third octave bandpass filters which cover the 0–9-kHz frequency range (Irii et al., 1987). These

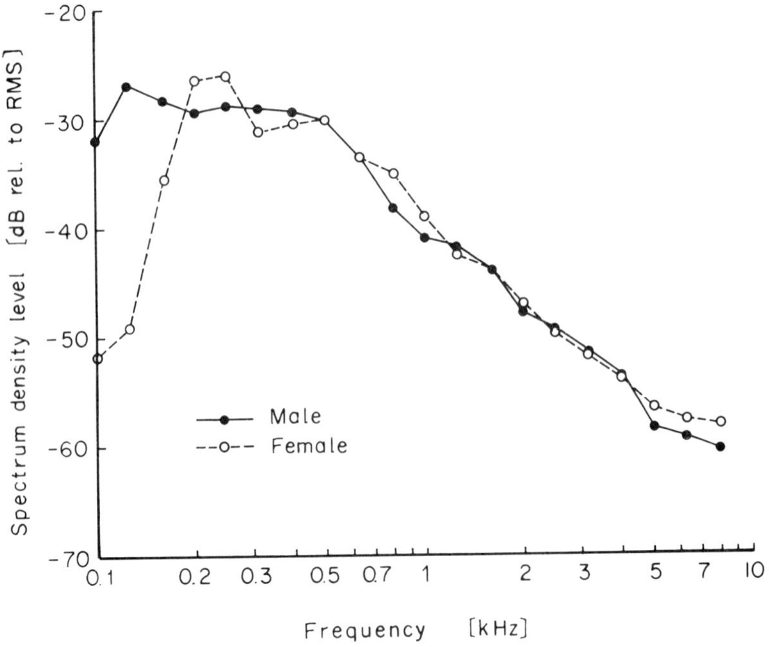


Fig. 2.10 Long-time averaged speech spectrum calculated for utterances made by 80 speakers.

results were also obtained using the utterances made by 80 speakers of 20 languages. As is clear, only a slight difference exists between male and female speakers, except for the low-frequency range where the spectrum is affected by the variation in fundamental frequency. The difference is also noticeably very small between languages.

Based on these results, the typical speech spectrum shape is represented by the combination of a flat spectrum and a spectrum having a slope of −10 dB/octave (oct). The former is applied to the frequency range of less than 500 Hz, while the latter is applied to that of more than 500 Hz. Although the long-time averaged spectra calculated through the above-mentioned method demonstrate only slight differences between speakers, those calculated with high-frequency resolution definitely feature individual differences (Furui, 1972).

### 2.5.3 Variation in Fundamental Frequency

Statistical analysis of temporal variation in fundamental frequency during conversational speech for every speaker indicates that the mean and standard deviation for female voices are roughly twice those for male voices as shown in Fig. 2.11 (Saito et al., 1958). The fundamental frequency distributed over speakers on a logarithmic frequency scale can be approximated by two normal distribution functions which correspond to male and female voices, respectively, as shown in Fig. 2.12. The mean and standard deviation for male voices are 125 and 20.5 Hz, respectively, whereas those for female voices are two times larger. Intraspeaker variation is roughly 20% smaller than interspeaker variation.

Analysis of the temporal transition distribution in the fundamental frequency indicates that roughly 18% of these are ascending and roughly 50% are descending. Frequency analysis of the temporal pattern of the fundamental frequency, in which the silent period is smoothly connected, shows that the frequency of the temporal variation is less than 10 Hz. This implies that the speed of the temporal variation in the fundamental frequency is relatively slow.

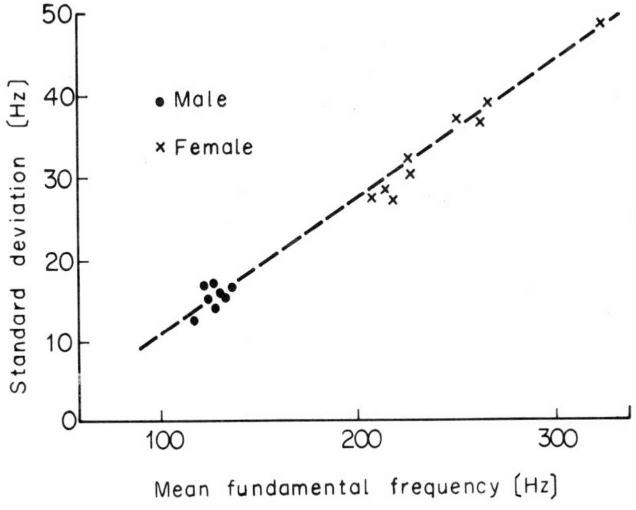


Fig. 2.11 Mean and standard deviation of temporal variation in fundamental frequency during conversational speech for various speakers.

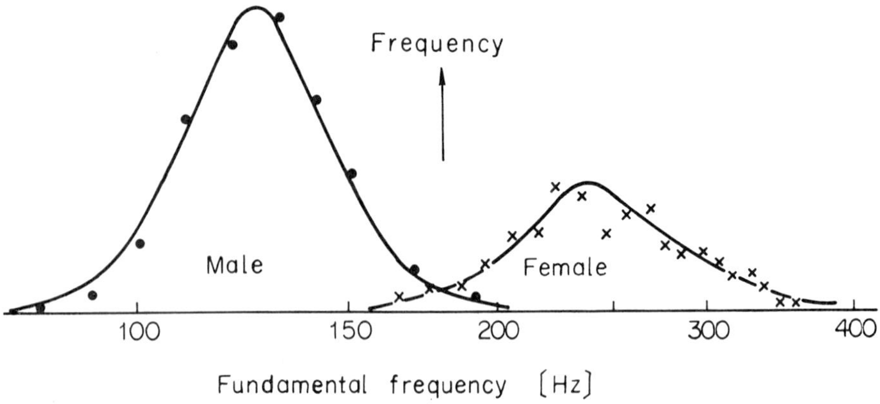


Fig. 2.12 Fundamental frequency distribution over speakers.

### 2.5.4 Speech Ratio

Conversational speech includes speech as well as pause periods, and the proportion of actual speech periods is referred to as the speech ratio. In conversational speech, the speech ratio for each speaker is roughly $\frac{1}{3}$, changing, of course, as a function of the speech rate. An experiment which increased and decreased the speech rate to 30–40% indicated that the expansion or contraction at pause periods becomes 65–69%, although during the speech period it is 13–19% (Saito, 1961). This means that the variation in the speech rate is mainly accomplished by changing the pause periods. Moreover, expansion or contraction during vowel periods is generally larger than that during consonant periods.

# 3

# Speech Production Models

## 3.1 ACOUSTICAL THEORY OF SPEECH PRODUCTION

As described in Sec. 2.3, the speech wave production mechanism can be divided into three stages: sound source production, articulation by vocal tract, and radiation from the lips and/or nostrils (Fant, 1960). These stages can be further characterized by electrical equivalent circuits based on the relationship between electrical and acoustical systems.

Specifically, sound sources are either voiced or unvoiced. A voiced sound source can be modeled by a generator of pulses or asymmetrical triangular waves which are repeated at every fundamental period. The peak value of the source wave corresponds to the loudness of the voice. An unvoiced sound source, on the other hand, can be modeled by a white noise generator, the mean energy of which corresponds to the loudness of voice. Articulation can be modeled by the cascade or parallel connection of several single-resonance or antiresonance circuits, which can be realized through a multistage digital filter. Finally, radiation can be modeled as arising from a piston sound source attached to an infinite, plane baffle. Here, the radiation impedance is represented by an L-r cascade circuit, where r is the energy loss occurring through the radiation.

The speech production process can accordingly be characterized by combining these electrical equivalent circuits as indicated in Table 3.1. The resonance characteristics depend on the vocal tract shape only, and not on the location of the sound source during both vowel-type and consonant-type production.

TABLE 3.1 Speech Production Process Models

| Type | Speech production model | System function |
|---|---|---|
| Vowel type | 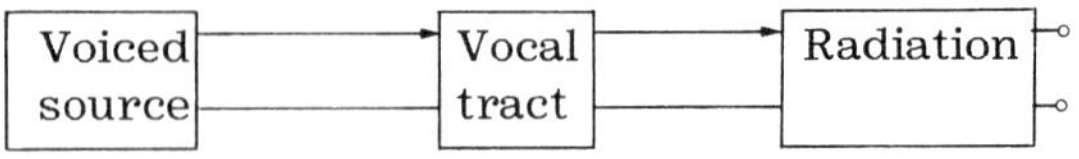  | Resonance only (all-pole model) |
| Consonant type | 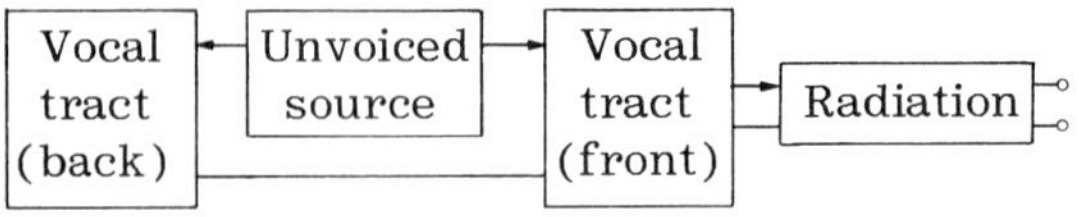  | Resonance and anti-resonance (pole-zero) |
| Nasal type (nasal & nasalized vowel) | 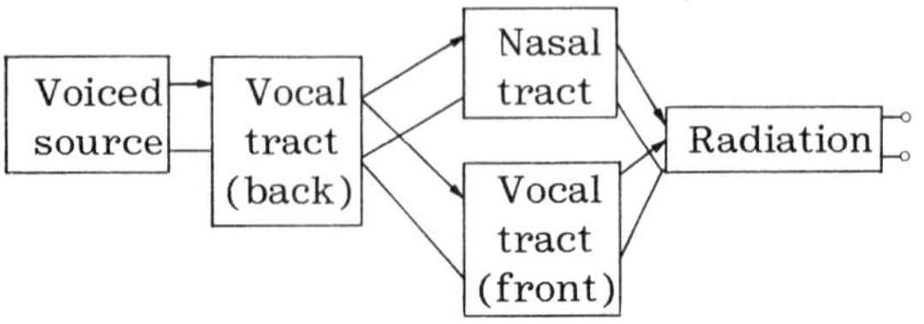  | Resonance and anti-resonance (pole-zero) |

Conversely, the antiresonance characteristics during consonant-type production depend primarily on the antiresonance characteristics of the vocal tract between the glottis and sound source position. The resonance and antiresonance effects are usually canceled in the low-frequency range, since these locations almost exactly coincide.

Resonance characteristics for the branched vocal tract, such as those for nasal-type production, are conditioned by the oral cavity characteristics forward and backward from the velum and by the nasal tract characteristics from the velum to the nostrils. The antiresonance characteristics of nasalized consonants (nasal sound) are determined by the forward characteristics of the oral cavity starting from the velum. On the other hand, the antiresonance characteristics of nasalized vowels depend on the nasal tract characteristics starting from the velum. Figure 3.1 exemplifies the spectral change caused by the nasalization of the vowel /a/.

When the radiation characteristics are approximated by the above-mentioned model, the normalized radiation impedance for the unit plane's free vibration can be represented by

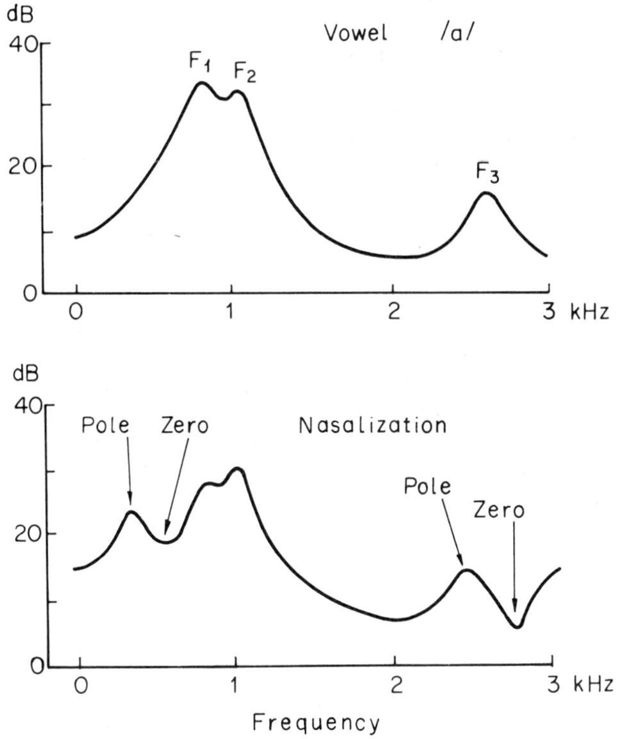


Fig. 3.1 An example of spectral change caused by the nasalization of vowel /a/. It is characterized by pole-zero pairs at 300–400 Hz and at around 2500 Hz. $F_1$, $F_2$, $F_3$ are formants.

$$Z_r = \frac{(ka)^2}{2} + j\,\frac{8ka}{3\pi} \qquad (ka \ll 1) \tag{3.1}$$

where a is the radius of the vibration plane, $k = \omega/c$, $\omega$ is the angle frequency, and c is the sound velocity (Flanagan, 1972). This equation is obtained for small values of ka. The first component in Eq. (3.1) represents the energy loss associated with the radiation of the speech wave. The second component indicates that the vocal tract is equivalently extended by $8a/3\pi$ having a cross section which is equal to the opening section. The radiation characteristics are usually approximated by considering the 6-dB/oct derivative characteristics only and not the phase characteristics.

Radiation impedance decreases all resonance frequencies with a constant ratio, but increases their bandwidths. The fact that the glottal source impedance is finite increases all resonance frequencies and bandwidths. These effects for high-frequency resonances, however, can be neglected.

## 3.2 LINEAR SEPARABLE EQUIVALENT CIRCUIT MODEL

Present speech information processing techniques are based on the linear separable equivalent circuit model of the speech production mechanism detailed in Fig. 3.2. This model is constructed by simplifying the model outlined in the previous section. Specifically, this involves completely separating the source $G(\omega)$ from the articulation (resonance and antiresonance) $H(\omega)$ and representing the production model for the speech wave $S(\omega)$ as

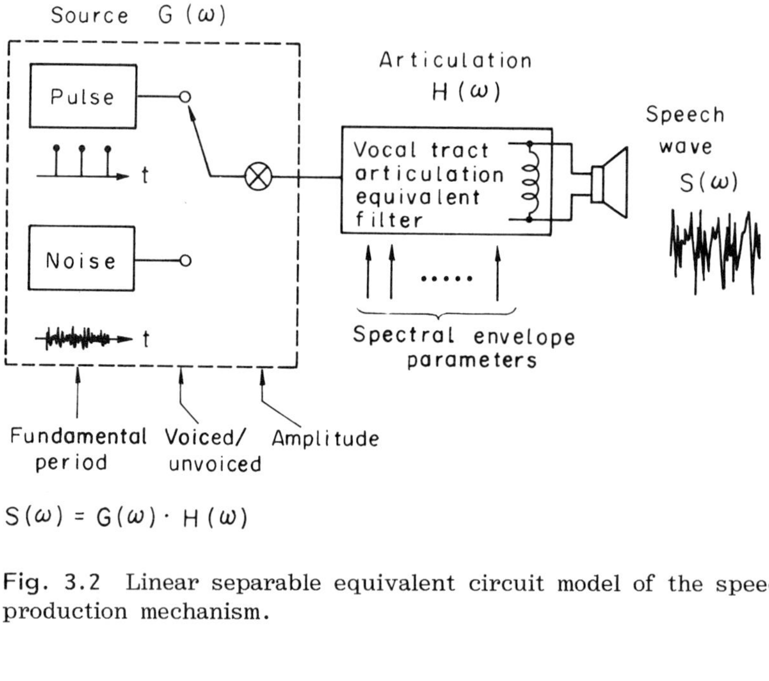


Fig. 3.2 Linear separable equivalent circuit model of the speech production mechanism.

the cascade connection of each electrical equivalent circuit without mutual interaction such that

$$S(\omega) = G(\omega)H(\omega) \tag{3.2}$$

The sound source is approximated by pulse and white noise sources, and the vocal tract articulation is represented by the filter characteristics of the all-pole model or the pole-zero model. The overall spectral characteristics of the glottal wave are included in the vocal tract filter characteristics together with the radiation characteristics. Consequently, the spectral characteristic of $G(\omega)$ is flat, and $H(\omega)$ is a digital filter having time-variable coefficients, which includes the source spectral envelope and radiation characteristics in addition to the vocal tract filter characteristics. Since the temporal variation of the vocal tract shape during the utterance of continuous speech is relatively slow, the transmission characteristics of the time-variable parameter digital filter can be regarded as having nearly constant characteristics in short periods, such as those 20–40 ms in length.

## 3.3 VOCAL TRACT TRANSMISSION MODEL

From the perspective of determining sonority as a linguistic sound, the most important of the three speech wave production mechanism subprocesses is vocal tract articulation. The vocal tract length of adults is roughly 15–17 cm, and the wave lengths $\lambda$ of the speech wave in the vocal tract are roughly 35 cm and 7 cm at 1 kHz and 5 kHz, respectively. Furthermore, the equivalent radius of the vocal tract is less than 2 cm when the vocal tract cross section approximates a circle. Therefore, in the frequency range of less than 4–5 kHz, $\lambda/4$ is larger than the equivalent radius of the vocal tract.

The vocal tract is thus appropriately analyzed as being a distributed parameter system of the one-dimensional acoustic tube whose cross section is continuously changing. This means that the transmission of the speech wave can be regarded as that of the plane wave. Although the nasal tract actually exists as a part of the vocal tract, it is omitted from the present discussion of the principal vocal tract characteristics for simplicity purposes.

Heat conduction losses, viscous losses, and leaky losses, which accompany sound wave transmission, are small enough to be neglected under normal conditions. These losses are therefore usually disregarded in the modeling. The vocal tract characteristics can be more precisely represented by equivalently locating these losses at the glottis and lips. Also, it is usually assumed for the sake of simplicity that the vocal tract model is linear and that it is not coupled to the glottis.

### 3.3.1 Progressing Wave Model

Sound wave transmission along the axis in a lossless one-dimensional sound tube featuring a nonuniform cross section can be represented by two simultaneous partial differential equations which consist of the momentum equation and the mass conservation equation (Rabiner and Schafer, 1978):

$$-\frac{\partial U}{\partial t} = \frac{A(x)}{\rho}\frac{\partial P}{\partial x}$$

and

$$-\frac{\partial P}{\partial t} = \frac{\rho c^2}{A(x)}\frac{\partial U}{\partial x} \tag{3.3}$$

Here, x is the distance from the glottis along the axis, U is volume velocity, P is sound pressure, A(x) is the area function of the vocal tract cross section, $\rho$ is air density, and c is sound velocity.

To accurately portray the vocal tract characteristics, let us now divide the vocal tract every $\Delta x$ and approximate each segment by a small acoustic tube having a constant cross-sectional area (in other words, by a distributed parameter system). The length of $\Delta x$ is determined by the frequency bandwidth F (Hz) of the speech wave with which we are concerned.

Approximating the segment having a length of $\Delta x$ by a set of distributed parameters requires that $\Delta x$ be less than a quarter of the wavelength of the sound wave; that is, it is necessary that $\Delta x \leqq c/4F$. If F = 4 kHz, for example, $\Delta x$ must be less than roughly 1 cm. The solution of the one-dimensional wave equation for volume velocity and sound pressure can then be represented by the linear combination of the forward propagation wave from the glottis toward the lips and the backward propagation waves. When the forward and backward waves and the size of the cross section of the nth ($n \geqq 1$) small segment from the lips are represented by $f_n(t)$, $b_n(t)$, and $A_n$, respectively, and when the propagation time for half of one section is represented by $\Delta t$ ($\Delta t = \Delta x/2c$), the volume velocity and sound pressure can be given by

$$U_n(t) = f_n(t - \Delta t) - b_n(t + \Delta t)$$

and

$$P_n(t) = \frac{\rho c}{A_n} \{f_n(t - \Delta t) + b_n(t + \Delta t)\} \tag{3.4}$$

The volume velocity relationship is expressed in Fig. 3.3. The equation for the sound pressure is obtained by putting the volume velocity equation into Eq. (3.3).

Owing to the continuity of both volume velocity and sound pressure at the boundary, two equations can then be obtained:

$$f_n(t - \Delta t) - b_n(t + \Delta t) = f_{n-1}(t + \Delta t) - b_{n-1}(t - \Delta t)$$

and

$$f_n(t - \Delta t) + b_n(t + \Delta t) = \frac{A_n}{A_{n-1}} \{f_{n-1}(t + \Delta t) + b_{n-1}(t - \Delta t)\} \tag{3.5}$$

The continuity condition for the volume velocity is also indicated in Fig. 3.3. When the two equations expressed as Eq. (3.5) are combined, we get

$$-b_n(t + \Delta t) = \frac{A_{n-1} - A_n}{A_{n-1} + A_n} f_n(t - \Delta t) \tag{3.6}$$

Since $b_n(t + \Delta t)$ can be regarded as the reflection of $f_n(t - \Delta t)$ at the boundary indicated in Fig. 3.3,

$$\kappa_n = \frac{A_{n-1} - A_n}{A_{n-1} + A_n} \tag{3.7}$$

is defined as the reflection coefficient. The reflection coefficient satisfies $-1 \leqq \kappa_n \leqq 1$, since the area function has positive values. By modifying Eq. (3.7), we can then obtain

$$\frac{A_n}{A_{n-1}} = \frac{1 - \kappa_n}{1 + \kappa_n} \tag{3.8}$$

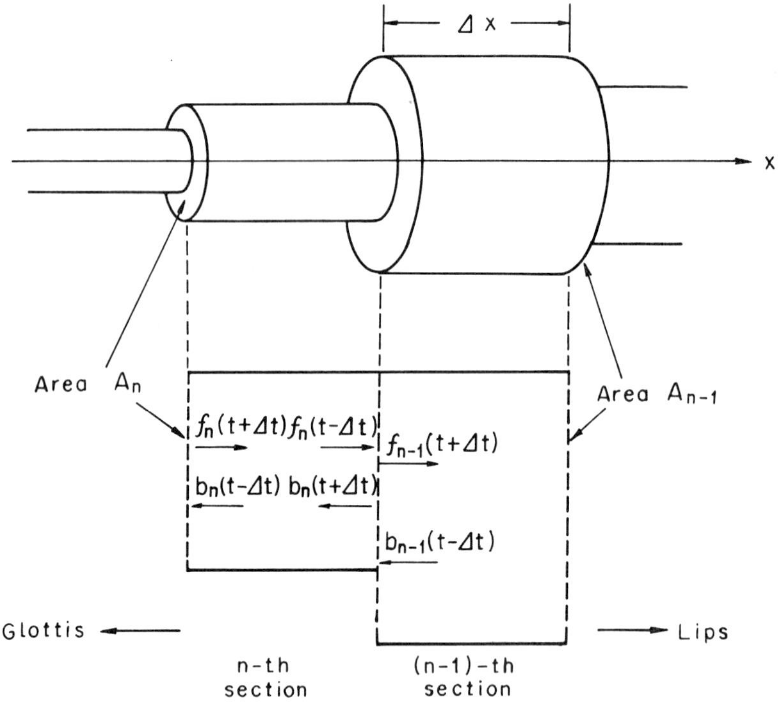


$$f_n(t - \Delta t) - b_n(t + \Delta t) = f_{n-1}(t + \Delta t) - b_{n-1}(t - \Delta t)$$

$$U_n(t) = f_n(t - \Delta t) - b_n(t + \Delta t)$$

Fig. 3.3 Definition of forward and backward waves with respect to volume velocity at the nth cross section, and continuity condition for the volume velocity at the boundary between the (n − 1)th and nth sections.

When areas $A_n$ and $A_{n-1}$ at the two segments are equal, $\kappa_n = 0$ and no reflection occurs.

Let us now calculate the sum and difference of Eqs. (3.5) and divide them by 2. When Eq. (3.8) is applied to these results, we are left with

$$f_n(t - \Delta t) = \frac{f_{n-1}(t + \Delta t) - \kappa_n b_{n-1}(t - \Delta t)}{1 + \kappa_n}$$

and

$$b_n(t + \Delta t) = \frac{-\kappa_n f_{n-1}(t + \Delta t) + b_{n-1}(t - \Delta t)}{1 + \kappa_n} \tag{3.9}$$

When these equations are solved for $f_{n-1}(t + \Delta t)$ and $b_n(t + \Delta t)$, two fundamental equations are obtained:

$$f_{n-1}(t + \Delta t) = \kappa_n b_{n-1}(t - \Delta t) + (1 + \kappa_n) f_n(t - \Delta t)$$

and

$$b_n(t + \Delta t) = (1 - \kappa_n) b_{n-1}(t - \Delta t) - \kappa_n f_n(t - \Delta t) \tag{3.10}$$

Figure 3.4(a) depicts the signal flow graph of these fundamental equations.

When sound pressure is used as the fundamental quantity instead of volume velocity, the continuous equations become

$$f_n(t - \Delta t) + b_n(t + \Delta t) = f_{n-1}(t + \Delta t) + b_{n-1}(t - \Delta t)$$

and

$$f_n(t - \Delta t) - b_n(t + \Delta t) = \frac{A_n}{A_{n-1}} \{f_{n-1}(t + \Delta t) - b_{n-1}(t - \Delta t)\} \tag{3.11}$$

The fundamental equations are then expressed as

$$f_{n-1}(t + \Delta t) = \kappa_n b_{n-1}(t - \Delta t) + (1 - \kappa_n) f_n(t - \Delta t)$$

and

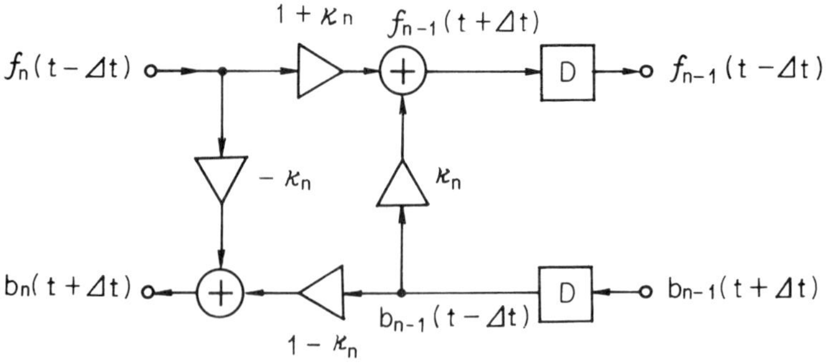


(a)

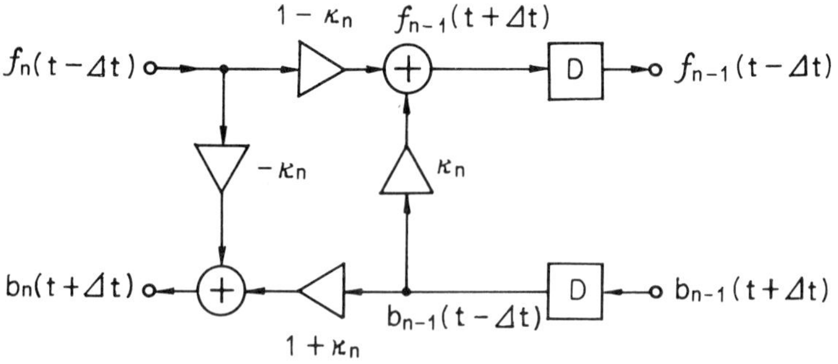


(b)

Fig. 3.4 Transmission model of acoustic waves in the vocal tract (D = time delay of $2\Delta t$): (a) transmission with respect to volume velocity; (b) transmission with respect to sound pressure.

$$b_n(t + \Delta t) = (1 + \kappa_n)b_{n-1}(t - \Delta t) - \kappa_n f_n(t - \Delta t) \quad (3.12)$$

The signal flow graph for these equations is indicated in Fig. 3.4(b).

In both figures, the state at $t + \Delta t$ depends on only the states of the sections adjacent to both sides at $t - \Delta t$. Therefore, the new state can be obtained by calculating these equations successively for each segment, and then by substituting these new calculated values for all previous values. The calculation can be done every $2\Delta t$. If $\Delta x \leqq c/4F$ is satisfied as mentioned before, $2\Delta t = \Delta x/c \leqq 1/4F$ is satisfied, which means that the sampling theory holds. This then indicates that the sound wave propagation in the vocal tract can be completely described by area ratios or by equivalent reflection coefficients. This model is called Kelly's speech production model (Kelly, 1962).

### 3.3.2 Resonance Model

When parameter P is eliminated from Eq. (3.3), what is known as Webster's horn equation is obtained:

$$-\frac{1}{c^2}\frac{\partial^2 U}{\partial t^2} + A(x)\frac{\partial}{\partial x}\left(\frac{1}{A(x)}\frac{\partial U}{\partial x}\right) = 0 \quad (3.13)$$

Since the variables of this partial derivative equation are separable, the following full derivative equation can be formulated, assuming that $U(x,t) = U(x)e^{j\omega t}$:

$$A(x)\frac{d}{dx}\left(\frac{1}{A(x)}\frac{dU}{dx}\right) + \left(\frac{\omega}{c}\right)^2 U = 0 \quad (3.14)$$

Moreover, because the area A(x) is positive, we can derive the equation

$$\frac{d}{dx}\left(\frac{1}{A(x)}\frac{dU}{dx}\right) + \lambda\frac{U}{A(x)} = 0, \qquad \lambda = \left(\frac{\omega}{c}\right)^2 \quad (3.15)$$

which is the Stürm-Liouville derivative equation. The transmission function of the vocal tract can be calculated when this equation is solved for U under a given area function A(x) and an appropriate boundary condition. The vocal tract transmission function can then be calculated by $H(\omega) = U(1,t)/U(0,t)|_\omega$ based on the U values at $x = 0$ (glottis) and $x = 1$ (lips).

The eigenvalue $\lambda$ corresponds to the resonance angle frequency $\omega$ of the system. There are two methods for obtaining eigenvalues. One is the algebraic method which solves the derivative equation by converting it into a differential equation. The other focuses on the calculus of variations. The resonance frequencies of the vocal tract are the formant frequencies described in Sec. 2.4. If the angle frequency of the nth formant and its frequency bandwidth are represented by $\omega_n$ and $\pm\sigma_n$, respectively, the amplitude spectral characteristics $|H(\omega)|$ can be written as

$$|H(\omega)| = \prod_{n=1}^{\infty} |V_n(\omega)| = \prod_{n=1}^{\infty} \left| \frac{s_n s_n^*}{(s - s_n)(s - s_n^*)} \right|_{s=j\omega}$$

$$= \prod_{n=1}^{\infty} \frac{\omega_n^2 + \sigma_n^2}{\sqrt{(\omega - \omega_n)^2 + \sigma_n^2}\ \sqrt{(\omega + \omega_n)^2 + \sigma_n^2}} \tag{3.16}$$

Here, $|V_n(\omega)|$ is the amplitude spectrum of the nth formant, which has three specific characteristics, as indicated in Fig. 3.5 (Fant, 1959):

1. The spectrum is almost flat at $\omega < \omega_n$.
2. It has a resonance peak at $\omega \simeq \omega_n$, the level of which is decided by $\omega_n/\sigma_n$.
3. It decreases at high frequency with the inclination of −12 dB/oct at $\omega > \omega_n$.

As is clear, the $\omega_n$ value controls not only the resonance position but also the spectral level of the high-frequency region. On the other hand, $\sigma_n$ primarily influences the spectral shape near $\omega_n$.

In the above-mentioned model, the impedance-matching connection with the sound source part is assumed, and the losses in the vocal tract are taken into account only equivalently by the backward propagation wave into the sound source part. The actual vocal tract wall is not completely rigid, however, but has a finite mass and resistance. This effect increases the resonance frequency and bandwidth, especially for the lower-order formants.

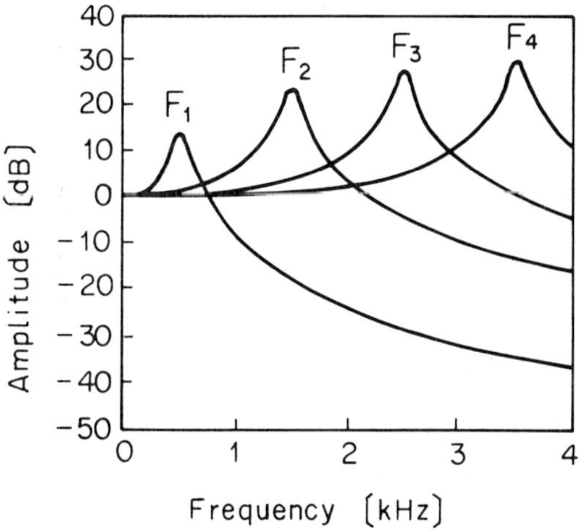


Fig. 3.5 Contribution of each formant to the amplitude spectrum.

## 3.4 VOCAL CORD MODEL

The vocal cord sound source is comprised of five principal physical characteristics (Stevens, 1977):

1. The fundamental frequency fluctuates both rapidly and slowly.
2. The volume velocity variation in the fundamental period is almost exactly proportional to the temporal variation of the open area function at the glottis, and can be approximated by asymmetrical triangular waves.
3. For a strong voice, the glottal-closed-interval increases and the triangular wave becomes sharper.
4. The frequency spectral envelope of the glottal wave has an inclination of -12--18 dB/oct.
5. Interaction with the vocal tract cannot be neglected in the frequency region below 500 Hz, and it influences the waveform at the onset of vocal cord vibration.

A two-mass model was investigated as a vocal cord vibration model which successfully expresses the actual vibration of human vocal cords (Ishizaka and Flanagan 1972; Flanagan et al., 1975). In this model, the vocal cord is separated into two parts which are connected to each other in terms of stiffness $k_c$, as indicated in Fig. 3.6. The vocal cords are assumed to move in only the vertical direction for simplicity's sake.

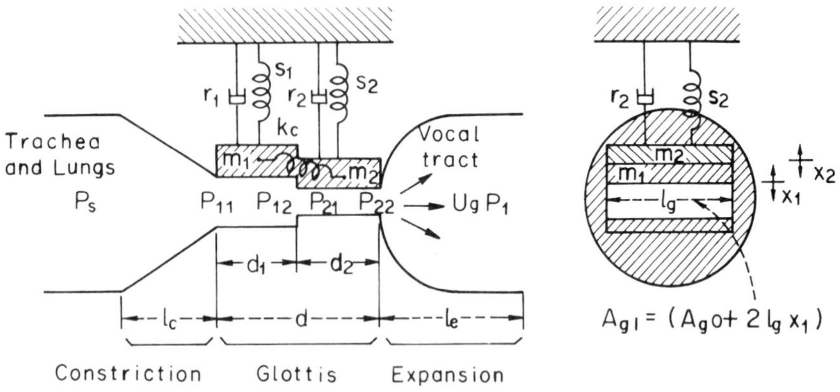


Fig. 3.6 Configuration of two-mass model; cross section of glottis ($A_{g1}$ = area at $d_1$ section; $A_{g0}$ = area in the neutral state at $d_1$ section).

Several physiological conditions and actually measured values were used in the simulation experiment based on this model. Additionally, an equivalent electrical circuit including the coupling to the vocal tract was introduced to achieve a high level of simulation. The simulation experiment made clear the conditions for the occurrence of vocal cord vibration (oscillation condition), vibration modes, temporal variation of the glottal area and volume velocity, and the vibration frequency of the vocal cords.

The results indicate that the variation rate of vocal cord vibration frequency according to the variation of subglottal pressure is 2–3 Hz per 1 cm $H_2O$, and that it is only slightly influenced by the vocal tract shape. In addition, a strong correlation is observable between the vocal tract shape (resonance characteristics) and vocal cord waveform. Furthermore, the phase difference between the vibration modes for the upper and lower parts of the vocal cord is found to be between $0^\circ$ and $60^\circ$. Finally, the model shows that vocal cord vibration can be determined by deciding on the subglottal pressure, vocal cord tension, glottal opening area during the neutral state, and the vocal tract shape.

Figure 3.7 indicates the glottal area, vocal cord vibration waveform (glottal volume velocity), and sound pressure at the lips for the vowel /a/ produced by this model. These results correspond well with our knowledge of vocal cord vibration.

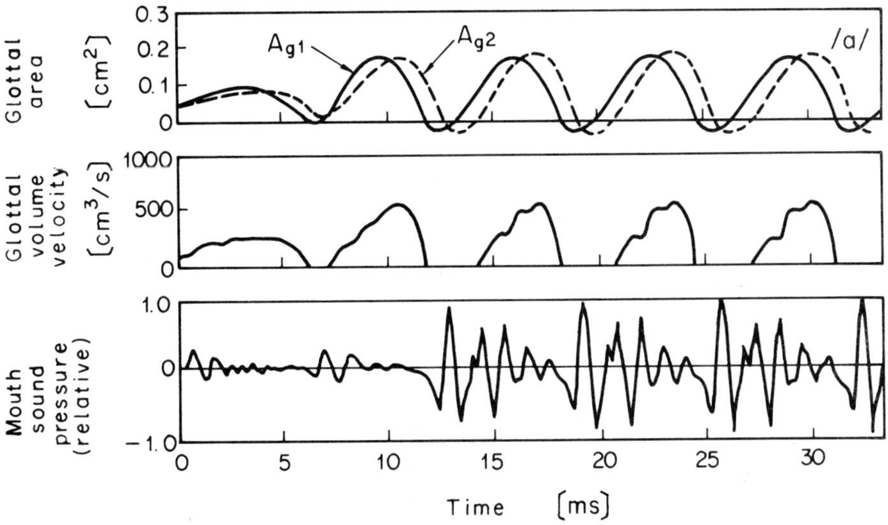


Fig. 3.7 Simulation of speech production for vowel /a/ using the two-mass model.

A speech production physical model which combines vocal cords and vocal tract characteristics based on the above-mentioned model is outlined in Fig. 3.8 (Flanagan et al., 1980). During experimentation, each control parameter of this speech production model was estimated by the analysis-by-synthesis method (A-b-S method; see Sec. 4.5) so that the analyzed results of an actual speech wave and synthesized voice using this model fit as closely as possible in the logarithmic spectral and cepstral domains. This model is the first system capable of completely taking into account the effect of vocal tract loss on the vocal cord vibration as well as the terminal effect of the glottis on the vocal tract characteristics. Consequently, the model is expected to fully contribute to the improvement of synthesized speech quality and to the progress of continuous speech recognition.

As for the noise source, models of turbulent flow production which incorporate the interaction with the vocal tract have been investigated (Stevens, 1971; Flanagan et al., 1975). These models should be able to realize an increase in the consonant resonance bandwidth accompanying the increased loss resulting from

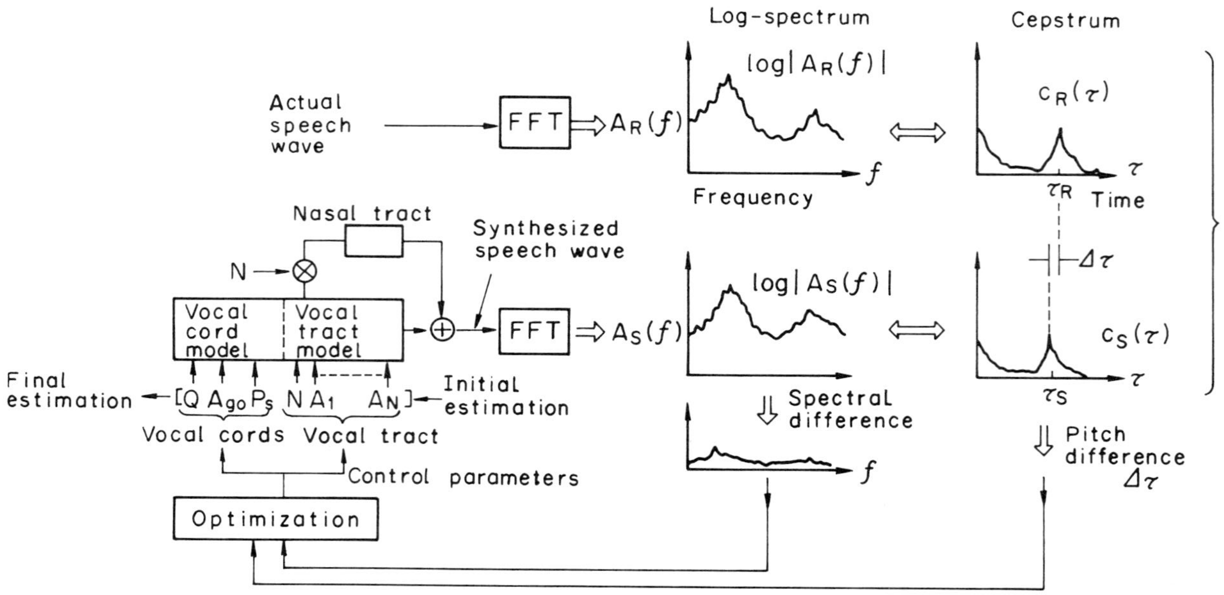


Fig. 3.8 Estimation procedure for the control parameters of the speech production model using the A-b-S method (Q = vocal cord tension; $A_{g0}$ = glottal area in the neutral state; $P_s$ = subglottal pressure; N = nasal coupling; $\{A_i\}$ = vocal tract area function).

turbulent sound source production. Such turbulent flow production upon constriction in the vocal tract and the diminishing of the turbulent flow caused by the release of this constriction are nonlinear hysteresis phenomena mediated by the Reynolds number. These phenomena will consequently require a highly complicated analysis.

## 3.5 ARTICULATORY MODEL

Another kind of physical speech production model, which we call the articulatory model, attempts to provide an efficient representation of the vocal tract area function. This model is based on the direct representation of the dynamic characteristics of the articulatory organs (Shirai and Honda, 1980). The model assumes that the nonlinear function $y = h(x)$ is given as shown in Fig. 3.9. Here, $y = h(x)$ transforms the articulatory parameters x representing the location of the articulatory organs into acoustic features of speech y. The values x are then estimated from y, by solving the nonlinear optimization problem.

The structure of the articulatory model and its articulatory parameters are detailed in Fig. 3.10. The tongue surface is

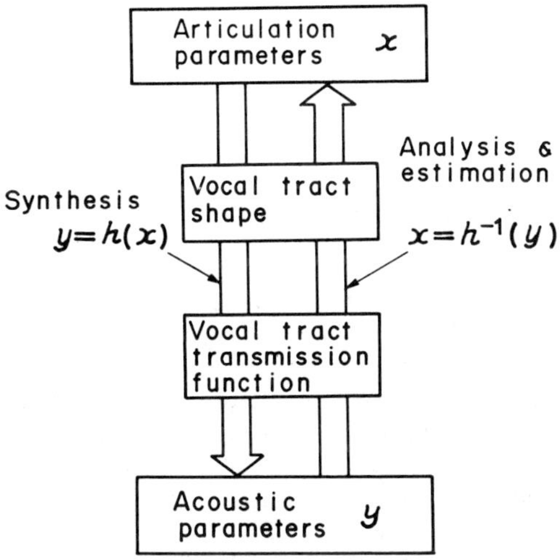


Fig. 3.9 Relationship between articulatory parameters and acoustic features in the articulatory model.

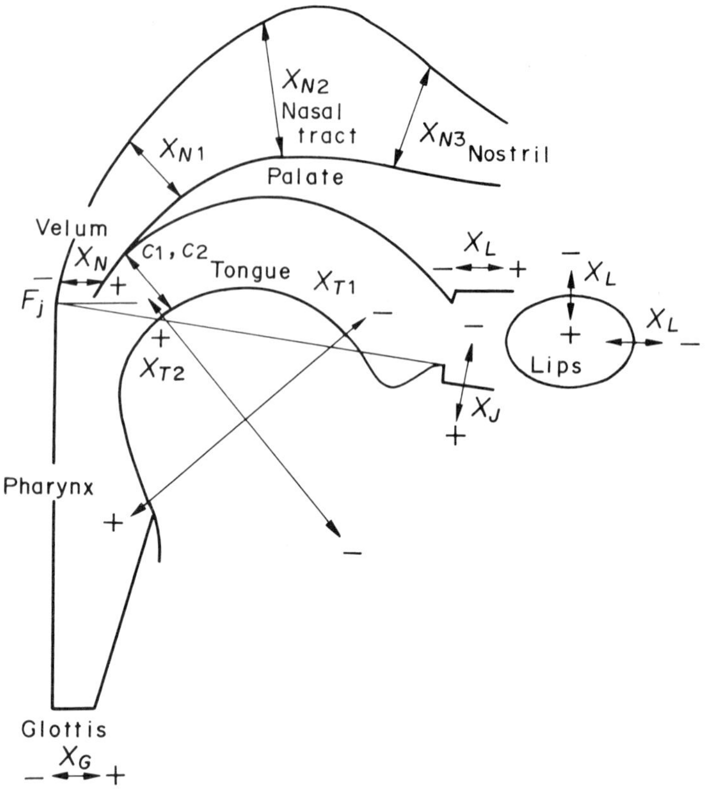


Fig. 3.10 Configuration of the articulatory model.

assumed to swing around the fixed center of $F_j$ as a result of the lower jaw opening, and its location is represented by the semipole coordinate. The location of the lower jaw is given by the opening angle $X_J$. The tongue surface shape normalized by the jaw opening is represented by the tongue articulatory parameters $X_{T1}$ (front-back) and $X_{T2}$ (high-low). The opening area and protruding value of the lips are represented by $X_L$, and the opening of the glottis is given by $X_G$. The location of the glottis is changed in accordance with the articulatory parameters of the lips and is indicated relative to the reference point $F_j$. Additionally, a nasalization parameter $X_N$ which represents the opening of the velum, is incorporated to represent the vocal tract shape configuration for nasalized sounds.

Hence, when a set of articulatory parameters $x = (X_{T1}, X_{T2}, X_J, X_L, X_G, X_N)$ is given, the vocal tract area can be decided and the transmission characteristics of the vocal tract according to the area function can be obtained. In other words, the set of acoustic features y for the speech wave is represented as a function of x, such that $y = h(x)$. The articulation condition can be estimated from a given speech wave by adjusting x so that it produces $\hat{y}$, which is close to the actual acoustic parameter set of the speech wave, based on an evaluation function. The A-b-S method, which is similar to the method employed in the physical model presented in the previous section, is used for the estimation. The mean vocal tract length is estimated for each speaker and used in the system to determine the overall physical size of the articulatory organs of each speaker.

An experiment based on this model using five connected vowels indicated that the spectral matching error is 1.8–3.6 dB, and that the mean formant frequency errors for the first to third formants are 13.2, 28.4, and 98.5 Hz, respectively. Furthermore, the experiment confirmed that the estimated articulatory parameter values are fairly reasonable. Speech recognition has also been attempted using these articulatory parameters.

# 4

# Digital Processing of Speech in Time and Frequency Domains

## 4.1 DIGITIZATION

The speech signal, or speech wave, can be changed into a processible object by converting it into an electrical signal using a microphone. The electrical signal is usually transformed from an analog into a digital signal prior to almost all speech processing for two reasons (Oppenheim and Schafer, 1975). First, digital techniques facilitate highly sophisticated signal processing which cannot otherwise be realized by analog techniques. Second, digital processing is far more reliable and can be accomplished by using a compact circuit. Rapid development of computers and integrated circuits in conjunction with the growth of digital communications networks have encouraged the application of digital processing techniques to speech processing.

Analog-to-digital conversion, commonly referred to as digitization, consists of the sampling, quantizing, and coding processes. Sampling is the process for depicting a continuously varying signal as a periodic sequence of values. Quantization involves approximately representing a waveform value by one of a finite set of values. Coding concerns assigning an actual number to each value. For such a task, binary coding, which uses binary number representation, is usually used. These processes thus enable a continuous analog signal to be converted into a sequence of codes selected from a finite set.

### 4.1.1 Sampling

In the sampling process, an analog signal x(t) is converted into a sequence (sampled sequence) of values $\{x_i\} = \{x(iT)\}$ at a periodic time $t_i = iT$ (i is an integer), as plotted in Fig. 4.1. Here, T [s] is called the sampling period, and its reciprocal, S = 1/T [Hz], is termed the sampling frequency. If T is too large, the original signal cannot be reproduced from the sampled sequence; conversely, if T is too small, useless samples for the original signal reproduction are included in the sampled sequence. Along these lines, Shannon-Someya's sampling theorem for the relationship between the frequency bandwidth of the analog signal to be sampled and the sampling period was proposed as a means for resolving this problem (Shannon and Weaver, 1949).

This sampling theorem says that when the analog signal x(t) is band-restricted between 0 and W [Hz] and when x(t) is sampled at every T = 1/2W [s], the original signal can be completely reproduced by

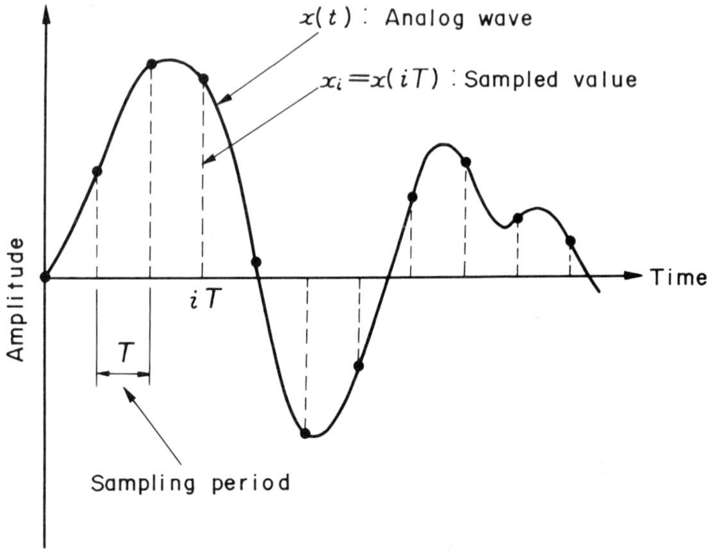


Fig. 4.1 Sampling in the time domain.

$$x(t) = \sum_{i=-\infty}^{\infty} x\left(\frac{i}{2W}\right) \frac{\sin\{2\pi W(t - i/2W)\}}{2\pi W(t - i/2W)} \qquad (4.1)$$

Here, $x(i/2W)$ is a sampled value of $x(t)$ at $t_i = i/2W$ ($i$ is an integer). Furthermore, $1/T = 2W$ [Hz] is called the Nyquist rate.

For example, a regular telephone signal can be sampled every $T = 1/8000$ [s], since its bandwidth W is restricted under 4 kHz. The sampling frequency for digitally processing speech signals is usually set between 6 and 16 kHz. Even for several special consonants, setting the sampling frequency at 20 kHz is sufficient. For those signals the frequency bandwidths of which are not known, a low-pass filter is used to restrict the bandwidths before sampling. When a signal is sampled contrary to the sampling theorem, aliasing distortion occurs, which distorts the high-frequency components of the signal, as shown in Fig. 4.2. The sampled signal, which is discontinuous in the time domain but still continuous in the amplitude domain, is called a discrete signal.

### 4.1.2 Quantization and Coding

During quantization, the entire continuous amplitude range is divided into finite subranges, and waveforms, the amplitudes of which are in the same subrange, are assigned the same amplitude values. Figure 4.3 exemplifies the input-output characteristics of an eight-level (3-bit) quantizer, where $\Delta$ is the quantization step size. In this example, each code is assigned so that it directly represents the amplitude value. The quantization characteristics depend on both the number of levels and on the quantization step size $\Delta$. When the signal is assumed to be quantized by B [bit], the number of levels is usually set to $2^B$ to ensure the most efficient use of the binary code words. $\Delta$ and B must be selected together to properly cover the range of the signal. If we assume that $|x_i| \leqq x_{max}$, then we should set

$$2x_{max} = \Delta 2^B \qquad (4.2)$$

The difference between the sampled value after quantization $\hat{x}_i$ and the original analog value $x_i$, $e_i = \hat{x}_i - x_i$, is called the quantization error, quantization distortion, or quantization noise. It can be seen in Fig. 4.3 that the quantization noise satisfies

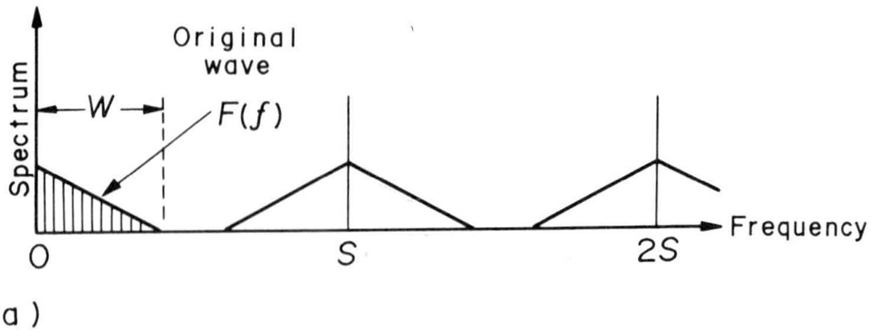


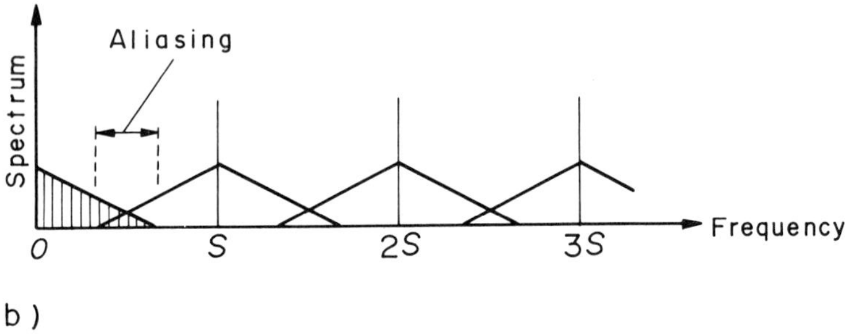


Fig. 4.2 Sampling in the frequency domain: (a) Correct sampling ($S \geqq 2W$); (b) incorrect sampling ($S < 2W$).

$$-\frac{\Delta}{2} \leqq e_i \leqq \frac{\Delta}{2} \tag{4.3}$$

when $\Delta$ and B are set to satisfy Eq. (4.2).

A statistical model incorporating three characteristics can be assumed to serve as the quantization noise (Rabiner and Schafer, 1975). The first characteristic is that the quantization noise is a stationary white noise process. The second is that the quantization noise is uncorrelated with the input signal. The third is that the distribution of quantization errors is uniform over each quantization interval, and that the following equation is satisfied since all quantization intervals have the same length:

$$\begin{aligned} \text{Prob}(e_i) &= \frac{1}{\Delta} \qquad -\frac{\Delta}{2} \leqq e_i \leqq \frac{\Delta}{2} \\ &= 0 \qquad \text{otherwise} \end{aligned} \tag{4.4}$$

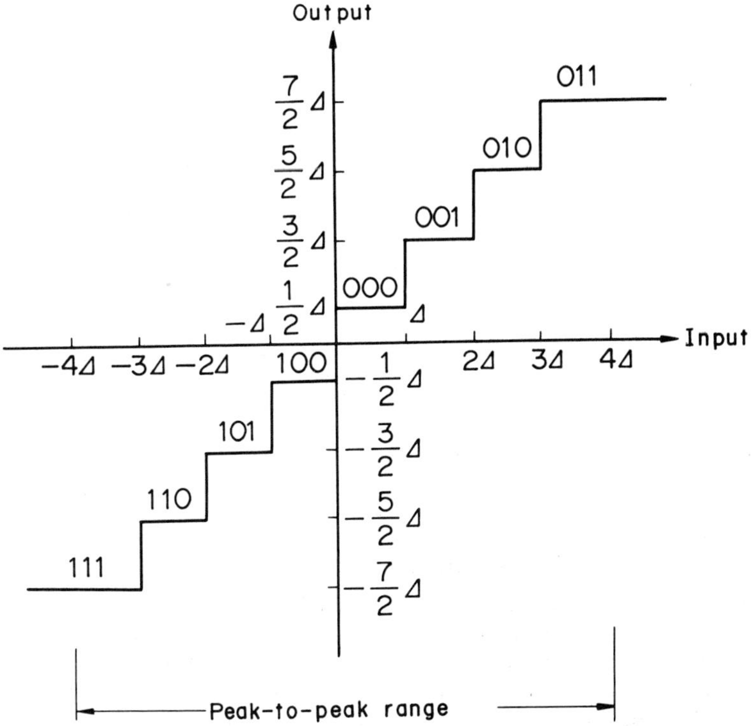


Fig. 4.3 An example of the input-output characteristics of eight-level (3-bit) quantization.

The signal-to-quantization noise ratio (SNR) is defined as

$$\mathrm{SNR} = \frac{\sigma_x^2}{\sigma_e^2} = \frac{E[x_i^2]}{E[e_i^2]} = \frac{\Sigma x_i^2}{\Sigma e_i^2} \qquad (4.5)$$

When the above-mentioned assumptions and Eq. (4.2) are satisfied,

$$\sigma_e^2 = \frac{\Delta^2}{12} = \frac{1}{12}\left(\frac{2x_{max}}{2^B}\right)^2 = \frac{x_{max}^2}{3 \times 2^{2B}} \qquad (4.6)$$

Therefore,

$$\mathrm{SNR} = \frac{3 \times 2^{2B}}{(x_{max}/\sigma_x)^2} \tag{4.7}$$

or, when represented in the dB scale,

$$\mathrm{SNR\ [dB]} = 10 \log_{10}\left(\frac{\sigma_x^2}{\sigma_e^2}\right)$$

$$= 6B + 4.77 - 20 \log_{10} \frac{x_{max}}{\sigma_x} \tag{4.8}$$

When the quantization range is set to $x_{max} = 4\sigma_x$,

$$\mathrm{SNR\ [dB]} = 6B - 7.2 \tag{4.9}$$

### 4.1.3 A/D and D/A Conversion

Conversion from analog to digital signals is called A/D conversion, and, conversely, the opposite process is known as D/A conversion. The low-pass filtering necessary before A/D conversion is also necessary after D/A conversion to remove the distortion present in the higher harmonic components. The relationship between the low-pass filter characteristics and the D/A conversion frequency must satisfy the same requirement as that fundamental to the sampling process.

In speech signal processing, preemphasis, namely, the compression of the signal dynamic range by flattening the spectral tilt, is effective in raising the SNR. This is usually done by emphasizing the higher-frequency components roughly 6 dB/oct prior to low-pass filtering for A/D conversion. Preemphasis can also be accomplished after A/D conversion through differential calculation or through application of the first-order digital filtering

$$H(z) = 1 - \alpha z^{-1} \tag{4.10}$$

where $\alpha$ is set to a value close to 1. Maximizing the SNR as much as possible, however, necessitates that preemphasis be applied prior to A/D conversion. The process of adding a tilt of

6 dB/oct to reproduce the original spectral tilt is called deemphasis.

Since the dynamic range of the speech wave is larger than 50 dB, 10 bits or more is necessary for A/D conversion. However, when block normalization is applied at every short period to normalize the amplitude variation by multiplying a constant value assigned to the short period by the speech wave, a sufficient quantization resolution can be obtained even at a bit rate of 6 to 7 bits. Since the peak factor of speech is 12 dB, the permissible maximum level of an A/D converter must be set 12 dB higher than the effective level of the input speech signal.

## 4.2 SPECTRAL ANALYSIS

### 4.2.1 Spectral Structure of Speech

As discussed in Sec. 2.4, the speech wave is usually analyzed using spectral features, such as the frequency spectrum and autocorrelation function, instead of directly using the waveform. There are two important reasons for this. One is that the speech wave is considered to be reproducible by summing the sinusoidal waves, the amplitude and phase of which change slowly. The other is that the critical features for perceiving speech by the human ear are mainly included in the spectral information, with the phase information not usually playing a key role.

The power spectral density in a short interval, that is, the short-time spectrum of speech, can be regarded as the product of two elements: the spectral envelope, which slowly changes as a function of frequency, and the spectral fine structure, which changes rapidly. The spectral fine structure produces periodic patterns for voiced sounds but not for unvoiced sounds, as shown in Fig. 4.4. The spectral envelope, or the overall spectral feature, reflects not only the resonance and antiresonance characteristics of the articulatory organs, but also the overall shape of the glottal source spectrum and radiation characteristics at the lips and nostrils. On the other hand, the spectral fine structure corresponds to the periodicity of the sound source.

Methods for spectral envelope extraction can be divided into parametric analysis (PA) and nonparametric analysis (NPA). In PA, a model which fits the objective signal is selected and applied to the signal by adjusting the feature parameters representing the model. On the other hand, NPA methods can generally be applied to various signals since they do not model the signals. If the model thoroughly fits the objective signal, PA

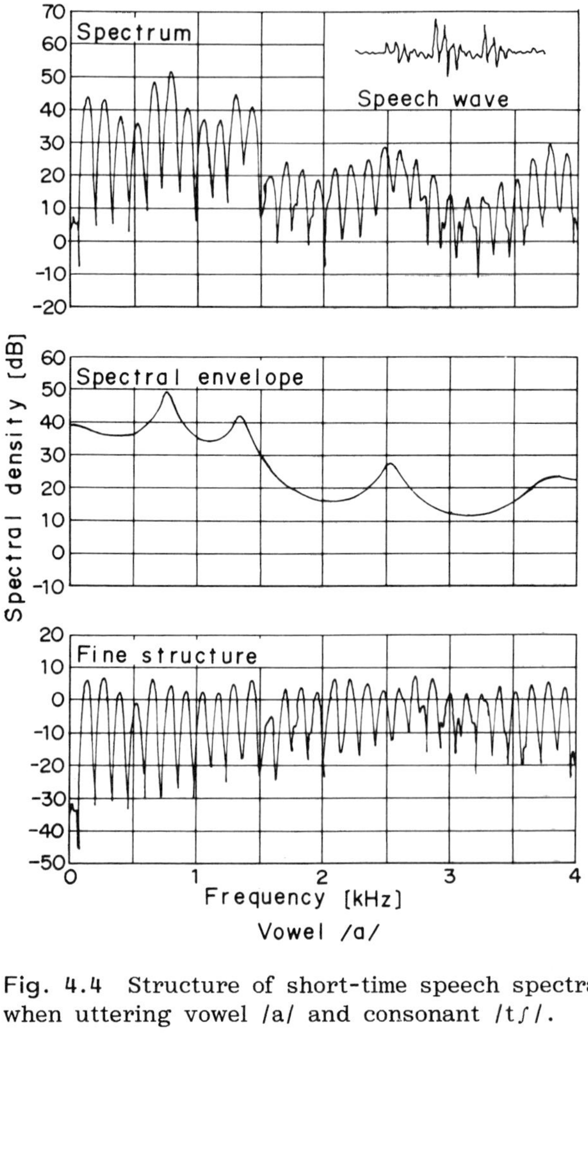


Fig. 4.4 Structure of short-time speech spectra for male voices when uttering vowel /a/ and consonant /tʃ/.

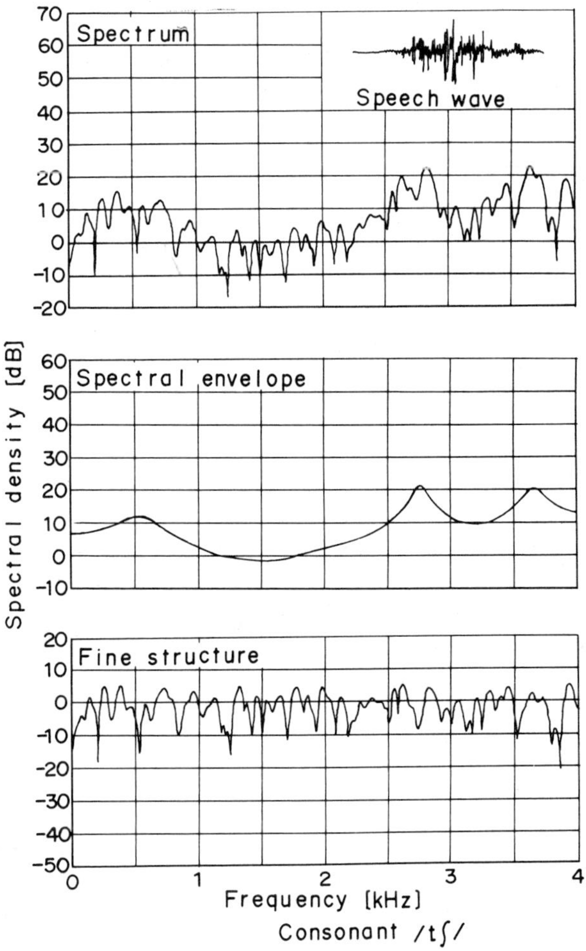


Fig. 4.4 (Continued)

methods can represent the features of the signal more effectively than can NPA methods. The major methods for analyzing the speech spectrum and spectral features are shown in Table 4.1 (Itakura and Tohkura, 1978). Of these, linear predictive coding analysis will be described precisely in Chap. 5.

### 4.2.2 Autocorrelation and Fourier Transform

When a sampled time sequence is written by x(n) (n is an integer), its autocorrelation function $\phi(m)$ is defined as

$$\phi(m) = \frac{1}{N} \sum_{n=0}^{N-1-|m|} x(n)x(n + |m|) \qquad (|m| = 0,1,\ldots,N-1) \tag{4.11}$$

where N is the number of samples in the short-time analysis interval. The length of the interval, NT (T is a sampling period), is usually set at around 30 ms. Specifically, intervals of around 20 and 40 ms often bring good results for female and male voices, respectively.

The short-time spectrum $S(\omega)$ and $\phi(m)$ constitute the Fourier transform pair (Wiener-Khintchine theorem)

$$S(\omega) = \frac{1}{2\pi} \sum_{m=-(N-1)}^{N-1} \phi(m) \cos \omega m$$

and

$$\phi(m) = \int_{-\pi}^{\pi} S(\omega) \cos \omega m \, d\omega \tag{4.12}$$

where $\omega$ is a normalized angle frequency which can be represented by $\omega = 2\pi fT$ (f is a real frequency). $S(\omega)$ is usually computed directly from the speech wave using the discrete Fourier transform (DFT) facilitated by the fast Fourier transform (FFT) algorithm:

$$S(\omega) = \frac{1}{2\pi N} \left| \sum_{n=0}^{N-1} x(n)e^{-j\omega n} \right|^2 \tag{4.13}$$

TABLE 4.1 Major Methods for Analyzing Speech Spectra and Their Principal Features

| Type | Analysis method | Parameters | Features |
|---|---|---|---|
| NPA | (i) Short-time autocorrelation | $\phi(m)$ | Spectral envelope and fine structure are convoluted. Simple, easy algorithm facilitates hardware realization. |
| | (ii) Short-time spectrum | $S(\omega)$ | Spectral envelope and fine structure are multiplied. Fast algorithm can be realized by FFT. |
| | (iii) Cepstrum | $c(\tau)$ | Spectral envelope and fine structure can be separated in quefrency domain. Two FFTs and log transform are necessary. |
| | (iv) Band-pass filter bank | rms of filter output | Global spectral envelope can be obtained. Appropriate for real-time processing. |
| | (v) Zero-crossing analysis | Zero-crossing rate | Formant freq. can be obtained by combination with (iv). Realized by simple hardware. |
| PA | (i) Analysis-by-synthesis | Formant, bandwidth, etc. | Precise modeling is possible. Accurate formant freq. can be obtained. Complicated iteration is necessary. |
| | (ii) Linear predictive coding | | Simple all-pole spectrum modeling. Parameters can be estimated from autocorr. or covariance without iteration. |
| | (ii-a) Maximum likelihood method | $\alpha_i$ | Stability of synthesis filter is guaranteed. Time window is necessary. Number of calculations $\propto p^2$ |

TABLE 4.1 (Continued)

| Type | Analysis method | Parameters | Features |
|---|---|---|---|
| PA (cont.) | (ii-b) Covariance method | $\alpha_i$ $k_i$ | Stability of synthesis filter is not guaranteed. Suitable for short-time analysis. Number of calculations $\propto p^3$ |
| | (ii-c) PARCOR method | $k_i$ | Normal equation can be solved by lattice filter. Equivalent to (a) and (b). Number of calculations $\propto p^2$ |
| | (ii-d) LSP method | $\omega_i$ | Quantization and interpolation characteristics are good. Similar to formant. Number of calculations is slightly larger than for PARCOR. |

NPA = nonparametric analysis; PA = parametric analysis; rms = root mean square; p = order of linear predictive coding model.

The autocorrelation function can also be calculated more simply by using the DFT (FFT) compared with the conventional correlation calculation method when higher-order correlation elements are needed. With this method, the autocorrelation function is obtained as the inverse Fourier transform of the short-time spectrum, which is calculated by using Eq. (4.13).

### 4.2.3 Window Function

In order to extract the N-sample interval from the speech wave for calculating the autocorrelation function and spectrum, the speech wave must be multiplied by an appropriate time window. Therefore, $x(n)$, indicated in Eqs. (4.11) and (4.13) for calculating $\phi(m)$ and $S(\omega)$, respectively, is usually not the original waveform but rather the waveform multiplied by the window function.

The multiplication of the speech wave by the window function has two effects. First, it gradually attenuates the amplitude at both ends of the extraction interval to prevent an abrupt change at the endpoints. Second, it produces the convolution for the Fourier transform of the window function and the speech spectrum, or the weighted moving average in the spectral domain. It is thus desirable that the window function satisfy two characteristics in order to reduce the spectral distortion caused by the windowing. One is a high-frequency resolution, principally, a narrow and sharp main robe. The other is a small spectral leak from other spectral elements produced by the convolution, in other words, a large attenuation of the side robe. The definition and properties of the convolution are specifically described in Appendix A.

Since these two requirements are actually contrary to each other, and because it is impossible to satisfy both, several compromise window functions have been proposed. Among these, the Hamming window $W_H(n)$, defined as

$$W_H(n) = 0.54 - 0.46 \cos\left(\frac{2n\pi}{N - 1}\right) \qquad (4.14)$$

is usually used as the window function for speech analysis. The Hamming window is advantageous in that its resolution in the frequency domain is relatively high and its spectral leak is small since the attenuation of the side robe is more than 43 dB.

On the other hand, a rectangular window, $W_R(n) = 1$ $(0 \leqq n \leqq N - 1)$, which corresponds to the simple extraction of N-sample points of the speech wave, has the largest frequency resolution, whereas the attenuation of its first side robe is only 13 dB. The rectangular window thus is not suited to the analysis of a speech wave having a large dynamic range of spectral components.

Another window, called the Hanning window,

$$W_N(n) = 0.5 - 0.5 \cos\left(\frac{2n\pi}{N - 1}\right) \qquad (4.15)$$

is also employed. Although the advantage of this window is that its higher-order side robes are lower than those of the Hamming window, the attenuation of the first side robe is only roughly 30 dB. The shapes of these windows and the spectra for 10 periods of 1-kHz sinusoidal waves extracted by using these windows are shown in Fig. 4.5.

The relationship between the sampling period T [s], number of samples for analysis N, and nominal frequency resolution of the calculated spectrum $\Delta f$ [Hz] is expressed as

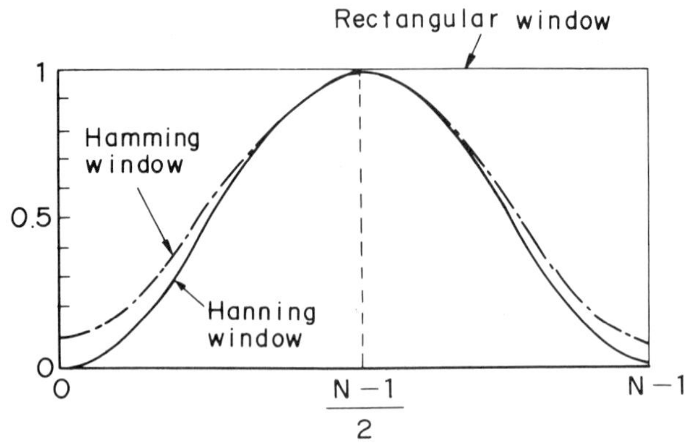


(a)

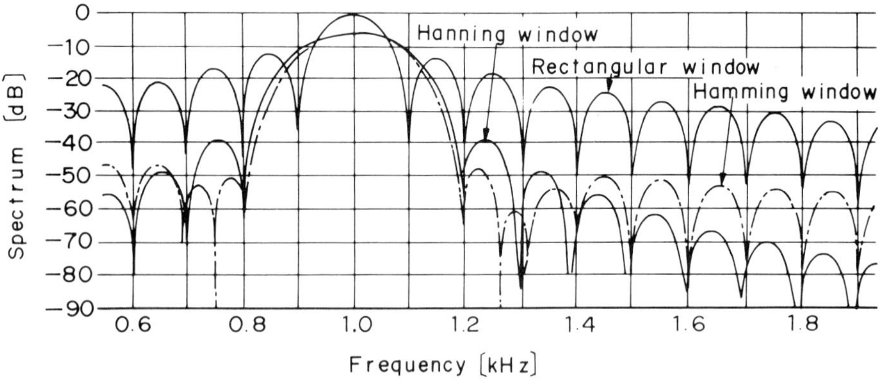


(b)

Fig. 4.5 Major window functions (a) and the spectrum for the 10 periods of a 1-kHz sinusoidal wave extracted using each of the windows (b).

$$\Delta f = \frac{1}{TN} \tag{4.16}$$

From this, it is clear that the resolution increases in proportion to the length of the speech interval for analysis. For example, when T = 0.125 ms (8-kHz sampling) and N = 256 (32-ms duration),

$$\Delta f = \frac{10^3}{0.125 \times 256} \simeq 31 \text{ [Hz]} \tag{4.17}$$

When the analysis window length increases, the frequency resolution increases as the time resolution decreases. On the other hand, when the analysis window length shortens, the time resolution increases as the frequency resolution decreases. These relationships can be easily understood from the fact that the multiplication of the waveform by a window function corresponds to the moving average of the spectrum in the frequency domain.

Furthermore, when the waveform is multiplied by either the Hamming or the Hanning window, the effective analysis interval length becomes approximately 40% shorter since the waveforms near both ends of the window are compressed, as indicated in Fig. 4.5. This results in a consequent 40% decrease in the frequency resolution.

Hence, the multiplication of the speech wave by an appropriate window reduces the spectral fluctuation due to the variation of the pitch excitation position within the analysis interval. This is effective in producing stable spectra during the analysis of voiced sounds featuring clear pitch periodicity. Since multiplication by the window function decreases the effective analysis interval length, the analysis interval should be overlappingly shifted along the speech wave to facilitate tracing the time-varying spectra.

The short-time analysis interval multiplied by a window function and extracted from the speech wave is called a frame. The length of the frame is referred to as the frame length, and the frame shifting interval is termed the frame interval.

A block diagram of a typical speech analysis procedure is shown in Fig. 4.6. Also indicated at each stage are typical parameter values and examples of speech waves.

### 4.2.4 Sound Spectrogram

Sound spectrogram analysis is a method for plotting the time function of the speech spectrum using density plots. The special device used for measuring and plotting the sound spectrogram is called the sound spectrograph. Figure 4.7 is an example of sound spectrograms for the Japanese word /ko:geN/, or "plateau," uttered by a male speaker. As indicated, the sound spectrogram provides two types of representations: light and dark and contour. Light-and-dark representations illustrate the magnitude of the frequency component by darkness, in other

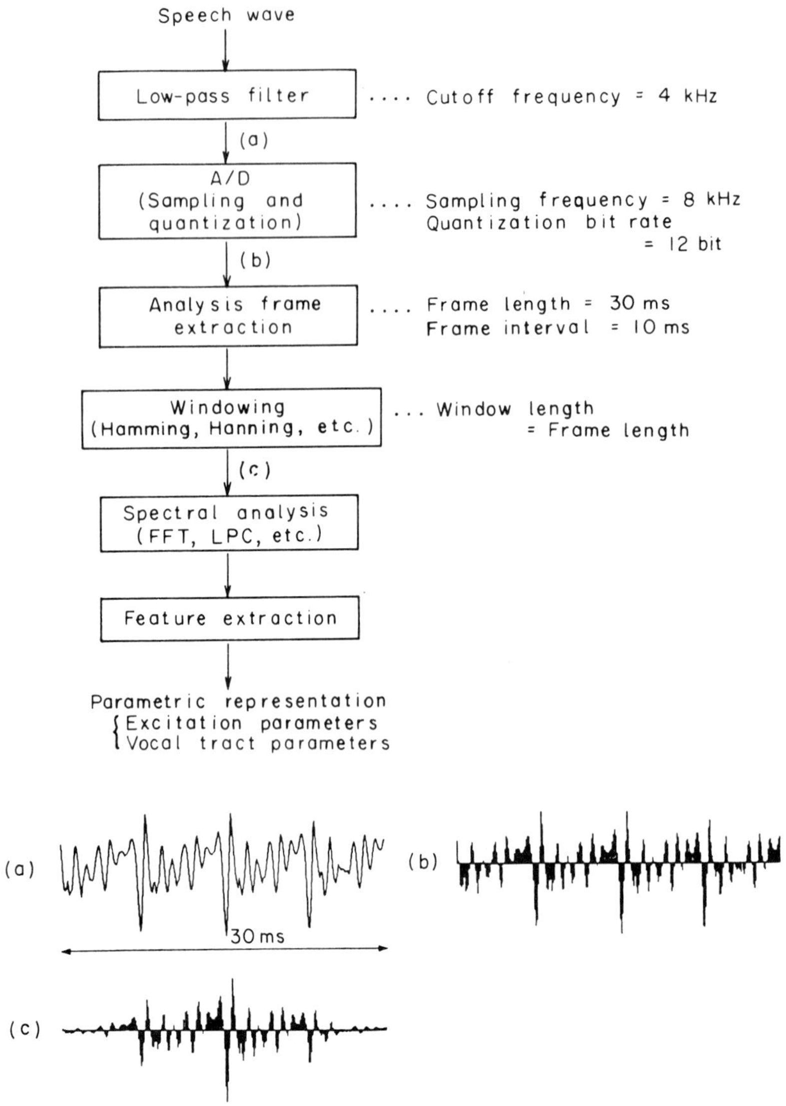


Fig. 4.6 Block diagram of a typical speech analysis procedure. Typical parameter values and examples of speech waves at each stage are also indicated.

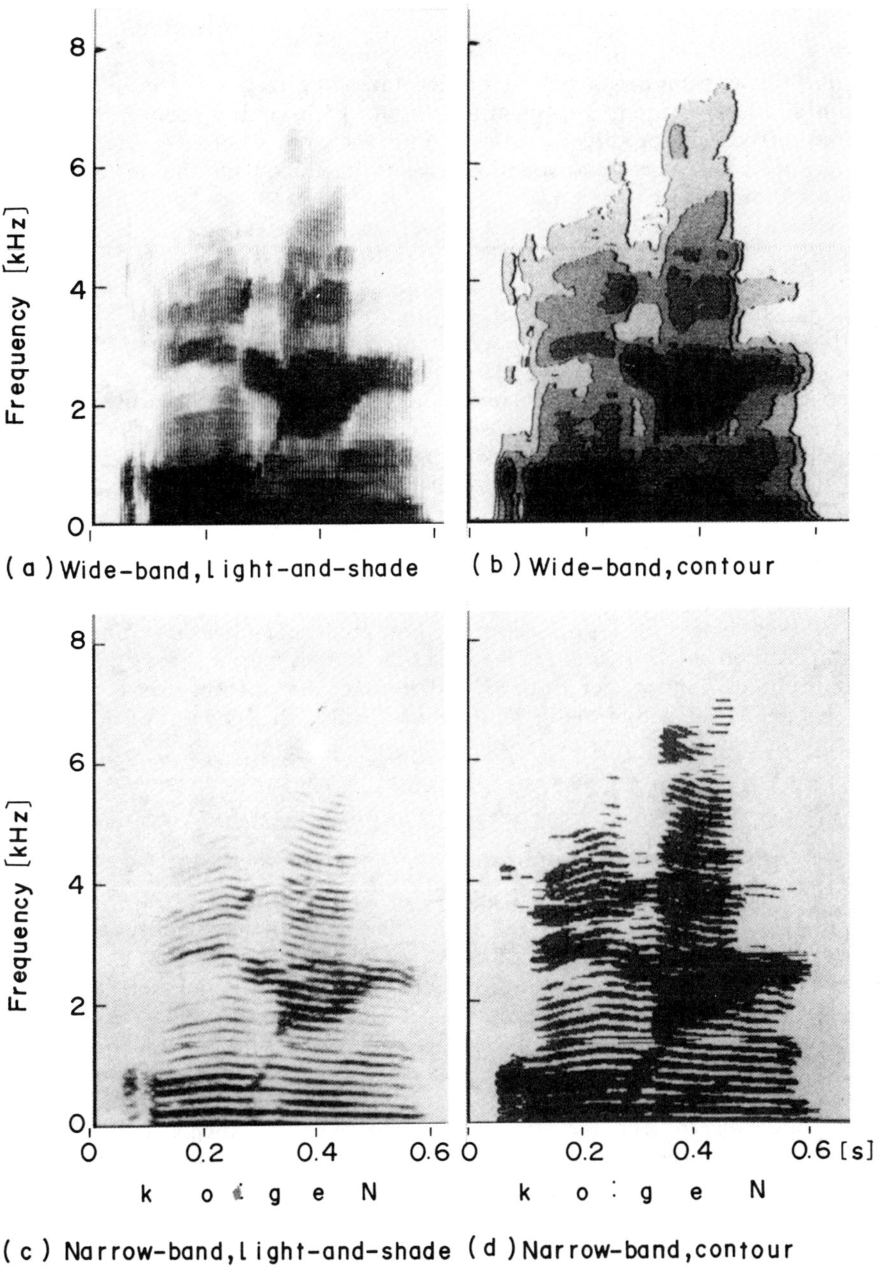


Fig. 4.7 Examples of sound spectrograms for a male voice when uttering the Japanese word /ko:geN/.

words, the darker areas reveal higher-intensity frequency components. With contour representations, as with contour maps, the magnitude is roughly quantized, and the area where the magnitude is in the same quantization level is produced by the same shade of darkness.

Usually the bandwidth of the band-pass filter (see Sec. 4.4.1) for the frequency analysis, i.e., the frequency resolution, is either 300 Hz or 45 Hz, depending on the purpose of the analysis. When the frequency resolution is 300 Hz, the effective length of the speech analysis interval is roughly 3 ms, and when the resolution is 45 Hz, the length becomes 22 ms. Since this trade-off occurs between the frequency and time resolutions, the pitch structure of speech is indicated by a vertically-striped fine repetitive pattern along the time axis in the case of the 300-Hz frequency resolution, and by a horizontally-striped equally fine repetitive pattern along the frequency axis in the case of the 45-Hz resolution, as shown in Fig. 4.7.

Many of the sound spectrograms originally produced by analog technology using the sound spectrograph are now produced by digital technology through computers and their peripherals. The digital method is particularly beneficial in that it permits easy adjustment of various conditions, and in that the spectrograms can be produced sequentially and automatically with good reproducibility.

## 4.3 CEPSTRUM

### 4.3.1 Cepstrum and Its Application

The cepstrum, or cepstral coefficient, $c(\tau)$ is defined as the inverse Fourier transform of the short-time logarithmic amplitude spectrum $|X(\omega)|$ (Bogert et al., 1963; Noll, 1964; Noll, 1967). The term cepstrum is essentially a coined word which includes the meaning of the inverse transform of the spectrum. The independent parameter for the cepstrum is called quefrency, which is obviously formed from the word frequency. Since the cepstrum is the inverse transform of the frequency domain function, the quefrency becomes the time-domain parameter. The special feature of the cepstrum is that it allows for the separate representation of the spectral envelope and fine structure.

Based on the linear separable equivalent circuit model described in Sec. 3.2, voiced speech $x(t)$ can be regarded as the response of the vocal tract articulation equivalent filter driven by a pseudoperiodic source $g(t)$. Then $x(t)$ can be given by the convolution of $g(t)$ and vocal tract impulse response $h(t)$ as

$$x(t) = \int_0^t g(\tau)h(t - \tau)\, d\tau$$

which is equivalent to

$$X(\omega) = G(\omega)H(\omega) \tag{4.18}$$

where $X(\omega)$, $G(\omega)$, and $H(\omega)$ are the Fourier transforms of $x(t)$, $g(t)$, and $h(t)$, respectively.

If $g(t)$ is a periodic function, $|X(\omega)|$ is represented by line spectra, the frequency intervals of which are the reciprocal of the fundamental period of $g(t)$. Therefore, when $|X(\omega)|$ is calculated by the Fourier transform of a sampled time sequence for a short speech wave period, it exhibits sharp peaks with equal intervals along the frequency axis. Its logarithm $\log|X(\omega)|$ is

$$\log|X(\omega)| = \log|G(\omega)| + \log|H(\omega)| \tag{4.19}$$

The cepstrum, which is the inverse Fourier transform of $\log|X(\omega)|$, is

$$c(\tau) = F^{-1} \log |X(\omega)| = F^{-1} \log |G(\omega)| + F^{-1} \log |H(\omega)| \tag{4.20}$$

where $F$ is the Fourier transform. The first and second terms on the right side of Eq. (4.19) correspond to the spectral fine structure and the spectral envelope, respectively. The former is the periodic pattern, and the latter is the global pattern along the frequency axis. Accordingly, large differences occur between the inverse Fourier transform functions of both elements indicated in Eq. (4.20).

Principally, the first function on the right side of Eq. (4.20) indicates the formation of a peak in the high-quefrency region, and the second function represents a concentration in the low-quefrency region from 0 to 2 or 4 ms. The fundamental period of the source $g(t)$ can then be extracted from the peak at the high-quefrency region. On the other hand, the Fourier transform of the low-quefrency elements produces the logarithmic spectral envelope from which the linear spectral envelope can be obtained through the exponential transform. The maximum order of low-quefrency elements used for the transform determines the smoothness of the spectral envelope. The process of separating the cepstral elements into these two factors is called liftering, which is derived from filtering.

When the cepstrum value is calculated by the DFT, it is necessary to set the base value of the transform, N, large enough to eliminate the aliasing similar to that produced during waveform sampling. The cepstrum then becomes

$$c_n = \frac{1}{N} \sum_{k=0}^{N-1} \log |X(k)| e^{j2\pi kn/N} \qquad (0 \leq n \leq N-1) \tag{4.21}$$

The process steps for extracting the fundamental period and spectral envelope using the cepstral method are given in Fig. 4.8, with examples of the extracted results shown in Fig. 4.9 (Noll, 1967). The cepstrum values indicated in the latter figure are the squared values of the cepstrum $c_n$ defined above.

### 4.3.2 Homomorphic Analysis and LPC Cepstrum

Cepstral analysis, which is the process of separating two convolutionally related properties by transforming the relationship into a summation, is a kind of homomorphic analysis or filtering (Oppenheim and Schafer, 1968). In general, homomorphic analysis implies signal processing, which decomposes the nonlinear system into independent factors, similar to the filtering which differentiates the linearly added signals. Homomorphic analysis makes use of several special methods to transform the relationship into an additive one.

Let us consider the cepstrum in a special case in which $X(\omega) = H(z)|_{z=\exp(j\omega T)}$. Here, H(z) is the z-transform of the impulse response of an all-pole speech production system estimated by the linear predictive coding (LPC) analysis method (see Chap. 5). Accordingly,

$$H(z) = \frac{1}{1 + \sum_{i=1}^{p} \alpha_i z^{-i}} \tag{4.22}$$

The definition and properties of the z-transform are described in Appendix A.

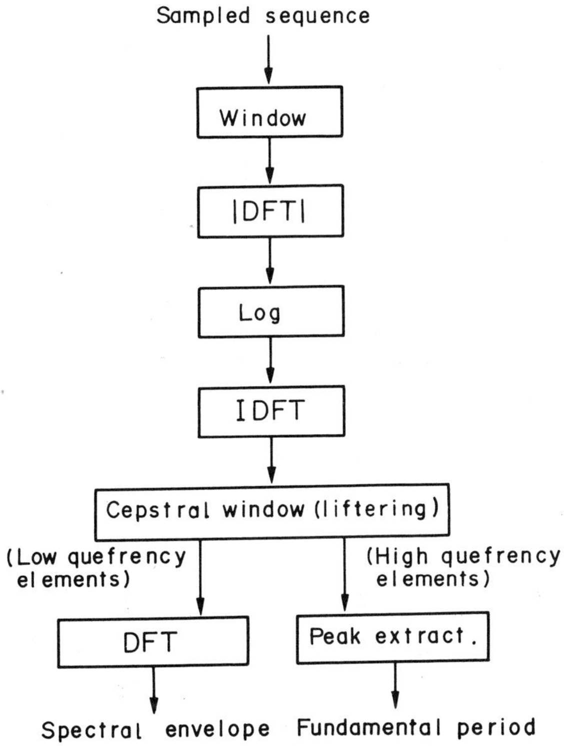


Fig. 4.8 Block diagram of cepstrum analysis for extracting spectral envelope and fundamental period.

Equation (4.22) means that the all-pole spectrum H(z) is used for the spectral density of the speech signal. This is accomplished by expanding the cepstrum into a complex form by replacing the DFT, logarithmic transform, and inverse discrete Fourier transform (IDFT) in Fig. 4.8 with a dual z-transform, complex logarithmic transform, and inverse dual z-transform, respectively (Atal, 1974). When this complex cepstrum for a time sequence x(n) is represented by $\hat{c}_n$, and their dual z-transforms are indicated by X(z) and C(z), respectively,

$$\hat{C}(z) = \log [X(z)] \tag{4.23}$$

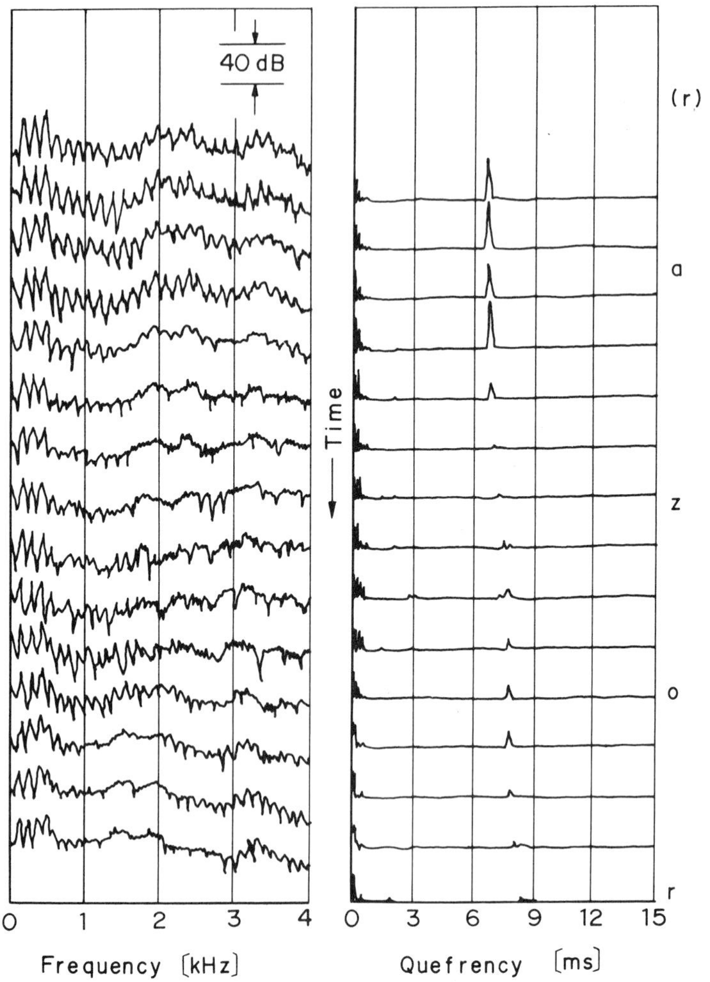


Fig. 4.9 Examples of short-time spectra (left) and cepstra (right) for male voice when uttering "(r)azor." Sampling frequency 10 kHz; Hamming window length 40 ms; frame interval 10 ms.

If we now differentiate both parts of this equation by $z^{-1}$, and then multiply by X(z), we have

$$X(z)\hat{C}'(z) = X'(z) \tag{4.24}$$

This equation permits recursive equations to be obtained:

$$\hat{c}_1 = -\alpha_1$$

$$\hat{c}_n = -\alpha_n - \sum_{m=1}^{n-1}\left(1 - \frac{m}{n}\right)\alpha_m\hat{c}_{n-m} \qquad (1 < n \leqq p) \tag{4.25}$$

$$\hat{c}_n = -\sum_{m=1}^{p}\left(1 - \frac{m}{n}\right)\alpha_m\hat{c}_{n-m} \qquad (p < n)$$

This cepstrum is referred to as the LPC cepstrum, since it is derived through the LPC model. The original cepstrum is sometimes called the FFT cepstrum to distinguish it from the LPC cepstrum.

Figure 4.10 compares the spectral envelope calculated using the cepstrum directly extracted from the waveform with that calculated using the LPC cepstrum (Furui, 1981). In this figure, the short-time spectrum and the spectral envelope extracted by LPC (maximum likelihood method) are also shown for reference. The spectral envelope derived from the LPC cepstrum clearly tends to follow the spectral peaks more strictly than does the spectral envelope obtained through the FFT cepstrum.

## 4.4 FILTER BANK AND ZERO-CROSSING ANALYSIS

### 4.4.1 Digital Filter Bank

The digital filter bank, more specifically, a set of band-pass filters, is one of the NPA techniques mentioned in Sec. 4.2.1. The filter bank requires a relatively small amount of calculation and is therefore quite suitable for hardware implementation. Since there is a definite trade-off between the time and frequency resolution of each band-pass filter, as indicated in Sec. 4.2.3, it is necessary to design various parameters according to the purposes intended. Generally, the band-pass filters are arranged

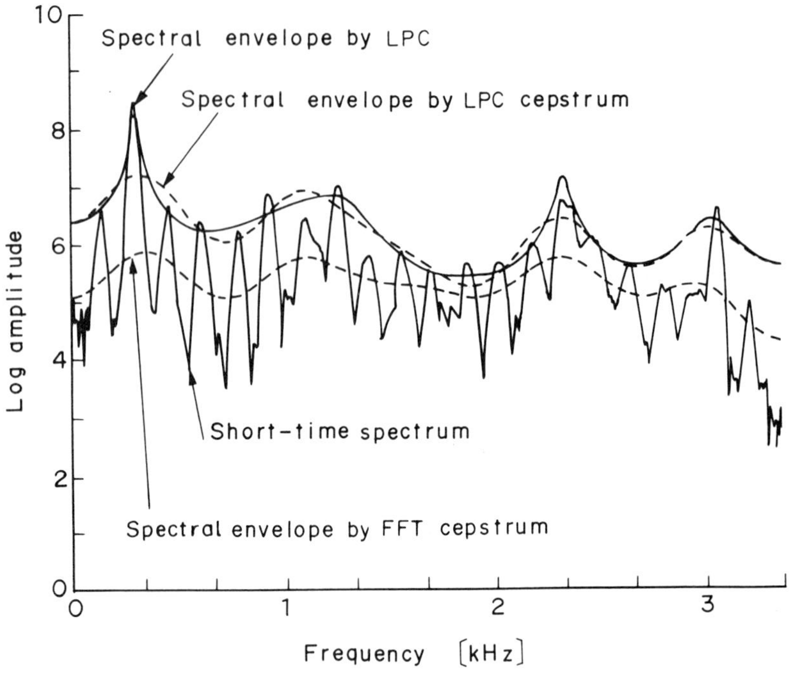


Fig. 4.10 Comparison of spectral envelopes by LPC, LPC cepstrum, and FFT cepstrum methods.

so that the center frequencies are distributed with equal intervals on the logarithmic frequency scale, taking human auditory characteristics into account, and so that the 3-dB attenuation points of the adjacent filters coincide. The output of each bandpass filter is rectified, smoothed by rms (root mean square) value calculation, and sampled every 5 to 20 ms to obtain values which represent the spectral envelope.

The spectral analysis part of the sound spectrogram analysis described in Sec. 4.2.4 is usually performed using a single bandpass filter whose center frequency is continuously changed. There the recorded speech wave is iteratively played back and analyzed by the filter.

### 4.4.2 Zero-Crossing Analysis

The zero-crossing number of the speech wave in a predetermined time interval, which is counted as the number of times when adjacent sample points have different positive and negative signs, approximately corresponds to the frequency of the major spectral component. Based on this principle, formant frequencies can be estimated by zero-crossing analysis as follows. First, the speech wave is passed through a set of four or five octave band-pass filters, and the power and zero-crossing number of the rectified and smoothed output of each filter are measured at short intervals, such as 10 ms. When the power of a filter exceeds the predetermined threshold, this frequency range is regarded as having a formant, with the formant frequency being estimated by the zero-crossing rate. This zero-crossing rate can also be used to detect the periodicity of the sound source as well as to estimate the fundamental period. Although the zero-crossing analysis method is well suited to hardware implementation, its drawback is that it is sensitive to additive noise.

## 4.5 ANALYSIS-BY-SYNTHESIS

Analysis-by-synthesis (A-b-S), presented in Fig. 4.11, is the process of determining the parameters which characterize the system based on an assumed signal production model (Bell et al., 1961). The model parameters are adjusted in the course of iterative feedback control so that the error between the observed value and that produced by the model is minimized. Important in A-b-S are selection of the assumed production model, the initial parameter values, the error evaluation measure, and the minimization algorithm. A-b-S is useful not only for speech parameter extraction but also for many applications in which a production model can be used.

During formant frequency extraction based on the A-b-S technique, the following parameters are adjusted: the first through the third or fourth formant frequencies and bandwidths, the fundamental frequency as well as the spectral envelope of the voice source, and the overall spectral compensation characteristics including the higher-order formant characteristics. The mean square error between the logarithmic power spectra of the modeled and observed speech is typically used as the error evaluating measure. Formant frequency extraction resolutions of

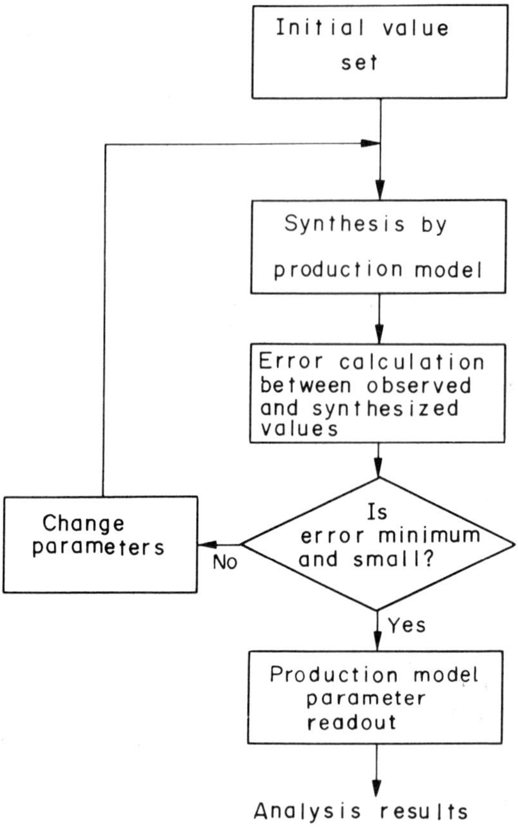


Fig. 4.11 Principle of A-b-S method.

±10 Hz and ±20 Hz were respectively obtained experimentally for the first and second formants.

Athough the A-b-S method is better than any other in principle, it is problematic in that considerable computation is required. Specifically, it needs a large number of iterations of feedback control during actual speech analysis because of the mutual interactions between the various parameter effects on spectral envelope production.

## 4.6 INFORMATION REDUCTION AND CODING FOR SPEECH SIGNALS

### 4.6.1 Waveform Coding and Analysis-Synthesis Systems

The speech signal exhibits large redundancies owing to the physical mechanism of vocal tract speech production and to the characteristics of the linguistic structure. The dynamic and frequency ranges of our hearing are restricted because of the physical mechanism of our auditory organs. As mentioned in Sec. 2.2, for example, an auditory masking phenomenon is involved in which low-frequency, high-level sound prevents the listener from hearing high-frequency sound existing simultaneously with the former. As a result of this phenomenon, low-level noise or distortion under the noise threshold, which is related to the spectral envelope of speech as shown in Fig. 4.12, cannot be heard (Crochiere and Flanagan, 1983). A strong formant tends to mask the noise in its frequency locality as long as the noise is about 15 dB below the signal. Using these redundancies and restrictions in both speech production and perception, information for representing speech signals can be reduced to achieve highly efficient transmission or low-capacity storage.

Coding methods for speech signals can be divided into the waveform coding method and the analysis-synthesis method. In the waveform coding method, the waveform is represented as precisely as possible by the decreased amount of information. In the analysis-synthesis method, the speech wave is transformed into a set of parameters based on the speech production model. Although precise comparisons between these two methods will be presented in Chaps. 5 and 6, a brief comparison is given in Table 4.2 for clarification. In addition, information compression techniques used in various waveform coding methods and the characteristics of speech waves on which these methods are based are indicated in Fig. 4.13.

Figure 4.14 diagrams the relationship between the coding bit rate and speech quality. When speech is quantized (coded by PCM) based on its amplitude variation characteristics, high-quality speech can be obtained at roughly 64 kbps. When the correlation characteristics of the waveform are used along with the spectral characteristics, the bit rate can be reduced to 32 or even 24 kbps. The bit rate can be further reduced to 9.6 kbps if we take into account the harmonic structure and apply noise shaping, which is a technique for controlling the distortion

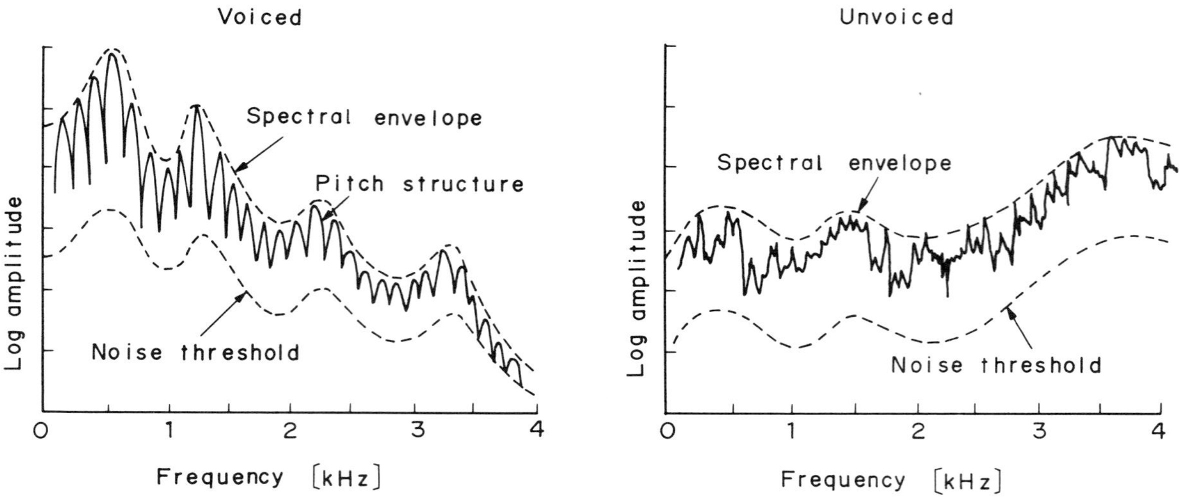


Fig. 4.12 Noise threshold for auditory masking associated with spectral envelope.

TABLE 4.2 Comparison between Waveform Coding and Analysis-Synthesis Methods

| Features | Method: Waveform coding | Method: Analysis-synthesis |
|---|---|---|
| Coding information | Waveform | Spectrum envelope (short-time spectrum) and source information (pitch, amplitude, and voiced/unvoiced) |
| Quantizing bit rate | 9.6–64 kbps (medium or wideband) | 2.4–4.8 kbps (narrowband) |
| Coding objective | Any sound | A single speaker's voice |
| Objective evaluation measure | SNR | Spectrum distortion |
| Problems | Difficult to reduce the bit rate into narrowband range. | Vulnerable to noise and transmission error. Speech quality is limited. Processing is complicated. |
| Examples | Time-domain coding: PCM, ADPCM, ΔM, ADM, APC<br>Frequency domain: SBC, ATC<br>Combination: APC-AB | Channel vocoder, formant vocoder, phase vocoder, LPC (maximum likelihood, PARCOR, LSP) vocoder, cepstrum vocoder |

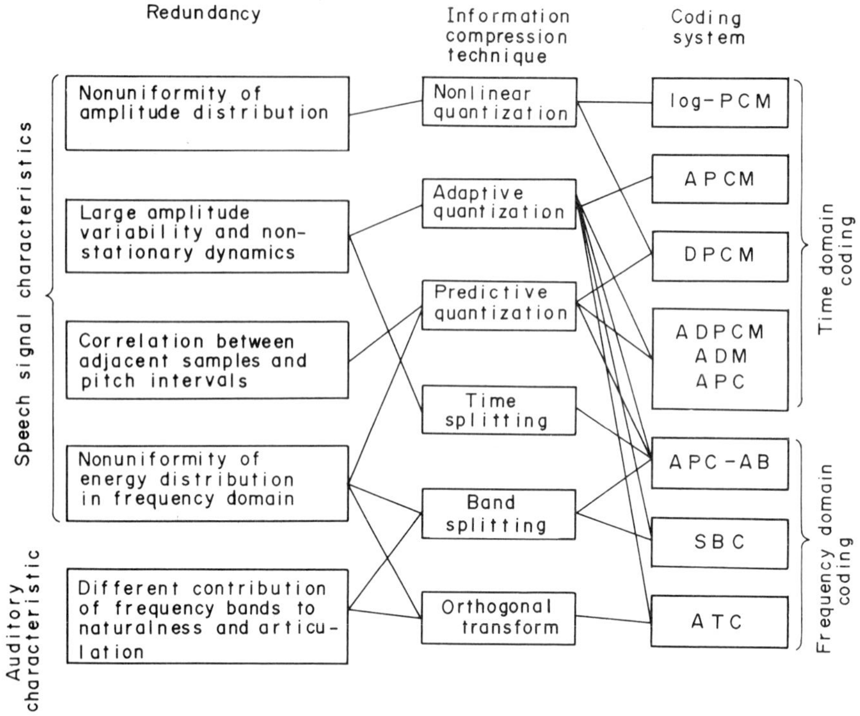


Fig. 4.13 Information compression techniques and characteristics of speech signals as well as hearing which support the techniques.

so that it remains below the noise threshold in all frequency bands. When the bit rate is reduced even further by using the waveform coding technique, the quality of coded speech rapidly decreases.

On the other hand, although the analysis-synthesis method can reduce the bit rate to around 2.4 kbps, it limits the quality possible, even if the amount of information is increased. Recently, a highly sophisticated approach for very low bit rate coding at 200 to 300 bps has been investigated (see Sec. 6.5.6). From 4.8 to 9.6 kbps methods of combining the advantages of the waveform coding and analysis-synthesis methods have been investigated. These include the residual-, speech-, multi-pulse-, or code-excited LPC methods.

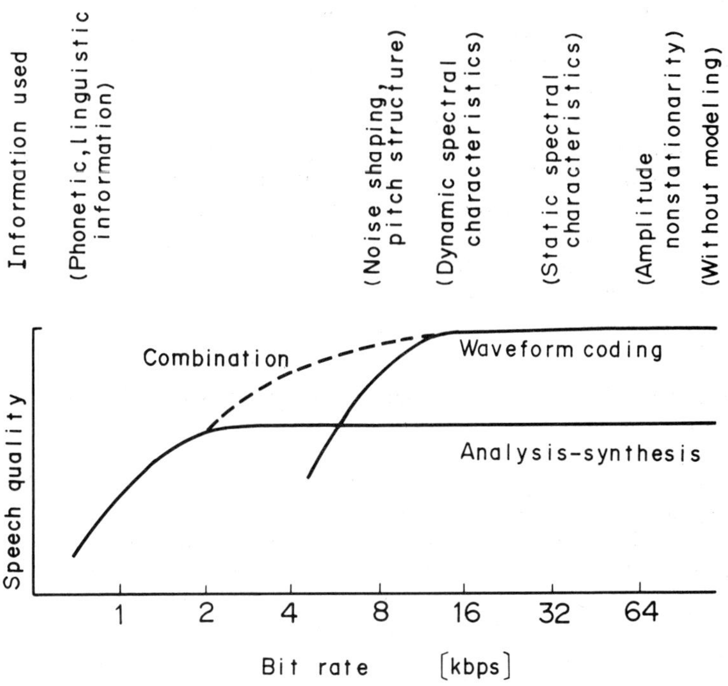


Fig. 4.14 Relationship between the coding bit rate and speech quality.

### 4.6.2 Analysis-Synthesis System Structure

In analysis-synthesis systems, the speech wave is reproduced (synthesized) using source and articulation parameters which are extracted based on the linearly separable equivalent circuit for the speech production mechanism described in Sec. 3.2. These parameters designate four types of information:

1. Distinction between voiced sound (pulse source) and unvoiced sound (noise source)
2. Fundamental period or fundamental frequency of voiced sounds
3. Source amplitude
4. Linear filter (resonance) characteristics

The first three provide source information, whereas the last parameter set gives spectral envelope (articulation) information.

A careful investigation into the three principal procedures of speech analysis-synthesis systems is essential to ensure improved synthesized speech quality. The first is extracting those parameters which precisely convey only the important auditory information by neglecting the redundant information included in speech waves. The second is coding the feature parameters efficiently. The third is reproducing the original speech as precisely, clearly, and naturally as possible by using the coded feature parameters.

### 4.6.3 Examples of Analysis-Synthesis Systems

Major examples of speech analysis-synthesis systems are summarized in Table 4.3 (Itakura, 1981). As indicated, the prototype of the speech analysis-synthesis system is the vocoder, invented in 1939 by H. Dudley of Bell Laboratories (Dudley, 1939). The term vocoder is an abbreviation for voice coder. The structure of the vocoder is diagrammed in Fig. 4.15, in which spectral analysis is applied to the speech wave through a band-pass filter bank at the analysis part (transmitter) (Schroeder, 1966). At the same time, the presence of periodicity and the fundamental period for the periodic signals are analyzed. These signals are then transmitted to the synthesis part (receiver) where source signals are produced by a pulse or noise generator, depending on the presence of periodicity. The source signals are amplitude-controlled at each frequency band and passed through the band-pass filters, which are similar to the transmitter. The output signals of the band-pass filters are then summed to reproduce the original speech.

The word vocoder is being widely used today to represent all speech analysis-synthesis systems. The original vocoder, which uses a band-pass filter bank for spectral analysis, is now referred to as the channel vocoder (Gold and Rader, 1967). Although the channel vocoder has been improved in quality through increasing the number of channels, it is limited in its ability to reproduce natural speech.

The formant vocoder is problematic in its accurate extraction of formant frequencies, and the correlation vocoder has difficulty in accurately reproducing the spectrum. With the pattern matching vocoder, phonemes in the speech wave are identified based on the time-frequency pattern of the band-pass filter output, with the phoneme symbols being transmitted (Smith, 1969).

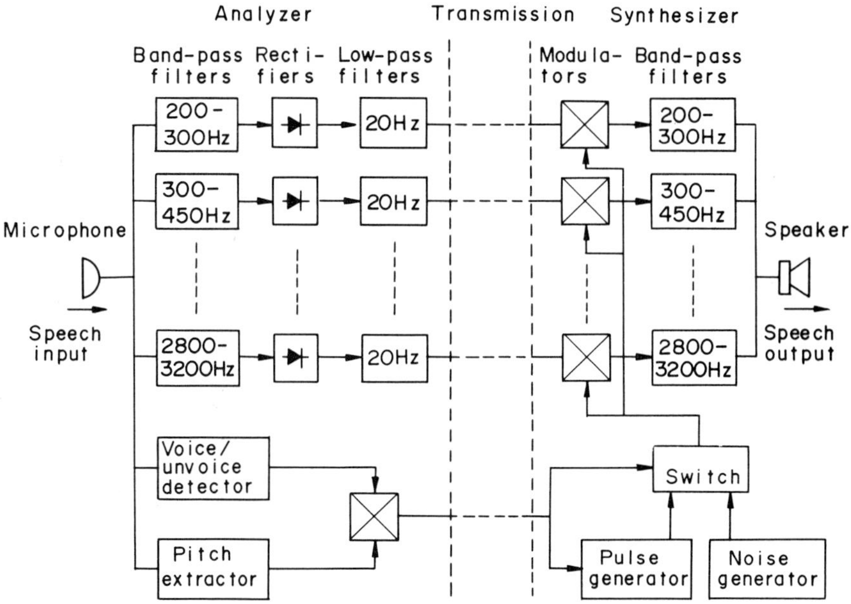


Fig. 4.15 Structure of the (channel) vocoder.

Although this technique realizes the highest compression rate, it presents several unsolved problems. One is how to extract the phonemes from continuous speech. Another is how to measure the similarity between input speech and reference patterns. Still another is how to synthesize natural speech based on the phoneme symbol sequence.

With the homomorphic vocoder, the spectral envelope is represented by the cepstral coefficients of lower-order quefrencies (for example, 30 elements) by using the method described in Sec. 4.3. In addition, the pitch estimation and voiced/unvoiced decision are made based on higher-order quefrency elements. At the synthesizer, an approximate value for the impulse response is produced by using the transmitted low-quefrency elements. Simultaneously, the excitation function (impulse sequence or random noise), which is produced based on pitch, voiced/unvoiced, and amplitude information, is convoluted by the impulse response. When the DFT of the lower-order quefrency elements are exponentially and inverse Fourier transformed, the zero-phase impulse response is obtained.

TABLE 4.3 Major Examples of Speech Analysis-Synthesis Systems

| Vocoder | Proposer | Spectral analysis method | Feature parameters | Channel capacity |
|---|---|---|---|---|
| Channel vocoder | H. Dudley (1939) | Band-pass filter bank analysis | Filter output amplitude | 300 Hz (analog)<br>2400 bps (digital) |
| Formant vocoder | W. A. Munson (1950) | Band-pass filter bank, zero-cross analysis | Filter output amplitude, zero-cross rate | 300 Hz<br>2400 bps |
| Pattern matching vocoder | C. P. Smith (1957) | Band-pass filter bank analysis | Phoneme spectral pattern | 900 bps |
| Correlation vocoder | M. R. Schroeder (1959) | Short-time autocorrelation analysis | Autocorrelation function, $\phi(M)$ | 400 Hz |

| | | | | |
|---|---|---|---|---|
| Phase vocoder | J. L. Flanagan (1966) | Band-pass filter bank analysis | Filter output amplitude and phase | 1500 Hz 7200–9600 bps |
| Maximum likelihood vocoder | F. Itakura S. Saito (1968) | Maximum likelihood method | Linear predictive coefficients, $\alpha_i$ | 5400 bps |
| Homomorphic vocoder | A. V. Oppenheim (1969) | Cepstrum analysis | Cepstrum $c(\tau)$ | 7800 bps |
| PARCOR vocoder | F. Itakura S. Saito (1969) | PARCOR analysis | PARCOR coefficients | 2400–9600 bps |
| LPC vocoder | B. S. Atal (1971) | Covariance method | Linear predictive coefficients, $\alpha_i$ | 3600 bps |
| LSP vocoder | F. Itakura N. Sugamura (1979) | Line spectrum analysis | LSP, $\omega_i$ | 1600–4800 bps |

If the lower-order quefrency elements are multiplied by the following lifter, the minimum phase impulse response is obtained:

$$l(n) = \begin{cases} 1 & n = 0 \\ 2 & 0 < n < n_0 \\ 0 & \text{other } n \end{cases} \tag{4.26}$$

Experimental results indicate that the best-quality speech can be synthesized under the minimum phase condition, which is close to natural speech (Oppenheim, 1969).

Another speech synthesis method based on the homomorphic vocoder has recently surfaced, which uses a filter set directly approximating logarithmic amplitude characteristics (Imai and Kitamura, 1978). The synthesis filter set in this method is constructed through the cascade connection of several filters having the system function $H_n(z)$:

$$H_n(z) = \frac{1 + \frac{1}{2} c(n)z^{-n} + \frac{1}{12} (c(n)z^{-n})^2}{1 - \frac{1}{2} c(n)z^{-n} + \frac{1}{12} (c(n)z^{-n})^2} \tag{4.27}$$

The synthesized voice is directly produced without transforming the cepstrum into an impulse response. The logarithmic amplitude characteristics of the filter constructed by cascade connection of these $(n_0 + 1)$-stage filters is

$$\ln |H(e^{j\omega})| \simeq \sum_{n=0}^{n_0} c(n)\cos(n\omega) \tag{4.28}$$

Since the cepstrum multiplied by the lifter $l(n)$ of Eq. (4.26) is used as $c(n)$ in this equation, the synthesis filter features minimum-phase characteristics. It has been ascertained that high-quality synthesized voice can be obtained by using this method at a relatively low bit rate.

The analysis-synthesis systems based on the LPC method (linear predictive vocoder, maximum likelihood vocoder, PARCOR vocoder, LSP vocoder, etc.) offer a considerable number of advantages which will be precisely described in Chap. 5.

## 4.7 PITCH EXTRACTION

In speech analysis-synthesis systems, it is necessary to extract source parameters in parallel with spectral envelope parameter extraction. The source parameters include the presence of vocal cord vibration (voiced/unvoiced), fundamental frequency for voiced sound, and source amplitude. Although the accurate extraction of the fundamental frequency (pitch extraction) has been one of the most important study concerns since the beginning of speech analysis research, no definite approach has yet been established.

This difficulty with pitch extraction stems from three factors. First, vocal cord vibration does not necessarily have complete periodicity especially at the beginning and end of voiced sounds. Second, it is difficult to extract the vocal cord source signal from the speech wave separately from the vocal tract effects. Third, the dynamic range of the fundamental frequency is very large.

With these in mind, recent pitch extraction research has been undertaken from three viewpoints. One is how to reliably extract the periodicity of quasi-periodic signals. Another is how to correct the pitch extraction error owing to the disturbance of periodicity. The other is how to remove the vocal tract (formant) effects. Major errors in pitch extraction are classified into double-pitch and half-pitch errors. The former are those errors occurring when extracting a frequency which is twice as large as the actual value. The latter are errors arising when extracting the half-value of the actual fundamental frequency. The tendency toward which error is most apt to occur depends on the extraction method employed.

The major pitch extraction methods are outlined in Table 4.4 (Itakura, 1978). They can generally be grouped into waveform processing (I), correlation processing (II), and spectral processing (III). Group I is composed of methods for detecting the periodic peaks in the waveform. Group II methods are those most widely used in digital signal processing of speech, since the correlation processing is unaffected by phase distortion in the waveform, and since it can be realized by a relatively simple hardware configuration. Among the methods in Group III, the principle of pitch extraction using cepstral analysis has already been described in Sec. 4.3. The modified correlation method and simplified inverse filter tracking (SIFT) algorithm (Markel, 1972), which are correlation methods, and the cepstral method

TABLE 4.4 Classification of Major Pitch Extraction Methods and Their Principal Features

| Classification | Pitch extraction method | Principal features |
|---|---|---|
| I. Waveform processing | Parallel processing method | Uses majority rule for pitch periods extracted by many kinds of simple waveform peak detectors. |
| | Data reduction method | Removes superfluous waveform data based on various logical processing and leaves only pitch pulses. |
| | Zero-crossing count method | Utilizes iterative patterns in waveform zero-crossing rate. |
| II. Correlation processing | Autocorrelation method | Employs autocorrelation function of waveform. Applies center and peak clipping for spectrum flattening and computation simplification. |
| | Modified correlation method | Utilizes autocorrelation function for residual signal of LPC analysis. Computation is simplified by LPF and polarization. |
| | SIFT (simplified inverse filter tracking) algorithm | Applies LPC analysis for spectrum flattening after down-sampling of speech wave. Time resolution is recovered by interpolation. |
| | AMDF method | Uses average magnitude differential function (AMDF) for speech or residual signal for periodicity detection. |
| III. Spectrum processing | Cepstrum method | Separates spectral envelope and fine structure by inverse Fourier transform of log-power spectrum. |
| | Period histogram method | Utilizes histogram for harmonic components in spectral domain. Pitch is decided as the common divisor for harmonic components. |

are generally the most efficient since they explicitly remove the vocal tract effects. The modified correlation method will be described in detail in Sec. 5.4.

The voiced/unvoiced decision is usually made using a method for pitch extraction, since, for the sake of simplicity, the cues for periodic/unperiodic decision are usually regarded as those for voiced/unvoiced decisions. The peak values of the autocorrelation or modified autocorrelation functions are generally implemented in the decision. Because these methods do not work effectively for unperiodic voiced sounds, improvement in decision accuracy has been attempted by employing several other parameters as additional cues (Atal and Rabiner, 1976). These parameters include the speech energy, zero-crossing rate, first-order autocorrelation function, first-order linear predictor coefficient, and energy of the residual signal.

# 5

# Linear Predictive Coding (LPC) Analysis

## 5.1 PRINCIPLES OF LPC ANALYSIS

Since the term linear prediction was first coined by N. Wiener (Wiener, 1966), the technique has become popularly employed in a wide range of applications based on a number of formulations. This technique, first used for speech analysis and synthesis by Itakura and Saito (Itakura and Saito, 1968) and Atal and Schroeder (Atal and Schroeder, 1968), has produced a very large impact on every aspect of speech research (Markel and Gray, 1976). The importance of linear prediction stems from the fact that the speech wave and spectrum characteristics can be efficiently and precisely represented using a very small number of parameters. Additionally, these parameters are obtained by relatively simple calculation.

Let us express the discrete speech signal sampled at every $\Delta T$ [s] by $\{x_t\}$ (t is an integer). When the frequency range of the speech signal is 0–W [Hz], $\Delta T$ must satisfy $\Delta T \leqq 1/2W$ [s]. Let us then assume the following first-order linear combination between the present sample value $x_t$ and the previous p samples,

$$x_t + \alpha_1 x_{t-1} + \cdots + \alpha_p x_{t-p} = \varepsilon_t \tag{5.1}$$

where $\{\varepsilon_t\}$ is an uncorrelated statistical variable having a mean value of 0 and a variance of $\sigma^2$.

This linear difference equation means that the present sample value $x_t$ can be linearly predicted using the previous sample values. That is, if the linearly predicted value $\hat{x}_t$ for $x_t$ is represented by

$$\hat{x}_t = -\sum_{i=1}^{p} \alpha_i x_{t-i} \tag{5.2}$$

the following equation can be obtained from Eqs. (5.1) and (5.2):

$$x_t - \hat{x}_t = \varepsilon_t \tag{5.3}$$

We thus consider Eq. (5.1) to be the linear prediction model having linear predictor coefficients $\{\alpha_i\}$. $\varepsilon_t$ is designated as the residual error.

Let us now define the linear predictor filter as

$$F(z) = -\sum_{i=1}^{p} \alpha_i z^{-i} \tag{5.4}$$

and define $\hat{X}(z) \longleftrightarrow \hat{x}_t$ and $X(z) \longleftrightarrow x_t$ as the pairs of z-transforms and their sample values. The z-transform of Eq. (5.2) is then expressed by

$$\hat{X}(z) = F(z)X(z) \tag{5.5}$$

Based on Eqs. (5.2) and (5.3), the linear prediction model in z-transform notation can be given by

$$X(z)(1 - F(z)) = E(z) \tag{5.6}$$

or

$$X(z)A(z) = E(z) \tag{5.7}$$

where

$$A(z) = 1 + \sum_{i=1}^{p} \alpha_i z^{-i} = 1 - F(z) \tag{5.8}$$

and $E(z) \longleftrightarrow \varepsilon_t$. A(z) is called the inverse filter (Markel, (1972). Based on these definitions, the linear predictive model using the linear predictor filter F(z) and inverse filter A(z) can be block diagrammed as in Fig. 5.1. This diagram shows that LPC, that is, the process of applying the linear predictive model to the speech wave, minimizes the output $\sigma^2$ by adjusting the

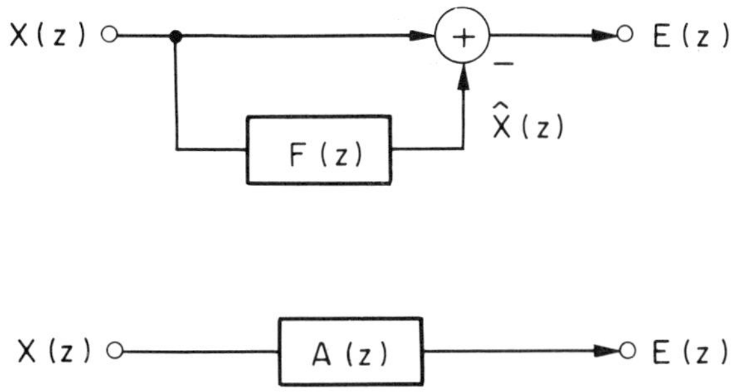


Fig. 5.1 Linear prediction model block diagram.

coefficients $\{\alpha_i\}$ of either the linear predictor filter or the inverse filter.

Based on the linear separable equivalent circuit model of the speech production mechanism (Sec. 3.2), the speech wave is regarded as the output of the vocal tract articulation equivalent filter excited by a vocal source impulse. The characteristics of the equivalent filter, which include the overall spectral characteristics of the vocal cords as well as the radiation characteristics, can be assumed to be passive and linear. The speech wave is then considered to be the impulse response of the equivalent filter, and, therefore, the equivalent filter characteristics can be theoretically obtained as the solution of the linear differential equation. Accordingly, the speech wave can be predicted, and the speech spectral characteristics can be extracted by the linear predictor coefficients.

Although linear predictive analysis is based on these assumptions, they actually vary and do not hold completely. This is because the vocal tract shape is temporally changing slowly, of course, and because the vocal source is not a single impulse but rather the iteration of impulses or triangular waves accompanied by noise sources.

## 5.2 LPC ANALYSIS PROCEDURE

Let us here consider the method for estimating the linear predictor coefficients $\{\alpha_i\}$ by applying the least mean square error method to Eq. (5.3). Specifically, let us determine the coefficients $\{\alpha_i\}_{i=1}^{p}$ so that the squared sum of the error $\varepsilon_t$ between the sample values of $x_t$ and the linearly predicted values $\hat{x}_t$ over a predetermined period of $[t_0, t_1]$ is minimized.

The total squared error $\beta$ is

$$\beta = \sum_{t=t_0}^{t_1} \varepsilon_t^2$$

$$= \sum_{t=t_0}^{t_1} \left( \sum_{i=0}^{p} \alpha_i x_{t-i} \right)^2$$

$$= \sum_{t=t_0}^{t_1} \sum_{i=0}^{p} \sum_{j=0}^{p} \alpha_i \alpha_j x_{t-i} x_{t-j} \tag{5.9}$$

where $\alpha_0 = 1$. Defining

$$c_{ij} = \sum_{t=t_0}^{t_0} x_{t-i} x_{t-j} \tag{5.10}$$

$\beta$ can then be equivalently written as

$$\beta = \sum_{i=0}^{p} \sum_{j=0}^{p} \alpha_i c_{ij} \alpha_j \tag{5.11}$$

Minimization of $\beta$ is obtained by setting to zero the partial derivation of $\beta$ with respect to $\alpha_j$ $(j = 1, 2, \ldots, p)$ and solving. Therefore, from Eq. (5.11),

$$\frac{\partial \beta}{\partial \alpha_j} = 2 \sum_{i=0}^{p} \alpha_i c_{ij} = 0 \qquad (j = 1, 2, \ldots, p) \tag{5.12}$$

The predictor coefficients $\{\alpha_i\}$ can be obtained by solving this set of p linear simultaneous equations. The known parameters $c_{ij}$ $(i = 0, 1, 2, \ldots, p;\ j = 1, 2, \ldots, p)$ are defined from the sample data by Eq. (5.10), which shows that the samples $x_t$ from $t_0 - p$ to $t_1$ are essential to the solution.

For the actual solution based on a sequence of N speech samples, $\{x_t\} = \{x_0, x_1, \ldots, x_{N-1}\}$, two specific cases have been investigated in detail. These are referred to as the covariance method and the autocorrelation method.

The covariance method is defined by setting $t_0 = p$ and $t_1 = N - 1$ so that the error is minimized only over the interval $[p, N - 1]$, whereas all the N speech samples are used in calculating the covariance matrix elements $c_{ij}$ (Atal and Hanauer, 1971). Accordingly, Eq. (5.12) is solved using

$$c_{ij} = \sum_{t=p}^{N-1} x_{t-i} x_{t-j} \tag{5.13}$$

The covariance method draws its name from the fact that $c_{ij}$ represents the row i, column j element of a covariance matrix.

The autocorrelation method is defined by setting $t_0 = -\infty$ and $t_1 = \infty$, and by letting $x_t = 0$ for $t < 0$ and $t \geqq N$ (Markel, 1972). These limits allow $c_{ij}$ to be simplified as

$$\begin{aligned} c_{ij} &= \sum_{t=-\infty}^{\infty} x_{t-i} x_{t-j} \\ &= \sum_{t=-\infty}^{\infty} x_t x_{t+|i-j|} \\ &= \sum_{t=0}^{N-1-|i-j|} x_t x_{t+|i-j|} \\ &= r_{|i-j|} \end{aligned} \tag{5.14}$$

Thus, $\alpha_i$ is obtained by solving

$$\sum_{i=0}^{p} \alpha_i r_{|i-j|} = 0 \qquad (j = 1, 2, \ldots, p) \tag{5.15}$$

where

$$r_\tau = \sum_{t=0}^{N-1-\tau} x_t x_{t+\tau} \qquad (\tau \geqq 0) \tag{5.16}$$

Although the error $\varepsilon_t$ is minimized over an infinite interval, equivalent results are obtained by minimizing it only over $[0, N + p - 1]$. This is because $x_t$ is truncated to zero for $t < 0$ and $t \geqq N$ by multiplied by a finite-length window, such as a Hamming window. The autocorrelation method is so named from the fact that for the conditions stated, $c_{ij}$ reduces to the definition of the short-term autocorrelation $r_\tau$ at the delay $\tau = |i - j|$.

Equation (5.16) can be expressed by matrix representation as

$$\begin{bmatrix} r_0 & r_1 & \cdots & r_{p-1} \\ r_1 & r_0 & & \vdots \\ \vdots & & \ddots & r_1 \\ r_{p-1} & \cdots & r_1 & r_0 \end{bmatrix} \begin{bmatrix} \alpha_1 \\ \alpha_2 \\ \vdots \\ \alpha_p \end{bmatrix} = - \begin{bmatrix} r_1 \\ r_2 \\ \vdots \\ r_p \end{bmatrix} \tag{5.17}$$

The $p \times p$ correlation matrix of the left term has the form of a Toeplitz matrix, which is symmetrical, and has the same values along the lines parallel to the diagonal. This type of equation is called a normal equation or a Yule-Walker equation. Since the positive definiteness of the correlation matrix is guaranteed by the definition of the correlation function, an inverse matrix exists for the correlation matrix. Solving the equation then permits $\{\alpha_i\}$ to be obtained. On the other hand, the positive definiteness of the coefficient matrix is not necessarily guaranteed in the covariance method.

The equations for the covariance and correlation methods can be efficiently solved by the Cholesky decomposition method and by Durbin's recursive solution methods, respectively. Durbin's method is equivalent to the PARCOR (partial autocorrelation) coefficient extraction process which will be presented later in Sec. 5.6. Although the covariance and autocorrelation methods give almost the same results when $\{x_t\}$ is long ($N \gg 1$) and stationary, their results differ when $\{x_t\}$ is short and has temporal variations. The number of multiplications and divisions in Durbin's method are $p^2$ and p, whereas the number of multiplications, divisions, and square root calculations in the Cholesky decomposition are $(p^3 + 9p^2 + 2p)/6$, p, and p. Assuming that p = 10, computationally, the former method is three times more efficient than the latter method.

In linear system identification in modern control theory, the process exemplified by Eq. (5.1) is called the autoregressive (AR) process, in which $\varepsilon_t$ and $x_t$ are the system input and output, respectively. This system is also referred to as the all-pole model since it has an all-pole system function.

## 5.3 MAXIMUM LIKELIHOOD SPECTRAL ESTIMATION

### 5.3.1 Formulation of Maximum Likelihood Spectral Estimation

Maximum likelihood estimation is the method used to estimate parameters which maximize the likelihood based on the observed values. Here, the likelihood is the probability of occurrence of the actual observations (the speech samples) under the presumed parameter condition. The maximum likelihood method is better than any other estimation method in the sense that the variance of the estimated value is minimized when the sample size is sufficiently large.

In order to accomplish maximum likelihood spectral estimation, let us make two assumptions for the speech wave (Itakura and Saito, 1968):

1. The sample value $x_t$ can be regarded as the sample derived from a stationary Gaussian process characterized by the power spectral density $f(\lambda)$. (Here, $\lambda = W\Delta T$ is the normalized angle frequency; i.e., $\lambda = \pm\pi$ corresponds to the frequency $\pm W$.)
2. The spectral density $f(\lambda)$ is represented by an all-pole polynomial spectral density function of the form

$$f(\lambda) = \frac{\sigma^2}{2\pi} \frac{1}{\left| \prod_{i=1}^{p} (1 - z/z_i) \right|^2}$$

$$= \frac{\sigma^2}{2\pi} \frac{1}{\left| 1 + \sum_{i=1}^{p} \alpha_i z^{-i} \right|^2}$$

$$= \frac{\sigma^2}{2\pi} \frac{1}{A_0 + 2 \sum_{i=1}^{p} A_i \cos i\lambda} \tag{5.18}$$

where $z_i$ is the root of

$$1 + \sum_{i=1}^{p} \alpha_i z^{-i} = 0 \tag{5.19}$$

and $A_i$ is defined as

$$A_i = \sum_{j=0}^{p-|i|} \alpha_j \alpha_{j+|i|}, \quad \alpha_0 = 1 \qquad (i = 0, \pm 1, \ldots, \pm p) \tag{5.20}$$

Furthermore, $\sigma^2$ is the scaling factor for the magnitude of spectral density, and p is the number of poles necessary for approximating the actual spectral density. Here, a pair of conjugate poles is counted as two separate poles.

Although assumption 1 is easily approved for unvoiced consonants, it is not readily so for voiced sounds having a pitch-harmonic structure. In actual speech, however, the glottal source usually features temporal variation and fluctuation, and, therefore, harmonic components are broadened in the spectral domain. Hence, assumption 1 can be accepted for the spectral envelope characteristics of both voiced and unvoiced sounds.

Assumption 2 corresponds to the AR process described in the previous section. That is, the signal $\{x_t\}$, exhibiting the spectral density of Eq. (5.18), satisfies the relationship of Eq. (5.1) in the time domain. This correspondence can be understood if one traces back from Eq. (5.8) to Eq. (5.1).

Zeros are not included in the hypothesized spectral density for two reasons. First, the human auditory organs are sensitive to poles and insensitive to steep spectral valleys, such as those represented only by zeros (Matsuda, 1966). Second, removing zeros simplifies as well as facilitates the mathematical process and the parameter extraction procedure.

When $\{\varepsilon_t\}$ is Gaussian, the logarithmic likelihood $L(X|\tilde{\omega})$ for the N sample sequence $X = (x_0, x_1, \ldots, x_{N-1})$ can be approximated by

$$L(X|\tilde{\omega}) \simeq -\frac{N}{2}\left[\log 2\pi\sigma^2 + \frac{1}{\sigma^2}\sum_{\tau=-p}^{p} A_\tau \hat{v}_\tau\right]$$

$$= -\frac{N}{2}\left[2\log 2\pi + \frac{1}{2\pi}\int_{-\pi}^{\pi}\left\{\log f(\lambda) + \frac{\hat{f}(\lambda)}{f(\lambda)}\right\}d\lambda\right] \tag{5.21}$$

where $\tilde{\omega}$ indicates the parameter set $(\sigma^2, \alpha_1, \alpha_2, \ldots, \alpha_p)$ in Eq. (5.18). $\hat{f}(\lambda)$ and $\hat{v}_\tau$, which respectively express the short-term spectral density (periodogram) and short-term autocorrelation function for $\{x_t\}$, are defined as

$$\hat{v}_\tau = \frac{1}{N}\sum_{t=0}^{N-1-|\tau|} x_t x_{t+|\tau|} \tag{5.22}$$

and

$$\hat{f}(\lambda) = \frac{1}{2\pi}\sum_{\tau=-(N-1)}^{N-1} \hat{v}_\tau \exp(-j\tau\lambda) \tag{5.23}$$

$\hat{v}_\tau$ and $r_\tau$ in Eq. (5.14) are related by $\hat{v}_\tau = r_\tau/N$. Equation (5.21) shows that the logarithmic likelihood for a given X can be approximately represented using only the first p time delay elements of the short-term autocorrelation function, $\{\hat{v}_\tau\}_{\tau=1}{}^p$.

Let us maximize $L(X|\tilde{\omega})$ with respect to $\sigma^2$ first. From $\partial L(X|\omega)/\partial\sigma^2 = 0$, we obtain

$$\sigma^2 = J(\alpha_1, \alpha_2, \ldots, \alpha_p) = \sum_{\tau=-p}^{p} A_\tau \hat{v}_\tau \tag{5.24}$$

Then

$$L(X|\tilde{\omega}|_{\sigma^2=J} = -\frac{N}{2}[\log 2\pi e J(\alpha_1,\alpha_2,\ldots,\alpha_p)] \tag{5.25}$$

Therefore, the maximization of $L(X|\tilde{\omega})$ with respect to $\{\alpha_i\}_{i=1}^p$ is attained by the minimization of $J(\alpha_1,\alpha_2,\ldots,\alpha_p)$. Since

$$J(\alpha_1,\alpha_2,\ldots,\alpha_p) = \int_{-\pi}^{\pi} |1 + \alpha_1 \exp(-j\lambda) + \cdots$$

$$+ \alpha_p \exp(-jp\lambda)|^2 \hat{f}(\lambda)\, d\lambda$$

$$= \sum_{i,j=0}^{p} \alpha_i \alpha_j \hat{v}_{i-j} \geqq 0 \tag{5.26}$$

$\{\alpha_i\}_{i=1}^p$ can be derived by solving the linear simultaneous equations

$$\frac{\partial J(\alpha_1,\alpha_2,\ldots,\alpha_p)}{\partial \alpha_j} = \sum_{i=0}^{p} \alpha_i \hat{v}_{i-j} = 0 \qquad (j = 1,2,\ldots,p) \tag{5.27}$$

From Eqs. (5.24) and (5.26),

$$\sigma^2 = \sum_{\tau=0}^{p} \alpha_\tau \hat{v}_\tau \tag{5.28}$$

Since Eqs. (5.27) and (5.15) are equivalent, the $\{\alpha_i\}_{i=1}^p$ values obtained by Eq. (5.27) are equal to the values derived by the autocorrelation method. This means that linear predictive analysiś employing the autocorrelation method and maximum likelihood spectral estimation, respectively, solve the same passive linear system (acoustic characteristics of the vocal tract, including the source and radiation characteristics) in the time domain and frequency domain, respectively. The maximum likelihood spectral estimation method is equivalent to the process of adjusting the coefficients to minimize the output power $\sigma^2$ when the input signal is passed through an adjustable pth-order inverse filter. Hence, this method is often referred to as the inverse filtering method (Markel, 1972).

### 5.3.2 Physical Meaning of Maximum Likelihood Spectral Estimation

The function $f(\lambda)$ in Eq. (5.21) is restricted in that it takes on the form of Eq. (5.18). Without such a restriction, $f(\lambda)$, which maximizes Eq. (5.21) under the condition of a given $\hat{f}(\lambda)$, is equal to $\hat{f}(\lambda)$ $(-\pi \leqq \lambda \leqq \pi)$. The maximum value of L is

$$L_{max} = -\frac{N}{2}\left[2 \log 2\pi + \frac{1}{2\pi}\int_{-\pi}^{\pi} \{\log \hat{f}(\lambda) + 1\}\, d\lambda\right] \qquad (5.29)$$

Therefore,

$$E_1(f/\hat{f}) = \int_{-\pi}^{\pi} 2\left\{\log \frac{f(\lambda)}{\hat{f}(\lambda)} + \frac{\hat{f}(\lambda)}{f(\lambda)} - 1\right\} d\lambda \qquad (5.30)$$

which is defined by $8\pi(L_{max} - L(X|\tilde{\omega}))/N$, becomes zero only when $f(\lambda) = \hat{f}(\lambda)$ $(-\pi \leqq \lambda \leqq \pi)$, otherwise it has a positive value. Accordingly, $E_1(f/\hat{f})$ can be regarded as a matching error measure when the short-term spectral density is substituted by a hypothetical spectral density $f(\lambda)$. This means that the estimation of spectral information $\tilde{\omega}$, based on the maximum likelihood method, corresponds to the spectrum matching which minimizes the matching error measure in the same way as the A-b-S method.

If the integrand of $E_1(f/\hat{f})$ is represented by a function $d = \log(f(\lambda)/\hat{f}(\lambda))$, it becomes

$$G_1(d) = 2(d + e^{-d} - 1) \qquad (5.31)$$

which is shown by the solid curve in Fig. 5.2. On the other hand, in the conventional A-b-S method, $G_2(d) = d^2$ has usually been used as an integrand for measuring the spectral matching error. In the region $|d| < 1$, $G_1(d)$ and $G_2(d)$ are almost the same. When $d > 1$ and $d < -1$, however, $G_1(d)$ respectively increases linearly and exponentially as a function of d. $G_2(d)$ has a symmetrical curve around $d = 0$, whereas $G_1(d)$ is unsymmetrical. This means that in spectral matching using the maximum likelihood method, the matching error for neglecting a local valley in $\hat{f}(\lambda)$ is evaluated as being smaller than that for neglecting a local peak having the same shape. The nonuniform weighting in the maximum likelihood method is preferred over uniform weighting since the peaks play a dominant role in the perception of voiced speech.

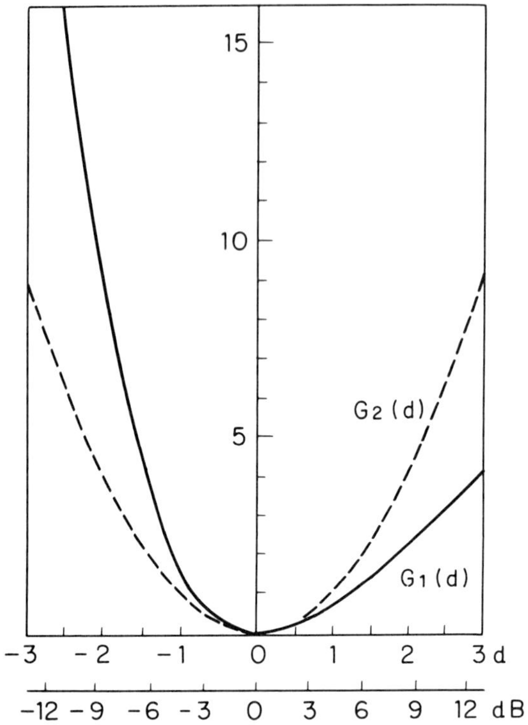


Fig. 5.2 Comparison of matching error measure in maximum likelihood method, $G_1(d)$, with that in analysis-by-synthesis (A-b-S) method, $G_2(d)$. $d = \log \{f(\lambda)/\hat{f}(\lambda)\}$; $f(\lambda)$ = model spectrum; $\hat{f}(\lambda)$ = short-term spectrum.

The poles of the spectral envelope, $z_i (i = 1,2,\ldots,p)$, can be obtained as roots of the equation

$$1 + \sum_{i=1}^{p} \alpha_i z^{-i} = 0 \tag{5.32}$$

in which complex poles correspond to quadrature resonances. Their resonance frequencies and bandwidths are given by the equations

$$F_i = \frac{\arg z_i}{2\pi\Delta T} \quad [\text{Hz}]$$

and

$$B_i = \frac{\log |z_i|}{\pi\Delta T} \quad [\text{Hz}] \tag{5.33}$$

where $\Delta T$ is the sampling period. The formants can be extracted by selecting the poles whose bandwidth-to-frequency ratios are relatively small.

Figure 5.3 compares the short-term spectral densities and spectral envelopes estimated by the maximum likelihood method

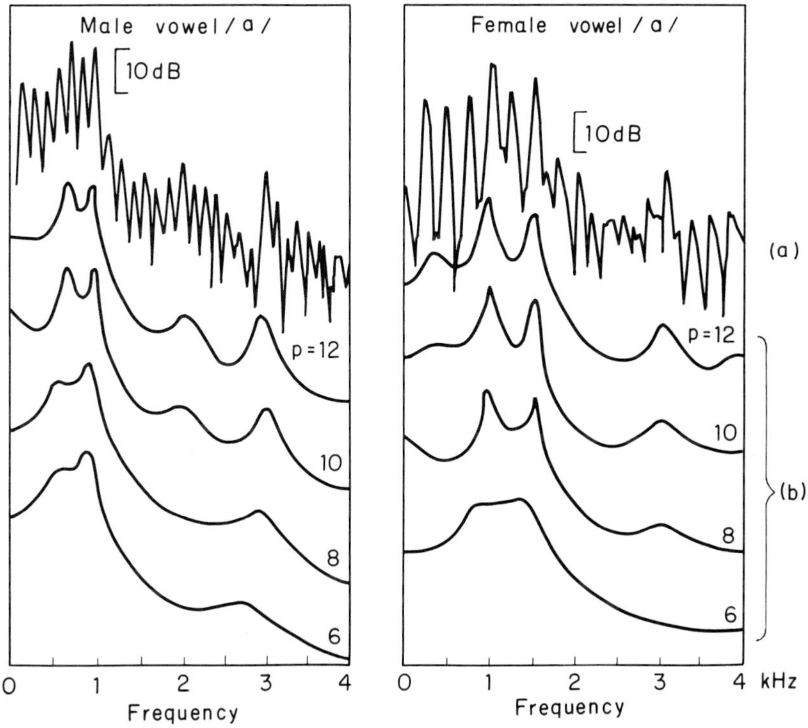


Fig. 5.3 Comparison of (a) short-term spectra and (b) spectral envelopes obtained by the maximum likelihood method.

for the male and female vowel /a/ when the number of poles is varied between 6 and 12. It is evident that major peaks in the short-term spectrum can be almost completely represented by f( λ) when the speech wave is band-limited between 0 and 4 kHz and p is set larger than or equal to 10.

Figure 5.4 exemplifies the time function of spectral envelopes for the Japanese test sentence beginning /bakuoNga/, or "A whir is ...," uttered by a male speaker (Tohkura, 1980). Here, the Hamming window length is 30 ms, the frame period is 5 ms, and p is set at 12.

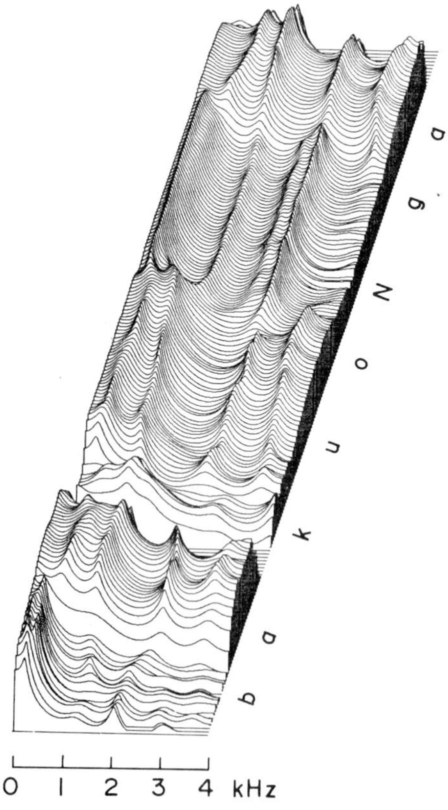


Fig. 5.4 Time function of spectral envelopes for the Japanese phrase /bakuNga/ uttered by a male speaker.

## 5.4 SOURCE PARAMETER ESTIMATION FROM RESIDUAL SIGNALS

Let us consider the spectral fine structure of the residual signal

$$\varepsilon_t = x_t - \hat{x}_t = \sum_{i=0}^{p} \alpha_i x_{t-i} \tag{5.34}$$

Since the fine structure is obtained by normalizing the short-term spectrum of input speech $\hat{f}(\lambda)$, using the spectral envelope $f(\lambda)$, it is almost flat along the frequency axis and exhibits a harmonic structure for periodic speech. Therefore, the autocorrelation function for the residual signal, called the modified autocorrelation function, produces large correlation values at the delays having the integer ratio of the fundamental period for voiced speech, whereas no specific correlation is demonstrated for unvoiced speech (Itakura and Saito, 1968).

In this way, the vocal source parameters can be obtained using the modified autocorrelation function regardless of the spectral envelope shape. The modified autocorrelation function can be easily calculated by the Fourier expansion of $\hat{f}(\lambda)/f(\lambda)$ as follows:

$$\begin{aligned}\omega_\tau &= \frac{1}{2\pi} \int_{-\pi}^{\pi} \frac{\hat{f}(\lambda)}{f(\lambda)} \cos \tau\lambda \, d\lambda \\ &= \frac{1}{\sigma^2} \int_{-\pi}^{\pi} \hat{f}(\lambda) \sum_{s=-p}^{p} A_s \cos(\tau - s)\lambda \, d\lambda \\ &= \frac{1}{\sigma^2} \sum_{s=-p}^{p} A_s \hat{v}_{\tau-s} \end{aligned} \tag{5.35}$$

where $A_s$ is a correlation function of linear predictor coefficients as previously defined by Eq. (5.20). Equation (5.35) means that $\omega_\tau$ can be calculated by the convolution of the short-term autocorrelation function and $\{A_s\}_{s=1}^{p}$ for input speech, followed by normalization using $\sigma^2$. $\omega_\tau$ can also be obtained by directly calculating the correlation function for $\varepsilon_t$ using Eq. (5.34).

Since actual speech often features intermediate characteristics between the periodic and unperiodic, the source characteristic function $V(\omega_\tau)$ is defined so that it expresses not only merely voiced or unvoiced sound but also the intermediate characteristics between these sounds.

In the course of pitch extraction, low-pass filtering is widely applied to speech waves or residual signals for improving the resolution of the extracted pitch period. Low-pass filtering is effective for removing the influence of high-order formants and for compensating for the insufficiency of the time resolution arising in the autocorrelation function. The latter effect is especially important for pitch extraction using this modified autocorrelation function. The double-period pitch error due to the time resolution insufficiency can be considerably minimized by employing low-pass filtering.

Figure 5.5 exemplifies waveforms, autocorrelation functions, and short-term spectra for speech waves, residual signals, and their low-passed signals for the vowel /a/ uttered by a male speaker (Tohkura, 1980). The cutoff frequency for the low-pass filter is 900 Hz. Comparison of the correlation functions for the speech waves and for the residual signals shows that the latter, specifically, the modified autocorrelation function, is more advantageous than the former correlation function. When the correlation function for the speech waves is used, formant-related components, which become large when the harmonic components of the fundamental frequency and the formant frequencies are close together, cause errors in maximum value selection. On the other hand, when the correlation function for the residual signals is used, peaks are observed only at the fundamental period and at its ratios of integers and are not affected by formants.

## 5.5 SPEECH ANALYSIS-SYNTHESIS SYSTEM BY LPC

The original speech wave can be reproduced based on the relationship $x_t = \hat{x}_t + \varepsilon_t$ or $X(z) = E(z)/A(z)$, using the speech synthesis circuit indicated in Fig. 5.6 and the residual signal $\varepsilon_t$ as the sound source. For the purpose of reducing information, pulses and white noise are utilized as sound sources to drive the speech synthesis circuit instead of employing $\varepsilon_t$ itself. Pulses and white noise are controlled based on the source periodicity information extracted from $\varepsilon_t$. The control parameters of the speech synthesis circuit are thus linear predictor coefficients $\{\alpha_i\}_{i=1}^{p}$, pulse amplitude $A_V$, and fundamental period T for the

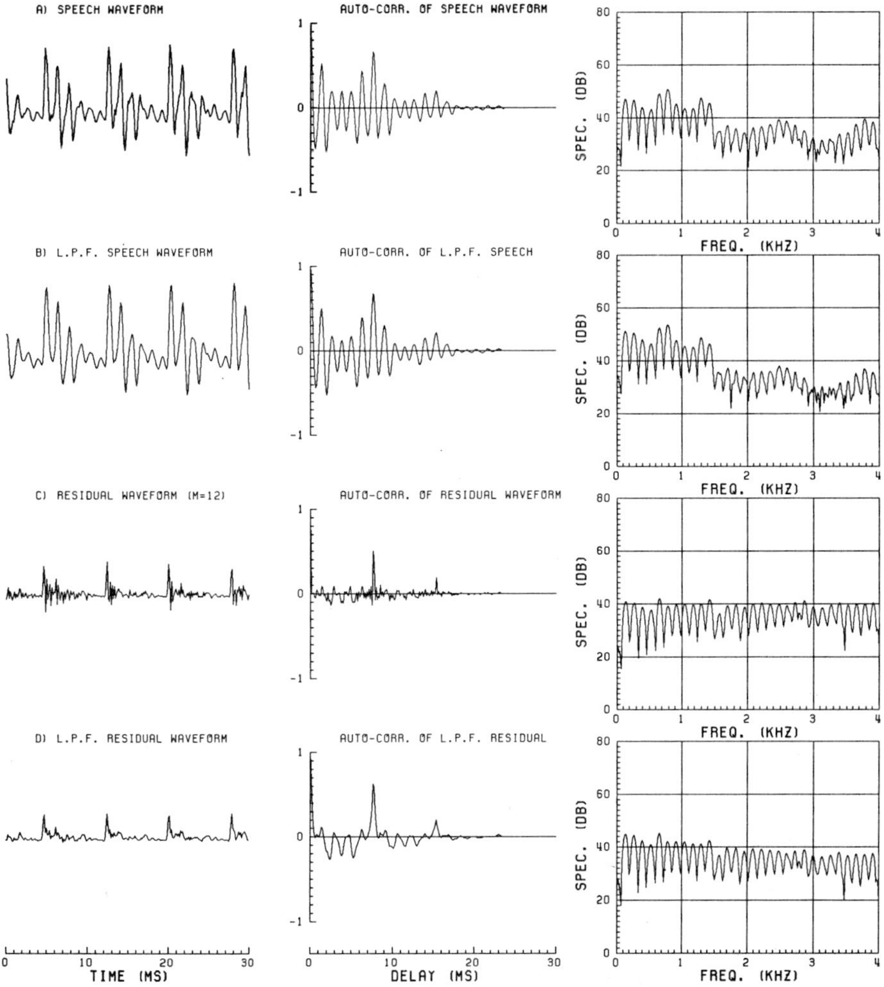


Fig. 5.5 Waveforms, autocorrelation functions, and short-term spectra for a speech wave, a residual signal, and their low-pass filtered signals for the vowel /a/ uttered by a male speaker.

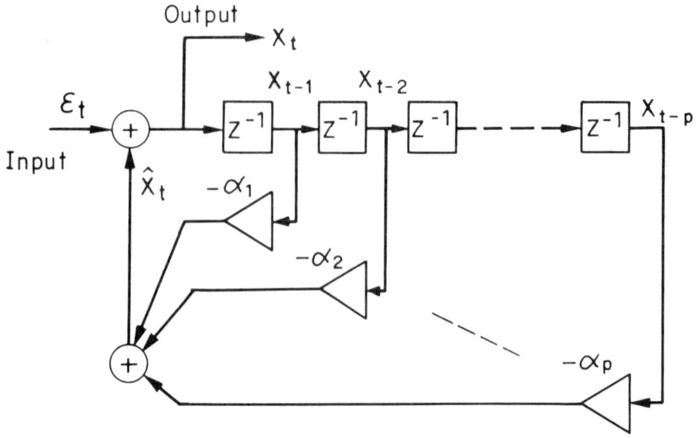


Fig. 5.6 Speech synthesis circuit based on linear predictive analysis method.

voice source. $A_V$ and T are replaced with noise amplitude $A_n$ for the unvoice source (Itakura and Saito, 1968).

The stability of the above-mentioned synthesis filter 1/A(z) must be carefully maintained since it has a feedback loop. Stability here, meaning that the output of the system for a finite input is itself finite, corresponds to the condition that the difference equation (5.1) has a stationary solution (see Appendix A.3). If the linear predictor coefficients are obtained through the correlation method of linear predictive analysis or through the maximum likelihood method, stability of the synthesis filter is theoretically guaranteed. The reason for this is that the spectral density function f( $\lambda$ ) always becomes positive definite when the short-term autocorrelation function $\{\hat{v}_\tau\}_{\tau=0}^{p}$ is a positive definite sequence.

During actual parameter transmission or storage, however, stability is not always guaranteed because of the quantization error. In such situations, there is no practical, clear criterion for the range of $\{\alpha_i\}_{i=1}^{p}$ which secures stability. This is one of the difficulties of using LPC or the maximum likelihood method in speech analysis-synthesis systems.

In order to minimize this problem, the spectral dynamic range, namely, the difference between the maximum and minimum values (peaks and valleys) in the spectrum, should be reduced as much as possible. Effective for this purpose is the application of a 6-dB/oct high-emphasis filter or a spectral equalizer adapted to the overall spectral inclination. The stability problem, however, has finally been solved theoretically as well as practically by the PARCOR analysis-synthesis method as described in the following section.

## 5.6 PARCOR ANALYSIS

### 5.6.1 Formulation of PARCOR Analysis

The same two assumptions made for the maximum likelihood estimation (see 5.3.1) are also made for the speech wave. When the prediction errors for the linear prediction of $x_t$ and $x_{t-m}$ using the sampled values $\{x_{t-i}\}_{i=1}^{m-1}$ are written as

$$\varepsilon_{ft}^{(m-1)} = \sum_{i=0}^{m-1} \alpha_i^{(m-1)} x_{t-i}$$

and

$$\varepsilon_{bt}^{(m-1)} = \sum_{i=1}^{m} \beta_i^{(m-1)} x_{t-i} \tag{5.36}$$

the PARCOR (partial autocorrelation) coefficient $k_m$ between $x_t$ and $x_{t-m}$ is defined by

$$k_m = \frac{E\{\varepsilon_{ft}^{(m-1)} \varepsilon_{bt}^{(m-1)}\}}{[E(\varepsilon_{ft}^{(m-1)})^2\} E\{(\varepsilon_{bt}^{(m-1)})^2\}]^{1/2}} \tag{5.37}$$

This equation means that the PARCOR coefficient is the correlation between the forward prediction error $\varepsilon_{ft}^{(m-1)}$ and the backward prediction error $\varepsilon_{bt}^{(m-1)}$ (Itakura and Saito, 1971). The definitional concept behind the PARCOR coefficient is presented in block diagram form in Fig. 5.7. Since the prediction errors, $\varepsilon_{ft}^{(m-1)}$ and $\varepsilon_{bt}^{(m-1)}$, are obtained after removing the linear effect of m sample values between $x_t$ and $x_{t-m}$ from these sample values, $k_m$ represents the pure or partial correlation between $x_t$ and $x_{t-m}$.

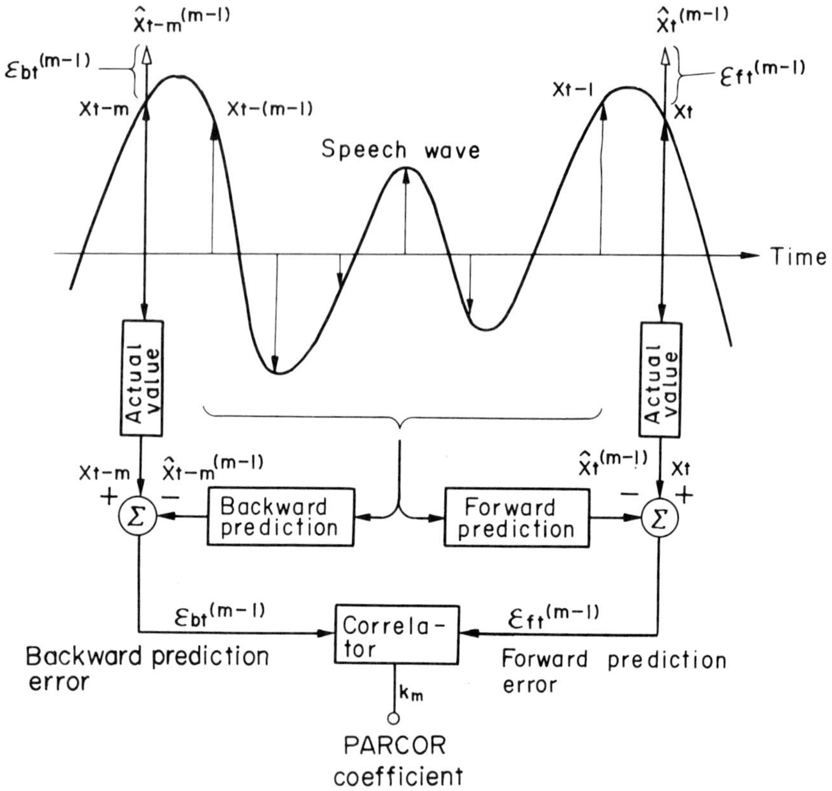


Fig. 5.7 Definition of PARCOR coefficients.

When Eq. (5.36) is put into Eq. (5.37), the PARCOR coefficient sequence $k_m(m = 1,2,\ldots,p)$ can be written as

$$k_m = \frac{\sum_{i=0}^{m-1} \alpha_i^{(m-1)} v_{m-i}}{\sum_{i=0}^{m-1} \alpha_i^{(m-1)} v_i}$$

$$= \frac{w_{m-1}}{u_{m-1}} \tag{5.38}$$

where $v_i$ is the short-term autocorrelation function for the speech wave. Although this autocorrelation function should be written as $\hat{v}_i$ in line with the notations made thus far, it is written as $v_i$ for simplicity's sake. $k_1$ is equal to $v_1/v_0$, i.e., to the first-order autocorrelation coefficient. This is also clear from the definition of $k_m$.

Using Eq. (5.38) and the fact that the prediction coefficients $\{\alpha_i^{(m-1)}\}_{i=0}^{m-1}$ and $\{\beta_i^{(m-1)}\}_{i=1}^{m}$ constitute the solutions of the simultaneous equations

$$\sum_{i=0}^{m-1} \alpha_i^{(m-1)} v_{i-j} = 0, \quad \alpha_0^{(m-1)} = 1 \qquad (j = 1,2,\ldots,m-1)$$

and

$$\sum_{i=1}^{m} \beta_i^{(m-1)} v_{i-j} = 0, \quad \beta_m^{(m-1)} = 1 \qquad (j = 1,2,\ldots,m-1)$$

$$\tag{5.39}$$

the following recursive equations can be obtained $(m = 1,2,\ldots,p)$:

$$\alpha_i^{(m)} = \alpha_i^{(m-1)} - k_m \beta_i^{(m-1)}, \quad \alpha_m^{(m-1)} = 0 \qquad (i = 1,2,\ldots,m)$$

$$\beta_i^{(m)} = \beta_{i-1}^{(m-1)} - k_m \alpha_{i-1}^{(m-1)}, \quad \beta_0^{(m-1)} = 0$$

$$(i = 1,2,\ldots,m+1)$$

$$u_m = u_{m-1}(1 - k_m^2) \tag{5.40}$$

Additionally, the following equation is obtained from Eq. (5.39):

$$\beta_i^{(m-1)} = \alpha_{m-i}^{(m-1)} \qquad (i = 1,2,\ldots,m-1) \tag{5.41}$$

Based on these results, the PARCOR coefficients $\{k_m\}_{m=1}^{p}$ and linear predictor coefficients $\{\alpha_m\}_{m=1}^{p}$ are obtained from $\{v_i\}_{i=1}^{p}$ through the flowchart in Fig. 5.8 by using Eqs. (5.38)

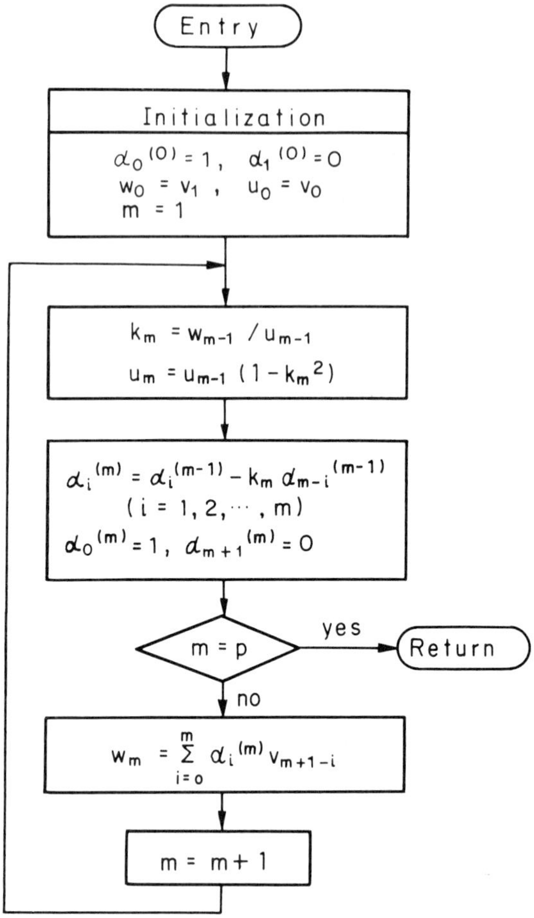


Fig. 5.8 Flowchart for calculating $\{k_m\}_{i=0}^p$ and $\{\alpha_i\}_{i=0}^p$ from $\{v_i\}_{i=0}^p$.

and (5.40). This iterative method is equivalent to Durbin's recursive solution for simultaneous linear equations. The numbers of multiplications, summations, and divisions necessary for this computation are roughly $p(p + 1)$, $p(p + 1)$, and $p$, respectively. When these computations are done using a short word length, the truncation error in the computation accumulates as the analysis progresses. In the iteration process, each $k_m (m = 1,2,\ldots,p)$ is obtained one by one, whereas the $\alpha_m$ values change at every iteration. Finally, $\alpha_m$ values are obtained as

$$\alpha_m = \alpha_m^{(p)} \qquad (1 \leqq m \leqq p) \tag{5.42}$$

Since the normalized mean square error $\sigma^2$ is equal to $u_p/v_0$ from its definition, $\sigma^2$ can be calculated using PARCOR coefficients, instead of linear predictor coefficients, from

$$\sigma^2 = \prod_{m=1}^{p} (1 - k_m^{\ 2}) \tag{5.43}$$

This equation is obtained from Eq. (5.40).

In order to derive $\{k_m\}_{m=1}^{p}$ directly from the signal $\{x_t\}$ let us define the forward and backward prediction error operators $A_m(D)$ and $B_m(D)$ as

$$A_m(D) = \sum_{i=0}^{m} \alpha_i^{(m)} D^i$$

and

$$B_m(D) = \sum_{i=1}^{m+1} \beta_i^{(m)} D^i \tag{5.44}$$

where D is the delay operator such that $D^i x_t = x_{t-i}$. Equations (5.36) can then be written as

$$\varepsilon_{ft}^{(m-1)} = A_{m-1}(D) x_t$$

and

$$\varepsilon_{bt}^{(m-1)} = B_{m-1}(D)x_t \tag{5.45}$$

From Eq. (5.40), we can arrive at the recursive equations

$$A_m(D) = A_{m-1}(D) - k_m B_{m-1}(D)$$

and

$$B_m(D) = D(B_{m-1}(D) - k_m A_{m-1}(D)) \tag{5.46}$$

Based on Eqs. (5.38), (5.45), and (5.46), the PARCOR coefficients $\{k_m\}$ can subsequently be produced directly from the speech wave $x_t$ using a cascade connection of variable parameter digital filters (partial correlators), each of which includes a correlator as indicated in Fig. 5.9(a). Since $E\{(\varepsilon_{ft}^{(m-1)})^2\}$ =

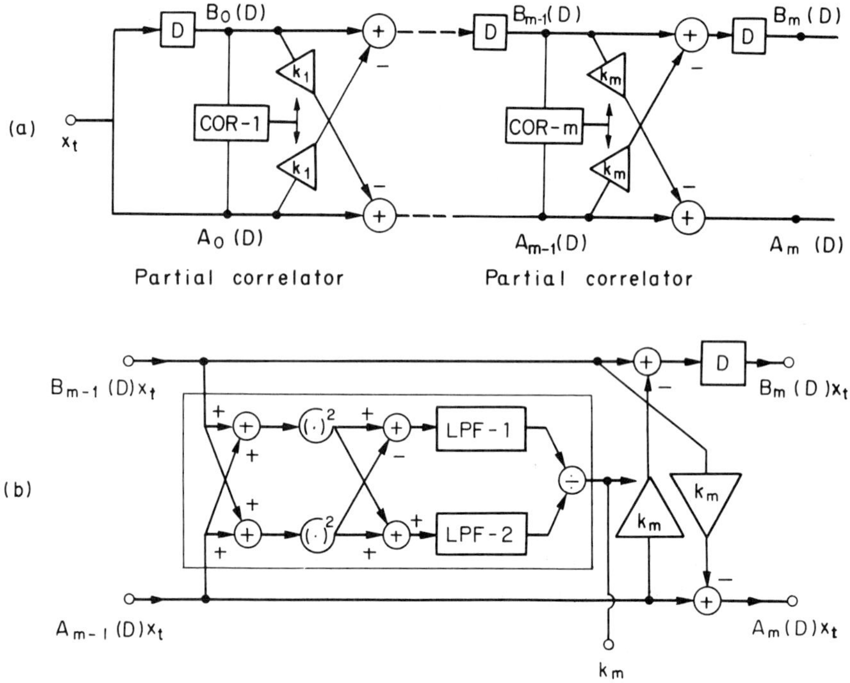


Fig. 5.9 (a) PARCOR coefficient extraction circuit constructed by cascade connection of partial autocorrelators and (b) construction of each partial autocorrelator.

$E\{(\varepsilon_{bt}^{(m-1)})^2\}$, the correlator can be realized by the structure indicated in Fig. 5.9(b), which consists of square, addition, subtraction, and division circuits and low-pass filters.

The process of extracting PARCOR coefficients using the partial correlators involves successively extracting and removing the correlations between adjacent samples. This is an inverse filtering process which flattens the spectral envelope successively. Therefore, when the number of partial correlators p is large enough, the correlation between adjacent samples, which corresponds to the overall spectral envelope information, is almost completely removed by passing the speech wave through the partial correlators. Consequently, the output of the final stage, namely, the residual signal, includes only the correlation between the distant samples which relates to the source (pitch) information. Hence, the source parameters can be extracted from the autocorrelation function for the residual signal, in other words, from the modified autocorrelation function.

The definition of the PARCOR coefficients confirms that $|k_m| \leqq 1$ is always satisfied. Furthermore, if $|k_m| < 1$, the roots for $A_p(z) = 0$ have also been verified to exist inside of the unit circle, and, therefore, the stability of the synthesis filter is guaranteed (Itakura and Saito, 1971).

### 5.6.2 Relationship Between PARCOR and LPC Coefficients

If either one of the set of $\{k_m\}_{m=1}^p$ or $\{\alpha_m\}_{m=1}^p$ is given, the other can be obtained by iterative computation. For example, when $\{k_m\}_{m=1}^p$ are given, $\{\alpha_m\}_{m=1}^p$ are derived by iterative computations (m = 1,2,...,p) using a part of Durbin's solution:

$$\alpha_m^{(m)} = -k_m$$

$$\alpha_i^{(m)} = \alpha_i^{(m-1)} - k_m \alpha_{m-i}^{(m-1)} \qquad (1 \leqq i \leqq m-1) \qquad (5.47)$$

On the other hand, $\{k_m\}_{m=1}^p$ can be drawn from $\{\alpha_m\}_{m=1}^p$ using the iterative computations in the opposite direction (m = p,p−1,...,2,1) as indicated below, where the initial condition is $\alpha_m^{(p)} = \alpha_m$ $(1 \leqq m \leqq p)$:

$$k_m = -\alpha_m^{(m)}$$

$$\alpha_i^{(m-1)} = \frac{\alpha_i^{(m)} - \alpha_m^{(m)}\alpha_{m-i}^{(m)}}{1 - k_m^2} \qquad (1 \leq i \leq m - 1)$$

(5.48)

## 5.7 PARCOR ANALYSIS-SYNTHESIS SYSTEM

### 5.7.1 PARCOR Synthesis Filter

A digital filter which synthesizes speech waveform employing PARCOR coefficients can be realized by the inverse process of speech analysis incorporating partial autocorrelators. In other words, in the PARCOR synthesis process the correlation between sample values is successively provided to the residual signal, or resonance is added to the flat spectrum of the residual signal. More specifically, the synthesis filter features the inverse characteristics of the analysis filter $1/A_m(D)$.

Reversing the signal propagation direction for A in the recursive equation (5.46) produces the relationships

$$A_m(D) = A_{m+1}(D) + k_{m+1}B_m(D)$$

and

$$B_{m+1}(D) = D(B_m(D) - k_{m+1}A_m(D)) \qquad (5.49)$$

Let us assume that the synthesis filters having the transmission characteristics of $1/A_m(D)$ and $B_m(D)$ are already realized as shown within the solid rectangle in Fig. 5.10. In order to attain a synthesized output $y_t$ at the final output terminal Q, a

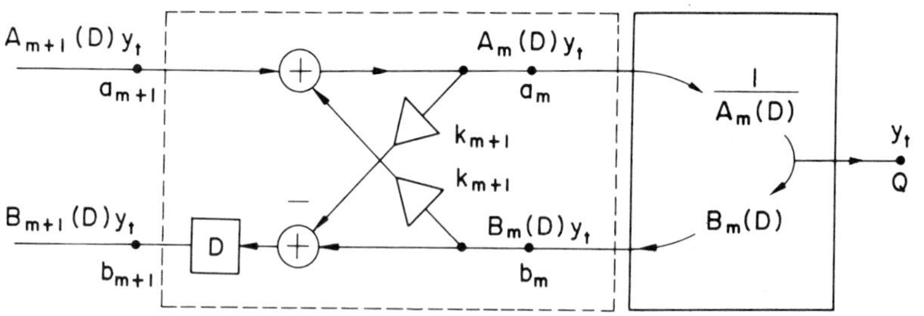


Fig. 5.10 Principal construction features of synthesis filter using PARCOR coefficients.

signal $A_m(D)y_t$ must be input to terminal $a_m$. This permits a signal $B_m(D)y_t$ to appear at terminal $b_m$. Let us next construct a lattice filter based on Eq. (5.49), as indicated within the dashed rectangle, and connect it to the circuit within the solid rectangle. If these combined circuits are viewed from terminal $a_{m+1}$, they exhibit an input-output relation of $1/A_{m+1}(D)$ since they produce output $y_t$ at terminal Q for input signal $A_{m+1}(D)y_t$. At the same time, signal $B_{m+1}(D)y_t$ appears at terminal $b_{m+1}$. Therefore, the structure indicated in Fig. 5.10 realizes one section (stage) of the PARCOR synthesis filter. Several equivalent transformations exist for this lattice filter, as indicated in Fig. 5.11.

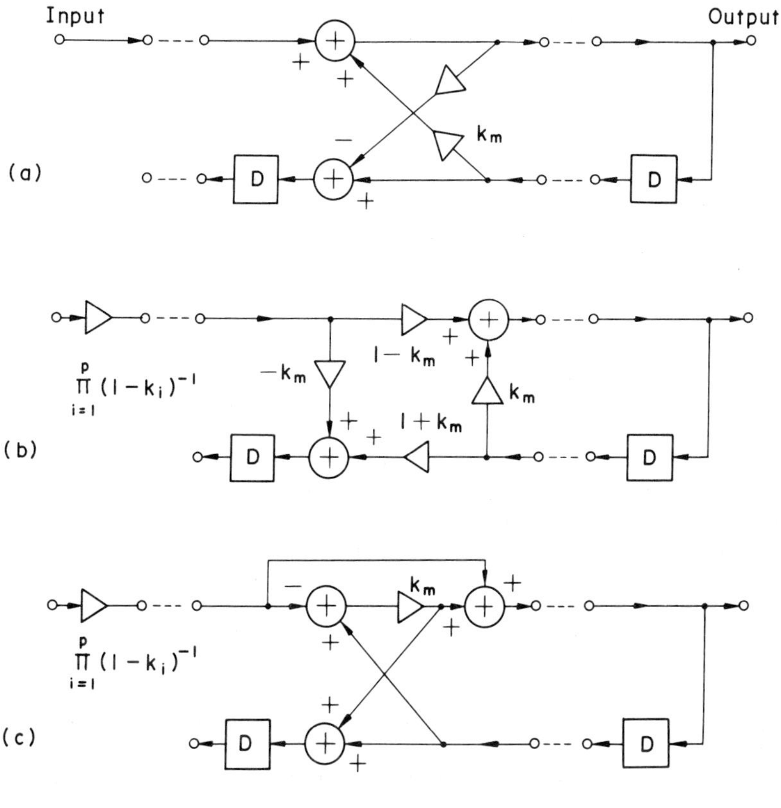


Fig. 5.11 Equivalent transformations for lattice-type digital filter.

A structural example of a speech analysis-synthesis system using PARCOR coefficients is presented in Fig. 5.12. Here, partial autocorrelators are used for the analysis. For comparison, Fig. 5.13 offers an example in which a recursive computation-based method is employed for the same purpose.

When the synthesis parameters of the PARCOR analysis-synthesis system are renewed at time intervals (frame intervals) different from the analysis intervals, the speaking rate is modified without an accompanying change in the pitch (fundamental frequency).

### 5.7.2 Optimization of PARCOR Analysis-Synthesis System

The four major system parameters determining the speech quality of analysis-synthesis systems having the structures indicated in Figs. 5.12 and 5.13 are

1. The number of PARCOR coefficients (maximum order): p
2. The sampling period of parameters (frame period): $T_r$ [s]
3. The quantizing bit rate for each PARCOR coefficient: $K_m(m = 1,2,...,p)$ [bit]
4. The quantizing bit rate for source parameters (fundamental period, and pulse and noise amplitudes): S[bit]

For the system diagramed in Fig. 5.12, the PARCOR coefficients extracted at every sampling period of the speech wave are sampled at every predetermined period (frame interval) since the coefficients at adjacent points indicate similar values. The source parameters are also sampled at the same frame interval. For the system shown in Fig. 5.13, the speech wave having a predetermined length (frame length) is extracted at every predetermined period (frame interval) and input into the autocorrelator. Usually the frame length and frame interval are set at 15 to 40 ms and 5 to 20 ms, respectively.

When input into the autocorrelator, the speech wave is usually multiplied by a time window, such as a Hamming window, so that the amplitude at both ends of each frame gradually decreases. This prevents the occurrence of spectral distortion due to the discontinuity of the speech wave. Since the effective length of the analysis period is shortened as a result of the windowing, as described in Sec. 4.2.3, adjacent frames are usually overlapped by setting the frame interval shorter than the frame length.

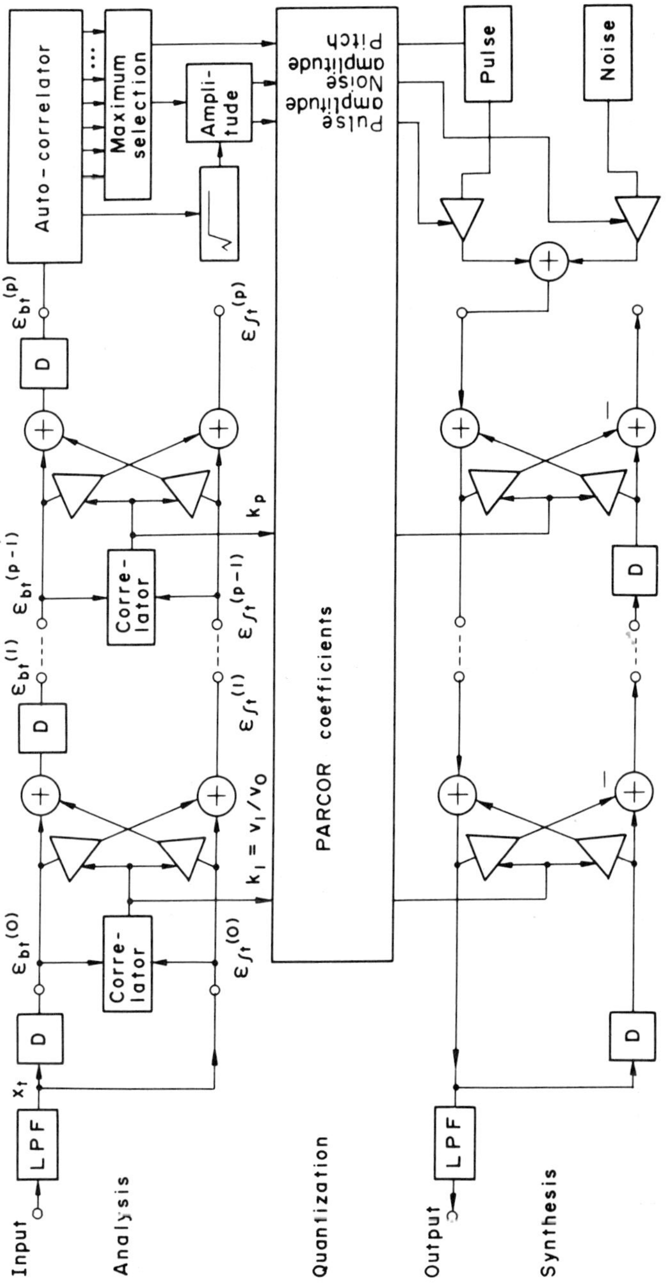


Fig. 5.12 Structure of PARCOR analysis-synthesis system.

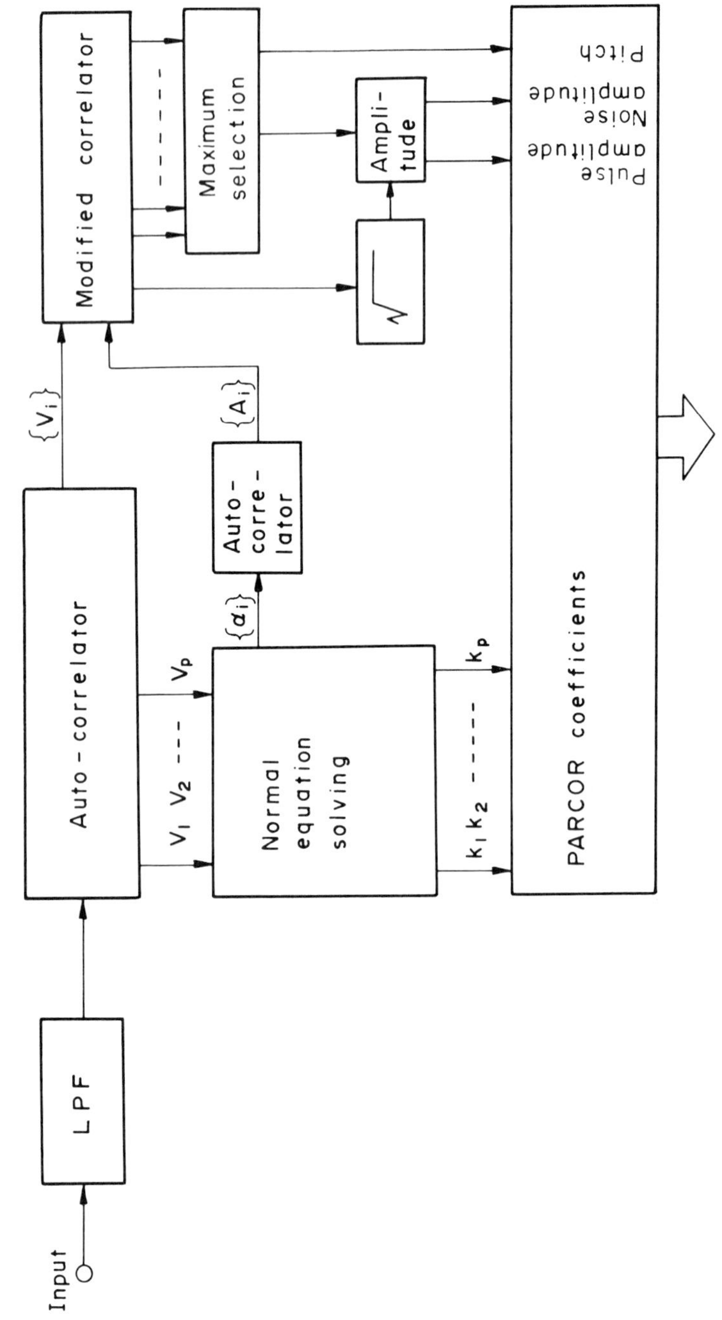


Fig. 5.13 Structure of PARCOR analyzer based on recursive computation method.

The amount of information $T_c$ at every second is then

$$T_c = \frac{1}{T_r}\left(\sum_{m=1}^{p} K_m + S\right) \text{[bit/s]} \tag{5.50}$$

As already mentioned in Sec. 5.3 concerning spectral estimation using the maximum likelihood method, the optimum value of p is 8 to 10 when the frequency range of the speech wave is limited to between 0 and 4 kHz. When $p \leqq 6$, the synthesized speech largely degrades as a result of the spectral distortion. Even if $p \geqq 12$, the quality is improved only slightly. As for the source information, the amplitude and source period can be quantized by 4–6 and 5–7 bits, respectively. The bit rate optimization procedure for PARCOR coefficients will be described in the next subsection.

### 5.7.3 Optimization Based on Spectral Distortion

When the amount of total information $T_c$ is given, the optimum sampling period and quantizing bit rate can be determined based on the quantitative analysis of the synthesized speech quality. Especially for the PARCOR coefficients, the effect of sampling and quantization can be evaluated by the spectral envelope deviation (spectral distortion) before and after processing. Furthermore, since there is an addition law concerning the two types of spectral distortion due to the sampling and quantization of each PARCOR coefficient, the total information amount can be optimally allotted based on the dynamic programming (DP) technique to minimize the overall spectral distortion (Kitawaki et al., 1978).

Figure 5.14 shows the relationship between the total bit rate of the PARCOR coefficients for each frame N and the spectral distortion $DS_Q$ when the allocation of the total bit rate $K_m$ is uniform and nonuniform with each coefficient. In this analysis, a female voice 10 s long is used, and p is set at 8. The bit rate for each PARCOR coefficient, $(K_1, K_2, \ldots, K_8)$, is indicated in parentheses in the figure. These results confirm that the nonuniform bit allocation, which assigns the larger information amount to the lower-order PARCOR coefficients $\{k_m\}$, is effective. This technique achieves smaller distortion than the uniform bit allocation at the same total bit rate N. The reason is that the larger the order m becomes the smaller the spectral distortion due to the reduced bit rate $K_m$ becomes. $DS_Q$ is referred to as quantization distortion.

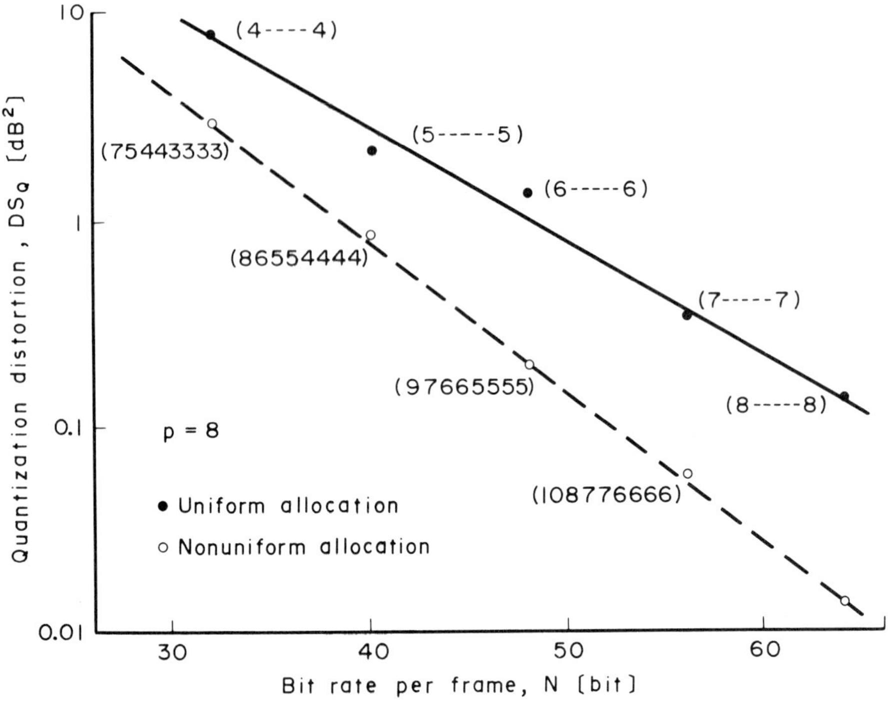


Fig. 5.14 Quantization distortion by uniform and nonuniform bit allocation.

The relationship between the frame interval $T_r$ and spectral distortion $DS_T$ measured against the standard distortion at $T_r$ = 5 ms is presented in Fig. 5.15. No improvement is notable in the auditory quality when $T_r < 5$ ms, and, clearly, a linear relationship exists between $DS_T$ and $T_r$ in the $T_r > 5$ ms region. $DS_T$ is referred to as temporal distortion.

The total distortion DS has been experimentally confirmed to be representable using the quantization distortion and the temporal distortion as

$$DS(N,T_r) \simeq DS_Q(N) + DS_T(T_r) \qquad (5.51)$$

The dependency relationship of $DS(N,T_r)$ and the articulation equivalent transmission loss (AEN) is demonstrated in Fig. 5.16.

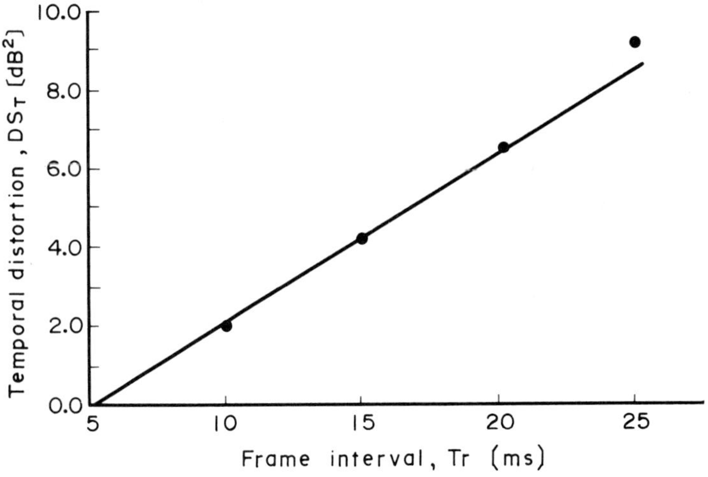


Fig. 5.15 Relationship between frame interval and temporal distortion.

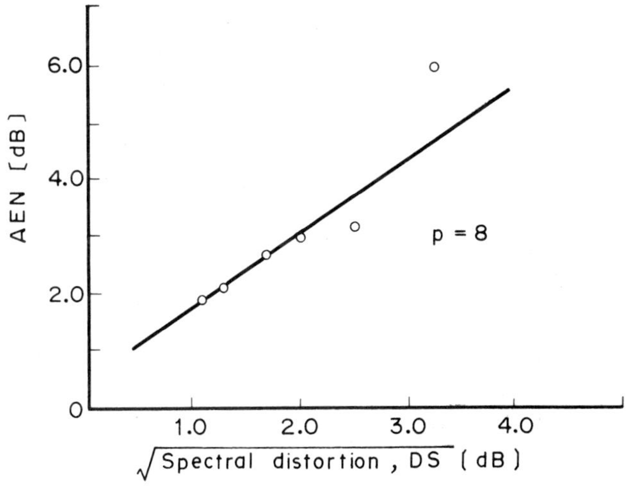


Fig. 5.16 Relationship between spectral distortion and articulation equivalent loss (AEN).

The AEN is the most basic measure of auditory degradation of synthesized speech (see Sec. 6.6). The results in the figure indicate that spectral distortion is a reasonable objective measure for evaluating the quality of PARCOR analysis-synthesis systems. A DS of 1 $dB^2$ roughly corresponds to the auditory detection limen (DL).

Although PARCOR coefficient values are theoretically restricted to between ±1, the spectral distortion (spectral sensitivity for quantization) largely differs between the region near ±1 and that around 0. Therefore, efficient quantization can be accomplished by applying the following nonlinear transformations to the first- and the second-order PARCOR coefficients which sometimes have values close to ±1:

$$g_m = \operatorname{arctanh}(k_m) = \frac{1}{2} \log \frac{1 + k_m}{1 - k_m} \tag{5.52}$$

and

$$\theta_m = \arcsin(k_m) \tag{5.53}$$

When these transformations are applied, the nonuniform bit allocation just mentioned becomes unnecessary. $g_m \times 2$, that is, $\log \{(1 + k_m)/(1 - k_m)\}$, is called the log area ratio.

Under the condition that the total information amount is restricted to below 2400 bps, three principal methods have been confirmed to be effective in improving the quality of synthesized speech (Tohkura and Itakura, 1979):

1. Spectral smoothing by a lag window, that is, weighting to the lower-order autocorrelation functions using a window such as a binomial coefficient window (this is effective especially for higher-pitched female voices)
2. Quantization taking the distribution of each PARCOR coefficient into consideration
3. Temporal smoothing of the spectrum by interpolating the variation of each PARCOR coefficient between adjacent frames

High-quality analysis-synthesis sound having an AEN of 3 dB has been confirmed to be achievable at 2400 bit/s using these techniques. As an example, Fig. 5.17 compares sound spectrograms for 2400-bps PARCOR analysis-synthesis speech with the original speech for the Japanese test sentence extended to /bakuoNga giNsekaino/, or "Over the place covered with snow, a whir is ...."

### 5.7.4 Vocal Tract Area Estimation Based on PARCOR Analysis

The signal flow graph of Kelly's speech synthesis model (Fig. 3.4(b) in Sec. 3.3.1) formally coincides with the speech synthesis digital filter used in PARCOR analysis-synthesis systems (Fig. 5.12). In other words, the PARCOR coefficient $k_n$ corresponds to the reflection coefficient $\kappa_n$. Also, the PARCOR lattice filter is regarded as an equivalent circuit for the vocal tract acoustic filter simulating the cascade connection of p equal-length acoustic tubes having different areas. Since a relationship exists between the reflection coefficient and area function as described in Sec. 3.3.1, the area function can expectantly be estimated from the PARCOR coefficients. However, several problems exist with this assumption.

From the speech production mechanism, the total system function S(z) for the speech production system is represented by the product of the system functions for source generation G(z), vocal tract resonance V(z), and radiation R(z) as

$$S(z) = G(z)V(z)R(z) \tag{5.54}$$

With PARCOR analysis, which is based on the linear separable equivalent circuit model described in Sec. 3.2, the vocal tract system function is obtained by assuming that the sound source consists of an impulse or random noise having a uniform spectral density. Therefore, the overall characteristics of S(z) including the source and radiation characteristics are derived instead of V(z). Consequently, when the area function is calculated according to the formal coincidence between the PARCOR coefficient $k_n$ and the reflection coefficient $\kappa_n$, the result widely differs from the actual area function.

Properly estimating the area function thus requires the removal of the effects of G(z) and R(z) from the speech wave prior to the PARCOR analysis, which is called inverse filtering or spectral equalization. Two specific methods have been investigated for inverse filtering.

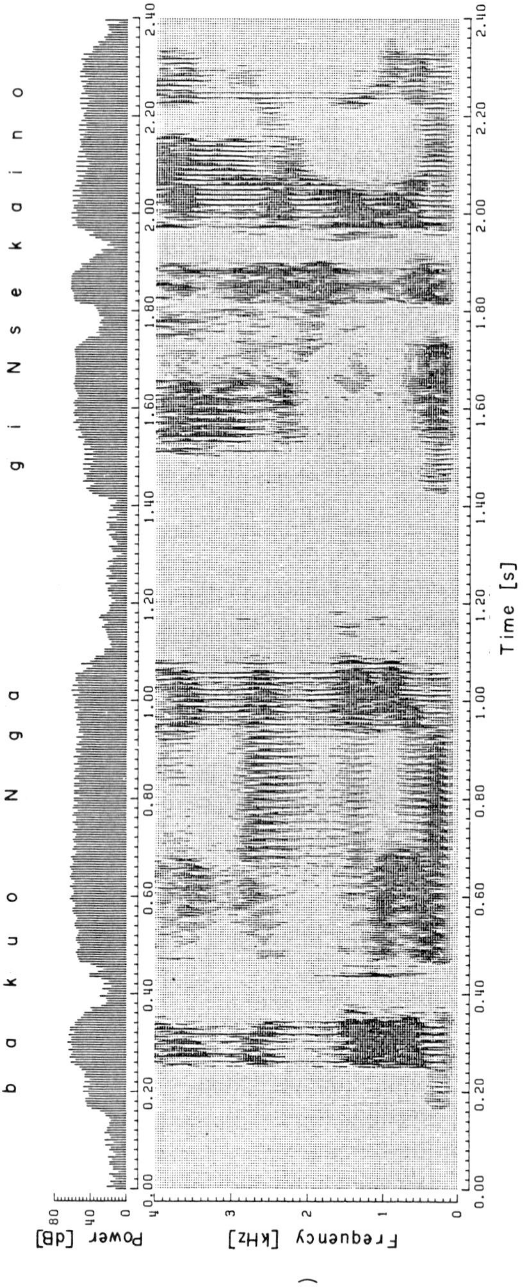


(a)

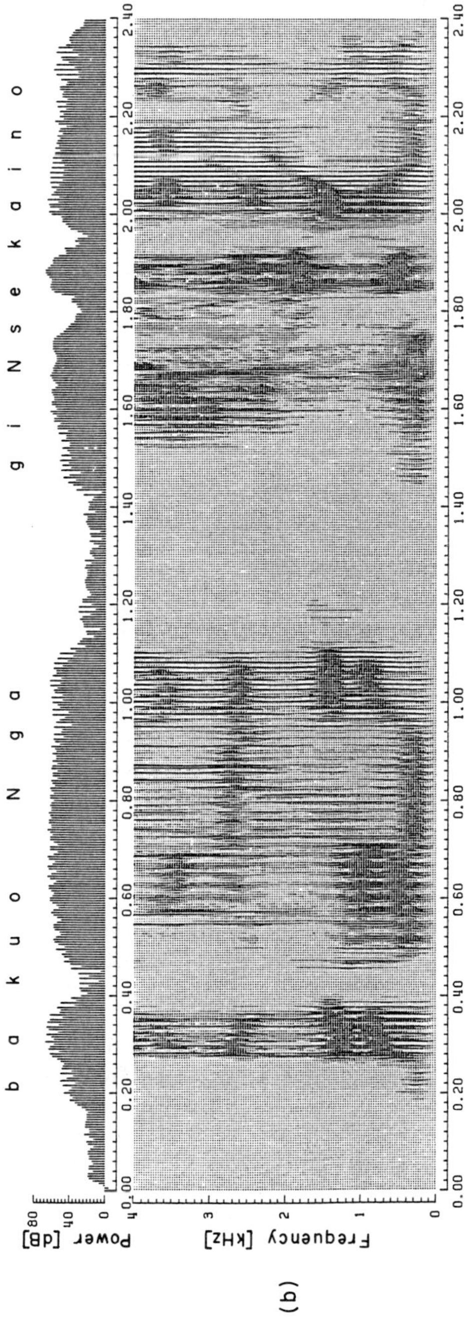


Fig. 5.17 Sound spectrograms for (a) original speech and (b) 2400-bps PARCOR analysis-synthesis speech.

1. First-order differential processing

As is well known, the frequency characteristics of the sound source $G(z)$ and radiation $R(z)$ can be roughly approximated as −12 dB/oct and 6 dB/oct, respectively. Based on this approximation, the sound source and radiation characteristics can be canceled by 6-dB/oct spectral emphasis (Wakita, 1973). This is actually done by analog differential processing of the input speech wave $\{x_t\}$ or by digital processing of digitized speech. The latter is accomplished by calculating $y_t = x_t - x_{t-1}$, which corresponds to the filter processing of $F(z) = 1 - z^{-1}$.

2. Adaptive inverse filtering

On the assumption that overall vocal tract frequency characteristics are almost flat and have hardly any spectral tilt, the spectral tilt in the input signal is adaptively removed at every analysis frame using lower order correlation coefficients (Nakajima et al., 1978). When the first-order inverse filter is applied, the first-order correlation coefficient, that is, the first-order PARCOR coefficient ($k_1 = r_1 = v_1/v_0$), is used to construct the $F(z) = 1 - k_1 z^{-1}$ filter. This is achieved by the computation of $y_t = x_t - k_1 x_{t-1}$ or by the convolution of the correlation coefficients. Using the convolution method, inverse filtering can easily be done even for the second- or third-order critical damping inverse filtering.

Appropriate boundary conditions at the lips and the glottis must also be established for properly estimating the area function. For this purpose, two cases have been considered for vowel-type speech production in which the sound source is located at the glottis and no connection exists with the nasal cavity.

1. Case 1

Lips: The vocal tract is open to the field having an infinite area (that is, $\kappa_0 = 1$) such that the forward propagation wave is completely reflected, and the circuit is short (impedance is $z = \rho c/A\,|_{A\to\infty} = 0$).

Glottis: The vocal tract is terminated by the characteristic impedance $\rho c/A_p$. The backward propagation wave flows out to the trachea without reflection and causes a loss. The input signal is supplied to the vocal tract through this characteristic impedance (Wakita, 1973; Nakajima et al., 1978).

2. Case 2

Lips: The vocal tract is terminated by the characteristic impedance $\rho c/A_1$. The forward propagation wave is emitted to the field without reflection and results in a loss.

Glottis: The vocal tract is completely closed (in other words, $\kappa_{p+1} = -1$) such that the backward propagation wave is completely reflected, and the input signal is supplied to the glottis as a constant flow source (Atal, 1970).

The vocal tract area ratio is successively determined from the lips in Case 1 and from the glottis in Case 2. Linear predictive analysis and PARCOR analysis correspond to Case 1. Comparing the results of these two cases, which are usually quite different from each other, Case 1 seems to give the most reasonable results. For final transformation from the area ratio to the area function, it is necessary to define the glottal area $A_p$ so that the final results become similar to the actual values determined through x-ray photography and other techniques. The relationship between the area function and PARCOR coefficients in Case 1 is shown in Fig. 5.18.

The vocal tract area function estimated from the actual speech wave based on the above method has been confirmed to globally coincide with the results observed by x-ray photographs. Figure 5.19 compares spectral envelopes and area functions (unit interval length is 1.4 cm) estimated by applying adaptive inverse filtering for the five Japanese vowels uttered by a male speaker (Nakajima et al., 1978).

If the vocal tract area could ever be estimated automatically and precisely from the speech wave, the estimation method achieving this will certainly become a fundamental speech analysis method. Furthermore, this method will be extremely useful for analyzing the speech production process and for improving speech recognition and synthesis systems. Several problems remain, however, in achieving the necessary precision of the estimated area function. These warrant further investigation into properly modeling the source characteristics in the estimation algorithm.

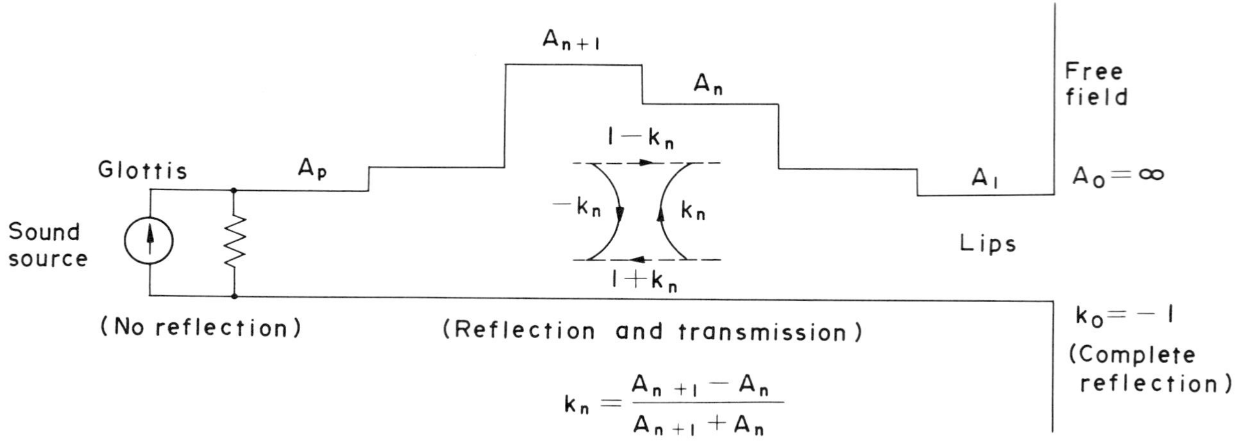


Fig. 5.18 Relationship between PARCOR coefficients $\{k_n\}$ and vocal tract area function $\{A_n\}$.

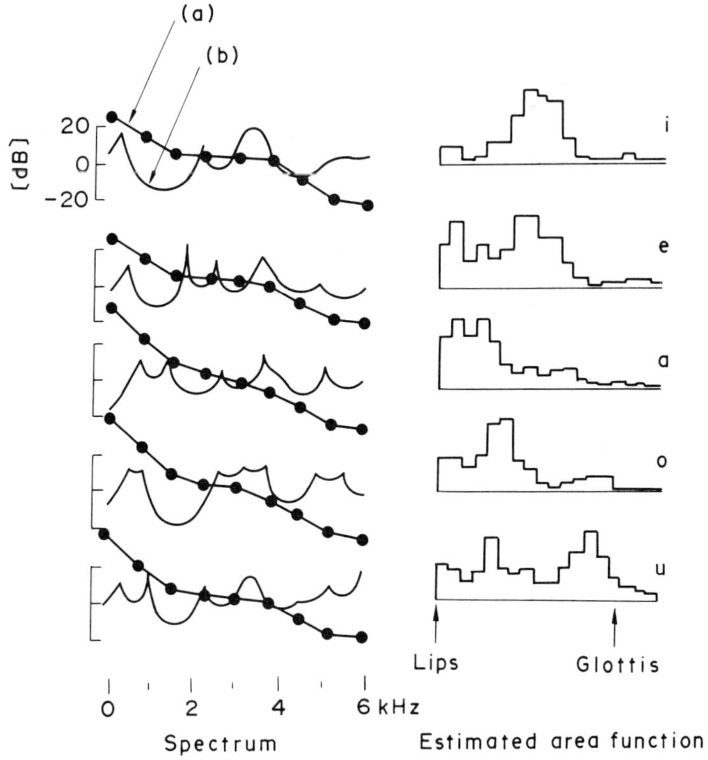


Fig. 5.19 Examples of spectral envelopes and estimated area functions for five vowels: (a) overall spectral envelope for inverse filtering (source and radiation characteristics); (b) spectral envelope after inverse filtering (vocal tract characteristics).

## 5.8 LINE SPECTRUM PAIR (LSP) ANALYSIS

### 5.8.1 Principle of LSP Analysis

Although the PARCOR analysis-synthesis method is superior to any other previously developed methods, it has the lowest bit rate limit, 2400 bps. If the bit rate falls below this value, synthesized voice rapidly becomes unclear and unnatural. The LSP method was thus investigated to maintain voice quality at smaller bit rates (Itakura, 1975). The PARCOR coefficients are essentially parameters operating in the time domain as are the autocorrelation coefficients, whereas the LSPs are parameters functioning in the frequency domain. Therefore, the LSP parameters are advantageous in that the distortion they produce is smaller than that of the PARCOR coefficients even when they are roughly quantized and linearly interpolated.

As with PARCOR analysis, LSP analysis is based on the all-pole model. The polynomial expression for z, which is the denominator of the all-pole model, satisfies the following recursive equations, as previously demonstrated in Eq. (5.46):

$$A_m(z) = A_{m-1}(z) - k_m B_{m-1}(z)$$

and

$$B_m(z) = z^{-1}(B_{m-1}(z) - k_m A_{m-1}(z)) \tag{5.55}$$

where $A_0(z) = 1$ and $B_0(z) = z^{-1}$ (initial conditions).

Let us assume that $A_p(z)$ is given, and represent two $A_{p+1}(z)$ types, P(z) and Q(z), under the conditions $k_{p+1} = 1$ and $k_{p+1} = -1$, respectively. The condition $|k_{p+1}| = 1$ corresponds to the case where the airflow is completely reflected at the glottis in the (pseudo) vocal tract model represented by PARCOR coefficients. In other words, this condition corresponds to the completely open or closed termination condition. The actual boundary condition at the glottis is, however, the iteration of opening and closing, as a function of vocal cord vibration.

Since the boundary condition at the lips in the PARCOR analysis is a free field ($k_0 = -1$) as mentioned in the previous section, the present boundary condition sets the absolute values of the reflection coefficients to 1 at both ends of the vocal tract. This means that the vocal tract acoustic system becomes a lossless system which completely shuts in the energy. The Q value at every resonance mode in the acoustic tube thus becomes infinite, and a pair of delta function-like resonance characteristics (a pair of line spectra) which correspond to each boundary condition at the glottis are obtained. The number of resonances are 2p.

### 5.8.2 Solution of LSP Analysis

From Eq. (5.55), P(z) and Q(z) can be represented as

$$P(z) = A_p(z) - B_p(z)$$

and

$$Q(z) = A_p(z) + B_p(z) \tag{5.56}$$

Although P(z) and Q(z) are both (p + 1)st-order polynomial expressions, P(z) has inversely symmetrical coefficients whereas Q(z) has symmetrical coefficients. Using Eq. (5.56), we get

$$A_p(z) = \frac{P(z) + Q(z)}{2} \tag{5.57}$$

On the other hand, from the recursive equations of (5.55),

$$\begin{aligned}
A_1(z) &= 1 - k_1 z^{-1} \\
B_1(z) &= z^{-1}(z^{-1} - k_1) = z^{(1+1)}A_1(z^{-1}) \\
A_2(z) &= 1 - k_1 z^{-1} - k_2 z^{-1}(z^{-1} - k_1) \\
&= 1 - k_1(1 - k_2)z^{-1} - k_2 z^{-2} \\
B_2(z) &= z^{-1}[z^{-1}(z^{-1} - k_1) - k_2(1 - k_1 z^{-1})] \\
&= z^{-1}[z^{-2} - k_1(1 - k_2)z^{-1} - k_2] \\
&= z^{-(1+2)}A_2(z^{-1})
\end{aligned} \tag{5.58}$$

Continuing this transformation, we can derive the general equation

$$B_p(z) = z^{-(p+1)}A_p(z^{-1})$$

$$= z^{-(p+1)} + z^{-p}\alpha_1 + \cdots + z^{-1}\alpha_p \tag{5.59}$$

If p is assumed to be even, P(z) and Q(z) are factorized as

$$P(z) = (1 - z^{-1}) \prod_{i=2,4,\ldots,p} (1 - 2z^{-1}\cos\omega_i + z^{-2})$$

and

$$Q(z) = (1 + z^{-1}) \prod_{i=1,3,\ldots,p-1} (1 - 2z^{-1}\cos\omega_i + z^{-2}) \tag{5.60}$$

The factors $1 - z^{-1}$ and $1 + z^{-1}$ are found by calculating P(1) and Q(−1) after putting Eq. (5.59) into Eq. (5.56). The coefficients $\{\omega_i\}$ which appear in the factorization of Eq. (5.60) are referred to as LSP parameters. $\{\omega_i\}$ are ordered as

$$0 < \omega_1 < \omega_2 < \cdots < \omega_{p-1} < \omega_p < \pi \tag{5.61}$$

Even-suffixed $\{\omega_i\}$ are proved to separate each element of odd-suffixed $\{\omega_i\}$, and vice versa. In other words, even-suffixed $\{\omega_i\}$ and odd-suffixed $\{\omega_i\}$ are interlaced. Furthermore, this interlacing is proved to correspond to the necessary and sufficient condition for the stability of the all-pole model: $H(z) = 1/A_p(z)$. Under the condition that p is odd, the LSP is obtained in the same way.

Using Eq. (5.57), the power transmission function for H(z) can be represented as

$$\begin{aligned}|H(e^{-j\omega})|^2 &= \frac{1}{|A_p(e^{-j\omega})|^2} \\ &= 4|P(e^{-j\omega}) + Q(e^{-j\omega})|^{-2} \\ &= 2^{1-p}\{\sin^2\frac{\omega}{2} \prod_{i=2,4,\ldots,p} (\cos\omega - \cos\omega_i)^2 \\ &\quad + \cos^2\frac{\omega}{2} \prod_{i=1,3,\ldots,p-1} (\cos\omega - \cos\omega_i)^2\}^{-2}\end{aligned} \tag{5.62}$$

The first term in braces approaches 0 when $\omega$ approaches 0 or one of the $\{\omega_i\}$ $(i = 2,4,\ldots,p)$, and the second term approaches 0 when $\omega$ approaches $\pi$ or one of the $\{\omega_i\}$ $(i = 1,3,\ldots,p-1)$. Therefore, when two LSP parameters, $\omega_i$ and $\omega_j$, are close together and when $\omega$ approaches both of them, the gain of $H(z)$ becomes large and resonance occurs. Strong resonance occurs at frequency $\omega$ when two or more $\omega_i$'s are concentrated near $\omega$. That is, the LSP method represents the speech spectral envelope through a distribution density of p discrete frequencies $\{\omega_i\}$.

Either of the following methods can be used to obtain the zeroes for $P(z)$ and $Q(z)$ with respect to $z^{-1}$ after deriving the coefficients for $A_p(z)$, that is, the linear predictor coefficients $\{\alpha_i\}$.

1. Root finding in algebraic equations
   Equation (5.60) can be transformed into

$$\prod_{j=1}^{m} (1 - 2z^{-1} \cos \omega_j + z^{-2}) = (2z^{-1})^m \prod_{j=1}^{m} \left( \frac{z + z^{-1}}{2} - \cos \omega_j \right) \qquad (5.63)$$

   Then, by replacing $(z + z^{-1})/2|_{z=\exp(-j\omega)} = \cos \omega$ with x, the equations $P(z)/(1 - z^{-1}) = 0$ and $Q(z)/(1 + z^{-1}) = 0$ can be solved as a pair of $(p/2)$th-order algebraic equations with respect to x using the Newton iteration method.
2. DFT for the coefficients of the equations
   The values of $P(z)$ and $Q(z)$ at $z_n = e^{-jn\pi/N}$ $(n = 0,\ldots,N)$ are first obtained through the DFT using the coefficients of $P(z)$ and $Q(z)$. Zeros can then be estimated by the interpolation of two points which produce a zero between them. The procedure for searching for the zeros is largely reduced using the relationship $0 < \omega_1 < \omega_2 < \cdots < \omega_p < \pi$. A value between 64 and 128 is considered large enough for N.

### 5.8.3 Composite Sinusoidal Model

The composite sinusoidal model (CSM) method is a speech analysis method closely related to the LSP method (Sagayama and Itakura, 1981). In the CSM method, the autocorrelation of the signal $r_\tau$ is represented by a linear combination of p/2 cosine waves as

$$r_\tau = \sum_{i=1}^{p/2} m_i \cos \lambda_i \tau \qquad (\tau = 0,1,\ldots,p-1) \tag{5.64}$$

where $m_i$ is a nonnegative coefficient called the CSM magnitude, and $\lambda_i$ is termed the CSM frequency. The parameter set $\{m_i, \lambda_i\}$ is uniquely determined from $r_\tau$ ($\tau = 0,1,\ldots,p-1$).

## 5.9 LSP ANALYSIS-SYNTHESIS SYSTEM

### 5.9.1 LSP Synthesis Filter

In LSP speech synthesis, a digital filter which corresponds to H(z) is constructed based on the LSP parameters $(\omega_1, \omega_2, \ldots, \omega_p)$. Since $H(z) = 1/A_p(z)$, this transfer function can be realized by inserting a filter having a transfer function of $A_p(z) - 1$ into a negative feedback path in the signal flow graph in the same way as in the LPC analysis-synthesis system (Itakura and Sugamura, 1979). Based on Eqs. (5.57) and (5.60), when p is even, we then have

$$\begin{aligned} A_p(z) - 1 &= \frac{1}{2}\,[(P(z) - 1) + (Q(z) - 1)] \\ &= \frac{z^{-1}}{2}\,\Big[\sum_{\substack{i=2 \\ i\ \mathrm{even}}}^{p} (c_i + z^{-1}) \prod_{\substack{j=0 \\ j\ \mathrm{even}}}^{i-2} (1 + c_j z^{-1} + z^{-2}) \\ &\quad - \prod_{\substack{j=2 \\ j\ \mathrm{even}}}^{p} (1 + c_j z^{-1} + z^{-2}) \\ &\quad + \sum_{\substack{i=1 \\ i\ \mathrm{odd}}}^{p-1} (c_i + z^{-1}) \prod_{\substack{j=-1 \\ j\ \mathrm{odd}}}^{i-2} (1 + c_j z^{-1} + z^{-2}) \\ &\quad + \prod_{\substack{j=1 \\ j\ \mathrm{odd}}}^{p-1} (1 + c_j z^{-1} + z^{-2})\Big] \end{aligned} \tag{6.65}$$

Here,

$$c_i = -2\cos\omega_i \quad (i = 1,2,\ldots,p), \qquad c_0 = c_{-1} = -z^{-1} \tag{6.66}$$

$A_p(z) - 1$ can thus be constructed by a pair of trunk circuits which respectively correspond to odd and even numbers of i, as shown in Fig. 5.20(a). Each trunk circuit is a p/2-stage cascade connection of quadratic antiresonance circuits: $1 - 2\cos\omega_i z^{-1} + z^{-2}$. The outputs at the middle of each stage on each trunk are successively summed up, and the outputs at the final stage are added or subtracted from the former value. The synthesis filter for odd p, represented in Fig. 5.20(b), is realized in the same way.

The numbers of computations necessary for synthesizing one sample of speech using this synthesis filter are p multiplications and 3p + 1 additions or subtractions. Although the number of multiplications is roughly half that for the two-multiplication-type PARCOR synthesis filter, the number of registers for delay is roughly twice that of the latter.

An example of an LSP analysis result for the complete Japanese test sentence /bakuoNga giNsekaino ko:geNni hirogaru/, or "A whir is spreading over the plateau covered with snow," is presented in Fig. 5.21. This figure indicates that LSPs are concentrated at the place where the speech spectrum is strong and that they resemble the movement of formants.

### 5.9.2 Coding of LSP Parameters

Optimum coding of LSP parameters can be realized by means of the same subjective and objective evaluation methods used for PARCOR analysis-synthesis systems (Sugamura and Itakura, 1981). Experimental studies on quantization characteristics have confirmed that if the distribution range of LSP parameters is considered in the quantization, the same spectral distortion can be realized by roughly 80% of the quantization bit rate compared with the PARCOR systems. As for the interpolation characteristics, the interpolation distortion has been demonstrated as being maintainable even if the parameter renewal rate is roughly 75% of the rate for PARCOR parameters. As the result of the combination of these two effects, the LSP method produces the same synthesized sound quality using only roughly 60% of the bit rate as compared with that needed employing the PARCOR method.

The advantages and disadvantages of the PARCOR and LSP methods are more closely compared in summarized form in Table 5.1.

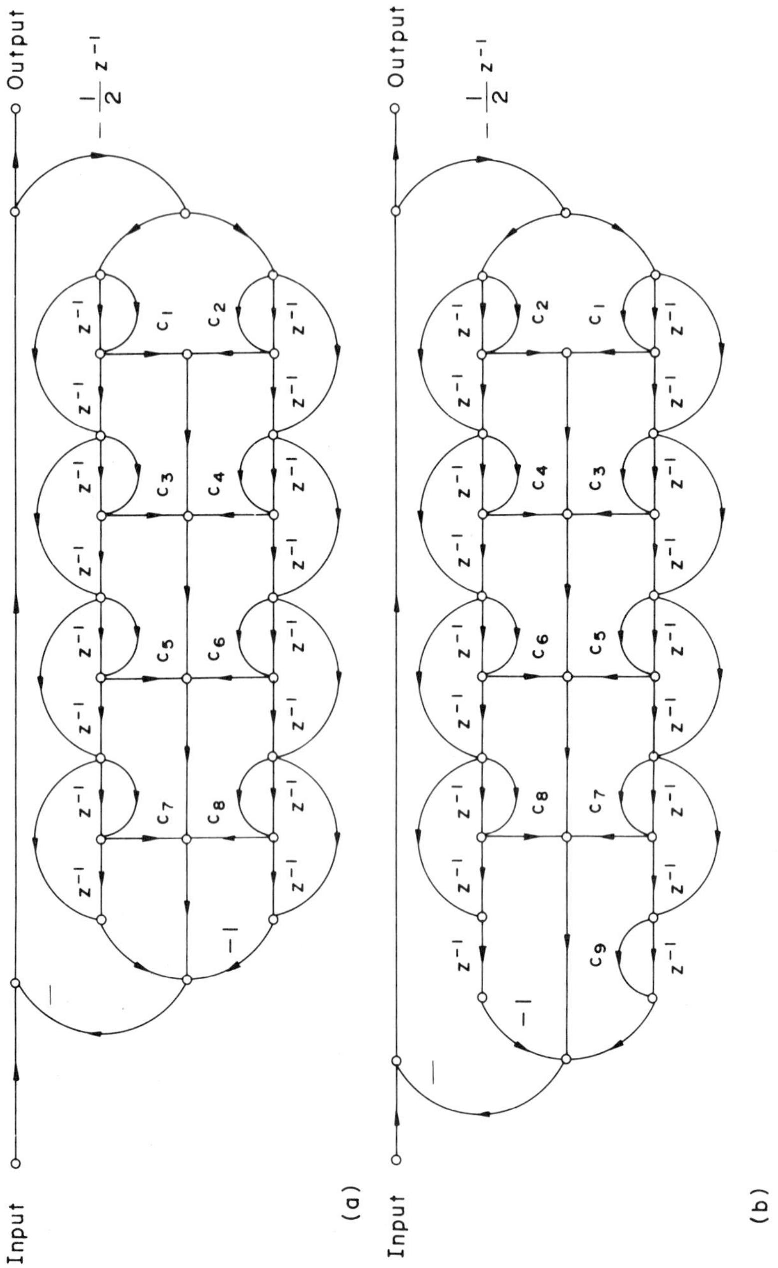


Fig. 5.20 Signal flow graph of LSP synthesis filter: (a) p = even; (b) p = odd.

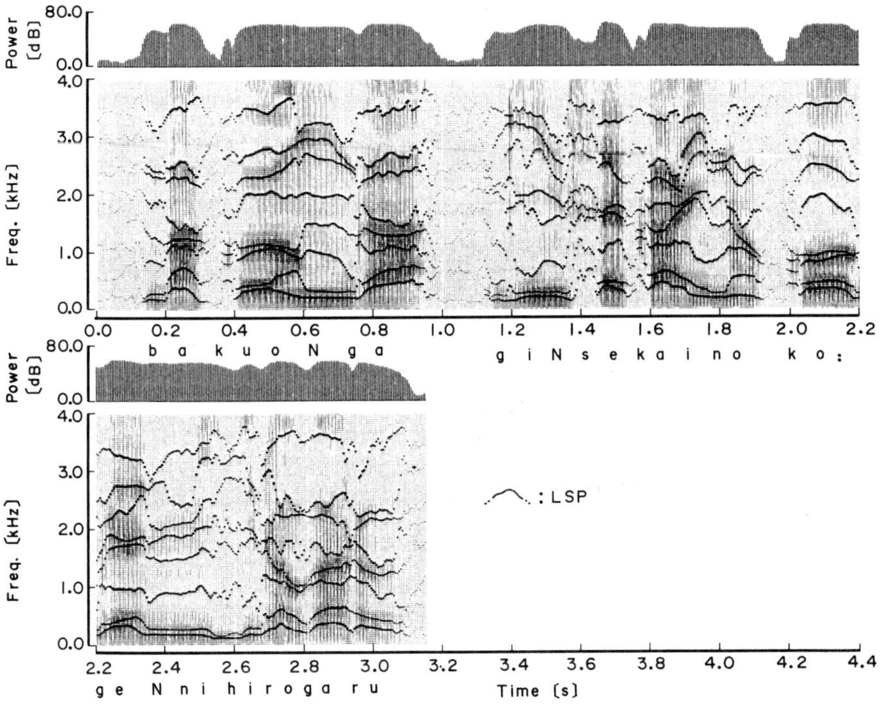


Fig. 5.21 LSP analysis result in which time functions of power, spectrum and LSP parameters are given for the spoken Japanese sentence indicated.

### 5.9.3 Mutual Relationships between LPC Parameters

The mutual relationships between each parameter obtained based on all-pole spectral modeling (LPC modeling) are indicated in Fig. 5.22 (Itakura, 1981). For reference, the relationships between the LPC cepstral coefficients and linear predictor coefficients $\{\alpha_i\}_{i=1}^{p}$ were described in Sec. 4.3.2.

The relationship existing between the autocorrelation function for the impulse response of the all-pole system $\tilde{r}_\tau$ and $\{\alpha_i\}_{i=0}^{p}$ can be expressed as

TABLE 5.1 Comparison of PARCOR and LSP Methods

| Method | Advantages | Disadvantages |
|---|---|---|
| PARCOR $\{k_i\}$ | a. $\lvert k_i \rvert <$ ensures stability | a. Poor interpolation characteristics |
| | b. Directly extracted by lattice-type analysis | b. Large spectral resolution variation over parameters |
| | c. $k_i$ values are independent of analysis order | c. Indirect correspondence to spectrum |
| LSP $\{\omega_i\}$ | a. $\omega_1 < \omega_2 < \cdots < \omega_p$ ensures stability | a. Computation amount for parameter extraction is slightly increased |
| | b. Good quantization and interpolation characteristics | b. $\omega_i$ values depend on analysis order |
| | c. Similar to formant | |

$$\sum_{i=0}^{p} \alpha_i \tilde{r}_{|i-j|} = 0 \qquad (j \geqq 1) \tag{5.67}$$

$\tilde{r}_\tau$, which is often called the LPC correlation function, agrees with the autocorrelation function for the signal $r_\tau$ in the range of $\tau = 1$ to p.

## 5.10 POLE-ZERO ANALYSIS

Although speech analysis based on the all-pole model has numerous advantages, the actual speech production models for nasal and consonant sounds are of the pole-zero type having formants and antiformants. The glottal source wave is also considered to have zeros in its spectrum. Therefore, it is more realistic to represent the speech production system function using both poles and zeros as

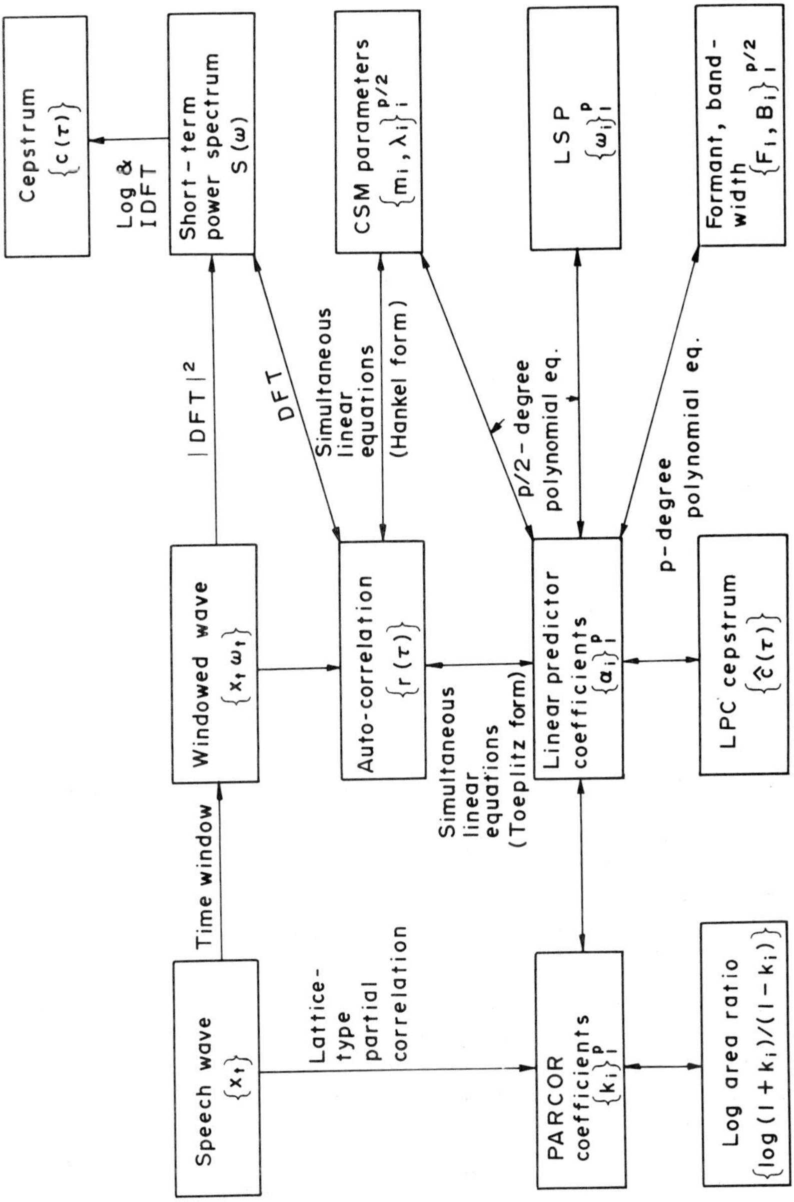


Fig. 5.22 Mutual relationships between parameters based on all-pole spectrum modeling.

$$H(z) = \frac{\prod_{i=1}^{q/2} (1 - \nu_i z^{-1})(1 - \nu_i^* z^{-1})}{\prod_{i=1}^{p/2} (1 - \gamma_i z^{-1})(1 - \gamma_i^* z^{-1})}$$

$$= \frac{1 + \beta_1 z^{-1} + \beta_2 z^{-2} + \cdots + \beta_q z^{-q}}{1 + \alpha_1 z^{-1} + \alpha_2 z^{-2} + \cdots + \alpha_p z^{-p}} \tag{5.68}$$

Here, $\nu_i$ and $\nu_i^*$ are conjugate zeros on the z-plane, $\gamma_i$ and $\gamma_i^*$ are conjugate poles, and q and p are the number of zeros and poles, respectively, except for those at the origin and infinite positions.

A relationship then results between the input $\{x_t\}$ and output $\{y_t\}$:

$$y_t + \sum_{i=1}^{p} \alpha_i y_{t-i} = x_t + \sum_{j=1}^{q} \beta_j x_{t-j} \tag{5.69}$$

Considering this relationship, the digital filter which synthesizes the speech wave based on Eq. (5.68) using a pulse train can be constructed as indicated in Fig. 5.23. The lower half of this figure is identical to the synthesis circuit based on the all-pole model (Sec. 5.5, Fig. 5.6). There are a number of variations in constructing H(z) such as the cascade or parallel connection of quadratic systems, each of which has a complex conjugate pole-zero pair.

Five principal methods have been proposed for parameter estimation based on the pole-zero model:

1. Homomorphic prediction (Oppenheim et al., 1976)
2. Iterative computation using inverse filtering (correlation matching) (Fukabayashi and Suzuki, 1977)
3. Iterative computation for poles and zeros using inverse spectrum (Ishizaki, 1977)
4. Expansion of Yule-Walker equation (application of the singular factorization method) (Morikawa and Fujisaki, 1984)
5. Maximum likelihood estimation for pole-zero parameters (Sagayama and Furui, 1977)

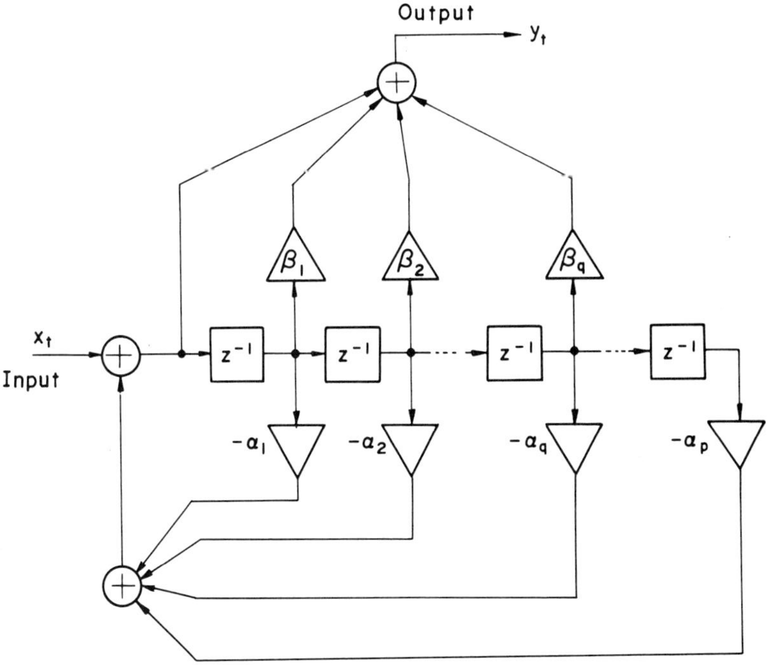


Fig. 5.23 Speech synthesis circuit derived from pole-zero modeling.

The pole-zero model is characteristic in that poles and zeros cancel each other. Furthermore, it is theoretically much more difficult to solve than the all-pole model because it causes nonlinear equations to arise for the numerator terms even in the simplest case when minimum square estimation is directly performed. These equations can be solved only by iterative methods, and convergence to the global optimum values is not guaranteed. Although both inputs and outputs of the system are usually given in the general linear system identification problems, the input wave (sound source) cannot be directly observed, and only the output wave is given in speech analysis. Therefore, an acceptable solution to the pole-zero model which can be reliably applied to actual speech has not yet been established.

# 6

# Coding of Speech Signals

## 6.1 PRINCIPAL TECHNIQUES FOR SPEECH CODING

### 6.1.1 Reversible Coding

Principal coding techniques can be classified into reversible coding which is not accompanied by information loss and irreversible coding which is so accompanied.

Reversible coding is based on Shannon's information source coding theory, which says that the coding efficiency is limited by the entropy of the information source (Jayant and Noll, 1984). This means that when the occurrence probability of each code is not homogeneous, the bit rate can be reduced by variable length coding. In variable length coding, therefore, the bit length of each code varies according to its entropy or occurrence probability. A short code is used for codes with a high occurrence probability, whereas a long code is used for low-occurrence probability codes. This coding, also referred to as entropy coding, is efficient in raising the signal-to-noise ratio (SNR), especially when it is combined with uniform quantization.

Shannon-Fano coding and Huffman coding are examples of entropy coding. Huffman coding has been ascertained to be the optimum (compact) coding since it achieves the minimum average code length when the occurrence probability is given. When a speech waveform of a relatively long period (block) is coded using Huffman coding, the approximate limit of the information source coding theory is realized. With Huffman coding, however, the complexity of both coding and decoding increases exponentially with the block length.

In order to cope with this difficulty, an arithmetic coding method has been proposed in which the complexity of coding and decoding increases linearly with the block length. Arithmetic coding can also realize the approximate limit of the information source coding theory. With these coding methods the probability distribution of the information source is assumed to be known.

On the other hand, a universal coding method has been proposed to devise a coding method which approaches the limit without the need to know the probability distribution. However, this method is disadvantageous in that the block length must be large in order to achieve the proper compression effect.

Variable-length coding, which is usually combined with one of several predictive coding methods, requires a time delay (buffering) making frame synchronization difficult.

### 6.1.2 Irreversible Coding and Information Rate Distortion Theory

Although no information is lost with reversible coding, a certain amount of distortion is usually permitted in speech coding as long as auditory comprehensibility is not impaired. Irreversible coding, which accompanies signal distortion, is based on the following rate distortion theory (Jayant and Noll, 1984). When a certain information source is coded so that the distortion is less than a certain value D, the average code length L for each information source has the lower limit of $L \geqq R(D)$. On the other hand, when the information rate R is given, the lower limit of quantization distortion D(R) exists. The lower limits of R(D) and D(R) are referred to as the rate distortion function and distortion rate function, respectively.

The rate distortion theory has no practical application, however, for two reasons. First, R(D) and D(R) are very difficult to calculate except for very simple cases. Second, actual coding methods cannot be derived from this theory.

As described in Sec. 4.6, the basic techniques for irreversible coding methods for a speech wave are as follows.

1. Nonlinear quantization
   The amplitude is compressed by nonlinear transformation (logarithmic transformation, etc.), based on the statistical characteristics of the speech amplitude. Figure 6.1 shows examples of linear and nonlinear quantization characteristics.

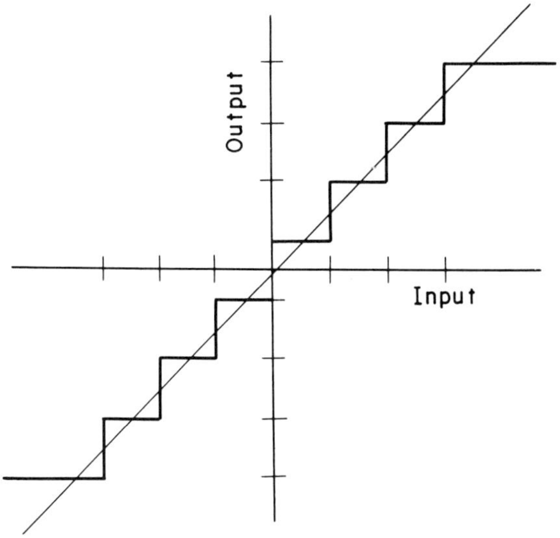


( a ) Linear quantization

Fig. 6.1 Input-output characteristics of linear and nonlinear quantization.

2. Adaptive quantization
   The step width of the quantizer is varied according to the amplitude variation in order to cope with the nonstationarity of the speech amplitude dynamics.
3. Predictive coding
   The transmission bit rate can be compressed by utilizing the correlation between adjacent samples as well as distant samples in a speech wave. The difference between adjacent samples or the difference between predicted and actual values (prediction residual) is encoded. In the latter case, the predicted value is calculated based on the correlation throughout the sample sequence of a certain period.
4. Time and frequency division
   Speech information is divided into several time periods or several frequency bands, with the larger amount of information being allocated to larger-amplitude periods or perceptually more important frequency bands.

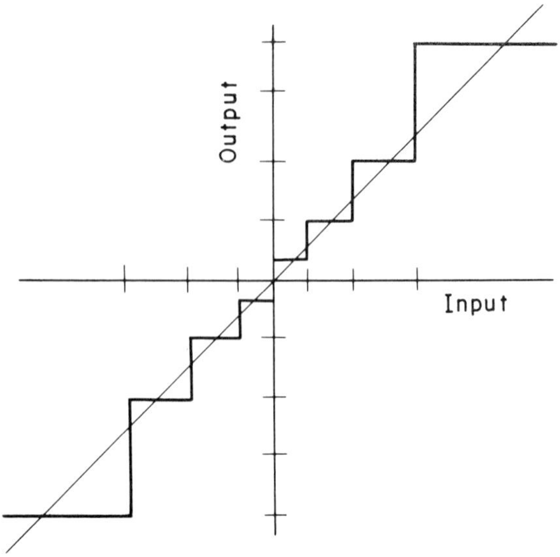


( b ) Nonlinear quantization

Fig. 6.1 (Continued).

5. Transform coding
   A speech wave of a certain period, such as 20 ms, which can be regarded as a stationary signal, is orthogonally transformed into a frequency domain by a method such as DCT and then encoded. This method is based on the perceptual redundancy of a speech wave.
6. Vector quantization
   Instead of coding individual samples, the information source sample sequence, group, or block is coded (quantized) all at once as a vector. The average code length per information source can be reduced to an approximate lower limit of R(D) by using this technique.

Each of the above techniques, including coding system examples, will be explained in the following sections.

## 6.2 CODING IN TIME DOMAIN

### 6.2.1 Pulse Code Modulation (PCM)

The simplest waveform coding method is linear pulse code modulation (PCM). In this method, analog signals are quantized in homogeneous steps similar to the usual A/D conversion. This method does not compress the information rate, since it uses no speech-specific characteristics. When the quantization step size and the range of signal amplitude are indicated by $\Delta$ and L, respectively, the quantization bits B must satisfy $\Delta 2^B \geqq L$ or $B \geqq \log_2(L/\Delta)$ (see Sec. 4.1.2). Since the SNR of a PCM signal quantized by B bits is roughly 6B−7.2 [dB] (Eq. (4.9)), the number of bits B must be decided so that the SNR of the quantized signal is larger than that of the signal before quantization. For example, a bit rate of roughly 100 kbps, in other words, 8-kHz sampling and 13-bit quantization, is necessary for quantizing 4-kHz-bandwidth telephone speech by linear PCM without producing detectable distortion arising from the quantization noise.

PCM used in the ordinary telephone system is called log PCM because the amplitude is compressed by logarithmic transformation before linear quantization and coding. This transformation is based on the statistical characteristics of speech amplitude. Since the amplitude of a speech signal has an exponential distribution, the occurrence probability for each bit is equalized by the logarithmic transformation. Therefore, the distortion can be minimized as suggested by the information theory. At the decoding stage, the amplitude is exponentially expanded.

Two kinds of transformation formulae, $\mu$-law and A-law, are usually used in actual PCM systems which produce high-quality speech at 56 or 64 kbps. Although, the difference between the two formulae is small, the $\mu$-law compression formula

$$F(x_t) = x_{max} \frac{\log\{1 + \mu|x_t|/x_{max}\}}{\log(1 + \mu)} \operatorname{sgn} x_t \qquad (6.1)$$

is usually used. Here, $x_t$ is a sample value of the speech wave, $x_{max}$ is the maximum permissible input level, and $\mu$ is the parameter controlling the amount of compression (Rabiner and Schafer, 1978). The larger $\mu$ becomes, the larger the amount of compression becomes. Typically, values between 100 and 500 are used for $\mu$.

### 6.2.2 Adaptive Quantization

In order to utilize the nonstationarity of the dynamic characteristics of speech amplitude for improving the SNR of quantized speech, the quantization step size is varied according to the rms value of the amplitude. This method is called adaptive PCM (APCM) (Jayant, 1973, 1974; Schafer and Rabiner, 1975). Since the speech signal can be considered to be stationary for a short period, the step size can be varied relatively slowly.

There are two methods for varying the step size. In the first method, which is called the forward (feedforward) adaptation method, the step size is changed at every block. In the second method, known as the backward (feedback) adaptation method, the step size is changed on a sample-by-sample basis according to the decoded samples. The principles of these two methods are indicated in Fig. 6.2.

In the forward adaptation method, the optimum step size is decided according to the rms value calculated for every block, and is then transmitted to the receiver as side information. In the backward adaptation method, the step size does not need to be transmitted, since it can be automatically generated sample by sample by using reconstructed samples at both ends. Although the adaptation might be more effective for the forward adaptation method, this method has a higher bit rate because of the side information. Various algorithms for renewing the step size have been proposed for the latter method and used in combination with several coding methods, such as ADPCM and SBC, which will be explained later. The former method is usually used in combination with APC, which will also be described later.

### 6.2.3 Predictive Coding

A speech signal has a correlation between adjacent samples as well as between distant samples. Therefore, information compression can be achieved by coding the difference between adjacent samples or the difference between the actual sample value and the predicted value calculated using the correlation (prediction residual). Since the difference and prediction residual have a smaller range of variation and smaller mean energy than that of the original signal, the quantization bits can be reduced. The method based on this principle is referred to as predictive coding, the actual structure of which is indicated in Fig. 6.3.

When the prediction is performed according to linear prediction, described in Chap. 5, the prediction residual

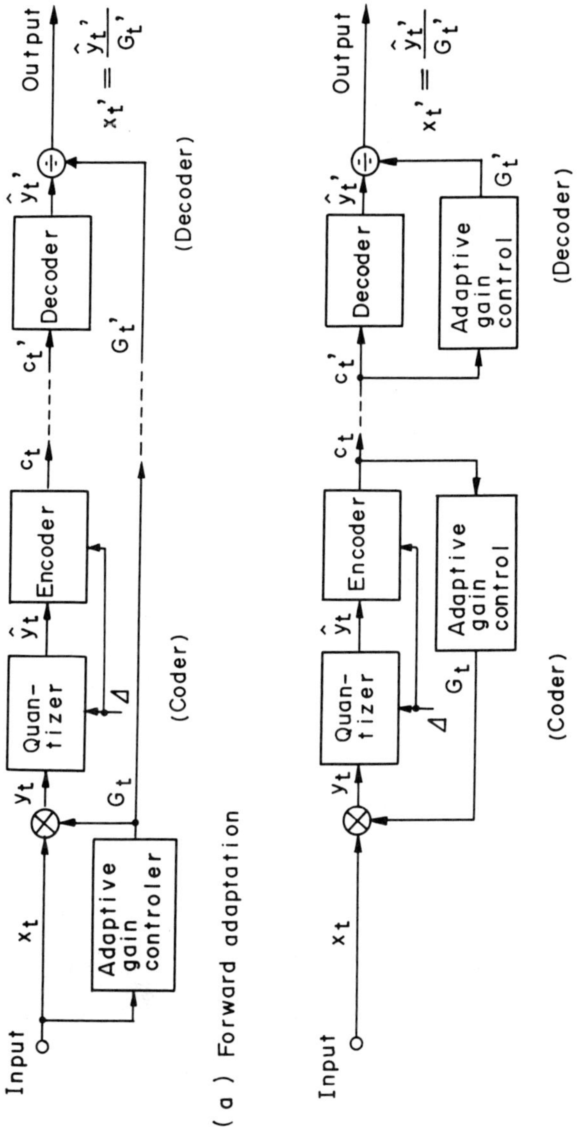


Fig. 6.2 Block diagram representation of adaptive PCM.

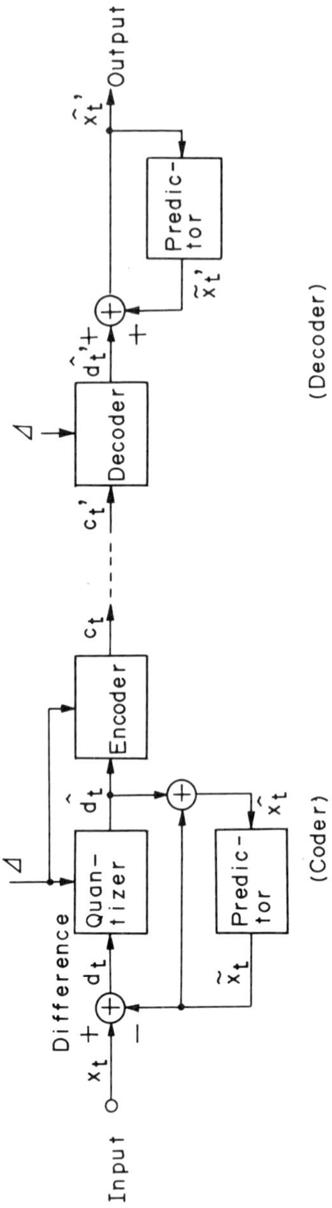


Fig. 6.3 Block diagram of predictive coding.

$$d_t = x_t + \sum_{i=1}^{p} \alpha_i x_{t-i} \tag{6.2}$$

is quantized and transmitted. In the simplest case of first-order linear prediction, the equation becomes $d_t = x_t + \alpha_1 x_{t-1}$. If the predictor coefficient is simply set as $\alpha_1 = -1$, the system merely transmits the difference between adjacent samples. This system is called differential PCM (DPCM).

In order to cope with the problem of accumulated encoder error and to achieve the maximum prediction gain, the method indicated in Fig. 6.3 is used. In this method, a local decoder which is identical to the decoder of the receiver is located in the transmitter, and the difference between the input signal and the output of the local decoder is encoded instead of simply encoding the difference between the input signal and a linear combination of past samples.

The reason for the improvement in SNR by predictive coding can be explained as follows. Since the output of the local decoder is equal to the encoder output at the receiver when no additive noise or transmission error is present, the equation

$$\begin{aligned} \hat{x}'_t &= \hat{x}_t = \tilde{x}_t + \hat{d}_t = \tilde{x}_t + (d_t + e_t) \\ &= \tilde{x}_t + (x_t - \tilde{x}_t + e_t) = x_t + e_t \end{aligned} \tag{6.3}$$

is obtained, where $e_t$ is the quantization error of the residual signal. Therefore, the SNR of this system becomes

$$\text{SNR} = \frac{E[x_t^2]}{E[e_t^2]} = \frac{E[x_t^2]}{E[d_t^2]} \, \frac{E[d_t^2]}{E[e_t^2]} \tag{6.4}$$

where E[ ] indicates the expectation value. This equation indicates that the SNR, which originally has the SNR value of the quantizer $q = E[d_t^2]/E[e_t^2]$, is increased by the prediction gain $G = E[x_t^2]/E[d_t^2]$. The smaller the variance of the prediction residual becomes, the larger the prediction gain becomes.

The prediction gain when the pth-order linear prediction indicated by Eq. (6.2) is used is represented as

$$G \simeq \left(1 + \sum_{i=1}^{p} \alpha_i r_i\right)^{-1} \tag{6.5}$$

where $r_i$ is the autocorrelation coefficient for $x_t$ ($r_0 = 1$). The prediction gains for an actual speech signal with fixed prediction and adaptive prediction are shown in Fig. 6.4 (Noll, 1975). In the former case, the predictor coefficients are set at fixed values. In the latter case, they are changed in accordance with the variation in the speech signal. Prediction gains of around 10 dB and 14 dB can be expected using fixed prediction and adaptive prediction, respectively. When p = 1, Eq. (6.5) becomes

$$G \simeq (1 - r_1^{\,2})^{-1} \tag{6.6}$$

This means that G " 1 when $0 < |r_1| \leqq 1$.

In the case of DPCM, the equation

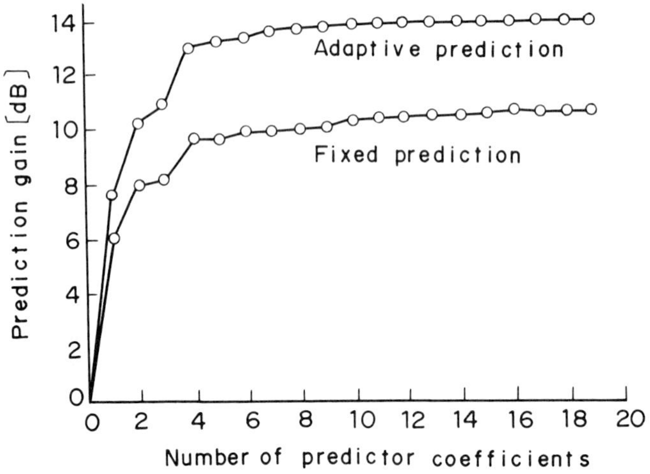


Fig. 6.4 Prediction gain for actual speech signals.

$$E[d_t^2] = E[(x_t - x_{t-1})^2]$$
$$= E[x_t^2] - 2E[x_t x_{t-1}] + E[x_{t-1}^2]$$
$$= 2E[x_t^2](1 - r_1) \tag{6.7}$$

can be obtained, where

$$r_1 = \frac{E[x_t x_{t-1}]}{E[x_t^2]} \tag{6.8}$$

Therefore,

$$G = \frac{E[x_t^2]}{E[d_t^2]} = \frac{1}{2(1 - r_1)} \tag{6.9}$$

This means that $G > 1$, or, more specifically, that the differential coding is effective when $r_1 > 0.5$.

The above-mentioned prediction methods are specifically called spectral envelope or short-term prediction methods, since the prediction is based only on the adjacent 4 to 20 samples. On the other hand, the prediction between speech samples at pitch period intervals, which will be described later, is called pitch prediction or long-term prediction. DPCM with adaptive prediction and/or adaptive quantization is referred to as adaptive differential PCM (ADPCM).

Similar to adaptive quantization, adaptive prediction is of two types: the forward type and the backward type. The former, in which optimum prediction is performed for every block of speech signal, is specifically called adaptive predictive coding (APC). APC in the narrowest sense designates a coding system involving pitch prediction and two-level quantization for the prediction residual (Atal and Schroeder, 1970). Backward adaptive prediction, in which the predictor coefficients are modified sample by sample to reduce the prediction residual, is sometimes called adaptive predictive DPCM (AP-DPCM).

### 6.2.4 Delta Modulation

Delta modulation (DM or ΔM) is an extreme method of differential quantization, in which the sampling frequency is raised so high that the difference between adjacent samples can be approximated by a 1-bit representation. This method, advantageous in its simple structure, is based on the fact that the correlation between adjacent samples increases as a function of the sampling frequency except for uncorrelated signals. As the correlation increases, the prediction residual decreases. Therefore, a coarse quantization can be used when signals are sampled at a high frequency. A high prediction gain can thus be obtained by such a differential coding structure. In the decoding of a delta-modulated signal, a Δ value is simply added to or subtracted from the previous sample according to the 1-bit (positive or negative) signal.

The method in which Δ is fixed is sometimes called linear delta modulation (LDM). In this method, when the speech amplitude becomes too large or changes too rapidly, the reconstructed sample does not exactly follow the original signal. Distortion in this case is referred to as slope overload distortion. On the other hand, when there is no speech, that is, during a period of silence, or when the speech wave changes only slightly and very slowly, the quantization output alternates between 0 and 1. The encoded waveform thus indicates an alternating increase and decrease with the stepping of Δ. This type of distortion, which is referred to as granular noise, produces a harsh noise. The mechanism producing these two kinds of distortion is shown in Fig. 6.5(a).

The slope overload distortion can be reduced by increasing the step Δ. When Δ is too large, however, the granular noise increases. Therefore, Δ is usually set at a compromise value which minimizes the mean square quantization error. In order to maintain a high-quality speech wave having a telephone bandwidth using this method, however, the sampling frequency must be as high as 100 to 200 kHz.

This problem has been handled more effectively by a coding method called adaptive delta modulation (ADM), in which Δ is changed adaptively with respect to the input speech waveform (Jayant, 1970). Most of the various ADM methods are based on the backward adaptation (feedback adaptation) technique, in which the minimum step size is adjusted according to the output code sequence. The general structure of this method is shown in Fig. 6.6.

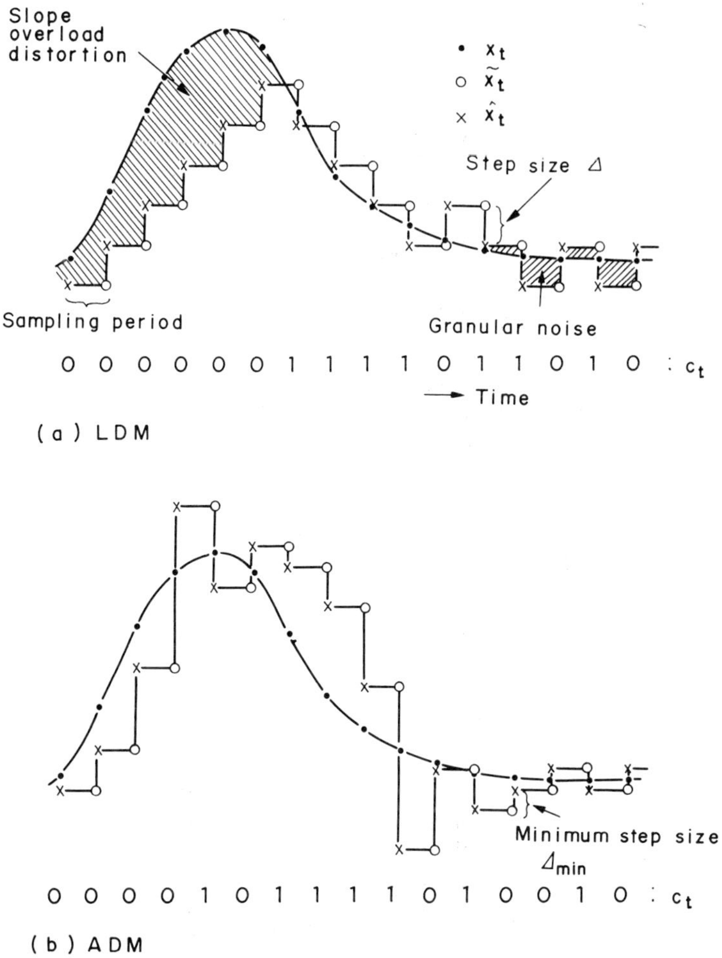


Fig. 6.5 Illustration of delta modulation.

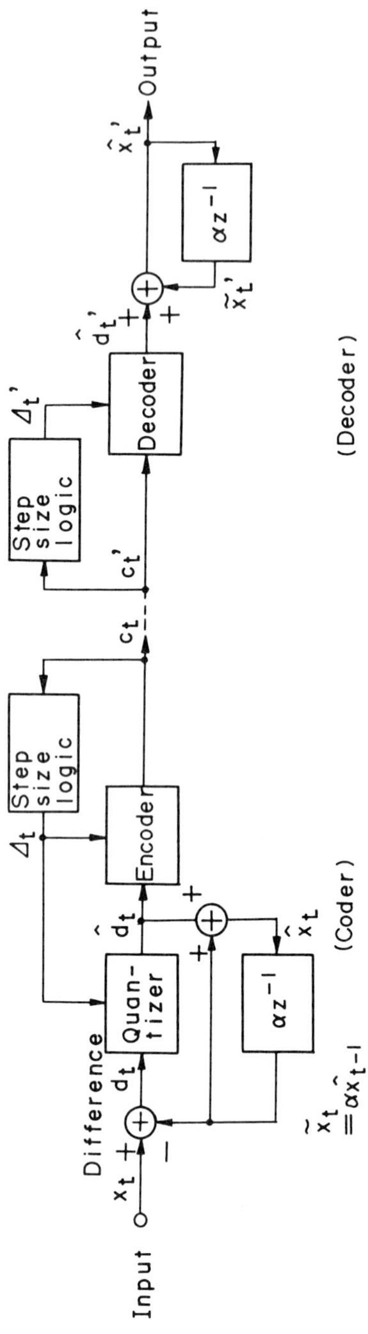


Fig. 6.6 Block diagram of adaptive delta modulation.

The step size is typically decided by the procedure

$$\Delta_t = M\Delta_{t-1} \qquad (\Delta_{min} \leqq \Delta_t \leqq \Delta_{max}) \tag{6.10}$$

where $\Delta_{min}$ and $\Delta_{max}$ are the predetermined lower and upper limits of the step size. When the output codes $c_t$ and $c_{t-1}$ are the same, a constant value $P > 1$ is given to M, whereas when $c_t$ and $c_{t-1}$ are different, a constant value $Q < 1$ is assigned. Experiments confirmed the optimum condition to be $P \times Q \simeq 1$. Figure 6.5(b) is an example of the quantization when $\alpha = 1$, $P = 2$, and $Q = \frac{1}{2}$.

Since the step size is varied exponentially in ADM, the slope overload distortion and the granular noise in ADM are smaller than those in LDM. Experimental evaluation indicates that an ADM with a sampling frequency of 56 kHz has almost the same quality as a 7-bit log PCM with 8-kHz sampling.

### 6.2.5 Adaptive Differential PCM (ADPCM)

ADPCM is a type of DPCM which includes backward adaptive quantization and/or backward adaptive prediction. This method is advantageous in that only the residual signals must be transmitted (Cummiskey et al., 1973). The method using backward (feedback) adaptive quantization and fixed prediction produces high quality in spite of its simple structure. In this method, the quantization step for the first-order difference using a fixed coefficient is controlled to adapt to input speech. This method produces an SNR of roughly 22 dB at 32 kbps (8-kHz sampling and 4-bit quantization), which is roughly 8 dB higher than that of log PCM at the same data rate. Subjective evaluation by the preference method indicates that the quality of 4-bit ADPCM is between that of 6-bit and 7-bit log PCM. This means that ADPCM can achieve an improvement of roughly 2.5 bits.

There are two reasons for this improvement by ADPCM. One is that ADPCM can cover a wider amplitude range than log PCM with the same bit rate. The other is that its power spectral distribution for the quantization noise is not homogeneous but is concentrated in the lower-frequency range. Therefore, the speech spectrum can easily mask the quantization noise.

A block diagram of an advanced ADPCM system incorporating both adaptive quantization and adaptive prediction capabilities is shown in Fig. 6.7. The dashed lines indicate the additional transmission information, $\Delta_t$ and $\{\alpha_t\}$, with forward-type quantization and prediction. A backward-type system at 32 kbps has

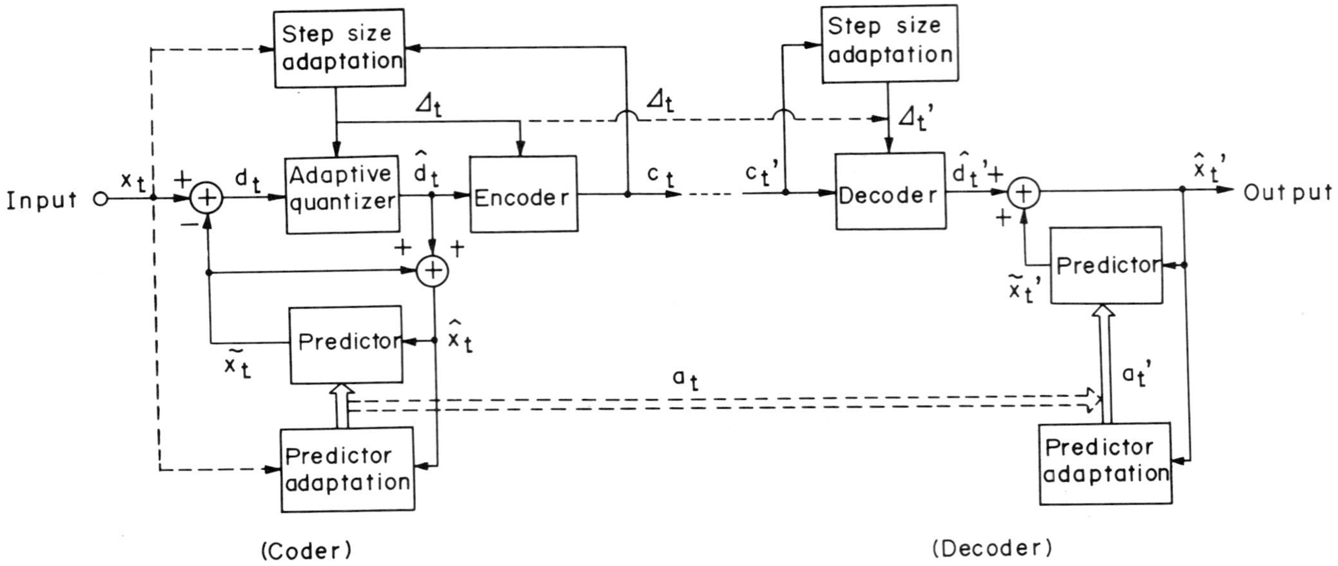


Fig. 6.7 ADPCM, including adaptive quantization and adaptive prediction.

been reported to produce an SNR of roughly 30 dB, and that one at 16 kbps (6.67-kHz sampling and 4th-order linear prediction) has the same intelligibility as 8-kHz sampling, 5-bit log PCM.

### 6.2.6 Adaptive Predictive Coding

Adaptive predictive coding is forward-type AP-DPCM in the broadest sense of the definition. In the narrowest sense, it is a system which includes pitch prediction as well, as shown in Fig. 6.8 (Atal and Schroeder, 1970). The prediction model in the latter case is

$$\hat{x}_t = -\beta\hat{x}_{t-M} - \sum_{k=1}^{p} \alpha_k(\hat{x}_{t-k} + \beta\hat{x}_{t-k-M}) \tag{6.11}$$

The speech signal is analyzed block by block to obtain the predictor coefficients $\{\alpha_i\}$, pitch period M, and amplitude of the pitch component $\beta$. This information and quantization step width q for the residual signal, which together are called side information, are transmitted along with the residual signal. The residual signal is quantized and 1-bit coded (two levels).

Since linear prediction is performed using all samples in each block, unlike ADM and ADPCM, a large prediction gain can be obtained. Subjective evaluation experiments indicated that when the sampling frequency is 6.67 kHz (a transmission bit rate for the residual signal is 6.67 kbps and a small amount of side information is additionally transmitted), the quality of coded speech is slightly lower than with 6-bit log PCM (SNR = 27 dB). The side information is not quantized in these experiments.

Although the predictor structure presented in Fig. 6.8(b) corresponds well to Eq. (6.11), it is redundant. Therefore, a different structure is usually used in which $P_1$ and $P_2$ are separated into different feedback loops.

### 6.2.7 Noise Shaping

Figure 6.9 is a block diagram of an APC system capable of noise shaping. As described in Sec. 4.6.1, noise shaping is the process of decreasing the auditory quantization noise using the auditory masking effect. This is accomplished by modifying the flat quantization noise spectrum into a spectrum which resembles that of speech (Makhoul and Berouti, 1979; Atal and Schroeder, 1979). This is done by feeding back the quantization noise.

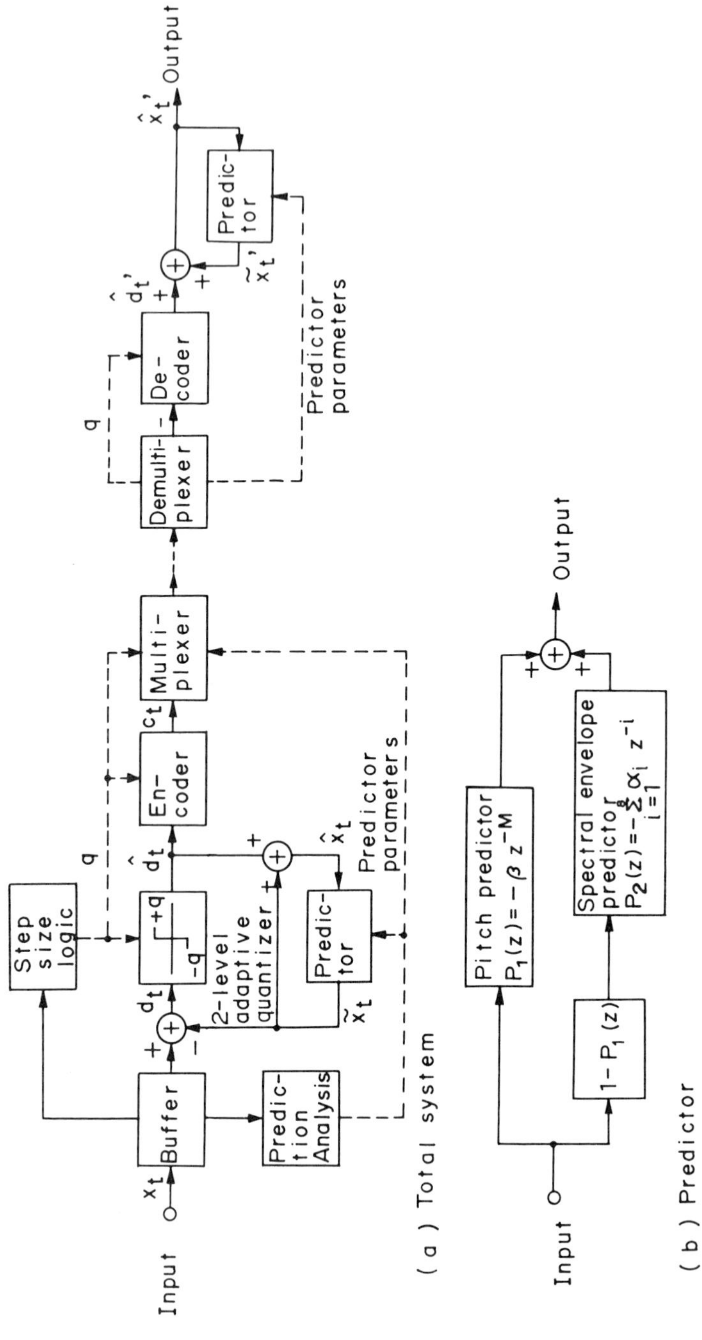


Fig. 6.8 Block diagram of APC.

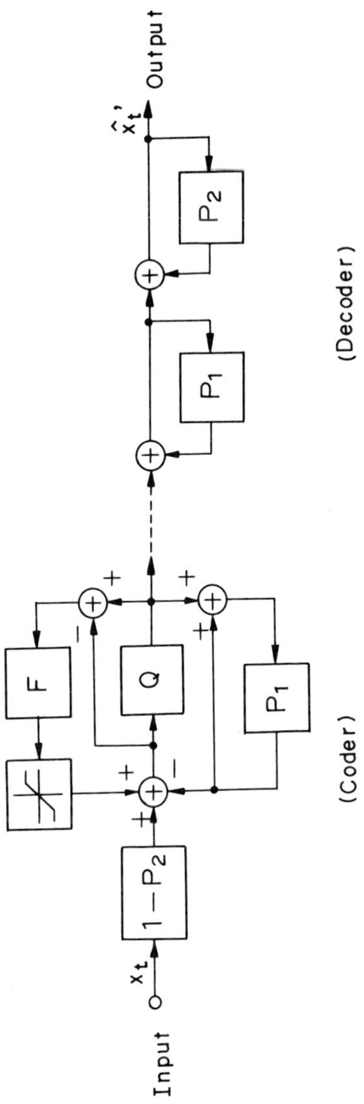


Fig. 6.9 APC with noise shaping. $P_1$ = pitch predictor; $P_2$ = spectral envelope predictor; F = feedback filter for quantization noise; Q = quantizer.

The transmission function of the feedback filter F is

$$F(z) = -\sum_{i=1}^{p} b_i z^{-i} \tag{6.12}$$

The filter coefficients are set at $\{b_i\} = \{\gamma^i \alpha_i\}$, where $\{\alpha_i\}$ are the coefficients of predictor $P_2$, and parameter $\gamma$ is set at $0 < \gamma < 1$. Accordingly, when $\gamma$ approaches 0, the quantization noise spectrum approaches the speech spectrum, and when $\gamma$ approaches 1 the noise spectrum flattens.

For practical purposes, $\gamma$ is set at an appropriate value derived from the results of the hearing test. Although the coding algorithm becomes slightly complicated by introducing this method, the subjective SNR is improved by 12 dB when $\gamma = 0.8$. When pitch prediction and sophisticated quantization algorithms are introduced, a quality equivalent to that of 7-bit log PCM can be obtained at 16 kbps.

An adaptive noise-shaping postfilter has also been proposed as a postprocessor for enhancing speech quality (Jayant and Ramamoorthy, 1968). The philosophy of the postfiltering technique can be explained using the simple illustration in Fig. 6.10. Part (a) of the figure shows a signal spectrum with two narrowband components in the frequency regions $W_1$ and $W_2$, and a flat noise spectrum that is 15 dB below the first signal component but 5 dB above the second signal component. Part (b) presents the spectra of the postfiltered signal and noise, when the postfilter transfer function is identical to the signal spectrum in (a). Although the resulting SNRs in regions $W_1$ and $W_2$ are same as those before postfiltering, the noise in the rest of the frequency range is much lower than the signal levels. This postfiltering operation perceptually enhances the signal.

Figure 6.11 is a block diagram of the adaptive postfiltering applied to the ADPCM decoder output. The coefficients of the postfilter are scaled versions of the coefficients of the adaptive predictor in ADPCM. The speech distortion inevitable in postfiltering can be mitigated by adapting the degree of postfiltering to the ADPCM performance.

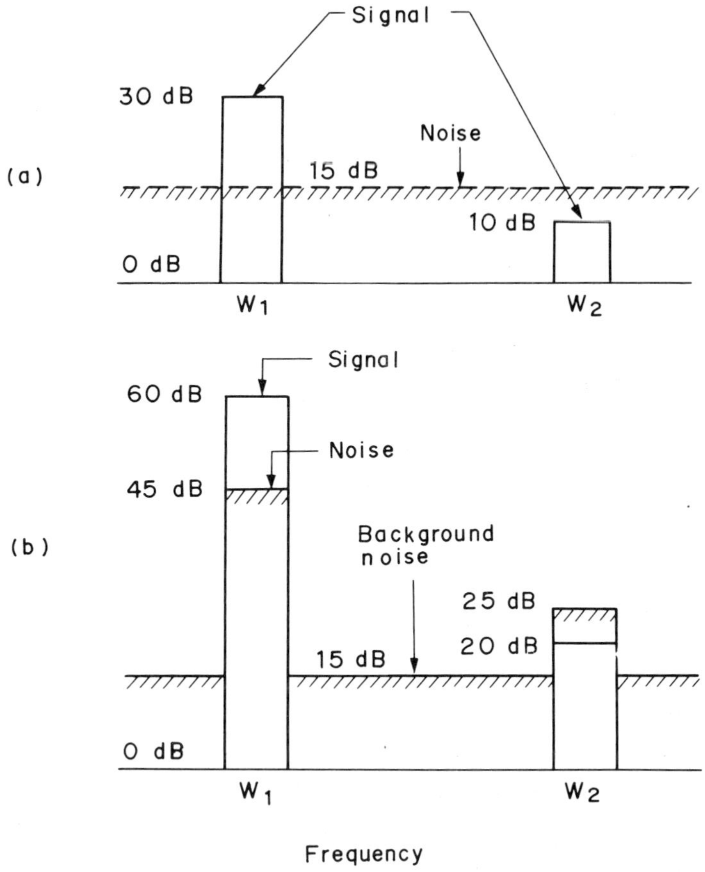


Fig. 6.10 An idealized explanation of the effects of postfiltering: (a) signal and noise spectra at the postfilter input; and (b) postfiltered spectra.

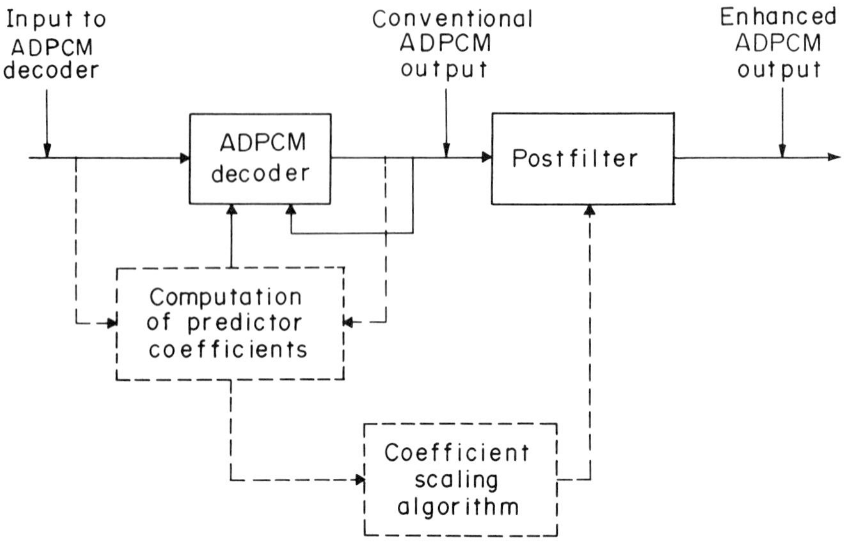


Fig. 6.11 Block diagram indicating adaptive postfiltering of the output of an ADPCM decoder.

## 6.3 CODING IN FREQUENCY DOMAIN

### 6.3.1 Subband Coding (SBC)

The coding method, in which a speech band is divided into several contiguous bands by a bank of band-pass filters (BPFs), and a specific coding strategy is employed for each band signal, is called subband coding (SBC, Crochiere et al., 1976). As shown in Fig. 6.12, the speech signal passing through each BPF is transformed into a baseband signal by low-frequency conversion, down-sampled at the Nyquist rate, and coded by an adaptive coding method such as APCM. The inverse procedures reproduce the original signal.

This method is advantageous for two reasons. One is that processing concerning human auditory characteristics such as noise shaping can easily be applied. The other is that a higher bit rate can be allocated to those bands in which higher speech energy is concentrated or to those bands which are subjectively more important. Therefore, this method can produce less perceptible quantization noise at the same or even at a lower bit

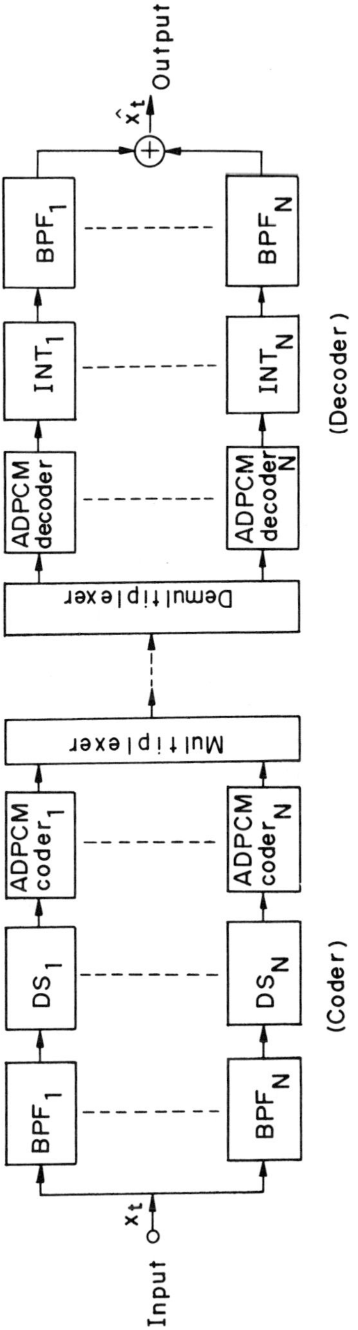


Fig. 6.12 Block diagram of SBC. DS = down-sampling; INT = interpolation.

rate. This method is also beneficial in that the quantization noise produced in one band does not influence any other band; that is, low-level speech input will not be corrupted by quantization noise in another band. Since a short-time frequency analysis of input signals is performed in the human auditory system, the method for controlling the quantization noise in the frequency domain is both effective and naturally appealing (Tribolet and Crochiere, 1979; Krasner, 1979).

The BPF bank necessary for this method is realized by general digital filters or by a charge-coupled device (CCD) filter which handles analog sampled values. The most reasonable way of dividing the frequency band is to equalize the contributions to the articulation index from all subbands. Since this method complicates low-frequency conversion, however, a far more practical and simpler way is through integer band sampling.

Figure 6.13 indicates the sampling process for each band. Assuming that m is an integer, the frequency range of each subband is set at [mf, (m + 1)f], and the output signal is sampled at 2f. The output is then coded and transmitted. At the receiver, the original signal in each subband is reproduced by passing the decoded signal through a BPF having a frequency range of [mf, (m + 1)f]. When the flexibility of the band division

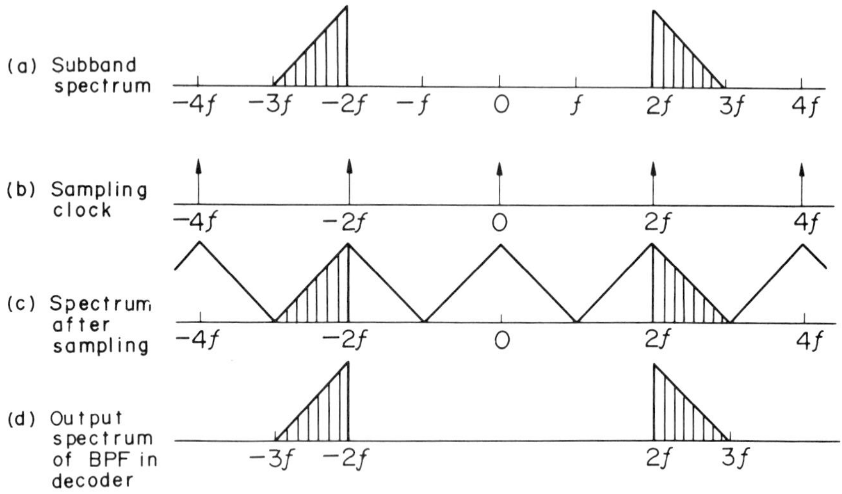


Fig. 6.13 Illustration of integer band sampling.

is restricted to a ratio of 2:1, a quadrature mirror filter (QMF) can be used (Esteban and Galand, 1977). Since a QMF advantageously provides for very simple processing and for the automatic cancellation of aliasing distortion, this method is frequently used for realizing SBC systems.

Experimental evaluation indicates that although the SNR for 16-kbps SBC is 11.1 dB, which is almost the same as 16-kbps ADPCM, the subjective quality is almost the same as that of 22-kbps ADPCM (Crochiere et al., 1976). Although SBC is classified as a type of frequency-domain coding in this book, it can also be defined as a time-domain coding method where input signals are subdivided into frequency bands and quantized.

### 6.3.2 Adaptive Transform Coding (ATC)

Adaptive transform coding (ATC) is a method in which a speech signal is divided into several frequency bands in a way similar to that with SBC. However, ATC is more flexible than SBC. In this method, a speech wave of around 20 ms, which can be considered stationary, is extracted as a block or a frame. The speech wave of every block is first orthogonally transformed into frequency-domain components, which are subsequently processed by adaptive quantization. At the decoder stage, the speech wave is reproduced by concatenating the inverse-transformed block waveforms (Zelinski and Noll, 1977; Tribolet and Crochiere, 1979). Although various kinds of orthogonal transforms are used, such as the DFT, discrete cosine transform (DCT), and Karhunen-Loeve transform (KLT), ATC usually refers to a system in which DCT and adaptive bit allocation are employed.

DCT for a block consisting of an M-sample speech signal, $\{x_t\}_{t=0}^{M-1}$, is defined as

$$X_k = \sum_{t=0}^{M-1} x_t c_k \cos \frac{(2t+1)\pi k}{2M} \qquad (k = 0,1,2,\ldots,M-1)$$

$$c_k = \begin{cases} 1 & k = 0 \\ \sqrt{2} & k = 1,2,\ldots,M-1 \end{cases} \tag{6.13}$$

The inverse DCT is defined as

$$x_k = \frac{1}{M} \sum_{k=0}^{M-1} X_k c_k \cos \frac{(2t + 1)\pi k}{2M} \qquad (t = 0,1,2,\ldots,M-1)$$

(6.14)

There are four advantages of using DCT:

1. Unlike KLT where input signals are transformed into their principal components, DCT corresponds to conversion into the conventional frequency domain. It thus facilitates the use of processes based on the auditory function of frequency analysis and the control of quantization noise in the frequency domain.
2. DCT takes a relatively small amount of calculation since an N-point DCT for each frame can be performed using a symmetric 2N-point FFT. Additionally, in contrast with KLT, it is not necessary to transmit the fixed base vectors.
3. The base vector of DCT is statistically closer to that of KLT, which is the optimum orthogonal transformation, than other well-known orthogonal transformations such as DFT and Walsh-Hadamard transformation. Accordingly, DCT is statistically more efficient than DFT in terms of coding performance.
4. DCT is less sensitive to the edge effect in waveform extraction than DFT (Tribolet and Crochiere, 1979). The distortion in the frequency domain is therefore naturally smaller with DCT.

The basic structure of ATC is shown in Fig. 6.14. The speech wave in each block is transformed by DCT into the frequency domain, and the resultant DCT coefficients are roughly divided into 20 subbands. The mean energy of each subband is calculated and coded as side information. A spectral envelope is obtained by interpolating the mean energy values of adjacent subbands (linear interpolation on a logarithmic scale). The number of quantization bits and corresponding quantization steps are optimally allocated to each DCT coefficient based on the spectral envelope values so as to maximize the resultant SNR.

The bit allocation maximizing the SNR corresponds to the allocation minimizing the squared sum of the quantization distortion for each spectral coefficient. This allocation produces a uniform level of quantization noise along the frequency axis. A system including noise shaping in the frequency domain, similar to the noise shaping used in APC, has also been proposed (Flanagan et al., 1979).

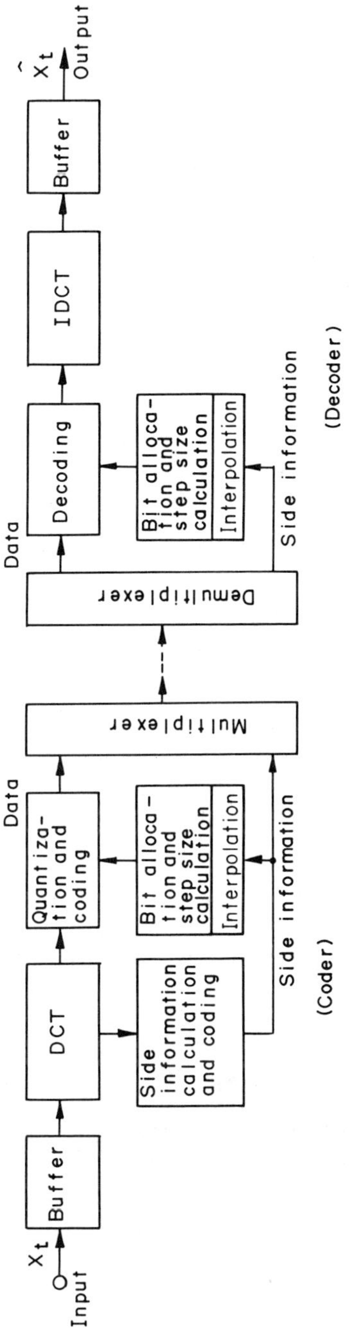


Fig. 6.14 Block diagram of ATC.

Accordingly, output signals from the coder are quantized DCT coefficients and side information which represents the spectral envelope. Roughly 2 kbps is necessary for the transmission of side information. An SNR improvement of 17 to 23 dB over that possible using log PCM can be achieved by ATC at 16 to 32 kbps (Tribolet and Crochiere, 1979). Vocoder-driven ATC in which LPC (PARCOR) coefficients and pitch information are used as side information has also been proposed (Tribolet and Crochiere, 1978). Vocoder-driven ATC of 16 kbps has been reported to be able to produce high-quality speech which is almost transparent, i.e., perceptually equivalent, to original speech.

### 6.3.3 APC with Adaptive Bit Allocation (APC-AB)

APC-AB, the principal structure of which is indicated in Fig. 6.15 (Honda and Itakura, 1984), is based on a combination of SBC and APC. A speech signal is divided into subbands, and each subband signal is down-sampled to a baseband. APC which includes pth-order linear predictive analysis is then applied to each baseband signal. Both short-term and long-term prediction (pitch prediction) are performed in APC.

For the residual signal, bit allocation for each subband is performed based on the energy distribution. Additionally, each pitch period is divided into L time intervals, and dynamic bit allocation is performed to adapt to the energy of each subinterval. Adaptive bit allocation is basically a process of minimizing the mean waveform distortion over all subintervals. In this system, predictor coefficients, residual energy, and the parameters for the subintervals (interval length corresponding to pitch period, and the relative position of the first pitch epoch in an analysis interval) are transmitted as side information. Signals are reproduced by procedures which are inverse to the coding.

The SNR gain $G_{FT}$ resulting from both the frequency-domain and time-domain bit allocation can be represented by the summation of the SNR gain in the frequency domain, $G_F$, and that in the time domain, $G_T$, as

$$G_{FT} = G_F + G_T \tag{6.15}$$

where $G_F$ is equal to the ratio of the algebraic mean to the geometric mean of the spectra $f(\lambda)$, such that

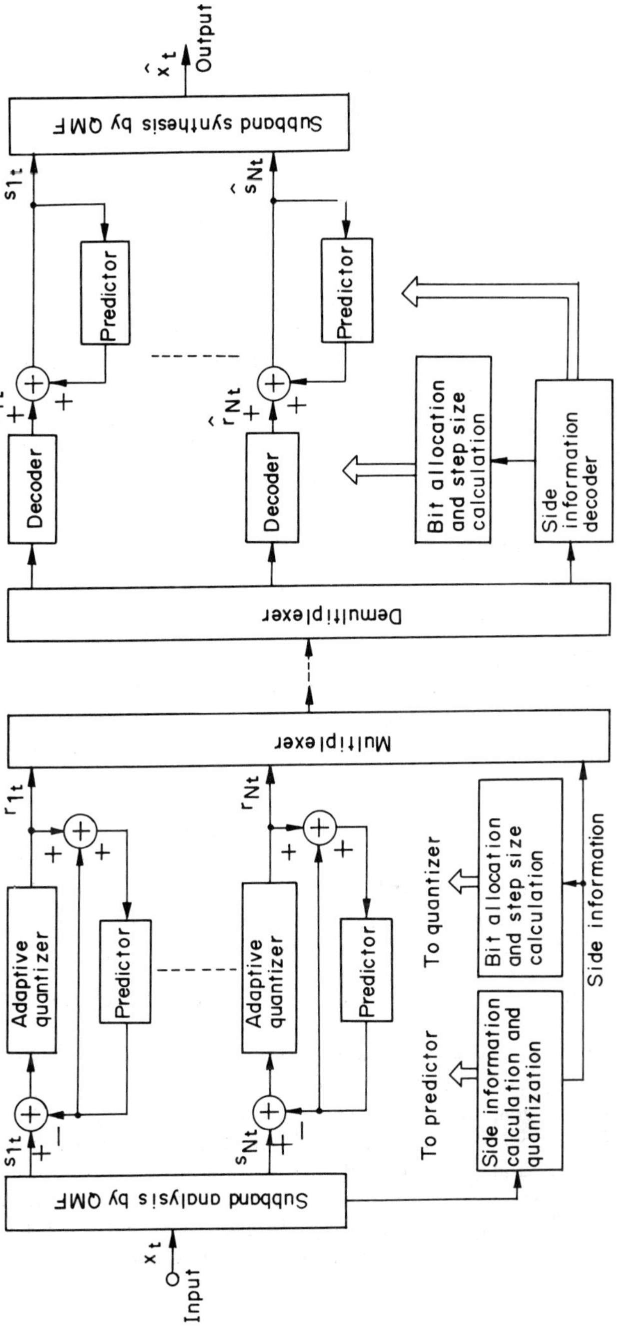


Fig. 6.15 Block diagram of APC-AB.

$$G_F = \ln \frac{\pi^{-1} \int_0^{\pi} f(\lambda)\, d\lambda}{\exp \pi^{-1} \int_0^{\pi} \ln f(\lambda)\, d\lambda} \tag{6.16}$$

Here, $f(\lambda)$ is represented by the combination of subband spectra, each of which is modeled by an all-pole spectrum. Therefore, if $f(\lambda) \simeq f'(\lambda)$, where $f'(\lambda)$ is the all-pole spectrum representing the spectrum for the entire frequency range, $G_F$ becomes equal to the prediction gain for the entire frequency range.

The subjective quality of the speech coded by APC-AB at 9.6, 16, and 24 kbps is equal to 6-, 7-, and 8-bit log PCM, respectively. In this experimental system, the LSP parameters (see Sec. 5.8) are used for transmitting LPC side information.

## 6.4 ANALYSIS-SYNTHESIS AND WAVEFORM CODING COMBINATION

### 6.4.1 Linear Predictive Coding Excited by Residual or Speech

Hybrid coding methods have been derived to serve as intermediate methods between the analysis-synthesis (vocoding) system using pulses and noise as sound sources and the waveform coding system. In these methods, the low-frequency components of either an input speech wave or an inverse-filtered input speech wave are coded as sound sources and transmitted with spectral information. At the decoder, the high-frequency components of the source signal are regenerated using the low-frequency components. All these components are then modified by spectral envelope information to reproduce the speech signal.

These methods offer four advantages.

1. The system is free from quality degradation due to source modeling.
2. A low-frequency waveform is exactly reproduced within the limit of the quantization error.
3. Spectral information for the entire frequency range is efficiently represented by the analysis-synthesis method such as the LPC analysis method.
4. Since pitch period estimation and voiced/unvoiced decision are not necessary, the system is free from both pitch estimation error and voiced/unvoiced decision error.

The first experimental system based on these methods was proposed as a modification of the channel vocoder, and was named the voice-excited vocoder or baseband vocoder (David et al., 1962). Subsequently, the residual-excited LPC vocoder (RELP) and voice-excited LPC vocoder (VELP) have been investigated by many researchers as systems which effectively modifiy the LPC method. In both systems, the spectral envelope is extracted by LPC analysis. The LPC spectral parameters, such as the PARCOR coefficients, are encoded for transmission. At the same time, the low-frequency components of either speech signals or residual signals are down-sampled and encoded. Usually, baseband signals lower than roughly 800 Hz are encoded by either log PCM, ADPCM, APCM, ADM, APC, or SBC.

At the decoder, high-frequency components are reproduced by combining nonlinear processing such as rectification and clipping, high-emphasis, spectral smoothing, and noise addition. The bit rate for these systems is 4.8 to 9.6 kbps in which roughly 2 kbps is used for the transmission of LPC parameters.

Block diagrams of three of these systems are presented in Fig. 6.16. RELP, outlined in Fig. 6.16(a), is a system in which the low-frequency components of an LPC residual signal are encoded and transmitted. A system which is also regarded as a modification of vocoder-driven ATC has been proposed as a modification of RELP (Tribolet and Crochiere, 1980). In this system, the low-frequency components of a residual signal are coded by DCT, and high-frequency components are reproduced by shifting the low-frequency DCT spectrum. This system is favorable in that it enables the realization of a system with any bit rate between that of a 2.5-kbps LPC vocoder and 16-kbps ATC.

In VELP shown in Fig. 6.16(b), the low-frequency components of a speech signal are encoded and transmitted. VELP-reproduced speech is said to be somewhat smoother than that produced by RELP. The problem with VELP, however, is that the LPC synthesizer excited by the speech signal produces an energy discrepancy in the low-frequency region due to resonances which occur at formant frequencies.

Figure 6.16(c) illustrates a system in which the low-frequency components are processed by waveform coding and the high-frequency components are processed by an LPC vocoder. Although this method is beneficial in that low-frequency waveforms are preserved, it also requires pitch extraction and voiced/unvoiced decision. Additionally, waveform coding along with vocoding in this system result in an overlap of low-frequency components.

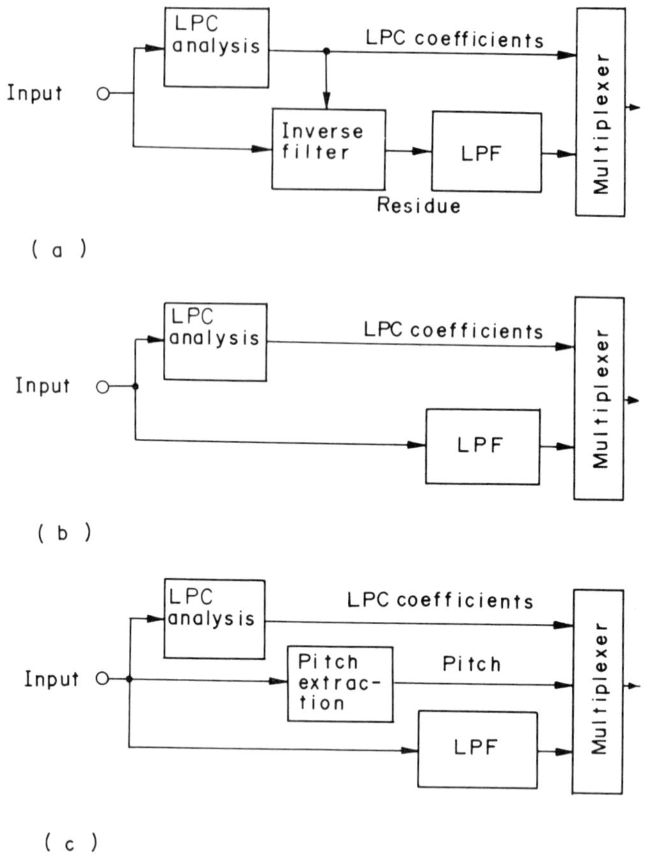


Fig. 6.16 Block diagrams of linear predictive coders excited by residual or speech: (a) RELP, (b) VELP, (c) combination of vocoder and waveform coder.

### 6.4.2 Multipulse-Excited Linear Predictive Coding (MPC)

Multipulse-excited LPC (MPC) is a system in which an LPC synthesis filter is excited by multiple pulses, regardless of whether the source is voiced or unvoiced, without modeling the source using pulses and noise (Atal and Remde, 1982). A schematic

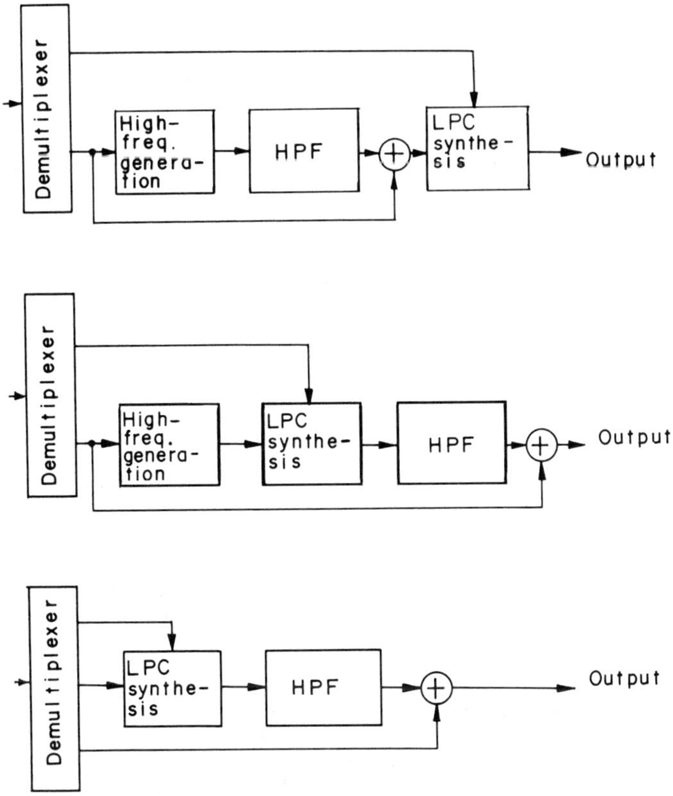


diagram of the synthesis filter for this method is presented in Fig. 6.17. The strong point of this method is that it is free from quality degradation due to source modeling and source parameter estimation errors such as pitch period estimation error. In this aspect, MPC is similar to RELP and VELP.

The problem with this method is its difficulty in determining optimum amplitudes and locations of multiple pulses. A method based on the A-b-S technique, as shown in Fig. 6.18, is usually used for this purpose. First, a speech wave roughly 20 ms long

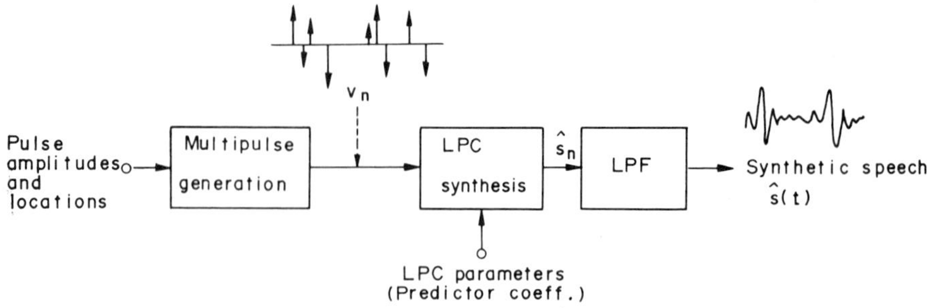


Fig. 6.17 Block diagram of MPC.

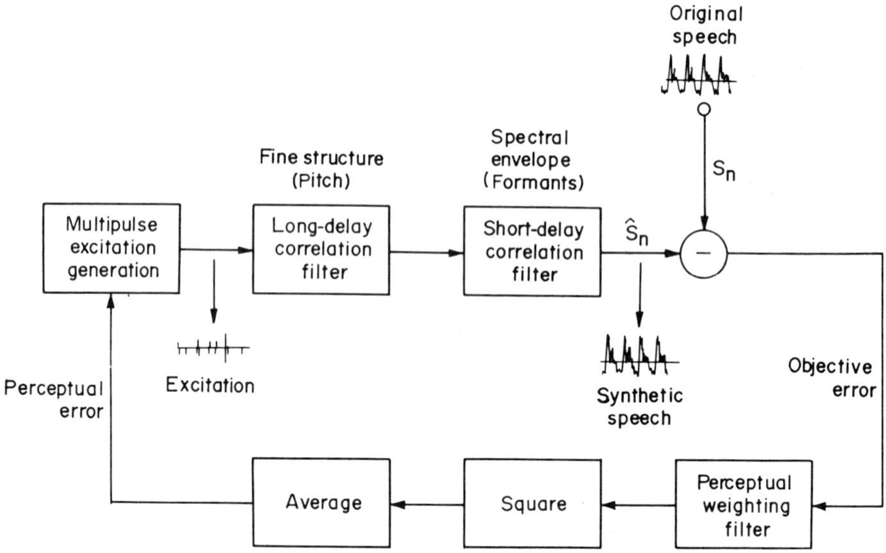


Fig. 6.18 Procedure for determining optimum excitation in MPC.

is extracted as a frame (block) approximately every 10 ms, and the spectral envelope is estimated using LPC analysis for this frame period. Next, multiple pulses are determined as a driving source function using the algorithm indicated in the figure at every 5 or 10 ms.

Here, we assume that the amplitudes and locations of a certain number of pulses are already determined. Accordingly, the multiple pulses $\{v_n\}$ are transformed into synthesized speech $\{s_n\}$ through the LPC synthesis filter corresponding to the estimated spectral envelope. The amplitude and location of a new pulse is determined to minimize the mean square error between the synthesized speech and original speech using perceptually based weighting. The synthesized speech produced by the pulses determined thus far is then subtracted from the speech wave. The procedure for determining a new pulse and subtracting the synthesized speech from the previous speech is repeated until the error becomes less than a certain predetermined threshold or the number of pulses reaches a predetermined number. The synthesized speech samples of the current frame are used as the initial condition for the next frame.

Perceptually based weighting is performed in the same way as the noise shaping described in Sec. 6.2.7. The transfer function of the weighting filter is

$$W(z) = \frac{1 + \sum_{i=1}^{p} \alpha_i z^{-i}}{1 + \sum_{i=1}^{p} \gamma^i \alpha_i z^{-i}} \tag{6.17}$$

where $\{\alpha_i\}_{i=1}^{p}$ are the linear prediction coefficients, and $\gamma$ is the weighting factor $(0 < \gamma < 1)$, which is empirically determined.

The autocorrelation function of the impulse response for the synthesis filter and the cross-correlation between this impulse response and the original speech signal can be used for sequentially determining the impulse amplitude and position as follows. The energy of error between the speech wave synthesized by K-pulses and the original speech wave is

$$\varepsilon_K = \sum_{n=1}^{N} \left\{ s_n - \sum_{i=1}^{K} g_i h_{n-m_i} \right\}^2 \tag{6.18}$$

where $h_n$ is the impulse response for the synthesis filter, N is the frame length, and $g_i$ and $m_i$ are the amplitude and position of the ith pulse in the frame, respectively. The weighting process is omitted in this equation for simplicity. To put it more precisely, the values after convolution with the impulse response of the weighting filter must be used instead of $s_n$ and $h_n$.

The pulse amplitude and position minimizing Eq. (6.18) can be obtained by maximizing the following equation, which is derived by setting the partial differential function for Eq. (6.18) concerning $g_i$ to zero:

$$g_K = \max_{1 \leq m \leq N} \left| \frac{\phi_{hs}(m) - \sum_{l=1}^{K-1} g_l R_{hh}(|m_l - m|)}{R_{hh}(0)} \right| \tag{6.19}$$

Here, $R_{hh}$ is the autocorrelation for the impulse response of the synthesis filter, and $\phi_{hs}$ is the cross-correlation between the impulse response and the original speech.

Experimental results indicate that eight pulses for every 10-ms period produce a speech quality in which little distortion can be perceived. Examples of original speech, synthesized speech, multipulses, and residual signals for a 100-ms period are shown in Fig. 6.19 (Atal and Remde, 1982). In this case, the number of poles (p) is 16, frame length is 20 ms, frame period is 10 ms, and multipulses are determined for every 5-ms period. This figure confirms that the waveform is accurately reproduced even for a transitional signal between voiced and unvoiced periods. A subjective evaluation test shows that quality equivalent to that of 6.4-bit log PCM can be obtained at 9.6 kbps (16 pulses for a 20-ms period; Ozawa et al., 1982). Pitch information has been confirmed to be useful for improving quality when the number of pulses is small (Ozawa and Araseki, 1986).

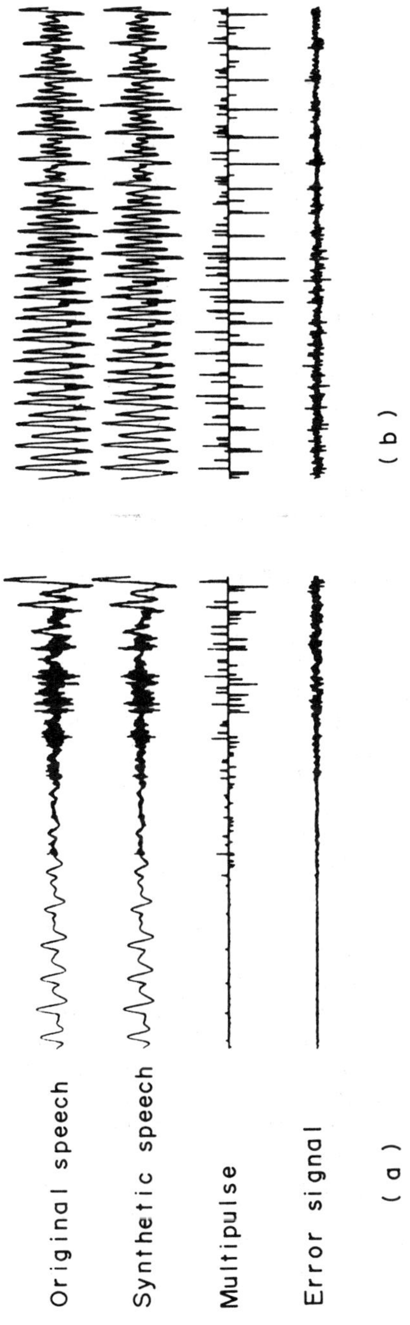


Fig. 6.19 Examples of waveforms at various stages of MPC: (a) consonant speech; (b) vowel speech.

### 6.4.3 Coding by Phase Equalization and Variable-Rate Tree Coding

Speech coding methods can be classified into waveform coding and analysis-synthesis, with the difference between them being whether the sound source is modeled or not. For example, the excitation information is compressed by quantizing the LPC residual in APC, whereas it is modeled dichotomously either using a periodic pulse train or random noise source in an LPC vocoder.

The residual waveform representation in an LPC vocoder is considered to be a process of both whitening the short-time power spectrum of the prediction residual and modifying the short-time phase into the zero phase or random phase. A phase modification process utilizing human perceptual insensitivity to the short-time phase change is highly effective for bit rate reduction.

Also with waveform coding, if the LPC residual can be modified into a pulselike wave, speech energy will be temporally localized, and, hence, coding efficiency can be increased by time-domain bit allocation. This is similar to the effectiveness of energy localization in the frequency domain which increases the prediction gain.

For this purpose, a highly efficient speech coding method has been proposed combining phase equalization in the time domain with variable-rate (time-domain bit allocation) tree coding (Moriya and Honda, 1986). Figure 6.20 shows a block diagram of this system. The phase equalization (PH) is realized through the matched filter principle. The characteristics of the phase equalization filter are determined to minimize the mean square error between the pseudoperiodic pulse train and the filter output for the residual signal. The impulse response of the phase equalization filter can be approximated as a time-reversed residual waveform under the assumption that adjacent samples are uncorrelated. The output residual of this filter is approximately zero-phased over a short period, and it becomes an impulse-train-like signal. The matched filter principle implies that the phase equalization filter corresponds to the filter which maximizes the amplitude at the pulse position under the fixed gain condition. Examples of phase-equalized waveforms, shown in Fig. 6.21, clearly indicate that the residual signal is modified to an impulse-train-like signal by phase equalization.

In this method, the phase-equalized residual signal is coded by variable-rate tree coding (VTRC). Variable-rate coding is effective for signals with temporally localized energy. Tree

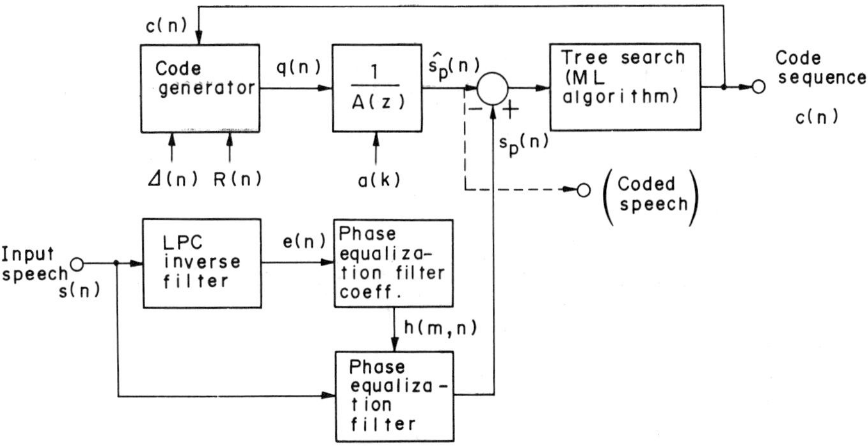


Fig. 6.20 Block diagram of coder based on phase equalization of prediction residual waveform and variable-rate tree coding.

coding is a method in which a tree structure of signals is used to search for the optimum excitation source signal sequence minimizing the error between the input speech signal and coded output (Anderson and Bodie, 1975; Fehn and Noll, 1982). The tree coder in this system is constructed by a code generator having a variable rate tree structure and an all-pole prediction filter. Each code in the code sequence minimizing the error between the phase-equalized speech wave and coded output over several sample values is successively determined using a method similar to the A-b-S procedure. The number of bits R(n) and quantization step size Δ(n) for each branch of the tree are allocated according to the temporal localization of the residual energy.

Decoding is performed by the excitation of the all-pole filter using a residual signal which is phase-equalized and tree-coded. Since the decoded speech waveform is processed by phase equalization, it is generally different from the original waveform.

The experimental results of evaluating this system (VTRC + PH) from the standpoints of subjective quality (opinion-equivalent SNR, $SNR_q$) and objective quality (segmental SNR, $SNR_{seg}$) are compared in Fig. 6.22 with those of APC, TRC (fixed-rate tree coding), MPC, APC-AB, and log PCM. The definition of $SNR_q$

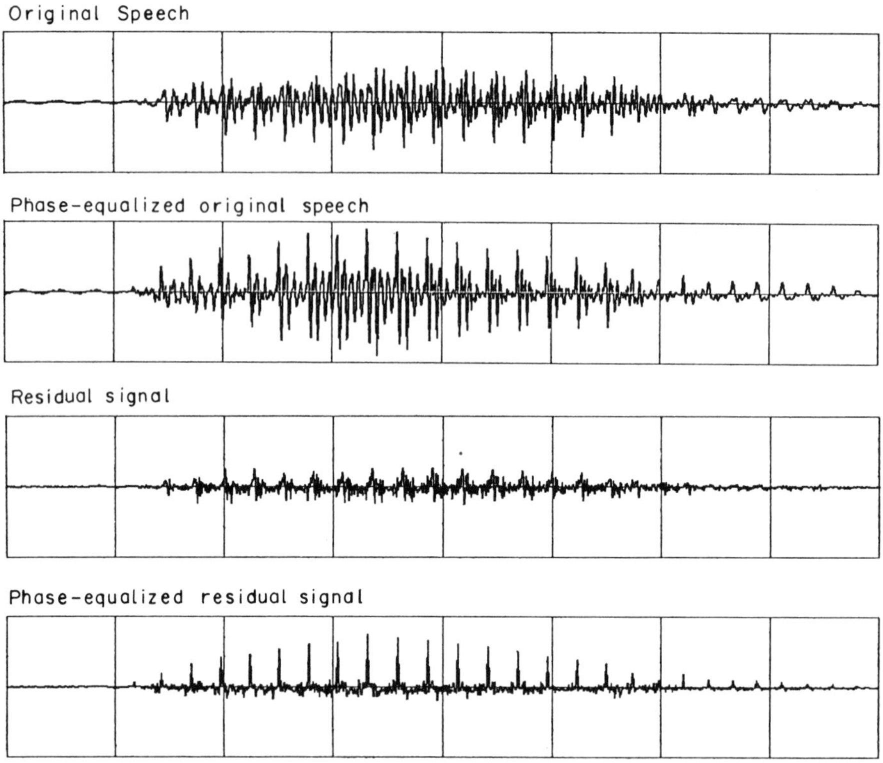


Fig. 6.21 Examples of phase-equalization processing for original speech and residual signal by a female speaker.

and $SNR_{seg}$ will be explained in Sec. 6.6. In the figure, VTRC and MPC are examined both with and without phase equalization (PH). In these experiments, the sampling frequency is 8 kHz, LPC analysis window length is 20 ms, frame period is 20 ms, and prediction order is 10. The bit rate without side information is 1 bit/sample in each coder except in the log PCM systems. The quality of speech when only processed by phase equalization is equivalent to that with 7.6-bit log PCM as indicated on the PCM axis in the figure. This means that degradation due to phase equalization is only slightly noticed. $SNR_{seg}$ and $SNR_q$ for VTRC + PH are 19.0 dB and 29.4 dB (equivalent to those with

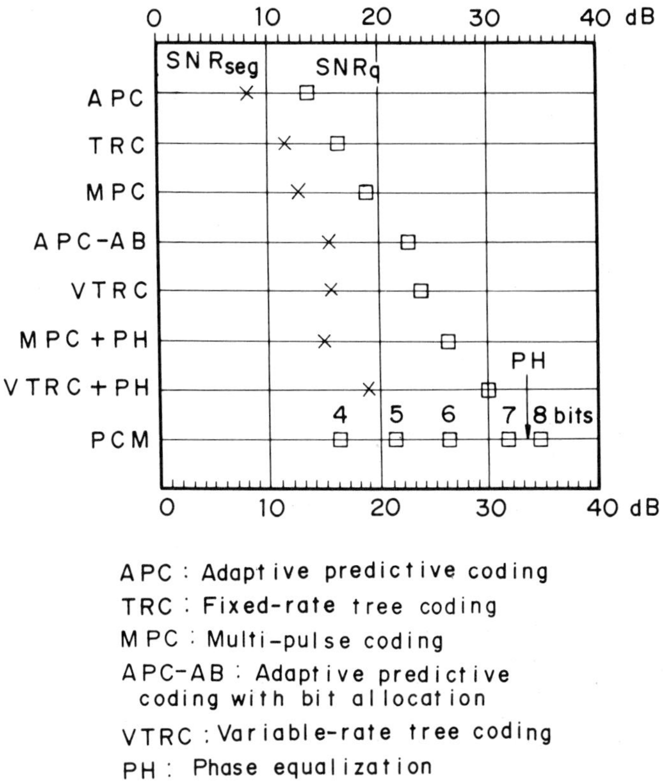


Fig. 6.22 Subjective quality ($SNR_q$) and objective quality ($SNR_{seg}$) of speech coded by the combination of phase equalization and variable-rate tree coding (VTRC + PH) compared with various other coders.

6.6-bit log PCM), respectively. These values are higher than those without phase equalization by 3.5 dB and 6 dB, respectively. The figure also indicates that phase equalization is largely effective in MPC as well, in which the improvements in $SNR_{seg}$ and $SNR_q$ are 2 dB and 7 dB, respectively.

The coding method based on phase equalization not only provides an efficient method of speech waveform representation, but also makes possible a unified modeling of the speech waveform in the same framework including waveform coding and the analysis-synthesis method. The latter capability is similar to that possible in the multipulse coding method.

### 6.4.4 Time-Domain Harmonic Scaling (TDHS) Algorithm

The TDHS algorithm is a method for compressing or expanding a harmonic structure to a ratio of between $\frac{1}{3}$ and 3 by processing it in the time domain. Mechanisms and procedures for harmonic scaling by TDHS are given in Figs. 6.23 and 6.24 (Malah et al., 1981; Crochiere et al., 1982). In this method, waveforms of adjacent pitch periods are mixed after being multiplied by an appropriate weighting factor. The weighting factor is set as a function of the location in time in order to produce a speech waveform without discontinuities.

With a compression to $\frac{1}{2}$, adjacent pitch segments which have a length of P are multiplied by a triangular-shaped weighting factor and added together as shown in Fig. 6.24(a). If the output segments are concatenated and played out at the original sampling period, a time-compressed signal results. If each segment is expanded to the length of 2P and sampled at a sampling period twice the length of the original period, a frequency-compressed signal results. Since the original waveforms at both ends of the 2P-sample-long period are preserved after compression, no waveform discontinuity will occur. The computation load is low because the actual computation process consists of only two multiplications and one addition for each output sample. Also, the sampling period after compression is longer than the original sampling period.

With double expansion, on the other hand, overlapping 2P-sample-long waveforms are multiplied by weighting factors and added together as shown in Fig. 6.24(b). If the original sampling period is retained, a time-expanded signal is obtained. And if this wave is compressed to a P-sample-long waveform and

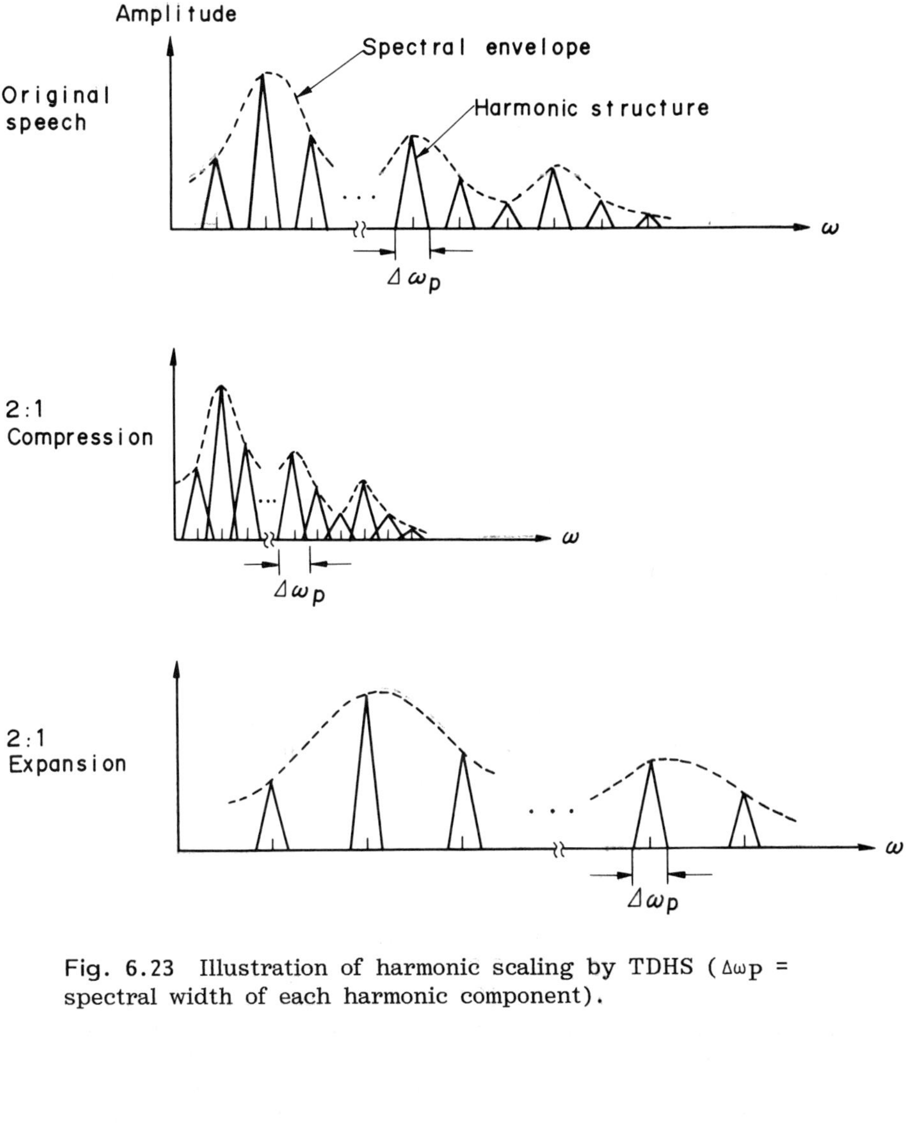


Fig. 6.23 Illustration of harmonic scaling by TDHS ($\Delta\omega p$ = spectral width of each harmonic component).

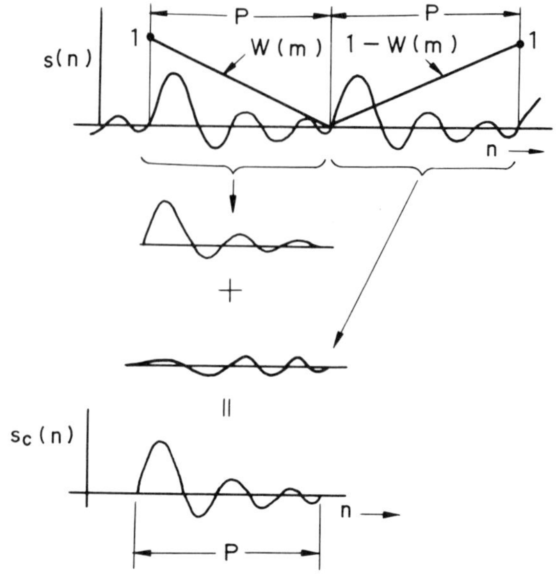


( a )

Fig. 6.24 Procedure of (a) compression and (b) expansion of harmonic structure by TDHS. s(n) = original speech wave; $s_c(n)$ = compressed wave; $\hat{s}_c(n)$ = compressed wave after coding and decoding; $\hat{s}(n)$ = reproduced wave after expansion; W(m) = weighting function.

sampled at a period half that of the original sampling period, a frequency-expanded signal is obtained.

Although the input signal is not necessarily reproduced as the output signal, this algorithm is advantageous in that it produces natural sound even for noisy speech. This robustness stems from the fact that the algorithm does not perform voiced/unvoiced decisions. Thus, the same algorithm is used for both voiced and unvoiced periods. The pitch detection error deteriorates synthesized speech quality fairly gradually in this algorithm, and it works well even with two or more than two speakers competing at the same time.

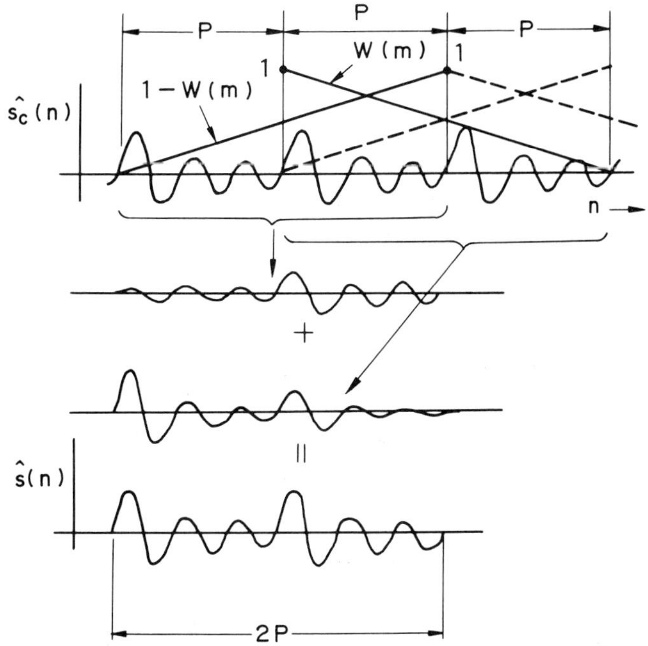


( b )

Fig. 6.24

When this algorithm is combined with various waveform coding methods as shown in Fig. 6.25, the bit rates of these coding methods can be reduced even further. For example, the SBC/HS method, which is a combination of SBC and TDHS, realizes at 9.6 kbps the quality equivalent to 16-kbps SBC. The ATC/HS method, a combination of ATC and TDHS, actualizes at 7.2 kbps the quality equivalent to ATC having a bit rate roughly 4 kbps higher. Cepstrum analysis is used in the TDHS parts of both methods for pitch extraction. Since the ATC method already uses pitch information for time-domain bit allocation, TDHS does not improve quality as much as SBC. Additionally, the SBC/HS method is superior to ATC in that it can realize higher quality with simpler hardware.

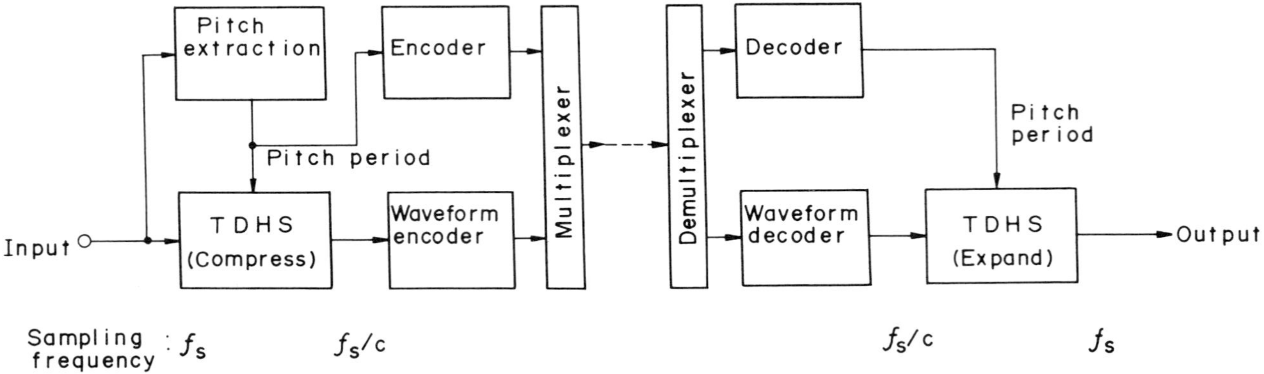


Fig. 6.25 Block diagram of the combination of TDHS and various waveform coding techniques.

## 6.5 VECTOR QUANTIZATION

### 6.5.1 Multipath Search Coding

Since the backward adaptive quantization method determines the present quantization step using only the information concerning past signals, it does not necessarily produce the minimum quantization distortion over several samples. On the other hand, tree coding can further reduce quantization distortion using a delayed decision strategy before more future samples are received. The method utilized to search for the optimum code maximizing the overall SNR on the assumption that some delay is involved is called multipath search coding or delayed decision encoding. This method includes tree (search) coding (Anderson and Bodie, 1975; Schroeder and Atal, 1982), trellis coding (Stewart et al., 1982), and vector quantization.

The structure of multipath search coding is presented in Fig. 6.26. Although error energy minimization is usually used as the criterion for selecting the optimum sequence $y_k$ for the input signal vector x, a criterion including frequency weighting has also been proposed. The M-L method (Jelinek and Anderson, 1971) and a method based on dynamic programming (DP) have been investigated as algorithms for deriving the optimum sequence. Application of the tree coding method to ADPCM realizes an SNR of roughly 20 dB at 16 kbps.

In contrast to multipath search coding, coding methods based only on present and/or past sample values, such as ΔM and DPCM, are referred to as types of single-path search coding. As can be expected, the circuit structure of multipath search coding is usually more complicated than that of single-path search coding.

### 6.5.2 Principles of Vector Quantization

Vector quantization (VQ) is a quantization method in which waveforms or spectral envelope parameters are not quantized on a sample-by-sample basis, but instead a set of scalars composing a vector is represented by a single code in waveform coding or in the analysis-synthesis method (Gersho and Cuperman, 1983). Conversely, the one-dimensional coding methods described so far are generally classified as forms of scalar quantization. VQ was first proposed as a highly efficient quantization method for LPC parameters (Linde et al., 1980), and was later applied to waveform coding. Figure 6.27 indicates the principle of VQ.

In VQ waveform coding (vector PCM, VPCM), a certain period of the sampled waveform is extracted, and the waveform

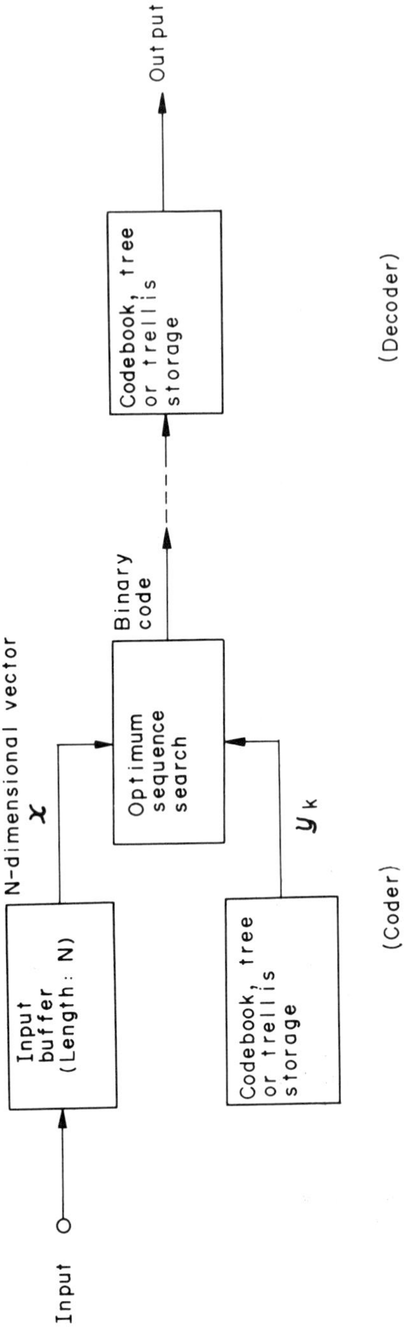


Fig. 6.26 Block diagram of multipath search coding.

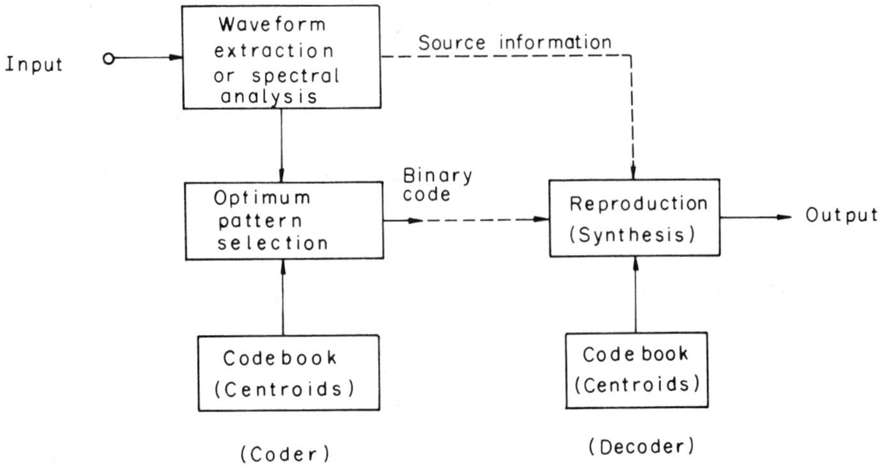


Fig. 6.27 Block diagram of VQ.

pattern in this period is represented by a single code. This procedure is accomplished by storing typical waveform patterns (code vectors or templates), and giving a code to each pattern. The table indicating the correspondence between patterns and codes is termed a codebook. An input waveform is compared with each pattern at every predetermined interval, and the waveform of each period is delineated by a code indicating the pattern having the largest similarity to the waveform.

The codebook should thus provide an appropriate set of patterns which minimize the overall distortion when various types of waveforms are depicted by a limited number of patterns. Solving a nonlinear optimization problem usually facilitates the construction of a set of these patterns based on the original pattern distribution. Since finding a globally optimal solution is usually computationally prohibitive, a locally optimal solution is generally obtained iteratively.

For this purpose, two codebook generation methods, the random learning and clustering-based methods, have been proposed. Random learning enables vectors to be randomly selected from training data and stored as code vectors. This method is used when the amount of training data is comparable to the number of code vectors. The clustering method is normally based on Lloyd's algorithm (K-means algorithm) (Lloyd, 1957; Max 1960).

In this method, training data are clustered into nonoverlapped groups, and corresponding centroids which minimize the average distortion are computed. These centroids are then stored as code vectors. Although the global optimality of this method is not guaranteed, the average distortion can be monotonically decreased by the iteration of codebook renewal, and a locally optimal solution can thus be obtained. The centroid depends on the distortion measure (distance measure, similarity) selected.

As an expansion of Lloyd's algorithm, the cluster-splitting method (LBG algorithm) was proposed (Linde et al., 1980). In this method, code vectors are obtained by Lloyd's algorithm, and the number of clusters is doubled at each stage of codebook renewal by adding new code vectors in the vicinity of previous vectors. This procedure is iterated starting with the one-cluster condition. The vector quantization algorithms are precisely explained in Appendix B.

Regarding VQ waveform coding, the following equation exists for the number N of patterns in the codebook, the dimension k of each vector (number of samples in each period), and the bit rate (bit/sample) r:

$$r = \frac{\log_2 N}{k} \tag{6.20}$$

When N is large enough,

$$\text{SNR [dB]} = 6\,\frac{\log_2 N}{k} + C_k \tag{6.21}$$

where $C_k$ is a k-dependent parameter (Gersho and Cuperman, 1983). Therefore, when the codebook doubles its size, the SNR increases by 6/k [dB]. The condition k = 1 corresponds to the scalar quantization. When r is given, the quantization distortion can generally be reduced to approach the minimum quantization distortion D(R) derived from the information rate distortion theory by increasing k.

VQ serves as a highly efficient coding method because it utilizes the statistical occurrence or the probability distribution function of the source, no matter how varied it is. VQ also employs the smooth continuity arising from the correlation or nonlinear dependency existing in a certain period of speech samples. Therefore, $C_k$ becomes larger than that possible with scalar quantization, and the bit rate can be reduced. For example, experimental results show that $C_8$ is 7 dB larger than $C_1$.

More formal results indicate that when the sampling frequency is 8 kHz, an SNR of 12 to 14 dB is obtained under the conditions of r = 2, k = 4, and N = 256, and an SNR of 8 to 10 dB can be derived when the conditions become r = 1, k = 8, and N = 256 (Abut et al., 1982).

### 6.5.3 Tree Search and Multistage Processing

Selecting the most appropriate pattern from the codebook as efficiently as possible is one of the important issues in VQ. One of the most practical selection methods is binary tree coding (BTC), indicated in Fig. 6.28 (Gersho and Cuperman, 1983). In this method, codebook patterns are stored in a binary tree structure, and patterns are sought by tracing the binary tree. When the size of the binary tree codebook is $N = 2^{kr}$, for example, the number of binary decisions is $\log_2 N = kr$. That is, N-dimensional space is successively divided, and the input vector is compared with two code vectors only at the last decision stage.

Another selection method is full search coding (FSC) in which the input vector is compared with all N-patterns stored in the codebook to calculate the similarities before selecting the closest pattern. Therefore, when the number of patterns is fixed, FSC can achieve a lower distortion than BTC. FSC is disadvantageous, however, in that its amount of similarity calculations is larger than that in BTC. On the other hand, since the codebook has

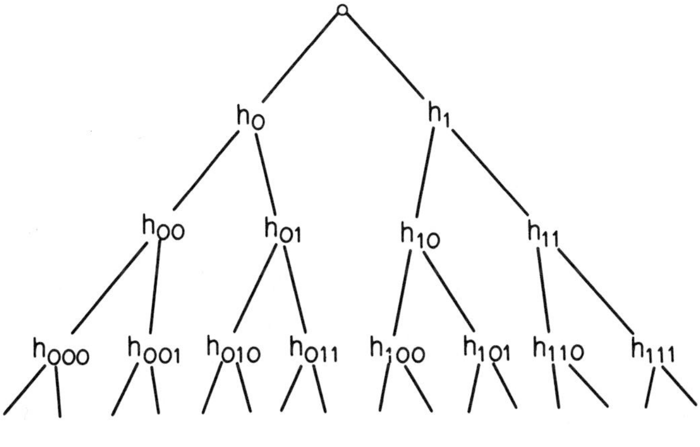


Fig. 6.28 Principle of BTC.

a binary tree structure in BTC, it must have a memory capacity corresponding to the number of nodes in the tree. Thus, BTC requires roughly twice the memory capacity of FSC.

A multistage VQ has been proposed to reduce the memory size and to simplify the coding process (Juang and Gray, 1982). Figure 6.29 expresses the principle of this method. The quantization errors of each stage are transmitted to the next stage, and the final code is constructed by a sequence of the code obtained at each stage. When the bit rate r is fixed and the dimension k is increased in FSC, the number of calculations and the memory size increase exponentially as a function of $N = 2^{kr}$ and $Nk = k2^{kr}$, respectively. However, when the number of stages S is proportional to k, the amount of processing increases only in proportion to $k^2$. Using a tree structure codebook at each stage of quantization further reduces the increase in the amount of processing.

Figures 6.30 and 6.31 indicate the amount of processing and memory capacity as a function of the number of vector dimensions under the condition of 1 bit/sample (Gersho and Cuperman, 1983). These results show that the increase in the amount of processing can be suppressed by combining multistage processing and binary tree coding, even when the number of dimensions increases.

A vector-scalar quantization has also been proposed in which a VQ using a small codebook is followed by a scalar quantization around each code vector. Adaptive transform coding with VQ (ATC-VQ) is a modification of ATC in which residual signals are transformed by DFT and vector-scalar quantized with adaptive bit allocation (Moriya and Honda, 1986).

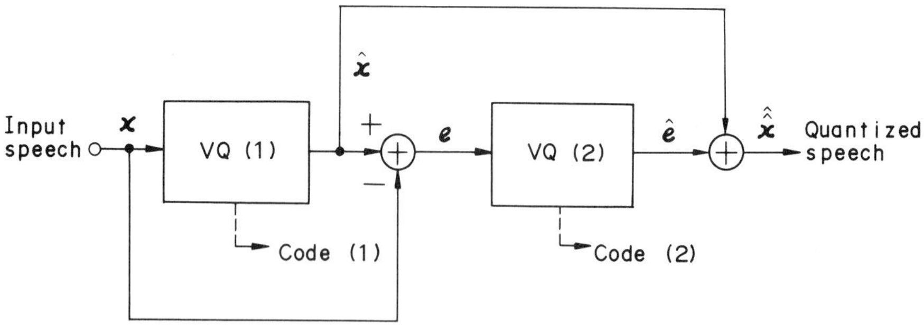


Fig. 6.29 Block diagram of multistage VQ.

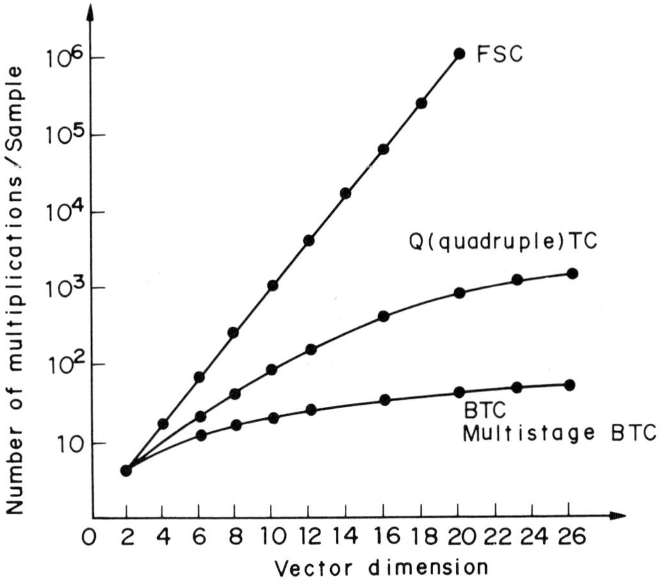


Fig. 6.30 Amount of VQ processing as a function of vector dimension.

Adaptive vector predictive coding (AVPC) is a modification of APC in which residual signals are vector quantized (Cuperman and Gersho, 1982). Experimental evaluation of this method indicates that an 18 to 20-dB SNR can be obtained when residual signals are vector-quantized under the conditions that the sampling frequency is 8 kHz, k = 5, and r = 2 (16 kbps). A modification of SBC in which VQ is applied to each subband signal has also been investigated.

### 6.5.4 Vector Quantization for Linear Predictor Parameters

In the VQ of LPC parameters, the 1st through pth-order LPC parameters (PARCOR coefficients, LSP parameters, etc.) are dealt with as a vector (pattern) and represented by a code. Using this method, a very-low-bit-rate coding which still maintains intelligibility can be realized at 150 to 800 bps, although the naturalness is inferior to that of high-bit-rate waveform coding (Smith, 1969; Buzo et al., 1980; Roucos et al., 1982a).

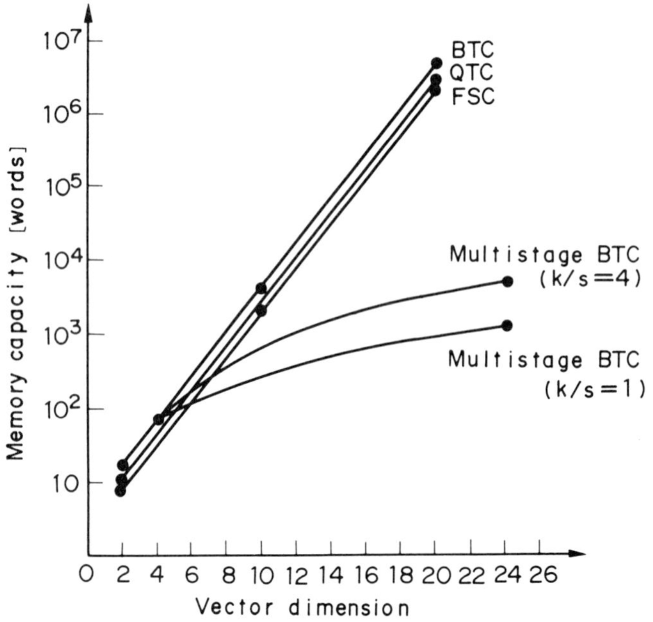


Fig. 6.31 Memory capacity for VQ as a function of vector dimension.

Figure 6.32 shows the spectral distortion for the speech coded by VQ or scalar quantization as a function of the amount of spectral envelope information per frame (Buzo et al., 1980). A spectral distortion of 1.8 dB is realized by FSC at 10 bits/frame, which is 27 bits/frame (73%) smaller than the bit rate of scalar quantization producing the same distortion. Additionally, the distortion by BTC at 10 bits/frame is 0.6 dB larger than FSC, and is equal to the distortion by FSC of 8 bits/frame. It has been reported that a VQ of 800 bps can realize almost the same quality produced by a 2.4-kbps LPC vocoder (Wong et al., 1982).

### 6.5.5 Code-Excited Linear Predictive Coding (CELP)

Code-excited LPC (CELP) or stochastically excited LPC is a method in which the residual signal is vector quantized by a stochastic or random sequence of pulses. The residual signal is produced

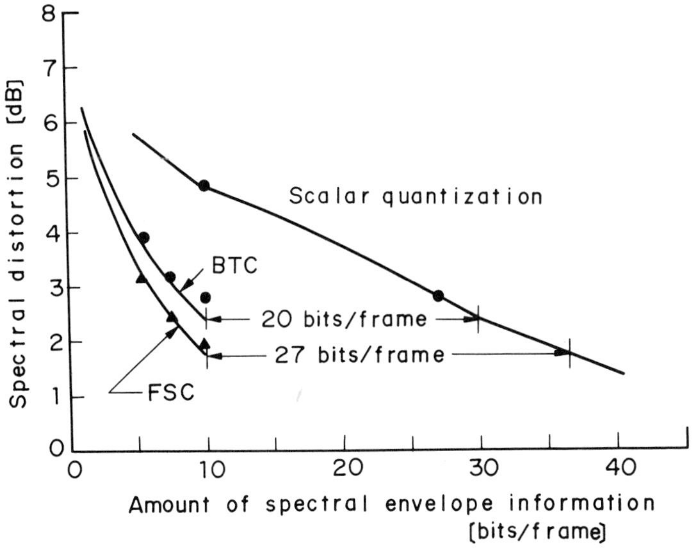


Fig. 6.32 Spectral distortion as a function of bit rate for spectral envelope parameters; comparison between VQ and scalar quantization.

by both the long-term prediction based on the long-term periodicity of the source and the short-term prediction based on the correlation between adjacent samples (Atal and Schroeder, 1984). This method can be regarded as a modification of MPC by replacing the multipulses with vector-quantized random pulse sequences.

Since each code vector is a random noise vector, L kinds of N sample vectors can be stored as a single (L + N) – sample noise wave instead of storing them separately. The different code vectors having N samples are then extracted from the single vector by shifting the starting position sample by sample. Each vector code is thus represented by the position in the (L + N) – sample vector from which the N-sample sequence is extracted. Selection of the optimum N-sample vector is performed so as to minimize the perceptually weighted sum of the squared error between the synthetic speech wave and the original speech wave as shown in Fig. 6.33 (Atal and Rabiner, 1986).

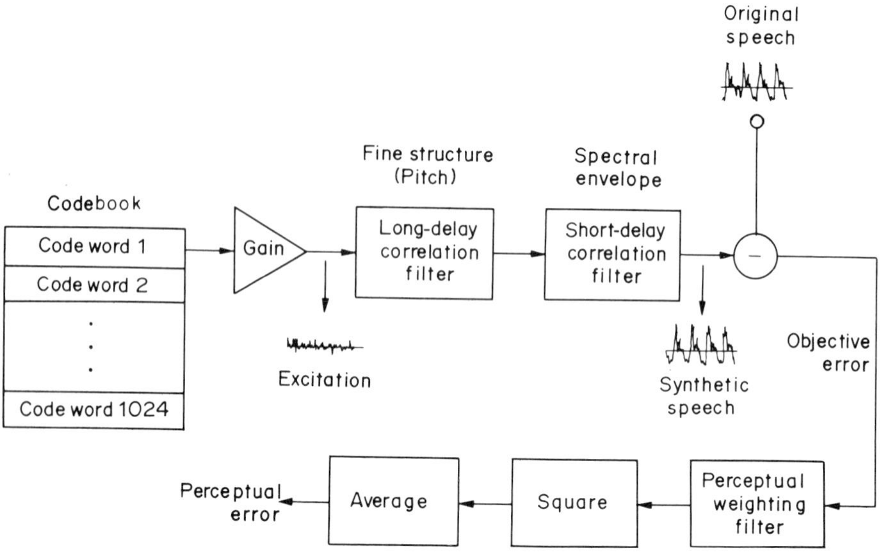


Fig. 6.33 Search procedure for determining best excitation code in CELP.

The same (L + N) − sample vector is stored in the decoder, and the N-sample vector at the position indicated by the transmitted signal is extracted from the (L + N) − sample vector as the excitation signal. High-quality speech with a mean SNR of roughly 15 dB was reported to be obtained under the conditions of N = 40 (5 ms) and a bit rate of 0.25 bit/sample (10 bits/40 samples) (Schroeder and Atal, 1985).

### 6.5.6 Matrix Quantization and Finite-State Vector Quantization

Matrix quantization (MQ) and finite-state VQ (FSVQ) have been investigated for the purpose of realizing a very-low-bit-rate coding. MQ is an expansion of VQ, in which a set of spectral parameters over multiple frames (spectral segment) is expressed by a single code (Wong et al., 1983). The speech spectral parameter sequence is depicted as the concatenation of spectral segments. On the other hand, FSVQ utilizes the transitional characteristics of the vector codes (Foster et al., 1985).

The principal MQ procedure consists of two processes: dividing the parameter sequence into multiple-frame segments (segmentation process), and matching each segment with code segments in the dictionary (quantization process) as shown in Fig. 6.34. MQ methods can be divided into two types, depending on whether the segment length (number of frames) is fixed (Roucos et al., 1982b) or variable (Shiraki and Honda, 1986). Variable-length MQ can further be divided into two types according to whether segmentation and quantization are performed separately or jointly. The latter method generally outperforms the former.

The phonocode method is a typical example of the variable-length MQ method in which the segmentation and quantization processes are performed jointly based on the spectral distortion minimization criterion. The structure of the phonocode method is shown in Fig. 6.35. Both the sequence of code segments and the segment lengths are efficiently determined using a dynamic programming procedure. Speech quality with a phoneme identification score of 78% was obtained by this method at roughly 200 bps using a 10-bit matrix codebook. The phonocode method is precisely explained in Appendix C.

FSVQ, the structure of which is shown in Fig. 6.36, is a kind of VQ in which the codebook is adapted at every frame based on the transitional characteristics of vector codes. FSVQ can be considered a VQ version of the backward adaptive quantization technique used in the waveform coding. In FSVQ, a code minimizing the distortion is selected from the codebook, depending on the state, and, at the same time, transition to the next state occurs according to the selected code. Since the state transition depends only on the initial state and code sequence, the decoder can reproduce vector codes by reconstructing the state transition based on the received code sequence.

Trellis coding has been proposed as a modification of FSVQ (Stewart et al., 1982; Juang, 1986). In this coding method, the vector code of each frame is determined to minimize the sum of distortion over several frames. Hidden Markov model (HMM) coding has also been suggested to delineate the dynamic characteristics of vector sequences (Farges and Clements, 1986). HMM is a stochastic finite-state model represented by the occurrence probability of each code vector at each state and interstate transitional probability. The principle and procedures of HMM are precisely explained in Appendix D. The amount of information necessary to depict the spectral envelope parameters can be reduced 30% below that needed by simple VQ using FSVQ, trellis, or HMM coding.

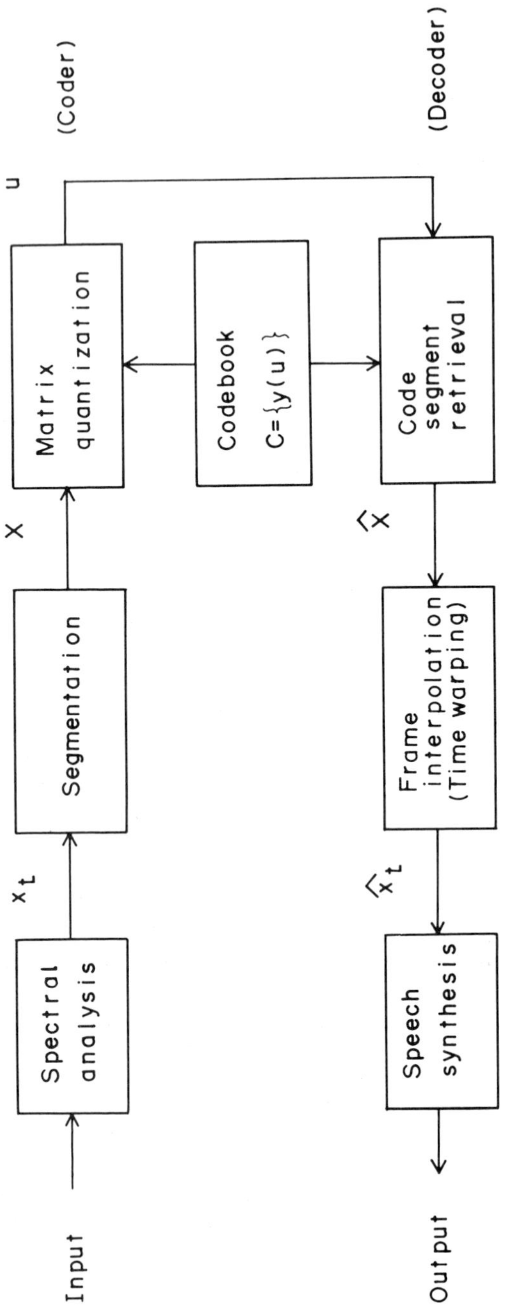


Fig. 6.34 Block diagram of MQ.

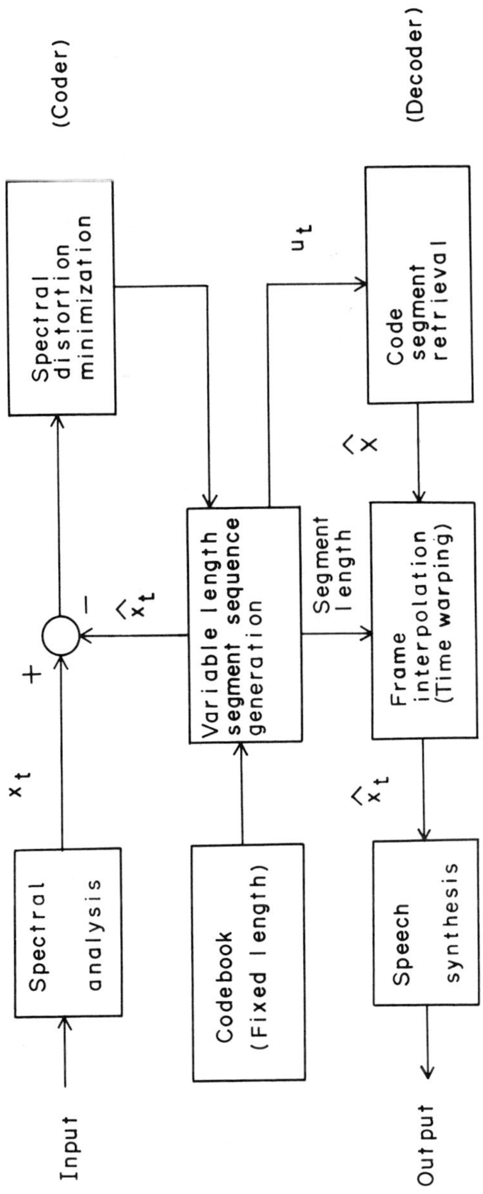


Fig. 6.35 Block diagram of phonocode method.

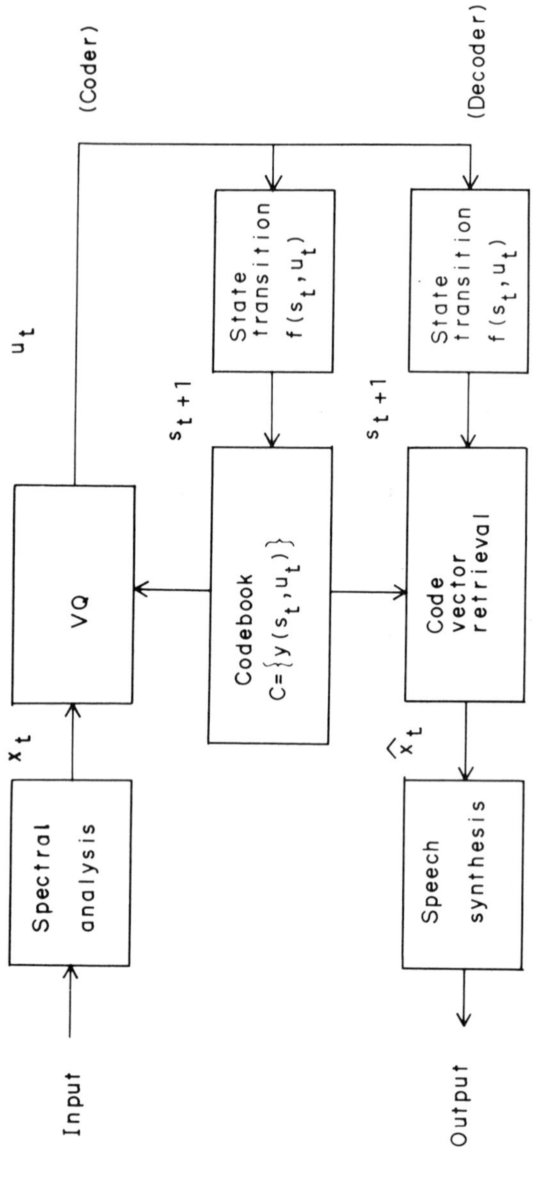


Fig. 6.36 Block diagram of FSVQ.

## 6.6 EVALUATION OF CODING METHODS

Techniques for evaluating the quality of speech coded by various methods can be divided into subjective evaluation and objective evaluation techniques. Subjective evaluation includes opinion tests, pair comparison, sometimes called A-B tests, and intelligibility tests. The former two methods measure the subjective quality, including naturalness and ease of listening, whereas the latter method measures how accurately phonetic information can be transmitted.

In the opinion tests, quality is measured by subjective scores (usually by five levels: 5 is excellent, 4 good, 3 fair, 2 poor, and 1 bad). The mean opinion score (MOS) is then calculated, in which a mean value is determined for the many listeners. Since the MOS indicates only the relative quality in a set of test utterances, the opinion-equivalent SNR value ($SNR_q$) has also been proposed to ensure that the MOS is properly related to the objective measures (Richards, 1973). The $SNR_q$ indicates the signal-to-amplitude-correlated noise ratio of the reference signal which results in the same MOS as that for each test utterance. Amplitude-correlated noise is white noise which has been modified by the speech signal amplitude in order to give it the same characteristics as the quantization noise. The energy ratio of the original signal to the modified noise is called the signal-to-amplitude-correlated noise ratio.

In the pair comparison test, each test utterance is compared with various other utterances, and the probability that the test utterance is judged to be better than the other utterances is calculated as the preference score.

Intelligibility is measured using the correct identification scores for sentences, words, syllables, or phonemes (vowels and consonants). Analyzing the relationship between syllable and sentence intelligibility indicates that when the syllable identification (articulation) score exceeds 75%, the sentence intelligibility score approaches 100%. The intelligibility is often indicated by the AEN (articulation-equivalent loss), the calculation of which is based on the identification (articulation) score (Richards, 1973).

As indicated in Fig. 6.37, the AEN is the difference in transmission losses between the system to be measured and the reference system when the phoneme identification scores for both systems are 80%. In the calculation, the reference system is adjusted to reproduce the acoustic transmission characteristics between two people facing each other at a distance of 1 m in a free field. Importantly, the AEN values are more stable than the raw identification scores.

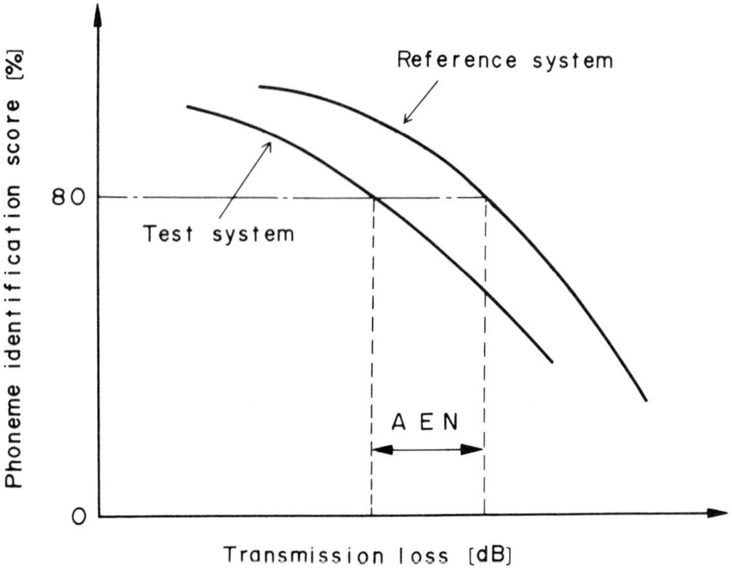


Fig. 6.37 Principle of AEN (articulation-equivalent loss) measure.

Although definitive evaluation of coding methods should be performed by human listeners, the subjective tests require a great deal of labor and time. Therefore, it is practical to build objective evaluation methods producing evaluation results which correspond well with the subjective evaluation results. Among the various objective measures proposed, the most fundamental is the SNR. Similar to this measure is the segmental SNR ($SNR_{seg}$), which is the SNR measured in dBs at short periods such as 30 ms, and averaged over a long speech interval. The $SNR_{seg}$ corresponds better with the subjective values than does the SNR, since the short-term SNRs of even relatively small amplitude periods contribute to this value.

In addition to this time-domain evaluation, spectral-domain evaluation methods have also been proposed. These methods are based on spectral distortion measured using various parameters such as the spectrum, predictor coefficients, autocorrelation function, and cepstrum. The most typical method is that using the cepstral distance measure defined as

$$CD = D_b \sqrt{2 \sum_{i=1}^{p} (c_i^{(x)} - c_i^{(y)})^2} \tag{6.22}$$

where $c_i^{(x)}$ and $c_i^{(y)}$ are cepstral or LPC cepstral coefficients for input and output signals of the coder, and $D_b$ is the constant for transforming the distance value into the dB value ($D_b = 10/\ln 10$) (Kitawaki et al., 1982).

Subjective evaluation results using the MOS for various coding methods including PARCOR and LSP analysis-synthesis systems are shown in Fig. 6.38 (Watanabe et al., 1982). The vertical axis indicates the $SNR_q$. $ADPCM_f$ and $ADPCM_v$ are ADPCM methods having a fixed predictor and an adaptive predictor, respectively. The results of objective evaluation using the $SNR_{seg}$ and spectral distortion measured by the cepstral distance (CD) for the same coding methods are presented in Fig. 6.39. Since the analysis-synthesis methods do not maintain the original waveform, only the spectral distortion is used as the objective measure for these systems. A comparison of the results shown in Figs. 6.38 and 6.39 verifies that the CD has a better correspondence to the subjective measure than does the $SNR_{seg}$.

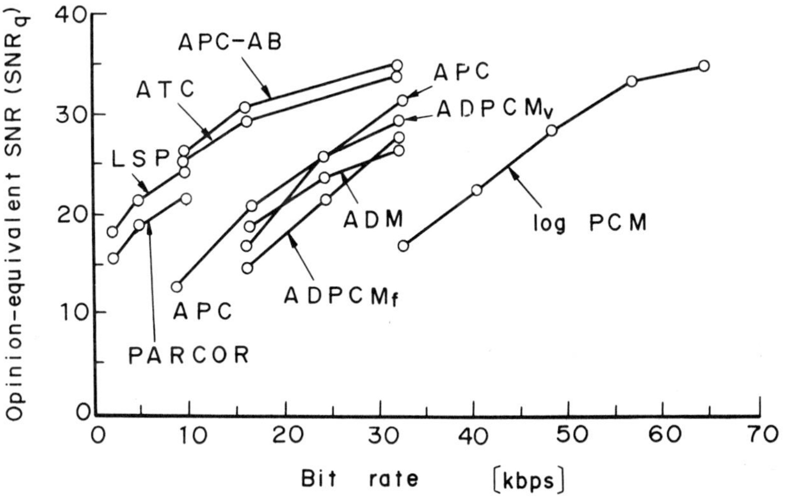


Fig. 6.38 Subjective evaluation results using opinion-equivalent SNR value ($SNR_q$) for various coding systems.

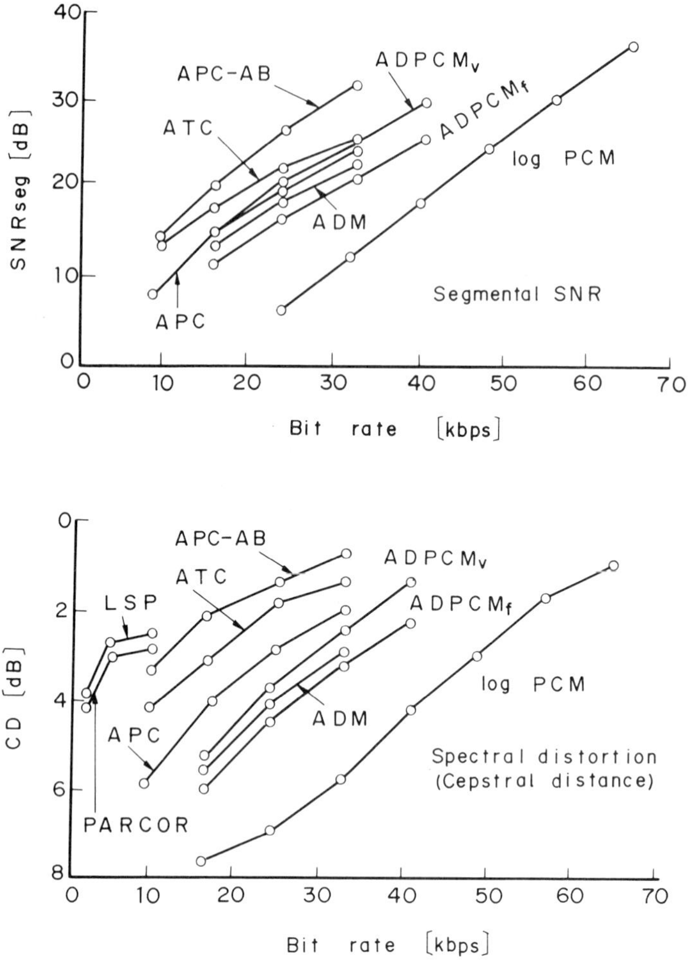


Fig. 6.39 Objective evaluation results using segmental SNR ($SNR_{seg}$) and cepstral distance (CD) for the same coding systems as in Fig. 6.38.

The relationship between the CD and MOS is demonstrated in Fig. 6.40 in which the regression equation between them obtained from the experiments is indicated by a quadratic curve. The standard deviation for the evaluation values from the regression curve is 0.18. These results indicate that quality equivalent to that of 7-bit log PCM can be obtained by 32-kbps ADPCM or 16-kbps APC-AB and ATC.

Although ADPCM, APC, and SBC systems are roughly 10 times more complex than PCM, ΔM, and DPCM systems, APC-AB and ATC systems are approximately 10 times more complex than them. As encoding and decoding algorithms become more complex, they require more powerful computational hardware for real-time coding purposes. Complex algorithms also introduce delays between the time the speaker utters a sound and the time a coded version of it enters the transmission system. Typically, APC-AB and ATC systems introduce delays of around 30 ms. Although coding delay is not a problem if the coder is used in only one stage of coding and decoding such as in voice storage, it can be objectionable in two-way telephone conversations. If the delay

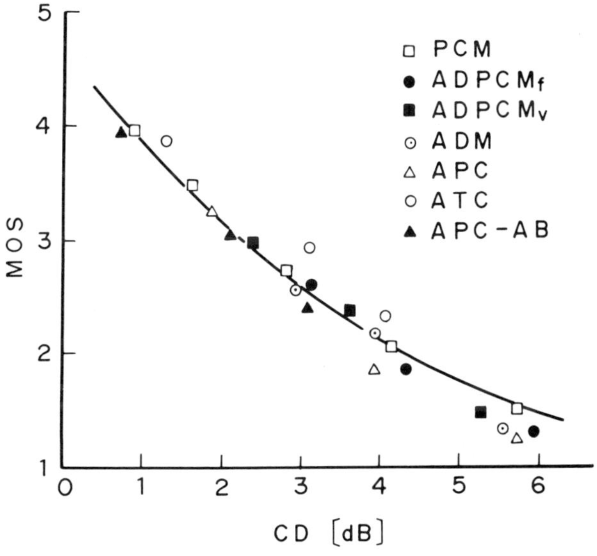


Fig. 6.40 Relationship between CD and MOS.

is undesirable only because of uncanceled echoes, however, it can be eliminated or mitigated by an echo canceler.

The objective and subjective measures do not correspond well in several cases such as in systems incorporating noise shaping. A universal objective measure which can be applied to all kinds of coding systems has not yet been established.

# 7

# Speech Synthesis

## 7.1 PRINCIPLES OF SPEECH SYNTHESIS

Speech synthesis is a process which artificially produces speech for various applications, diminishing the dependence on using a person's recorded voice. The speech synthesis methods enable a machine to pass on instructions or information to the user through "speaking."

As already mentioned, progress in LSI technology and LPC techniques in recent years have collectively helped to advance speech synthesis research. Moreover, information supply services are now available in a wider range of application fields. Speech synthesis research is closely related to research into deriving the basic units of information carried in speech waves and into the speech production mechanism.

Voice response technology designed to convey messages via synthesized speech presents several advantages for information transmission:

1. Anybody can easily understand the message without training or intense concentration.
2. The message can be received even when the listener is involved in other activities, such as walking, handling an object or looking at something.
3. The conventional telephone network can be used to realize easy, remote access to information.
4. This form of messaging is essentially a paper-free communication form.

The last item also means that no hard copy of the messages makes them difficult to scan. Thus, synthesized speech is sometimes inappropriate for conveying a large amount of complicated information to many people.

History's first speech synthesizer is said to have been constructed in 1779, more than 200 years ago. Figure 7.1 shows the structure of the speech synthesizer subsequently produced by von Kempelen in 1791 (Flanagan, 1972). This synthesizer, the first of its kind capable of producing both vowels and consonants, was intended to simulate the human articulatory organs. Sounds originated through the vibration of reeds were modulated by the resonance of the leather tube and radiated as a speech wave. Fricative sounds were produced through the "S" and "SH" whistles. This synthesizer is purported to have been able to produce words consisting of up to 19 consonants and 5 vowels. Early mechanically structured speech synthesizers, of course, could not generate high-quality synthesized speech, since it was difficult to continuously and rapidly change the vocal tract shape.

The first synthesizer incorporating an electric structure was made in 1922 by J. Q. Stewart. Two coupled resonant electric circuits were excited by a current interrupted at a rate analogous to the voice pitch. By carefully tuning the circuits, sustained vowels could be produced by this synthesizer.

The first synthesizer which actually succeeded in generating continuous speech was the voder, constructed by H. Dudley in 1939. It produced continuous speech by controlling the fundamental period and band-pass filter characteristics, respectively, using a foot pedal and 10 finger keys. The voder, which later served as the prototype of the speech synthesizer for the vocoder introduced in Sec. 4.6.3, became a principal foundation block for recent speech synthesis research. The voder structure, based on the linear separable equivalent circuit model, is still used in present speech synthesizers.

Present speech synthesis methods can be divided into three types:

1. Synthesis based on waveform coding, in which speech waves of recorded human voice stored after waveform coding or immediately after recording are used to produce desired messages
2. Synthesis based on the analysis-synthesis method, in which speech waves of recorded human voice are transformed into parameter sequences by the analysis-synthesis method and stored, with a speech synthesizer being driven by concatenated parameters to produce messages

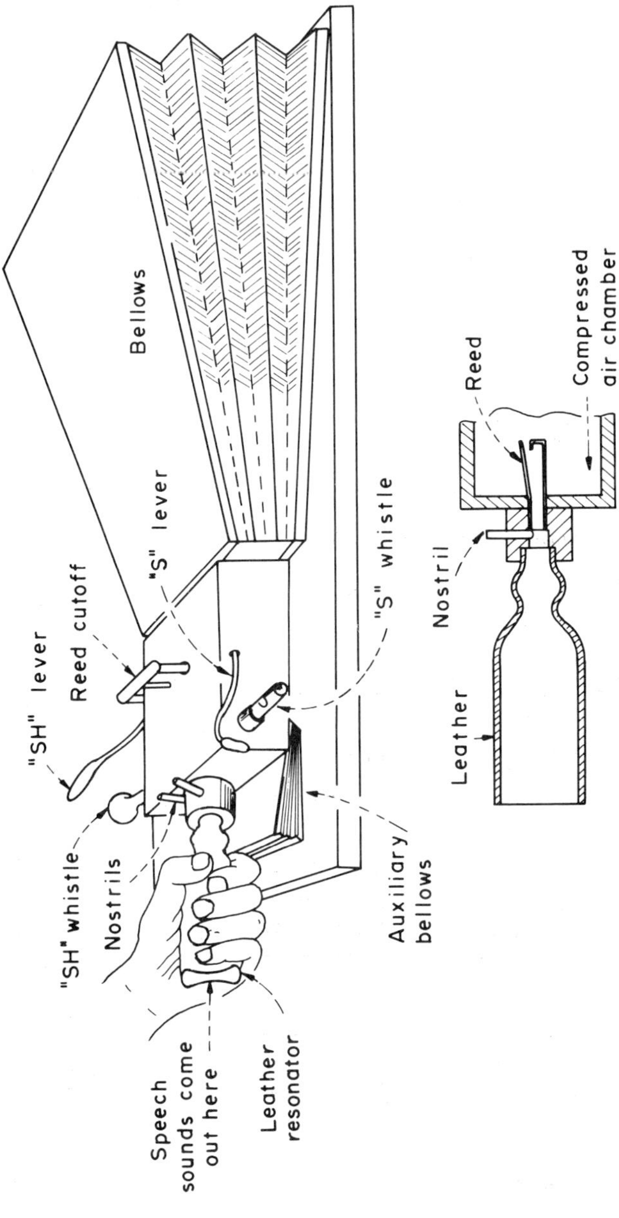


Fig. 7.1 Mechanical speech synthesizer by von Kempelen.

3. Synthesis by rule, in which speech is produced based on phonetic and linguistic rules from letter sequences or sequences of phoneme symbols and prosodic features.

The principles of these three methods and a comparison of their features are presented in Fig. 7.2 and Table 7.1, respectively. Synthesis systems based on the waveform coding method are simple and provide high-quality speech, but they also exhibit low versatility, only i.e., the messages can only be used in the form recorded. At the other extreme, synthesis-by-rule systems feature great versatility but are also highly complex, and, as yet,

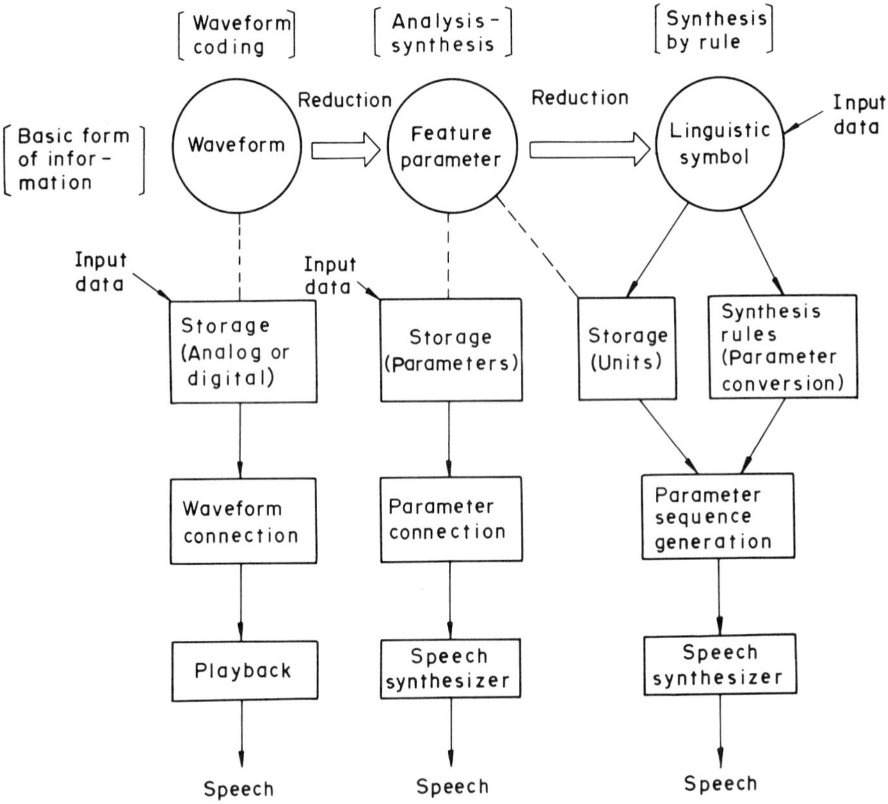


Fig. 7.2 Basic principles of three speech synthesis methods.

TABLE 7.1 Comparison of the Features of Three Speech Synthesis Methods

| Features | | Waveform coding | Analysis-synthesis | Synthesis by rule |
|---|---|---|---|---|
| Quality | Intelligibility | High | High | Medium |
| | Naturalness | High | Medium | Low |
| Vocabulary size | | Small (<500) | Large (1000 s) | Unrestricted |
| Bit rate | | 24–64 kbps | 2.4–9.6 kbps | 50–75 bps |
| Speech length stored in 1-Mbit memory | | 15–40 s | 100 s–7 min | Unrestricted |
| Stored units | | Words, syllables, sentences | Words, syllables, sentences | Phonemes, syllables (CV, VCV, CVC, morphs, etc.) |
| Complexity | | Low | Medium | High |
| Main hardware | | Memory | Memory and processor | Processor |
| Examples | | Analog or PCM recording, ADPCM | Channel vocoder LPC (PARCOR, LSP) | MITalk, DECtalk (synthesizers are terminal analog, LPC, cepstrum, etc.) |

of limited quality. In practical cases, it is desirable to select the method most appropriate for the objectives fully taking the performance and properties of each method into consideration.

The details of each method will be discussed in the following.

## 7.2 SYNTHESIS BASED ON WAVEFORM CODING

As mentioned, synthesis based on waveform coding is the method in which words or phrases of human voice are stored and the desired sentence speech is synthesized by reading and connecting the appropriate units. In this method, the quality of synthesized sentence speech is generally influenced by the quality of the continuity of acoustic features at the connections between units. Acoustic features include the spectral envelope, amplitude, fundamental frequency, and speaking rate. If large units such as phrases or sentences are stored and used, the quality (intelligibility and naturalness) of synthesized speech is better, although the variety of words or sentences which can by synthesized is restricted. On the other hand, when small units such as syllables or phonemes are used, a wide range of words and sentences can be synthesized, but the speech quality is largely degraded.

In practical systems typically available at present, words and phrases are stored, and words are inserted or connected with phrases to produce a desired sentence speech. Since the pitch pattern of each word changes according to its position in differing sentences, it is necessary to store variations of the same words with rising, flat, and falling inflections. The inflection selected also depends on whether the sentence represents a question, statement, or exclamation.

Major problems of simply concatenating words to produce sentences are as follows (Klatt, 1987). First, a spoken sentence is very different from a sequence of words uttered in isolation. In a sentence, words are as short as half their duration when spoken in isolation, making concatenated speech seem painfully slow. Second, the sentence stress pattern, rhythm, and intonation, which depend on syntactic and semantic factors, are disruptively unnatural when words are simply concatenated, even if several variations of the same word are stored.

In order to reduce requirements for memory size, the units are sometimes compressed by waveform coding methods such as ADPCM rather than simply storing with analog or digital speech waves. Synthesis based on the analysis-synthesis method, discussed below, is considered to be an advanced form of this method from the viewpoint of information reduction and controllability.

## 7.3 SYNTHESIS BASED ON ANALYSIS-SYNTHESIS METHOD

In synthesis based on the analysis-synthesis method, words or phrases of human speech are analyzed based on the speech production model and stored as time sequences of feature parameters. Parameter sequences of appropriate units are connected and supplied to a speech synthesizer to produce the desired spoken message. Since the units are stored by source and spectral envelope parameters, the amount of information is much less than with the previous method of storing by waveform, although the naturalness of synthesized speech is slightly degraded. Additionally, this method is advantageous in that changing the speaking rate and smoothing the pitch and spectral change at connections can be performed by controlling the parameters. Channel vocoders and speech synthesizers based on LPC analysis methods, such as LSP and PARCOR methods, are used for this purpose.

## 7.4 SYNTHESIS BASED ON SPEECH PRODUCTION MECHANISM

Two methods are capable of producing speech by electrically simulating the speech production mechanism. One is the vocal tract analog method, which simulates the acoustic wave propagation in the vocal tract. The other is the terminal analog method simulating the frequency spectrum structure, that is, the resonance and antiresonance characteristics, which simulates articulation as a result. Although in the early years these methods were realized by analog processing using analog computers or variable resonance circuits, digital processing has recently become popular owing to advances in digital circuits and computers and to their ease of control.

### 7.4.1 Vocal Tract Analog Method

The vocal tract analog method is based on the principle described in Sec. 3.3. More specifically, the vocal tract is represented by a cascade connection of straight tubes with various cross-sectional areas, each of which has a short length $\Delta x$. The acoustic waves in the tubes are separated into forward and backward waves. Acoustic wave propagation in the vocal tract is represented by the integration of reflection and penetration of forward and backward waves at each boundary between adjacent tubes. The amount of reflection and penetration at the boundary is determined by the reflection coefficient which indicates the amount of mismatching in acoustic impedance. The signal processing for speech synthesis based on this principle was already detailed in Fig. 3.4.

A method has also been investigated in which vocal tract characteristics are simulated by a cascade connection of $\pi$-type four-terminal circuits, each of which consists of L- and C-elements. The circuit is terminated by another circuit having a series of L- and R-elements, which is equivalent to the radiation impedance at the lips. The vocal tract model is excited by a pulse generator at the input terminal of the $\pi$-type circuit for voiced sounds, and by a white noise generator connected to a four-terminal circuit where turbulent noise is produced for consonants.

Rather than remaining with the modeling of the vocal tract area function, it would be better to take the next, more difficult step, and directly formulate a model based on the structure of the articulatory organs. In such a modeling system, locations and shapes of articulatory organs are used as control parameters for speech synthesis. In this method, synthesis rules are expected to be much clearer since the articulatory movements of the organs can be directly described and controlled. An example of this method, which is called the articulatory model, was described in Sec. 3.5. In another example of the speech synthesis system based on this method (Coker et al., 1978), the glottal area, gap between velum and pharynx, tongue location, shape of tongue tip, jaw opening, and the amount of narrowing and sticking of the lips are controlled to produce speech.

The speech synthesizer based on the vocal tract analog method is considered to be particularly effective in synthesizing transitional sounds such as consonants, since it can precisely simulate the dynamic manner of articulation in the vocal tract. Additionally, this method is considered to be easily related to the phonetic information conveyed by the speech wave. High-quality synthesized speech has not yet been obtained, however, since the movement of the articulatory organs has not been sufficiently clarified to offer suitable control rules.

### 7.4.2 Terminal Analog Method

The terminal analog method simulates the speech production mechanism using an electrical structure consisting of the cascade or parallel connection of several resonance (formant) and antiresonance (antiformant) circuits. The resonance or antiresonance frequency and bandwidth of each circuit are variable. This method is also called the formant-type speech synthesis method.

As indicated in Sec. 3.3.2 (resonance model), the complex frequency characteristics (Laplace transformation) of a resonance (pole) circuit can be represented as

$$H(s) = \frac{s_n s_n^*}{(s - s_n)(s - s_n^*)}$$

where

$$s = -\sigma + j\omega$$

$$s_n = -\sigma_n + j\omega_n \quad \text{and} \quad s_n^* = -\sigma_n - j\omega_n \tag{7.1}$$

Digital simulation of this circuit can be represented through its z-transformation

$$H(z) = \sum_{k=1}^{2} \frac{1}{1 - e^{T\theta_k} z^{-1}} \mathrm{Res}[H(\theta)]_{\theta = \theta_k}$$

$$= K_p \left( \frac{Az^{-1}}{1 + Cz^{-1} + Bz^{-2}} \right)$$

where

$$K_p = \frac{\sigma_n^2 + \omega_n^2}{\omega_n} \qquad A = e^{-\sigma_n T} \sin \omega_n T$$

$$B = e^{-2\sigma_n T} \quad \text{and} \quad C = 2e^{-\sigma_n T} \cos \omega_n T \tag{7.2}$$

T is the sampling period, and Res[ ] indicates the residue number. These equations imply that the digital simulation circuit can be represented as shown in Fig. 7.3(a). When the resonance frequency $f_n = \omega_n/2\pi$ [Hz] and bandwidth $b_n = \sigma_n/\pi$ [Hz] are given, the circuit parameters can be obtained. The antiresonance (zero) circuit indicated in Fig. 7.3(b) can be easily obtained from the resonance circuit, based on the inverse circuit relationships. Here, $K_z = \omega_n/(\sigma_n^2 + \omega_n^2)$.

The cascade connection of resonance and antiresonance circuits is advantageous in that mutual amplitude ratios between formants and antiformants are automatically determined. This is feasible because vocal tract transmission characteristics can be

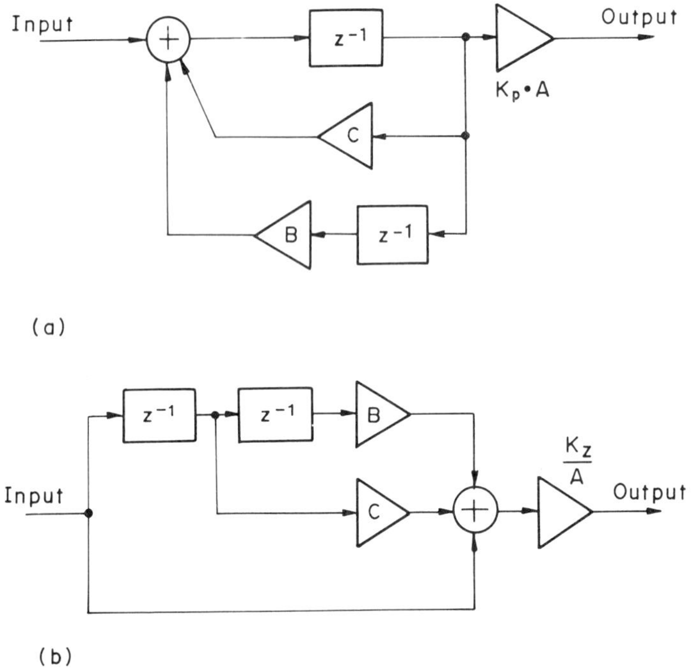


Fig. 7.3 Digital simulation of resonance and antiresonance circuits: (a) resonance (pole) circuit; (b) antiresonance (zero) circuit.

directly represented by this method. On the other hand, parallel connection is advantageous in that the final spectral shape can be precisely simulated. Such precise simulation is made possible by the fact that the amplitude of each formant and antiformant can be represented independently, even though this method does not directly indicate the vocal tract transmission characteristics. Therefore, cascade connection is suitable for vowel speech having a clear spectral structure, and parallel connection is best intended for nasal and fricative sounds featuring such a complicated spectral structure that their pole and zero structures cannot be extracted easily. Figure 7.4 shows a typical example of the structure of a synthesizer which is constructed based on these considerations (Klatt, 1980).

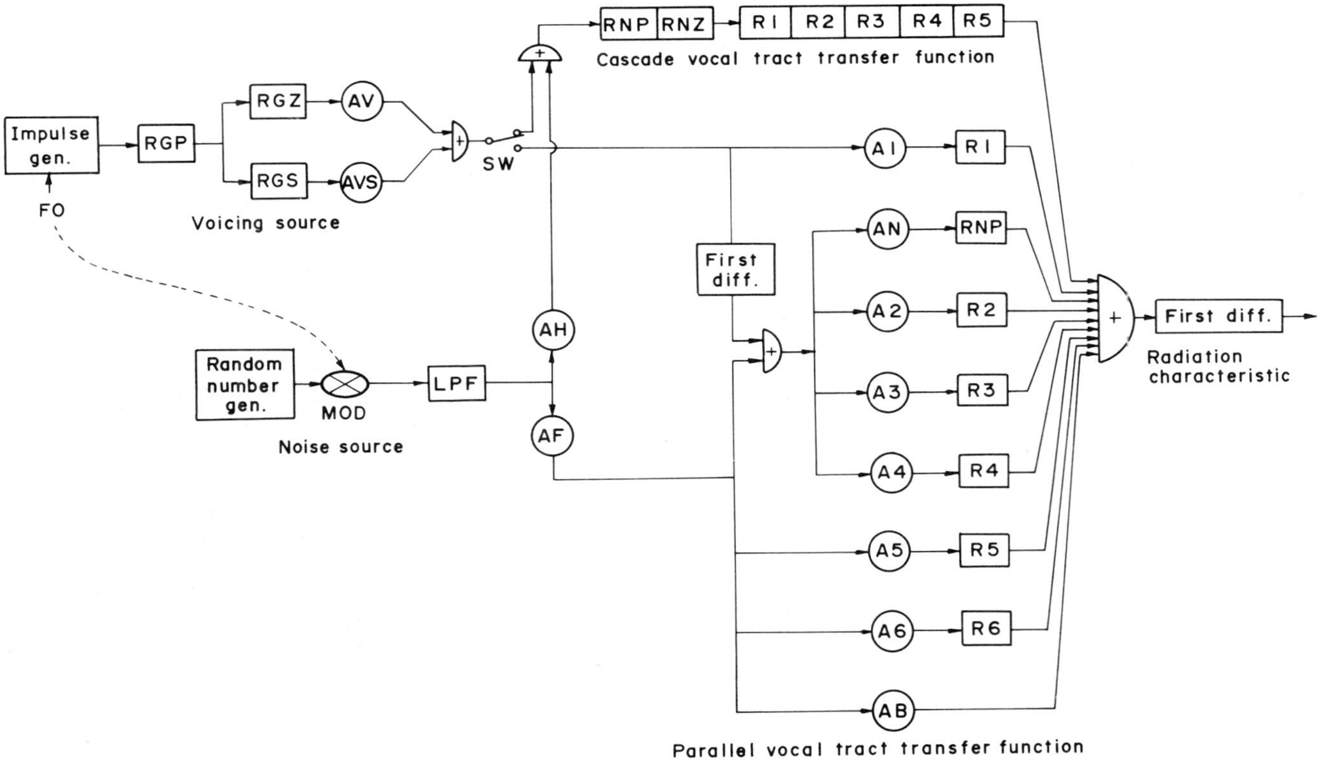


Fig. 7.4 Typical example of structure of terminal analog-type (formant-type) speech synthesizer (F0 = fundamental frequency; R~ = resonance circuits controlled by resonance frequency and bandwidth; RGP, RGS = glottal resonance circuits; RGZ = glottal antiresonance circuit; RNP, RNZ = resonance and antiresonance circuits for nasals; A~ = amplitude).

## 7.5 SYNTHESIS BY RULE

### 7.5.1 Principles of Synthesis by Rule

Synthesis by rule is a method for producing any words or sentences based on sequences of phonetic/syllabic symbols or letters. In this method, feature parameters for fundamental small units of speech such as syllables, phonemes or one-pitch-period speech, are stored and connected by rules. At the same time, prosodic features such as pitch and amplitude are also controlled by rules. The quality of fundamental units for synthesis as well as control rules (control information and control mechanisms) for acoustic parameters play crucially important roles in this method, and they must be based on phonetic and linguistic characteristics of natural speech. Furthermore, to produce natural and distinct speech, temporal transitions of pitch, stress, and spectrum must be smooth, and other features such as pause locations and durations must be appropriate.

Vocal tract analog, terminal analog, and LPC speech synthesizers are usually used for speech production. Feature parameters for fundamental units are extracted from natural speech or artificially created. When phonemes are taken as the fundamental units for speech production, the memory capacity can be greatly reduced, since the number of phonemes is generally between 30 and 50. However, the rules for connecting phonemes are so complicated that high-quality speech is hard to obtain. Therefore, units larger than phonemes are frequently used.

For the Japanese language, 100 CV syllables (C is a consonant, V is a vowel) corresponding to symbols in the Japanese "Kana" syllabary are often used as these units. CVC units have also been employed to obtain high-quality speech (Sato, 1984a). The number of CVC syllables appearing in Japanese is very large, somewhere between 5000 and 6000. Thus, combinations of roughly 1000 CVC syllables frequently appearing in Japanese along with roughly 200 CV/VC syllables have been used to synthesize Japanese sentences. Combinations of between 700 and 800 VCV units have also been tried (Sato, 1978).

For example, the Japanese word "sakura," or cherry blossom, can be represented by the concatenation of these units as

| | |
|---|---|
| CV units | sa + ku + ra |
| CVC units | sak + kur + ra |
| VCV units | sa + aku + ura |

CVC units are connected at consonants, and VCV units at vowel steady parts. Each method has its own advantages in ease of connection.

In contrast, the English language has more than 3500 syllables, which expand to roughly 10,000 when allophones (phonological variations) are taken into consideration. Therefore, syllables are usually decomposed into smaller units, such as dyads, diphones (both have roughly 400 to 1000 units; Dixon and Maxey, 1968), or demisyllables (roughly 1000 units; Lovins et al., 1979). These units basically consist of individual phonemes and transitions between neighboring phonemes. Although demisyllables are slightly larger than the other two units, all units are composed in such a way that they may be concatenated using simple rules.

In phoneme-based systems (Klatt, 1987), synthesis begins by selecting targets for each control parameter for each phonetic segment. Targets are sometimes modified by rules that take into account features of neighboring segments. Transitions between targets are then computed according to rules that range in complexity from simple smoothing to a fairly complicated implementation of the locus theory. Most smoothing interactions involve segments adjacent to one another, but articulatory/acoustic interaction effects that span more than the adjacent segment are also provided for in the rules.

Control parameters for intonation, accent, stress, pause, and duration used to be manually input into the system in order to synthesize high-quality sentence speech. Because of the difficulty of inputting these parameters, however, text-to-speech conversion, in which these control parameters are automatically produced based on letter sequences, has recently been introduced. This system can realize the human ability of reading written texts, that is, converting unrestricted text to speech. This is essentially the ultimate goal of speech synthesis. Building such a text-to-speech conversion system, though, necessitates clarifying how people understand sentences using our knowledge of syntax and semantics. To be totally effective, this process of understanding must then be converted into computer programs. The principles of text-to-speech conversion will be described in Sec. 7.6.

### 7.5.2 Control of Prosodic Features

In prosodic features, intonation and accent are most important in improving the quality synthesized speech. Fundamental frequency, loudness, and duration are related to these features.

In the period of speech between pauses, that is, the period of speech uttered in one breath, pitch frequency is usually high at the onset and gradually decreases toward the end due to the decrease in subglottal pressure. This characteristic is called the basic intonation component. The pitch pattern of each sentence is produced by adding the accent components of the pitch pattern to this basic intonation component. The accent components are determined by the accent position for each word or syllable.

Figure 7.5 shows an example of the pitch pattern production mechanism for the spoken Japanese sentence meaning "I received a pretty flower from Ms. Yamada." In the Japanese language, a pitch pattern can be approximately represented by the piecewise

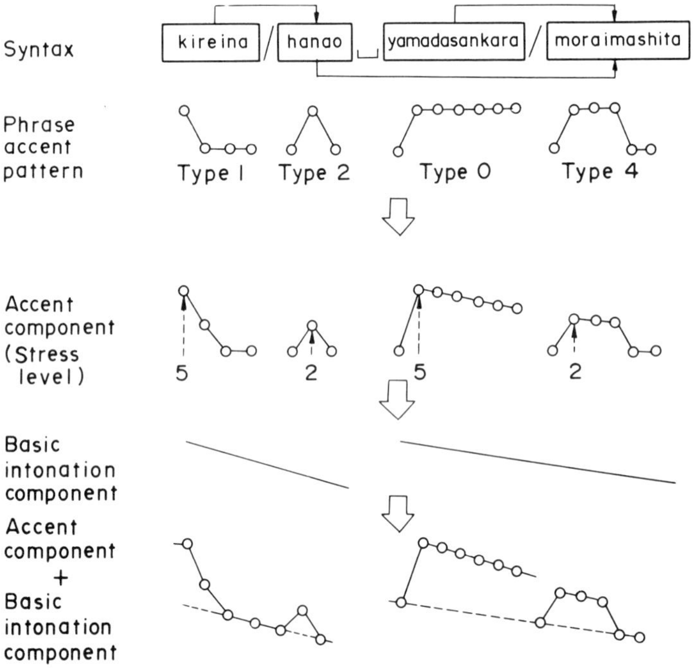


Fig. 7.5 Pitch pattern production mechanism for Japanese sentence speech. The meanings of the phrases are as follows: "kireina;" pretty; "hanao;" a flower; "yamadasankara;" from Ms. Yamada; and "moraimashita;" I recieved.

linear interpolation of the fundamental frequencies at vowel centers, which is called the point pitch pattern (Sagisaka and Sato, 1986). A Japanese phrase generally consists of an independent word followed by several dependent words, and phrases with N CV syllables have N + 1 types of accent patterns. Each pattern can be represented by the point pitch pattern as shown in the figure. The correct type for each phrase is usually attributed to the independent word, but is sometimes modified by its combination with other words. The accent component for each phrase is finally determined according to the syntactic relationships existing between phrases.

In a successful speech synthesis system for English (Klatt, 1987), the pitch pattern is modeled in terms of impulses and step commands fed to a linear smoothing filter. A step rise is placed near the start of the first stressed vowel in accordance with the "hat theory" of intonation. A step fall is placed near the start of the final stressed vowel. These rises and falls set off syntactic units. Stress is also manifested in this rule system by causing an additional local rise on stressed vowels using the impulse commands. The amount of rise is greatest for the first stressed vowel of a syntactic unit, and smaller thereafter. Finally, small local influences of phonetic segments are added by positioning commands to simulate the rises for voiceless consonants and high vowels. A gradual declination line (the basic intonation component) is also included in the inputs to the smoothing filter.

The top portion of Fig. 7.6 shows three typical clause final intonation patterns, and the bottom portion exemplifies a pitch "hat pattern" of rises and falls between the brim and top of the hat for a two-clause sentence. An example of the step and impulsive commands for the English sentence noted, as well as the pitch pattern generated by these commands and the rules, are given in Fig. 7.7.

Duration control for each phoneme is also an important issue in synthesizing high-quality speech. The duration of each phoneme in continuous speech is determined by many factors, such as the characteristics peculiar to each phoneme, influence of adjacent phonemes, and the number of phonemes as well as their location in the word (Sagisaka and Tohkura, 1984). The duration of each phoneme also changes as a function of the sentence context. Specifically, the final vowel of the sentence is lengthened, as are the stressed vowels and the consonants that precede them in the same syllable, whereas the vowels before voiceless consonants are shortened (Klatt, 1987).

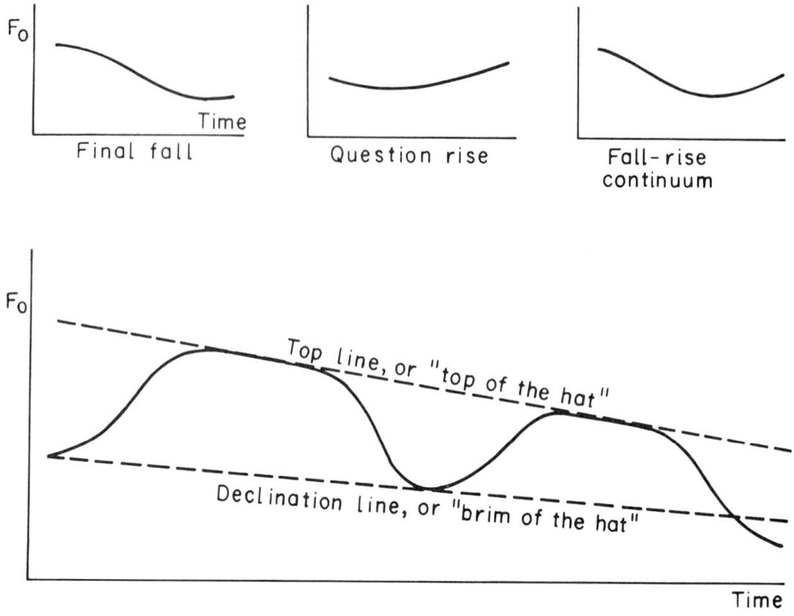


Fig. 7.6 Three typical clause-final intonation patterns (top), and an example of a pitch "hat pattern" of rises and falls (bottom).

## 7.6 TEXT-TO-SPEECH CONVERSION

Text-to-speech conversion is an ambitious objective and continues to be the focus of intensive research. A text-to-speech system produced will find a wide range of applications in a number of fields. These would range from accessing electronic mail and various kinds of databases by voice to reading for the blind. Figure 7.8 presents the chief elements of text-to-speech conversion (Crochiere and Flanagan, 1986). Input text often includes abbreviations, Roman numerals, dates, times, formulas, and punctuation marks. The system developed must be capable of first converting these into some reasonable, standard form and then translating them into a broad phonetic transcription. This is done by using a large pronouncing dictionary supplemented by appropriate letter-to-sound rules.

In the MITalk-79 system, which is one of the major pioneering English text-to-speech conversion systems yet developed,

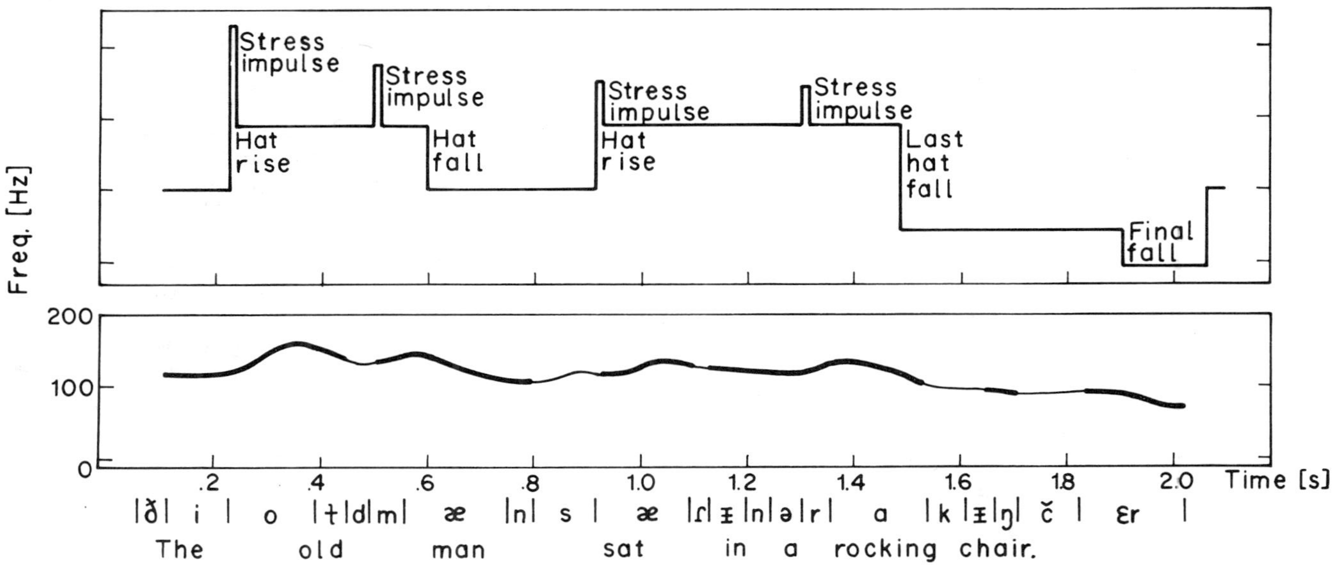


Fig. 7.7 An example of the step and impulsive commands for a sentence and the pitch pattern generated by sending these commands through a low-pass smoothing filter.

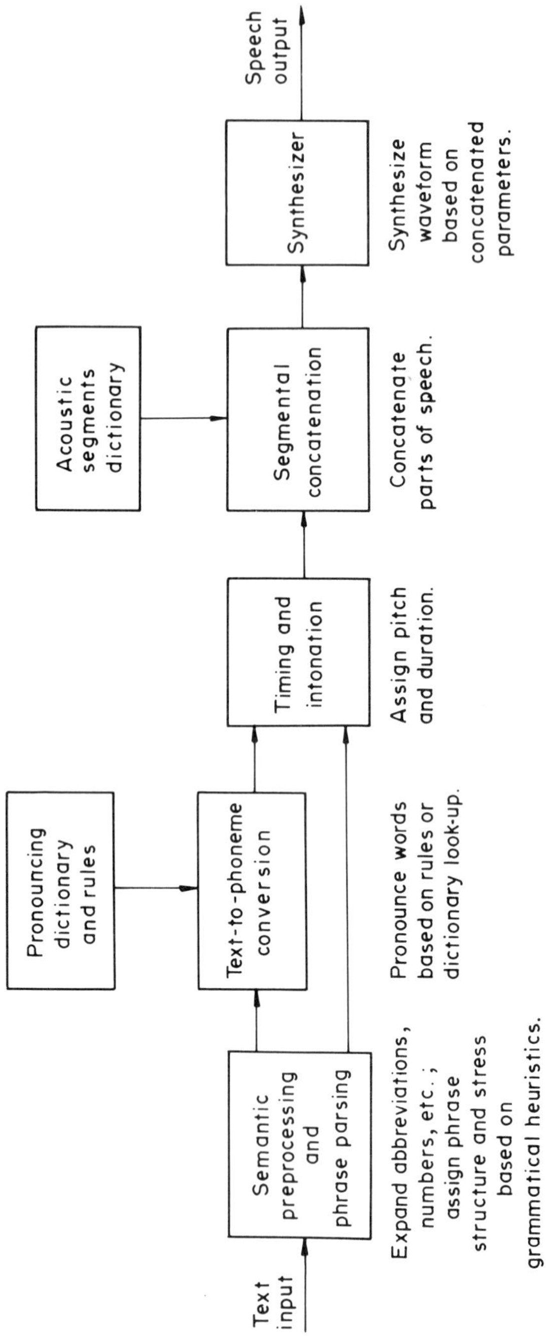


Fig. 7.8 Principal elements of text-to-speech conversion system.

12,000 morphs, covering 98% of ordinary English sentence, are used as basic acoustic segments (Allen et al., 1979). Morphs, which are smaller than words, are minimum units of letter strings having linguistic meaning. They consist of stems, prefixes, and suffixes. The word "changeable," for example, is decomposed into the morphs "change" and "able." The morph dictionary stores the spelling and pronunciation for each morph, rules for connecting with other morphs, and rules for syntax-dependent variations. Phoneme sequences for low-frequency words are produced by letter-to-sound rules, instead of preparing morphs for them. This is based on the fact that irregular letter-to-sound conversions generally occur for frequent words though the pronunciation of infrequent words tends to follow regular rules in English.

The MITalk-79 system converts word strings into morph strings by a left-to-right recursive process using the morph dictionary. Each word is then transformed into a sequence of phonemes. Additionally, stress in each word is decided according to the effects of prefixes, suffixes, the word compound, and the part of speech. Sentence level prosodic features are added according to syntax and semantics analysis, and sentence speech is finally synthesized using the terminal analog speech synthesizer introduced in Sec. 7.4.2 (Fig. 7.4).

The quality of the speech synthesized by the MITalk-79 system was evaluated by phoneme intelligibility in isolated words, word intelligibility in sentence speech, and sentence comprehensibility. Experimental results confirmed that the error rate for the phoneme intelligibility test was 6.9%, and that word intelligibility scores were, respectively, 93.2% and 78.7% in normal sentences and meaningless sentences. Figure 7.9 illustrates the results of the sentence comprehensibility test compared with reading performances. The listening comprehension results are broken down in this figure by first and second halves of the test. These results demonstrate that once a listener becomes used to the quality of the synthesized speech (second half of the test), it becomes almost as comprehensible as the written text from which it derives.

The DECtalk system, which is the most successful commercialized text-to-speech conversion system, is based on refinements of the technology used in the MITalk-79 system (Klatt, 1987).

Text-to-speech conversion systems for several other languages have also been investigated (Hirose et al., 1986). In a Japanese text-to-speech conversion system (Sato, 1984b), input

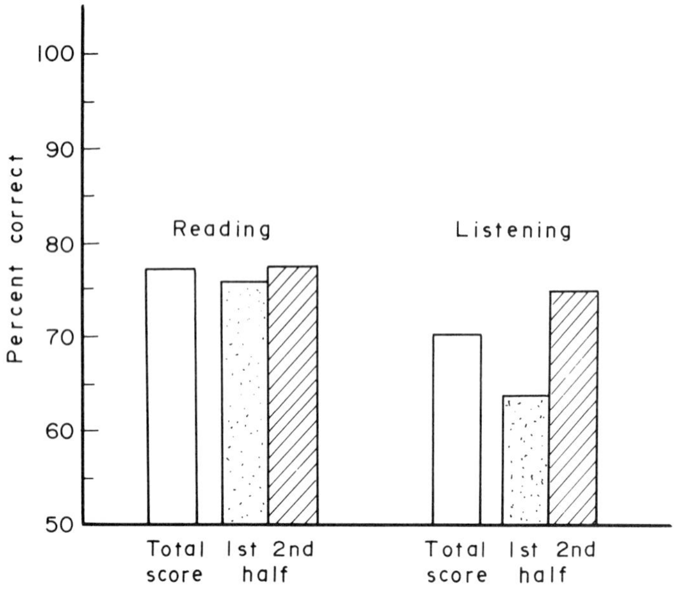


Fig. 7.9 Results of the evaluation of synthesized speech by MITalk-79 system (comparison of sentence comprehensibility with reading performances).

speech, which is written in a combination of Chinese characters, or Kanji and Japanese Kana syllabary, is analyzed by depth-first searching for the longest match using a 58,000-word dictionary and a word transition table. The transition table provides candidates for the following word. Compound and phrase accent and sentence prosodic characteristics are next determined by reconstruction of phrases on the basis of local syntactic dependency analysis. A continuous speech signal is finally synthesized by concatenating CV speech units.

# 8

# Speech Recognition

## 8.1 PRINCIPLES OF SPEECH RECOGNITION

### 8.1.1 Advantages of Speech Recognition

Speech recognition is the process of automatically extracting and determining linguistic information conveyed by a speech wave using computers or electronic circuits. Linguistic information, the most important information in a speech wave, is also called phonetic information. In the broadest sense of the word, speech recognition includes speaker recognition which involves extracting individual information indicating who is speaking. I will use the term speech recognition from here on, however, to mean the recognition of linguistic information only.

Automatic speech recognition methods have been investigated for many years aimed principally at realizing typewriters and robots capable of recognizing speech. The first technical paper to appear on speech recognition was published in 1952. It described Bell Labs' spoken digit recognizer Audrey (Davis et al., 1952). Research on speech recognition has since intensified, and speech recognizers for communicating with machines through speech have recently been constructed, although they remain only of limited use. Conversation with machines can be actualized by the combination of a speech recognizer and a speech synthesizer. This combination is expected to be particularly efficient and effective for data input since errors can be confirmed by hearing and then corrected promptly.

Similar to speech synthesizers, speech recognition features four specific advantages:

1. Speech input is easy to perform because it does not require a specialized skill as does typing or pushbutton operations.
2. Speech can be used to input information three to four times faster than typewriters and 8 to 10 times faster than handwriting.
3. Information can be input even when the user is moving or doing other activities involving the hands, legs, eyes, or ears.
4. Since a microphone or telephone can be used as an input terminal, inputting information is economical, with remote inputting capable of being accomplished over existing telephone networks.

Regardless of these positive points, however, speech recognition also has the same disadvantages as does speech synthesis. These include the facts that the input or conversation is not printed, and that noise canceling is necessary when used in a noisy environment.

In typical speech recognition systems, the input speech is compared with stored reference templates of phonemes or words, and the most similar reference template is selected as a candidate phoneme or word of input speech. Since speech waveforms are too complicated to compare, and since phase components which vary according to transmission and recording systems little affect human speech perception, it is desirable to remove the phase components from the speech wave. Therefore, short-time spectral density is usually extracted at short intervals and used for comparison with the reference templates.

### 8.1.2 Difficulties in Speech Recognition

Difficulties in speech recognition can be summarized as follows.

1. Coarticulation and reduction problems

The spectrum of a phoneme in a word or sentence is influenced by neighboring phonemes in consequence of coarticulation. Such a spectrum is very different from those of isolated phonemes or syllables, since articulatory organs do not move as much in continuous speech as in isolated utterances. Although this problem can be avoided in the case of isolated word recognition by using words as the reference templates, how best to cope with this problem is very important in continuous speech recognition. With continuous speech, the difficulty is compounded by elision, where the speaker runs words together and "swallows" most of the syllables.

2. Difficulties in segmentation

Spectra continuously change from phoneme to phoneme due to their mutual interaction. Since the spectral sequence of speech can essentially be compared to a string of handwritten letters, it is very difficult to precisely determine the phoneme boundaries which segment the time function of spectral envelopes. Although unvoiced consonants can be segmented relatively easily based on the amount of spectral variation and the onset and offset of periodicity, attempting to segment a succession of voiced sounds is particularly burdensome. Furthermore, it is almost impossible to segment a sentence of speech into words merely based on their acoustic features.

3. Individuality and other variation problems

Acoustic features vary from speaker to speaker, even when the same words are uttered, according to differences in manner of speaking and articulatory organs. To complicate matters, different phonemes spoken by different speakers often have the same spectrum. Transmission systems or noise also affect the physical characteristics of speech.

4. Insufficient linguistic knowledge

The physical features of speech do not always convey enough phonetic information in and of themselves. Sentence speech is usually uttered with an unconscious use of linguistic knowledge, such as syntactic and semantic constraints, and is perceived in a similar way. The listener can usually predict the next word according to several linguistic constraints, and incomplete phonetic information is compensated for by such linguistic knowledge.

### 8.1.3 Classification of Speech Recognition

Speech recognition can be classified as shown in Table 8.1 into isolated word recognition, in which words uttered in isolation are recognized, and continuous speech recognition, in which continuously uttered sentences are recognized. Continuous speech recognition can be further classified into connected word recognition and conversational speech recognition. The former recognizes a relatively small vocabulary aiming at recognizing each word correctly. The latter recognizes a relatively large vocabulary, on the other hand, but focuses on understanding the meaning of sentences rather than on recognizing each word. In conversational speech recognition, also called speech understanding, it is very important to use sophisticated linguistic knowledge.

TABLE 8.1 Classification of Speech Recognition Methods

| Object | Speaker dependency | |
|---|---|---|
| | Speaker-dependent | Speaker-independent |
| Isolated word recognition | X | X |
| Continuous speech recognition | | |
| { Connected word recognition | X | X |
| { Conversationl speech recognition (Speech understanding) | | |

X = Commercialized

Applying rules of grammar, which govern the sequence of words in a sentence, is but one example of this.

Speech recognition can also be classified from different points of view into speaker-independent recognition and speaker-dependent recognition. The former system can recognize speech uttered by any speaker, whereas, in the latter case, reference templates must be modified every time the speaker changes. Since speaker-independent recognition is much more difficult than speaker-dependent recognition, the former has been commercialized only for isolated word recognition, as shown in Table 8.1. It is of particular importance to develop speaker-independent recognition methods in order to broaden the range of possible uses.

Various units of reference templates from phonemes to words have been studied. When words are used as references, the digitized input signal is compared with each of the system's stored templates, i.e., sequences of values corresponding to the spectral pattern of a word, until one is found that matches. Conversely, phoneme-based algorithms analyze the input into a string of sounds that they convert to words through a pronunciation-based dictionary.

When words are used as references, word recognition can be expected to be highly accurate since the coarticulation problem can be avoided. A larger vocabulary requires a larger memory and more computation, however, making training troublesome. Additionally, the word references cannot solve the coarticulation problem arising within and between words in continuous speech recognition. Using phonemes as references does not greatly increase memory size requirements, on the other hand, nor the amount of computation as a function of vocabulary size. Furthermore, training can be performed efficiently. Moreover, coarticulation within and between words can be adequately taken into consideration. Since coarticulation rules have not yet been established, however, context-dependent multiple-phoneme reference templates are necessary. Additionally, phoneme-based recognition presents difficulty in that phoneme recognition error and segmentation error tend to lower overall recognition accuracy.

The most appropriate units for enabling recognition success depend on the type of recognition, that is, on whether it is isolated word recognition or continuous speech recognition, and on the size of the vocabulary. Along these lines, medium-size units between words and phonemes, such as CV syllables, VCV syllables, diphones, dyads, and demisyllables, have also been explored in order to overcome the disadvantages of using either words or phonemes.

With these smaller-than-word units, it is desirable to select more than one candidate in the unit recognition stage to form lattices and to transfer these candidates with their similarity values to the next stage of the recognition system. This method will help minimize the occurrence of serious errors at higher stages due to matching errors with these units and segmentation errors involved in the lower stages.

## 8.2 SPEECH PERIOD DETECTION

Detection of the speech period is the first stage of speech recognition. This is a particularly important stage because it is difficult to detect the speech period correctly in noisy surroundings and because a detection error ususally results in a serious recognition error. Consonants at the beginning or end of a speech period and low energy vowels are especially difficult to detect. Additional noise such as breath noise at the end of a speech period must also be ignored.

A speech period is usually detected by the fact that the short-time averaged energy level exceeds a threshold for longer than a predetermined period. The beginning point of a speech period is often determined as being a position which is a certain period prior to the position detected by the energy threshold. The energy level is often compared with two kinds of thresholds to make a reliable detection decision. In addition to the energy level, the zero-crossing number or the spectral difference between input signal and reference noise spectrum is often used for speech period detection.

Along with stationary noise which can be distinguished from the speech period using the above-mentioned methods, nonspeech sounds, such as coughing, the sound of turning pages, and even sounds uttered subconsciously when thinking or suddenly adjusting a sentence in midspeech, should be distinguishable from the actual speech. When the vocabulary is large, and the system must work speaker-independently, it is very troublesome to distinguish between speech and nonspeech sounds. Because this distinction is itself considered to be a speech recognition process, it is almost impossible to develop a perfect algorithm for determining it. Research on word spotting, specifically, the automatic detection of predetermined words from arbitrary continuous sentence speech, is expected to open the door to solving this problem.

Besides speech period detection, voiced/unvoiced decision is also important. Although ascertaining the presence of vocal cord vibration, that is, the existence of a periodic wave, is most reliable, this method requires a large amount of computation. Therefore, the energy ratio of high- to low-frequency ranges, such as the range higher than 3 kHz and that lower than 1 kHz, and similar measures are often used. When these methods are employed, it is necessary to normalize the effects of individuality and transmission characteristics to arrive at a reliable decision. Along these lines, a pattern recognition approach combining various parameters, such as autocorrelation coefficients, has also been attempted as previously mentioned (see Sec. 4.7).

## 8.3 SPECTRAL DISTANCE MEASURES

### 8.3.1 Distance Measures Used in Speech Recognition

As described before, in almost all speech recognition systems, short-time spectral distances or similarities between input speech and reference templates are calculated as the basis for the recognition decision. Spectral analysis is usually performed with one of five methods (see Sec. 4.2):

1. Using band-pass filter outputs for 10 to 30 channels
2. Calculating the spectrum directly from the speech wave using FFT
3. Employing cepstral coefficients

4. Utilizing an autocorrelation function
5. Deriving a spectral envelope from LPC analysis (maximum likelihood estimation)

Various distance (similarity) measures can be defined based on multivariate vectors representing short-time spectra which are obtained through these spectral analysis techniques. It is desirable that the distance measure d(x,y) between two vectors x and y satisfies the following equations for effective use in speech recognition:

(a) Symmetry: $$d(x,y) = d(y,x) \tag{8.1}$$

(b) Positive definiteness:
$$d(x,y) > 0, \quad x \neq y$$
$$d(x,y) = 0, \quad x = y \tag{8.2}$$

If d(x,y) is a distance in the mathematical sense of the word, it should satisfy the triangle inequality. This condition is not necessary in speech recognition, however, and it is more important to formulate algorithms for calculating d(x,y) efficiently.

Although the simple Euclidean distance is used in many cases for d(x,y), several modifications have also been tried. Among these are weighted distances based on auditory sensitivity and the distances in reduced multidimensional spaces obtained through statistical analyses of discriminant analysis or principal component analysis. Formant frequencies, which are important features for representing speech characteristics, have rarely been used in the most recent spectral distance-based speech recognition because they are very difficult to extract automatically.

### 8.3.2 Distances Based on Nonparametric Spectral Analysis

The following methods have been specifically investigated for obtaining spectral distances based on general spectral analysis techniques which do not incorporate modeling speech production mechanisms.

1. Band-pass filter bank method

Band-pass filter banks have been used for many years and are still being employed because of the ease with which hardware for real-time analysis purposes can be realized. Center frequencies of band-pass filters are usually set with equal spaces along the logarithmic frequency scale. Differences of logarithmic output for each band-pass filter between reference and input speech are averaged (summed) over all frequency ranges or averaged for their squared values to produce the overall distance.

2. FFT method

Although it is possible to directly calculate the distance between spectra obtained by FFT, spectral patterns smoothed by cepstral coefficients or window functions in the autocorrelation domain are usually used. This is because the spectral fine structure varies according to pitch, voice individuality, and many other factors. The spectral values obtained at equal intervals on a linear frequency axis are usually resampled with equal spaces on a logarithmic frequency scale taking the auditory characteristics into consideration. Equal space resampling on a Bark-scale or a Mel-scale frequency axis has also been introduced in an effort to simulate the auditory characteristics more precisely.

The Bark scale, which is based on the auditory critical bandwidth, corresponds to the frequency scale on the basilar membrane in the peripheral auditory system. It is defined as

$$B = 13 \arctan(0.76f) + 3.5 \arctan\left(\frac{f}{7.5}\right)^2 \tag{8.3}$$

where B and f represent the Bark scale and frequency in kilohertz.

The Mel scale corresponds to the auditory sensation of tone height. The relationship between frequency f in kilohertz and the Mel scale Mel is usually approximated by the equation

$$\text{Mel} = 1000 \log_2(1 + f) \tag{8.4}$$

The Bark and Mel scales are nearly proportional to the logarithmic frequency scale in the frequency range above 1 kHz.

3. Cepstrum method

It is clear from the definition of cepstral coefficients that the Euclidean distance between vectors consisting of lower-order cepstral coefficients corresponds to the distance between smoothed logarithmic spectra. Mel-cepstral coefficients transformed from the logarithmic spectrum resampled at Mel-scale frequency have also been used for this distance.

4. Autocorrelation function method

The distance between vectors consisting of the autocorrelation function multiplied by the lag window corresponds to the distance between smoothed spectra.

### 8.3.3 Distances based on LPC

Since LPC analysis has proven itself to be an excellent speech analysis method, as mentioned in Chap. 5, it is also being widely used in speech recognition. Notations of various LPC analysis-related parameters are indicated in Table 8.2, where $f(\lambda)$ and $g(\lambda)$ represent spectral envelopes based on the LPC model for a reference template and input speech, respectively. These are given as

$$f(\lambda) = \frac{1}{2\pi} \frac{u^{(f)}R^{(f)}}{\sum_{k=-p}^{p} A_k^{(f)} e^{jk\lambda}}$$

and

TABLE 8.2 Notations for LPC Analysis-Related Parameters

| Parameters | Reference template | Input speech |
|---|---|---|
| Spectral envelope | $f(\lambda)$ | $g(\lambda)$ |
| Energy | $u^{(f)}$ | $u^{(g)}$ |
| Autocorrelation coeff. | $r_j^{(f)}$ | $r_j^{(g)}$ |
| Predictor coeff. | $a_j^{(f)}$ | $a_j^{(g)}$ |
| Maximum likeihood parameter | $A_j^{(f)}$ | $A_j^{(g)}$ |
| Normalized residual | $R^{(f)}$ | $R^{(g)}$ |
| Cepstral coeff. | $c_n^{(f)}$ | $c_n^{(g)}$ |

$i = 1,\ldots,p,\ j = -p,\ldots,p$

$p$ = order of LPC model

$n = -n_0,\ldots,n_0$

$$A_j^{(\cdot)} = \sum_{i=0}^{p-j} a_i^{(\cdot)} a_{i+|j|}^{(\cdot)},\ a_0 = 1$$

$$g(\lambda) = \frac{1}{2\pi} \frac{u^{(g)}R^{(g)}}{\sum_{k=-p}^{p} A_k^{(g)} e^{jk\lambda}} \tag{8.5}$$

The following various distance measures using LPC analysis-related parameters have been proposed for determining the distance between $f(\lambda)$ and $g(\lambda)$.

1. Maximum likelihood spectral distance (Itakura-Saito distance)

Maximum likelihood spectral distance was introduced as an evaluation function for spectral envelope estimation from the short-time spectral density using the maximum likelihood method. This distance is represented by the equation (see Sec. 5.3.2)

$$E = \frac{1}{2\pi} \int_{-\pi}^{\pi} \left( \log \frac{f(\lambda)}{g(\lambda)} + \frac{g(\lambda)}{f(\lambda)} - 1 \right) d\lambda$$

$$= \log \frac{u^{(f)}R^{(f)}}{u^{(g)}R^{(g)}} + \frac{u^{(g)}}{u^{(f)}R^{(f)}} \sum_{k=-p}^{p} A_k^{(f)} r_k^{(g)} - 1 \tag{8.6}$$

This distance is also called the Itakura-Saito distance (distortion). As described in Sec. 5.3.2, by defining $d(\lambda) = \log f(\lambda) - \log g(\lambda)$ for examining the relationship between this distance and the logarithmic spectral distance, we obtain the equation

$$E = \frac{1}{2\pi} \int_{-\pi}^{\pi} (d(\lambda) + e^{-d(\lambda)} - 1)\, d\lambda \tag{8.7}$$

When the integrand of this equation is processed by Taylor expansion for $d(\lambda)$ at the region around 0,

$$d(\lambda) + e^{-d(\lambda)} - 1 = \sum_{i=2}^{\infty} \frac{1}{i!} \{-d(\lambda)\}^i \tag{8.8}$$

is derived. This means that when $|d(\lambda)|$ is small, the distance E is close to the squared logarithmic spectral distance. Equation (8.7) indicates that the integrand of this distance is in proportion to $d(\lambda)$ when $d(\lambda) \gg 0$ and in proportion to $e^{-d(\lambda)}$ when $d(\lambda) \ll 0$.

2. Log likelihood ratio distance

The log likelihood ratio distance is defined as the logarithm of the ratio of output residual energy values for input speech passing through two kinds of inverse filters. The transmission functions of these filters respectively correspond to the inverse characteristics of the spectral envelopes for the reference pattern and input speech itself. The residual energy passed through the latter inverse filter is known as the normalized residual energy or the minimum residual energy. The distance is represented by

$$H = \log \frac{\sum_{k=-p}^{p} A_k^{(f)} r_k^{(g)}}{R^{(g)}} \qquad (8.9)$$

This equation is also defined as the expression obtained by minimizing the maximum likelihood spectral distance E as a function of $u^{(f)}/u^{(g)}$, and by removing the constant.

3. Prediction residual

The prediction residual is obtained from the log likelihood ratio distance by removing the term related only to input speech. This is represented as

$$N = \sum_{k=-p}^{p} A_k^{(f)} r_k^{(g)} \qquad (8.10)$$

4. Cosh measure

The cosh measure was devised in order to remove the asymmetry associated with the weighting for the spectral difference in the maximum likelihood spectral distance E (Gray, Jr. and Markel, 1976). This measure, indicated in Eq. (8.11), is obtained by summing Eq. (8.6) and its modification in which $f(\lambda)$ and $g(\lambda)$ are inverted:

$$D = \frac{1}{2\pi} \int_{-\pi}^{\pi} 2\{\cosh(\log f(\lambda) - \log g(\lambda)) - 1\}\, d\lambda$$

$$= \frac{u^{(g)}}{u^{(f)}R^{(f)}} \sum_{k=-p}^{p} A_k^{(f)} r_k^{(g)} + \frac{u^{(f)}}{u^{(g)}R^{(g)}} \sum_{k=-p}^{p} A_k^{(g)} r_k^{(f)} - 2 \tag{8.11}$$

where, by definition,

$$\cosh(d(\lambda)) = \frac{e^{d(\lambda)} + e^{-d(\lambda)}}{2}$$

and

$$e^{d(\lambda)} = \frac{f(\lambda)}{g(\lambda)}$$

Using $d(\lambda)$, D is represented by

$$D = \frac{1}{2\pi} \int_{-\pi}^{\pi} (e^{d(\lambda)} + e^{-d(\lambda)} - 2)\, d\lambda \tag{8.12}$$

When the integrand of this equation is processed by Taylor expansion for $d(\lambda)$ at the region around 0,

$$e^{d(\lambda)} + e^{-d(\lambda)} - 2 = \sum_{i=1}^{\infty} \frac{2}{(2i)!} \{d(\lambda)\}^{2i} \tag{8.13}$$

This equation indicates that the distance D is very close to a squared logarithmic spectral distance when $|d(\lambda)|$ is small and that its integrand is proportional to the exponential function $e^{|d(\lambda)|}$ when $|d(\lambda)| \gg 0$.

5. LPC cepstral distance

The LPC cepstral distance is the distance between spectral envelopes represented by the LPC cepstral coefficients. It can be expressed as

$$L^2 = \sum_{n=-\infty}^{\infty} (c_n^{(f)} - c_n^{(g)})^2$$

$$= \left( \log \frac{u^{(f)} R^{(f)}}{u^{(g)} R^{(g)}} \right)^2 + 2 \sum_{n=1}^{\infty} (c_n^{(f)} - c_n^{(g)})^2$$

$$= \frac{1}{2\pi} \int_{-\pi}^{\pi} \{d(\lambda)\}^2 \, d\lambda \tag{8.14}$$

When this distance is actually used, the summation is truncated to $n = n_0$, such that it corresponds to that of the spectral envelopes smoothed by the cepstral coefficients. As for the relationship between the truncation order $n_0$ and the LPC analysis order p, $n_0 \geqq p$ is necessary. If $n_0 < p$, it is probable that the distance value becomes zero even between different spectra and that the positive definite characteristic of the distance measure cannot be maintained.

The LPC cepstral distance is a useful distance measure for three major reasons. First, it can be easily calculated from linear predictor coefficients, as described in Sec. 4.3.2. Second, it directly corresponds to the logarithmic distance between LPC spectral envelopes. Third, it satisfies the requirements for symmetry and the positive definite characteristic.

The weightings for $d(\lambda)$ in distance measures of E, D, and $L^2$ are compared in Fig. 8.1.

### 8.3.4 Peak-Weighted Distances Based on LPC Analysis

The peak-weighted distance measures based on LPC analysis techniques are produced by modifying the various LPC-based distance measures, thereby emphasizing the spectral differences at the peaks (Sugiyama and Shikano, 1981). That is, these distance measures are sensitive to discrepancies in spectral peaks such as formants where important information for speech recognition exists. This modification is accomplished by multiplying the integrand $U(\lambda)$ of the original distance measure by a weighting function $w(\lambda)$ emphasizing the spectral peaks before integration over all frequency ranges, as

$$P = \frac{1}{2\pi} \int_{-\pi}^{\pi} U(\lambda) w(\lambda) \, d\lambda \tag{8.15}$$

Experimental evaluation of various combinations of U and w, in terms of ease of computation, amount of weighting, and accuracy of recognizing phonemes in continuous speech, revealed

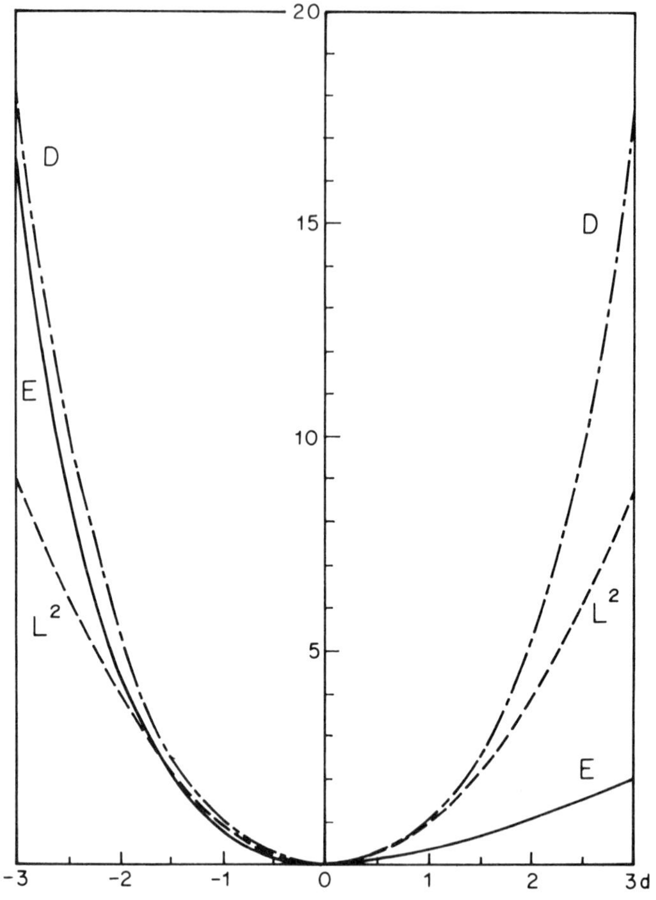


Fig. 8.1 Weighting factors for logarithmic spectral distance d($\lambda$) in maximum likelihood spectral distance E, cosh measure D, and cepstral distance $L^2$.

that using the WLR (weighted likelihood ratio) is better than any other measure (Sugiyama and Shikano, 1981). The WLR is calculated by

$$\mathrm{WLR} = \frac{1}{2\pi}\int_{-\pi}^{\pi}\left\{\left(\log\frac{f(\lambda)}{g(\lambda)} + \frac{g(\lambda)}{f(\lambda)} - 1\right)\frac{f(\lambda)}{u^{(f)}} + \left(\log\frac{g(\lambda)}{f(\lambda)} + \frac{f(\lambda)}{g(\lambda)} - 1\right)\frac{g(\lambda)}{u^{(g)}}\right\} d\lambda$$

$$= 2\sum_{n=1}^{\infty}\left(r_n^{(f)} - r_n^{(g)}\right)\left(c_n^{(f)} - c_n^{(g)}\right) \qquad (8.16)$$

In this measure, the integrand of the maximum likelihood spectral distance E is used as $U(\lambda)$, $f(\lambda)/u^{(f)}$ and $g(\lambda)/u^{(g)}$ are used as $w(\lambda)$, and the equation is modified so that the LPC parameters can be used directly. Weighting around the spectral peaks necessitates that spectral tilt in $f(\lambda)$ and $g(\lambda)$ be removed beforehand. Summation in Eq. (8.16) is truncated to the appropriate order $n_0$. Concerning the relationship between $n_0$ and the LPC analysis order p, $n_0 \geqq p$ must be satisfied.

The LPC correlation coefficients obtained using recursive equations for linear predictor coefficients based on Eq. (5.67) in Sec. 5.9.3 are used on orders larger than p. Although both correlation coefficients and LPC cepstral coefficients are necessary for calculating the WLR, the total amount of computation is almost the same as various conventional distance measures based on LPC analysis.

Weighting functions along the frequency axis can also be included in $w(\lambda)$ of Eq. (8.15). Recognition experiments for vowels in continuous speech confirmed that second-order filters with a peak around 1 kHz are effective in improving accuracy (Sugiyama and Shikano, 1982). It has also been empirically confirmed that the WLR is more effective than any other distance measure for large-vocabulary word recognition and speaker-independent word recognition (Sugiyama and Shikano, 1983). Another report importantly notes that the effectiveness of the WLR depends on the language spoken (Nocerino et al., 1985).

### 8.3.5 Weighted Cepstral Distance

A weighted cepstral distance measure was proposed and tested in a speaker-independent isolated word recognition system using word-based reference templates and a standard dynamic time warping (DTW) technique, described in Sec. 8.5.1 (Tohkura, 1986). The measure is a statistically weighted distance measure with weights equal to the inverse variance of the cepstral coefficients such that

$$d_{WCEP} = \sum_{n=1}^{p} w_n (c_n^{(f)} - c_n^{(g)})^2 \tag{8.17}$$

where $w_i$ is the inverse variance of the ith cepstral coefficient. Figure 8.2 presents experimentally observed cepstral coefficient variances and inverse variances.

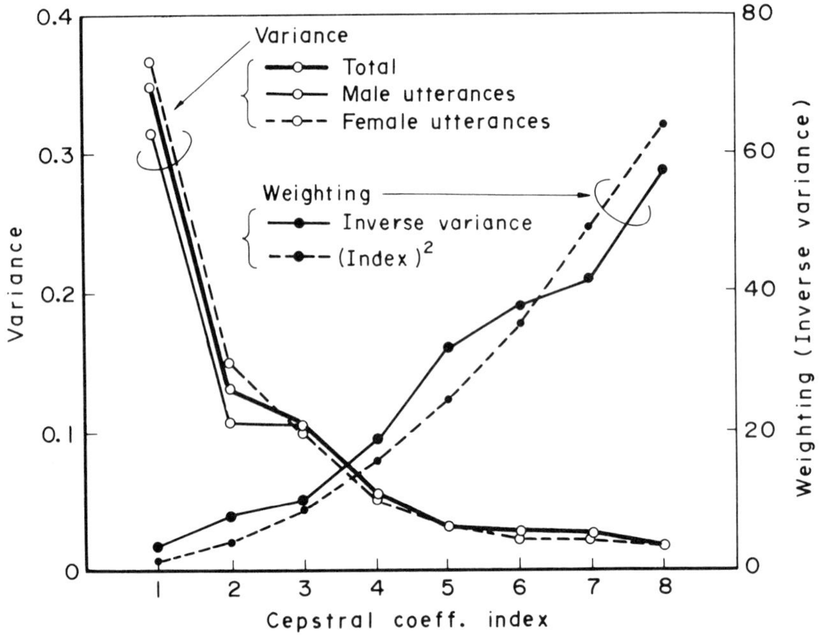


Fig. 8.2 Cepstral coefficient variances and inverse variances used as weighting in a weighted cepstral distance measure. Weighting for quefrency-weighted cepstral distance measure is also indicated.

Experimental results indicate that the weighted cepstral distance measure works substantially better than both the Euclidean cepstral distance and log likelihood ratio distance measures across two different databases, namely a 10-digit database and a 129-word airline vocabulary.

The most significant performance characteristic of the weighted cepstral distance is that it tends to equalize the performance of the recognizer across different talkers. Improvement due to weighting can be attributed to the fact that it deweights the lower-order cepstral coefficients rather than weights the higher-order cepstral coefficients. The results also demonstrate that when the number of cepstral coefficients is larger than 8, it is necessary to use some of the band-pass lifters (see Sec. 4.3.1) to reduce the weighting for higher-order cepstral coefficients.

The quefrency-weighted cepstral distance measure, which is another form of the weighted distance measure, has also been proposed (Paliwal, 1982). In this measure, $w_n = n^2$, namely, each cepstral coefficient is multiplied by its respective quefrency. Figure 8.2 also shows the weighting factor for this measure. Clearly, we find some similarity between $n^2$ and the inverse variance. The quefrency-weighted cepstral distance measure works well, and the error rate using this measure is only slightly larger than that obtained by using the inverse variance-weighted cepstral distance measure. The quefrency-weighted cepstral distance is equal to the weighted slope metric (Klatt, 1982), as follows:

$$
\begin{aligned}
d_{QCEP} &= \sum_{n=-\infty}^{\infty} n^2 (c_n^{(f)} - c_n^{(g)})^2 \\
&= \frac{1}{2\pi} \int_{-\pi}^{\pi} \left| \frac{\partial \log f(\lambda)}{\partial \lambda} - \frac{\partial \log g(\lambda)}{\partial \lambda} \right|^2 d\lambda \qquad (8.18)
\end{aligned}
$$

Summation in this equation is also truncated to the appropriate order, and some of the band-pass lifters are applied to higher-order cepstral coefficients.

### 8.3.6 Transitional Cepstral Distance

Dynamic spectral features (spectral transition) as well as instantaneous spectral features are believed to play an important role in human speech perception (Furui, 1986b). Based on this knowledge, a transitional cepstral measure was proposed (Furui, 1986a). Initially, spoken utterances are represented by time sequences of cepstral coefficients and logarithmic energy. Regression coefficients (or lower-order polynomial expansion coefficients) for these time functions are extracted for every frame t over an approximately 50-ms period ((t − K)th frame to (t + K)th frame). The regression coefficient for each cepstral coefficient, which gives a reliable estimation of the time derivative of the cepstrum time series (more specifically, the spectral slope in time), is represented as

$$\frac{\partial c_n(t)}{\partial t} \simeq \Delta c_n(t) = \frac{\sum_{k=-K}^{K} k h_k c_n(t+k)}{\sum_{k=-K}^{K} k^2 h_k} \tag{8.19}$$

Here, $h_k$ is a window (usually symmetric) of length 2K + 1 and is sometimes set to a unit value for simplicity.

A weighted Euclidean distance between two given transitional spectra is defined as

$$d_{\Delta CEP} = \sum_{n=1}^{p} w_n(\Delta c_n^{(f)} - \Delta c_n^{(g)})^2 \tag{8.20}$$

where the weighting coefficient $w_n$ is inversely proportional to the pooled variance of $\Delta c_n$. $w_n$ is sometimes also set to a unit value for simplicity. Transitional logarithmic energy, $\Delta u$, and its distance are defined in the same way. The transitional and instantaneous distances are usually linearly combined as

$$\begin{aligned} d_{CEP+\Delta CEP+\Delta ENERGY} = &\sum_{n=1}^{p} w_{1n}(c_n^{(f)} - c_n^{(g)})^2 \\ &+ \sum_{n=1}^{p} w_{2n}(\Delta c_n^{(f)} - \Delta c_n^{(g)})^2 \\ &+ w_3(\Delta u^{(f)} - \Delta u^{(g)})^2 \end{aligned} \tag{8.21}$$

where $w_{1n}$, $w_{2n}$, and $w_3$ are weighting coefficients.

The effectiveness of the transitional distance measure was confirmed by speaker-independent isolated word recognition (Furui, 1986a) and speaker identification (Soong and Rosenberg, 1986). The error rate for recognizing 100 Japanese city names was reduced from 6.2 to 2.4% by using the transitional cepstrum and energy in addition to the instantaneous cepstrum. This measure is advantageous in that its performance capability is resistant to transmission channel variations.

## 8.4 STRUCTURE OF WORD RECOGNITION SYSTEMS

The structures of isolated word recognition systems can be classified into two types, as shown in Fig. 8.3: systems using word

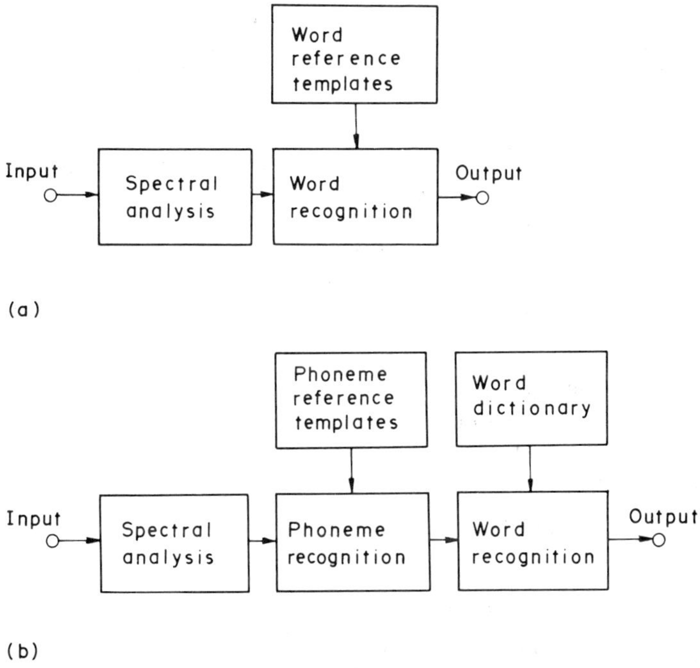


Fig. 8.3 Structure of word recognition systems: (a) word-based recognition; (b) phoneme-based recognition.

templates (a), and systems using reference templates smaller than words, such as phonemes or syllables, and a word dictionary (b). The word dictionary represents each word by a concatenation of phonemes or syllables.

With a word-template structure, input speech is compared with each word reference template, and the reference template with the smallest distance from the input speech is selected. With a phoneme- or syllable-template structure, on the other hand, short periods of input speech are compared with the phoneme or syllable reference templates to calculate the distances. The distances and word dictionary are then combined to make the decision.

With structure (b), therefore, the amount of distance calculation does not depend on the size of the vocabulary, and the memory size for string reference templates (word dictionary) and the amount of computation increases less than with structure (a) as the vocabulary increases. Structure (b) additionally features two other advantages. One is that the vocabulary can be easily increased or changed by rewriting the word dictionary. The other is that several types of pronunciation variations, such as vowel devocalization, can be manually added to the word dictionary based on the spelling of each word.

Representing each word by a concatenation of phonemes or syllables corresponds to a very rough quantization of spectral space, and it produces a large information loss. The system should thus incorporate a structure in which recognition errors in some phonemes and syllables are prevented from causing serious word recognition errors, as was described in Sec. 8.1.

Generally, structure (a) is better suited to a smaller vocabulary and (b) to a larger vocabulary. To effectively reduce the memory size and the amount of computation necessary with structure (a), nonuniform sampling has been attempted, in which the spectral transition is precisely sampled and the stationary part is roughly sampled (Fujisaki et al., 1977).

## 8.5 DYNAMIC TIME WARPING

### 8.5.1 DP Matching

Even if the same speaker utters the same word, the duration changes every time with nonlinear expansion and contraction. Therefore, with both structures (a) and (b) outlined in Sec. 8.4, DTW is essential at the word recognition stage. The DTW process nonlinearly expands or contracts the time axis to match the same phoneme positions between the input speech and reference templates.

This process can be efficiently accomplished by using the dynamic programming (DP) technique (Bellman, 1957), which will be described later. The DP technique was first applied to the DTW of speech by Slutsker (1968), Vintsyuk (1968), and Velichko and Zagoruyko (1970) of the USSR. A parallel investigation of this technique was conducted independently by Sakoe and Chiba (1971) of Japan. Results of these studies were published at almost the same time. This technique has had a very large impact on speech recognition, actually becoming an essential and widely applicable technique.

In exploring the DP technique, let us assume two time sequences for feature vectors which should be compared as

$$A = a_1, a_2, \ldots, a_I \quad \text{and} \quad B = b_1, b_2, \ldots, b_J \tag{8.22}$$

When we consider a plane spanned by A and B as shown in Fig. 8.4, the time warping function indicating the correspondence

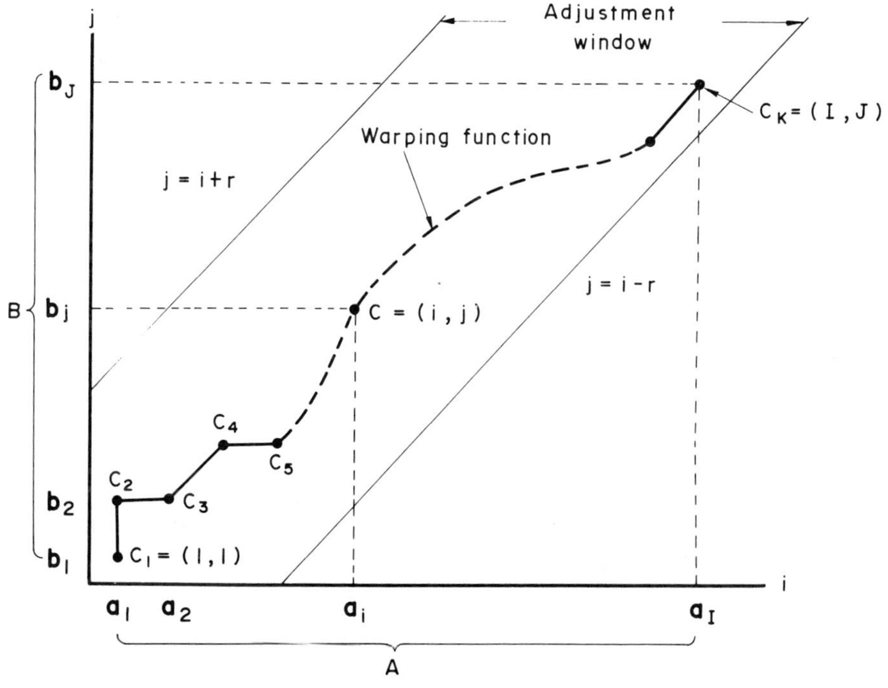


Fig. 8.4 DTW between two time sequences, A and B.

between the time axes of A and B sequences can be represented by a sequence of lattice points on the plane, $c = (i,j)$, as

$$F = c_1, c_2, \ldots, c_k, \ldots, c_K, \qquad c_k = (i_k, j_k) \tag{8.23}$$

When the spectral distance between two feature vectors $a_i$ and $b_j$ is represented by $d(c) = d(i,j)$, the sum of the distances from beginning to end of the sequences along F can be represented by

$$D(F) = \frac{\sum_{k=1}^{K} d(c_k) w_k}{\sum_{k=1}^{K} w_k} \tag{8.24}$$

The smaller this value is, the better is the match between A and B. Here, $w_k$ is a positive weighting function related to F.

Let us minimize Eq. (8.24) concerning F under the following conditions.

1. Monotony and continuity condition

$$0 \leqq i_k - i_{k-1} \leqq 1, \qquad 0 \leqq j_k - j_{k-1} \leqq 1 \tag{8.25}$$

2. Boundary condition

$$i_1 = j_1 = 1, \qquad i_K = I, \quad j_K = J \tag{8.26}$$

3. Adjustment window condition

$$|i_k - j_k| \leqq r, \qquad r = \text{constant} \tag{8.27}$$

Condition 3 is applied to prevent extreme expansion and contraction. Defining $w_k$ so that the denominator of Eq. (8.24) becomes constant independent of F simplifies the equation. For example, if $w_k = (i_k - i_{k-1}) + (j_k - j_{k-1})$ $(i_0 = j_0 = 0)$, $w_k$ becomes the city block distance, and

$$\sum_{k=1}^{K} w_k = I + J \tag{8.28}$$

Equation (8.24) then becomes

$$D(F) = \frac{1}{I + J} \sum_{k=1}^{K} d(c_k)w_k \tag{8.29}$$

Since the objective function to be minimized becomes additive, minimization can be efficiently solved without exhaustively examining all possibilities for F. Summation over a partial sequence of $c_1, c_2, \ldots, c_k$ ($c_k = (i,j)$) is

$$\begin{aligned} g(c_k) = g(i,j) &= \min_{c_1,\ldots,c_{k-1}} \left[ \sum_{m=1}^{k} d(c_m)w_m \right] \\ &= \min_{c_1,\ldots,c_{k-1}} \left[ \sum_{m=1}^{k-1} d(c_m)w_m + d(c_k)w_k \right] \\ &= \min_{c_{k-1}} \left[ \min_{c_1,\ldots,c_{k-2}} \left\{ \sum_{m=1}^{k-1} d(c_m)w_m \right\} + d(c_k)w_k \right] \\ &= \min_{c_{k-1}} \left[ g(c_{k-1}) + d(c_k)w_k \right] \end{aligned} \tag{8.30}$$

The above expresses the derivation of DP. Using all three conditions for F and the above-mentioned formulation of $w_k$, Eq. (8.30) can be rewritten as

$$g(i,j) = \min \begin{pmatrix} g(i,j-1) + d(i,j) \\ g(i-1,j-1) + 2d(i,j) \\ g(i-1,j) + d(i,j) \end{pmatrix} \tag{8.31}$$

Therefore, the distance between the two time sequences of A and B after DTW can be obtained as follows. First, let us set the initial conditions to $g(1,1) = 2d(1,1)$ and $j = 1$, and calculate Eq. (8.31) by varying i within the adjustment window. This calculation is iterated by increasing j until $j = J$. The overall distance between the two sequences is then obtained as $g(I,J)/(I + J)$. This method is called DP matching, meaning DTW employing the DP technique. The warping function F is sometimes called the DP path. When similarity instead of distance is used as d, it becomes a maximization problem which can be solved by the same formulation.

### 8.5.2 Variations in DP Matching

Various restrictions for the warping function F and various formulations of $w_k$ have been proposed and evaluated by recognition experiments. Good performance was confirmed for F and $w_k$, both symmetrical to the two time sequences, and for the slope constraint indicated in Fig. 8.5(a), which restricts the local slope between $\frac{1}{2}$ and 2 (Sakoe and Chiba, 1978). Speaker-dependent word recognition experiments for 50 Japanese city names uttered by four male and female speakers indicated that the error rate under the above-mentioned conditions for DP matching was 0.8%, whereas that for linear warping was 5.9%.

Asymmetrical DP matching is advantageous in that the number of summations depends only on the input or reference time sequence, and in that the number of summations is almost half that of the symmetrical method. Hence, the slope constraint indicated in Fig. 8.5(b) restricting the slope to between $\frac{1}{2}$ and 2, which is similar to (a), is also frequently used (Itakura, 1975).

Other modifications of DP matching include unconstrained endpoint DP matching, which was proposed as a means of coping with the variation in detected endpoint positions, and staggered array DP matching capable of performing unconstrained endpoint

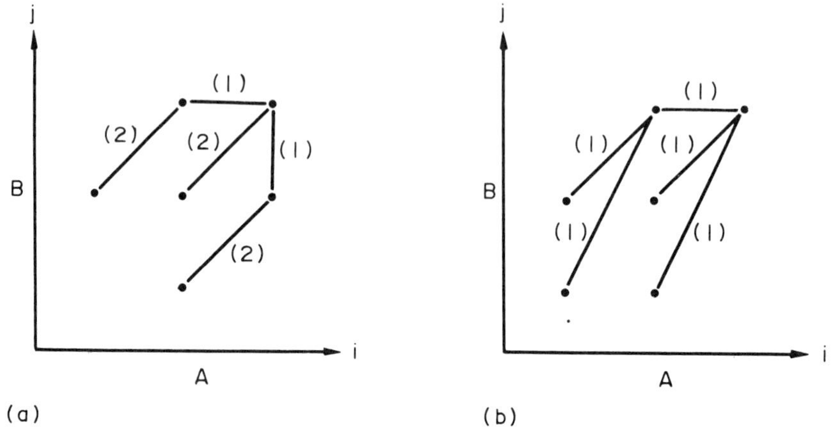


Fig. 8.5 Slope constraint restricting local slope between $\frac{1}{2}$ and 2, where ( ) indicates weighting function $w_k$: (a) symmetrical type; (b) asymmetrical type.

matching with reduced calculations. The staggered array DP matching method will be described in the next section.

The unconstrained endpoint method removes the boundary condition that the beginnings and endings of the two time sequences must be matched together, and allows for matching within a certain endpoint region. This method is free from speech period detection error and makes possible the true speech period being conversely determined according to the DP matching results. Although either the input or reference time sequence (A in Fig. 8.5(b)) can be matched to any part of the other time sequence in the asymmetrical method, unconstrained endpoint matching can be principally performed only at the final position of both time sequences in the symmetrical method. For the approximate realization of the unconstrained endpoint method at the initial position, a modified symmetrical method has also been proposed in which a special slope constraint was given to the initial area (Sugiyama and Shikano, 1983).

### 8.5.3 Staggered Array DP Matching

The staggered array DP matching method realizes complete symmetrical unconstrained endpoint matching and reduces the amount of computation by thinning out the lattice points in a plane spanned by two time sequences (Shikano and Aikawa, 1982). In this method, iterative computation for DP matching is only performed at every third point along the diagonal axis, as indicated by the symbol ⊙ in Fig. 8.6(a), and the warping function is constrained as shown in Fig. 8.6(b). The amount of computation thus necessary is one-third of that using the method outlined in Fig. 8.5(a). Accumulated distance values are compensated for by the distance values at neighboring points (indicated by the symbol · in the figure). Hence, precision is maintained in spite of thinning out the accumulation points.

Actual iteration is performed at the points (i,j), which satisfy

$$i + j = 3m + 2 \qquad \left( m = 0,1,2,\ldots,m_{max}; \quad m_{max} = \mathrm{int}\left[\frac{I + J - 2}{3}\right]\right) \tag{8.32}$$

within the allowable region of the warping function path for successive values of m. Here, int[x] is the integral number calculation. The intermediate accumulated value g(i,j) is stored in a

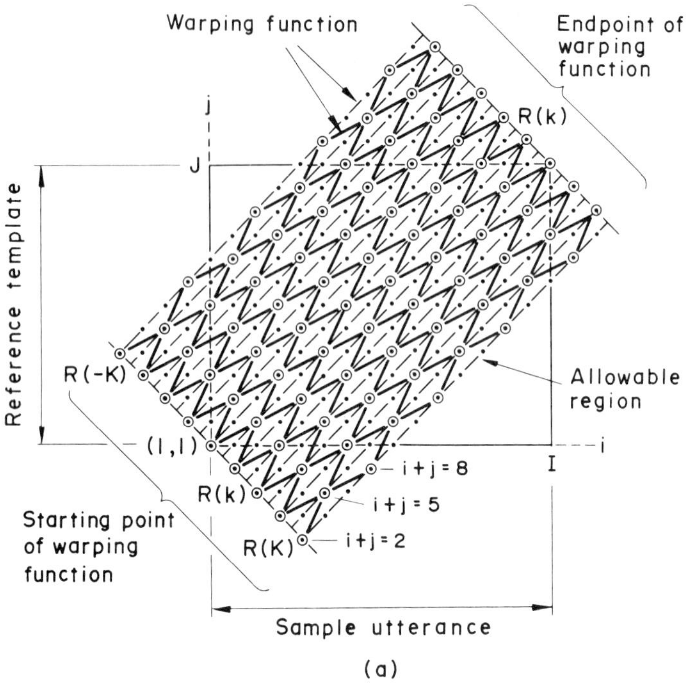


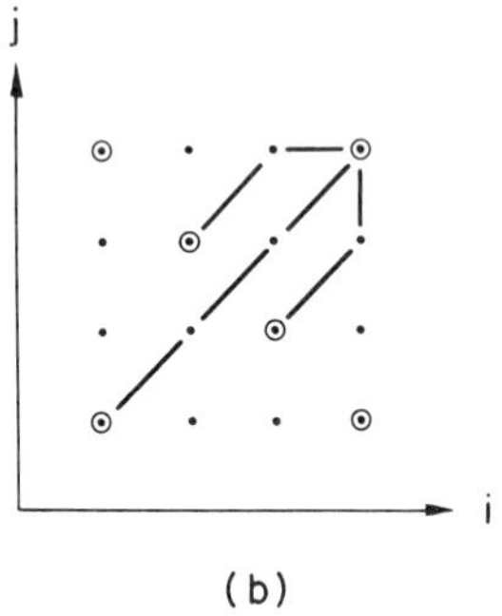


Fig. 8.6 DTW function (a) and its slope constraint (b) in staggared array DP matching.

register, $R(k) = R(i - j)$, as indicated in Fig. 8.6(a). When slope constraining and distance compensation are performed as shown in Fig. 8.6(b), the DP matching calculation is performed in the following way:

$$R(k) = \min \begin{pmatrix} R(k-1) + d(i-1,j) + d(i,j) \\ R(k) + \frac{4}{3}\{d(i,j) + d(i-1,j-1) + d(i-2,j-2)\} \\ R(k+1) + d(i,j-1) + d(i,j) \end{pmatrix} \tag{8.33}$$

Since the iterative process is performed by renewing the contents of the register $R(k)$, the memory capacity for DP matching is also less than with conventional symmetrical methods.

The unconstrained endpoint condition at both the beginning and end of the utterance is provided by using the spectral values before and after the speech period, that is, the frames before $a_1$ and $b_1$ and those after $a_I$ and $b_J$. The overall distance accumulated along the optimum warping function F is obtained by

$$D(F) = \frac{1}{I+J}\left\{ \min_{\substack{(i,j) \in i+j=I+J \\ k=i-j}} R(k) \right\} \tag{8.34}$$

Word recognition experiments indicated that a higher recognition accuracy than is possible with conventional pseudounconstrained endpoint methods can be obtained through this method. Various modifications of this method involving changing the thinned-out points or the points included in distance accumulation have also been investigated (Shikano and Aikawa, 1982).

## 8.6 WORD RECOGNITION USING PHONEME UNITS

### 8.6.1 Principal Structure

A typical example of the phoneme-based word recognition system derived from the method indicated in Fig. 8.3(b) is shown in Fig. 8.7 (Kohda et al., 1972; Furui, 1980). In this system, phonemes are not determined at the phoneme recognition stage, but similarity or distance values between each frame of input speech and each phoneme reference template are used for matching with the word dictionary. When the number of phoneme reference templates is increased so that various modifications are included as different templates, this method approaches that indicated in Fig. 8.3(a) using word templates. Importantly, this

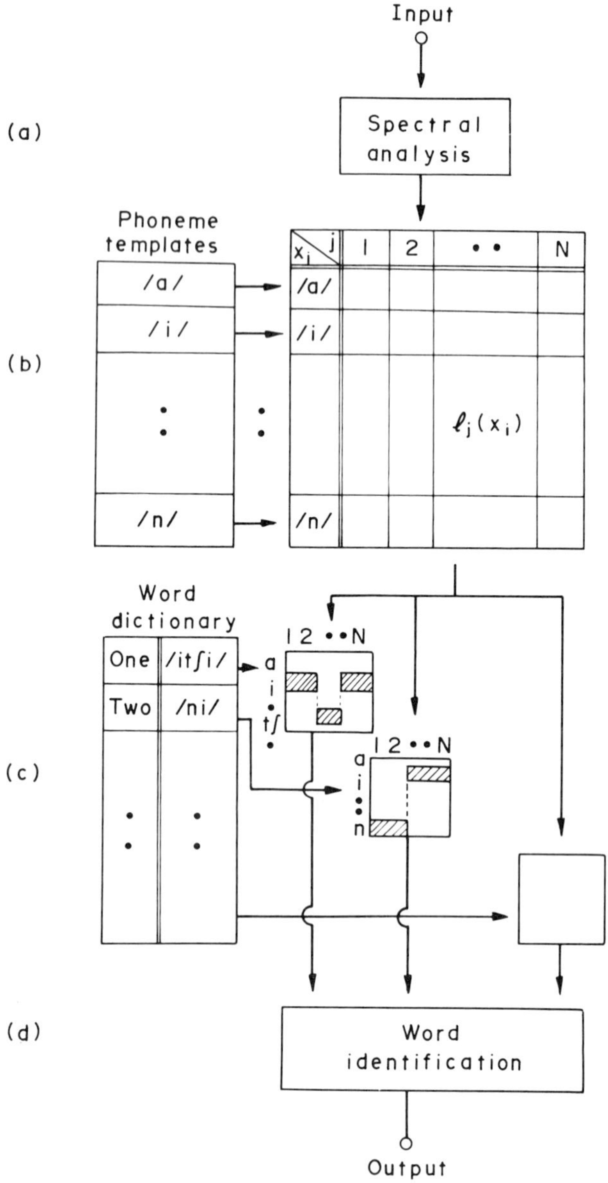


Fig. 8.7 Block diagram of phoneme-based word recognition system using phoneme reference templates and word dictionary: (a) spectral analysis; (b) computation of log likelihood matrix; (c) DTW and computation of total likelihood between each candidate word and input speech; (d) word identification.

means that the method using phoneme templates has a wide range of variations.

In the first stage of constructing the word recognition system, phoneme reference templates are created according to the size and content of the vocabulary. Each word is then represented by a sequence of phoneme reference templates and stored in the word dictionary. The number of phoneme reference templates in the system used to recognize 67 Japanese airport names is, for example, 44, including vowels, consonants, and several transitional templates. Plural templates are prepared for several phonemes to ensure that the variation due to coarticulation and devocalization can be adequately handled. In order to prevent an increase in the number of templates, a neutral pattern is commonly used for several phonemes considered unimportant for distinguishing words. Along with the sequence of phoneme labels, the upper and lower limits for the duration of each phoneme, and the presence and location of periods of silence in the word are stored for each word in the word dictionary.

When an unknown utterance is input into the system, the similarity between input speech and each phoneme reference template is calculated every 15-ms frame period. This is measured using the (relative) logarithmic likelihood ratio, that is, the negative value of the logarithmic prediction residual. All similarity values except those for silent periods are stored as a similarity matrix. The similarity matrix, word dictionary, and existence and location of the silence periods are subsequently used for word recognition. This is performed by DP matching between input speech and the phoneme reference template sequence of each word. Accumulated similarity between input speech and each word can be easily calculated using elements of the similarity matrix.

In the word dictionary, plural phoneme sequences are prepared for several words in order to cope with spectral variation due to devocalization and individual differences in the manner of pronunciation. Although the word dictionary is generally speaker-independent, phoneme reference templates need to be adjusted to each speaker using training utterances. Unlike recognition systems using word templates, however, the training utterances do not need to include all vocabulary words. In fact, spectral patterns averaged over all speech periods of each phoneme in training utterances are calculated and stored as a phoneme reference template. Each of the phoneme periods in the training utterances can be automatically determined by the DP matching method.

Recognition experiments using this system indicate that a mean recognition accuracy of 99.4% was obtained in the recognition of 67 Japanese airport names uttered by 30 male speakers.

### 8.6.2 SPLIT Method

To effectively apply the phoneme-based word recognition system to large-vocabulary word recognition, the number of phonemes was increased so that spectral variation could be sufficiently covered. These reference templates, which do not necessarily correspond to individual phonemes, are called phonemelike templates or pseudophonemes. Hence, this recognition method is called the SPLIT (strings of phonemelike templates) method (Sugamura and Furui, 1982; Sugamura et al., 1983), and is essentially a mixture of a conventional phoneme-based or word-based recognition system and the vector quantization (VQ) method used in speech coding (see Sec. 6.5).

Phonemelike templates are speaker-independently or speaker-dependently produced by clustering a set of short-time spectral patterns extracted from a large number of speech samples. This is the same technique as that used in producing a codebook in VQ. Since these templates are produced simply according to the distribution of spectral patterns, that is, according to distance relationships between patterns having no relation to linguistic knowledge, the correspondence between each template and phoneme is not clear. It is therefore impossible to produce a word dictionary directly based on orthographic knowledge. This means that this system is language-independent, specifically, that it can be applied to any language. A word dictionary is thus constructed for each word by assigning the nearest phonemelike template to each training utterance frame. A sequence of symbols indicating the templates is subsequently stored for each word.

Table 8.3 summarizes the comparative results of recognition experiments using the SPLIT method and the word-based template method for recognizing 641 Japanese city names uttered by four male speakers. These results clearly indicate that both methods produce nearly the same recognition accuracy. The experiment involving the SPLIT method used 256 phonemelike templates which were produced for each speaker using 64 word utterances arbitrarily extracted from the 641-word vocabulary. It should also be noted that the number of phonemelike templates can be reduced to 32 without a large decline in the recognition accuracy. When the phonemelike templates are produced speaker-independently,

TABLE 8.3 Comparison of Accuracies (5) of Recognized 641 City Names by SPLIT Method and Word-Based Reference Template Method (Results are averaged over four male speakers.)

| | Distance measure | |
|---|---|---|
| Reference | Cepstrum | WLR |
| Word-based template | 95.3 | 96.7 |
| SPLIT method | 95.4 | 96.3 |

SPLIT method: 256 phonemelike templates and word dictionary used as references

the number of templates ranges from 256 to 1024, depending on the vocabulary and required recognition accuracy. Memory size and the number of calculations necessary for the SPLIT method are roughly one-tenth those for the method using word-based templates. An important conclusion here is that the SPLIT method is effective for reducing system complexity while still maintaining performance.

As a modification of the SPLIT method, the double-SPLIT method in which input speech and word reference templates are both vector quantized was subsequently proposed (Shikano, 1982). Using this method in conjunction with adopting an efficient VQ technique for input speech, the amount of spectral distance calculation can be reduced since the distance value can simply be retrieved from the distance matrix. The distance matrix consisting of distance for every pair of phonemelike templates is stored prior to recognition.

### 8.6.3 Hidden Markov Model (HMM)

The word recognition method in which each word is represented by a hidden Markov model (HMM) has been widely investigated and used of late (Baker, 1975; Bahl and Jelinek, 1975; Jelinek, 1976, Rabiner et al., 1983; Rabiner and Juang, 1986). Figure 8.8 shows the principal structure of a word recognizer based on the HMM method. In this method, each word is modeled by a transition network which has a small number of states N such as the number of phonemes (five appear in the example shown in Fig. 8.9). Each state physically corresponds, in an indeterminable sense, to a set of temporal events in the spoken word.

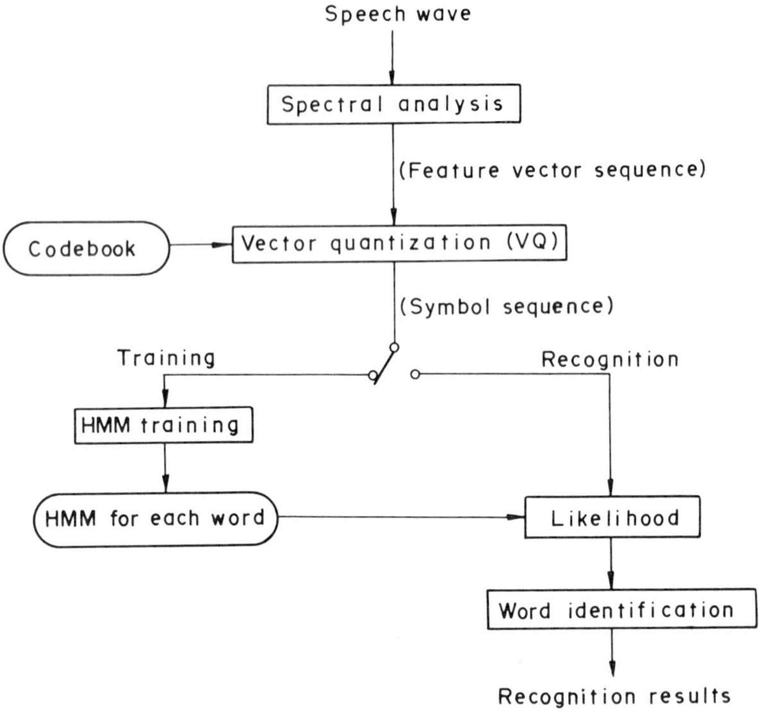


Fig. 8.8 Principal structure of word recognizer based on HMM model.

Although an event is observable at each state, the state itself cannot be observed. Hence this model is referred to as being "hidden."

The overall HMM is characterized by observation symbol probability $b_j(k)$ for the kth VQ codebook element (phonemelike template) at each state j, the state transition probability $a_{ij}$ that describes how the new state j may be reached from the old state i, and the initial state probability $\pi_i$. $\pi_i$ indicates the probability that the ith state is the initial state of transition. $A = (a_{ij})$ and $B = (b_j(k))$ are respectively called the state transition matrix and frequency probability matrix. A, B, and $\pi = (\pi_i)$ consequently represent temporal and spectral variations in each word. They are calculated using the training data.

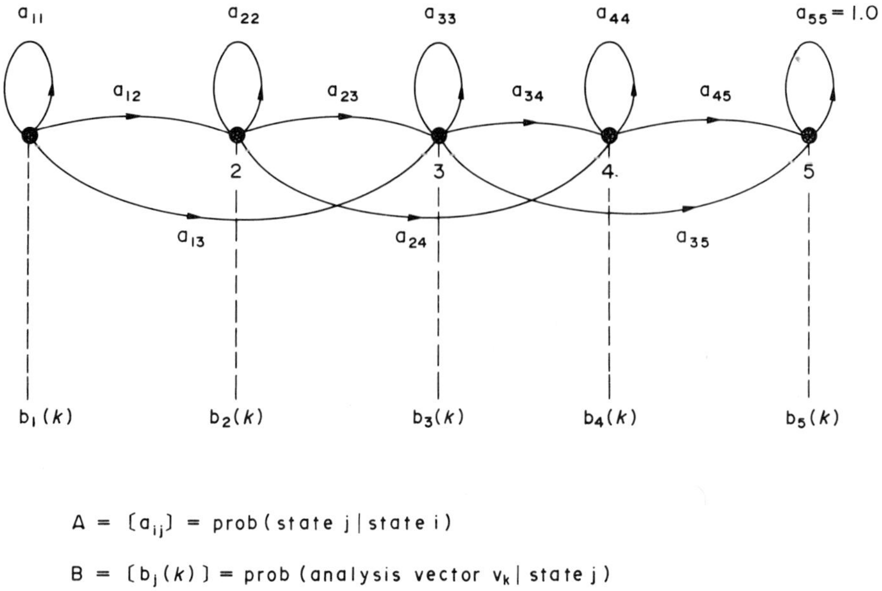


Fig. 8.9 Example of HMM for word recognition.

In the recognition phase for the unknown input, the probability (likelihood) that the observed sequence is generated from a state sequence for each vocabulary word is computed, and the word with the highest accumulated probability is selected as the correct identification. Time alignment is indirectly obtained through the sequence of states. Although the training process is complicated, the recognition process is very simple, with the HMM method producing almost the same recognition accuracy as the method based on DP matching. It has been indicated that when transitional probability is homogeneous, HMM is equivalent to DP matching.

In the training phase, when 100 training utterances,

$$O^{(n)} = \{O_t^{(n)}\}_{t=1}^{T_n}, \qquad T_n = \text{number of frames} \tag{8.35}$$

are obtained (n = 1,2,...,100), $(A^*,B^*,\pi^*)$, which satisfies

$$(A^*, B^*, \pi^*) = \underset{(A,B,\pi)}{\operatorname{argmax}} \prod_{n=1}^{100} \operatorname{Prob}(O^{(n)} | A, B, \pi) \tag{8.36}$$

is determined using the Baum-Welch algorithm (Baum, 1972). Here, $\operatorname{Prob}(O^{(n)} | A, B, \pi)$ indicates the conditional probability.

In the recognition phase $(m^*, q^*)$, which satisfies

$$(m^*, q^*) = \underset{(m,q)}{\operatorname{argmax}} \operatorname{Prob}(O, q | A_m, B_m, \pi_m) \tag{8.37}$$

is determined using the Viterbi algorithm, where $(A_m, B_m, \pi_m)$ is the mth word model ($m = 1, 2, \ldots, M$; $M$ = vocabulary size), $O = O_1 O_2 \cdots O_T$ is input speech ($T$ = number of frames), and $q$ is a state sequence (Viterbi, 1967). $\operatorname{Prob}(O, q | A_m, B_m, \pi_m)$ can be efficiently calculated using a forward-backward algorithm. These algorithms are precisely explained in Appendix D.

A continuous HMM method, in which feature vectors are not vector-quantized but directly applied to HMM, has also been investigated (Juang et al., 1985).

## 8.7 ISOLATED LETTER RECOGNITION

Word-based recognition has fairly much been limited to a vocabulary size of around 1000 words. This is due to the amount of computation required and to the trouble it takes in training to produce the reference templates for each new speaker. Therefore, one of the possible ways to recognize a much larger or unlimited vocabulary, such as one with thousands of everyday words or names of persons, is to have the speaker utter each letter in the word or name. In terms of examples, the Japanese language can be written using the 101 symbols in the "Kana" syllabary, most of which correspond to a CV (consonant-vowel) syllable, while English is written using the 26 letters of the alphabet. In order to realize recognition systems for spoken letters, however, it is necessary to build a system which can recognize difficult sets of CV syllables to a high degree of accuracy.

Since CV syllables are short and contain several groups having highly similar consonants, which must be discriminated according to transitional information at the onset of the syllables, a much more sophisticated algorithm is required than that used for normal word recognition. In many cases, the vowel and consonant parts of each syllable are recognized separately, and these results are combined for the final decision. Although DP matching is frequently used for consonant recognition, the extremely short transitional part does not greatly expand or contract. Moreover, transitional features bear important consonant information.

Accordingly, a method was proposed in which results of shift matching rather than DP matching for the transitional part are combined with the similarity of global spectral pattern features over the entire period of the syllable (Furui, 1982). In this context, shift matching means that one pattern is shifted along the time axis of the other pattern to find a matching position without the need for time warping. Consonant information included in the vowel part due to coarticulation is also extracted by the global spectral pattern features. The structure of this method is outlined in Fig. 8.10.

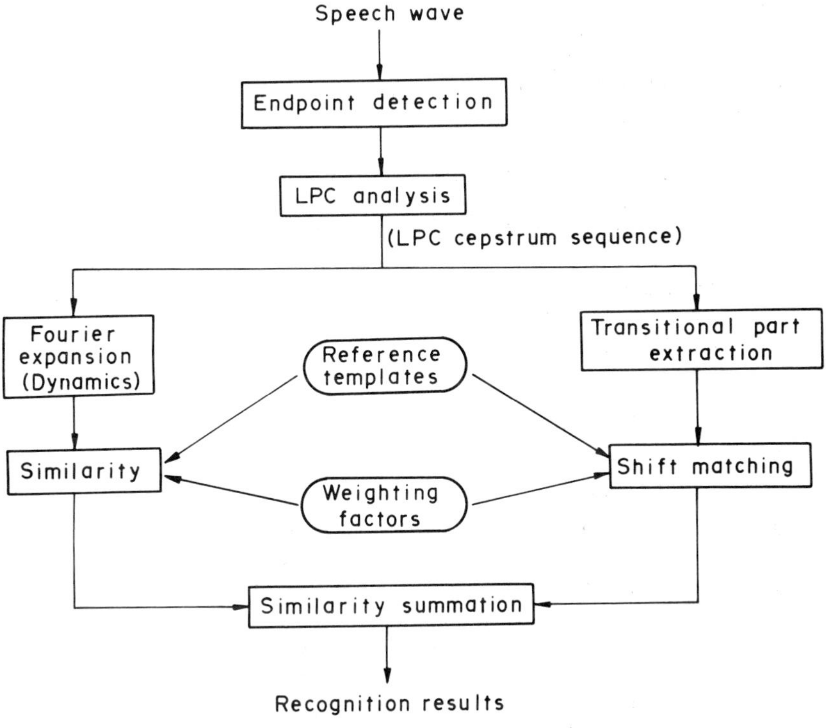


Fig. 8.10 Block diagram of Japanese CV syllable recognition system based on combination of shift matching of transitional part and similarity of global spectral features.

Recognition accuracies of 94 to 97% have been obtained using this method for Japanese CV syllable recognition, when speaker-dependent three to five multiple templates are used for each syllable. The relationship between syllable and word recognition accuracies has also been investigated theoretically and experimentally for a vocabulary of around 10,000 words uttered employing isolated syllables (Furui, 1982). The results show that 99 and 96% word recognition accuracies are obtained for four-syllable word vocabularies of 3203 and 12,813 words, respectively. Since each syllable must be uttered in complete isolation with this method, however, it is particularly troublesome and tiring for the speakers involved. Furthermore, the input speed cannot be increased. Importantly then, a new method must be formulated which allows speakers to utter whole words as connected syllables.

As a final example, an automated directory-listing retrieval system based on isolated letter speech recognition has been investigated (Aldefeld et al., 1980). In this system, each name is uttered by being spelled out letter by letter, with the telephone number being retrieved for the recognized name. Each letter utterance is recognized by the DP matching technique, with multiple letter candidates being produced. Although the recognition accuracy of producing correct letters as the top candidates in the speaker-dependent mode is only 70%, a word (name) recognition accuracy of 98% is obtained for 18,000 names owing to the redundancy in the letter strings of the names. In the speaker-independent mode, a 95% recognition accuracy is obtained using the multiple-template method to be described later (Rosenberg et al., 1980).

## 8.8 CONNECTED WORD RECOGNITION

### 8.8.1 Two-Level DP Matching and Its Modifications

The DP matching technique used in isolated word recognition can be expanded into a technique which is applicable to connected word recognition. The basic process involved in this expansion is to perform DP matching between input speech and all possible concatenations of reference word templates to ensure selecting the best sequence having the smallest accumulated distance.

Several problems persist, however, in finding the optimal matching sequence of reference templates. One is that the number of words in the input speech is generally unknown. Another is that the locations, in time, of the boundaries between words are unknown. The boundaries are usually unclear because the end of one word may merge smoothly with the beginning of the next word. Still another is that the amount of calculation becomes too large when all possible sequences and input speech are exhaustively matched using the method described in Sec. 8.5. This is because the number of ways of concatenating X words selected from the N-word vocabulary is $N^X$. It is thus very important to create an efficient means for ascertaining the optimal sequence.

Fortunately, several methods have fairly recently been devised that optimally solve the matching problem without giving rise to an exponential growth in the amount of calculation as the vocabulary or length of the word sequence grows. Specifically worth mentioning are four principal methods having different computation algorithms, but producing identical accumulated distance results.

1. Two-level DP matching

Since DP matching is performed on two levels in this method, it is called two-level DP matching (Sakoe, 1979). On the first level, semiunconstrained endpoint DP matching is performed between every short period of input speech and each word reference template. The starting position of the warping function is shifted frame by frame in input speech. The meaning of the semiunconstrained endpoint is that only the final position of the warping function is unconstrained. On the second level, the accumulated distance for the word sequence is calculated again using the DP matching method based on the results derived at the first level.

In exploring the method, let us assume that first-level DP matching has already been performed between partial periods of the input utterance starting from every position and each reference template. The word with the minimum distance from the input utterance between positions s and t is written as w(s,t), and its distance is written as D(s,t). w(s,t) and D(s,t) are obtained and stored for every partial period of input speech, more precisely, for every combination of s and t ($1 \leqq s < t \leqq T$, T = input speech length). These values are then used for second-level DP matching for obtaining the word sequence minimizing the accumulated distance over the entire input speech. That is, the recognition result is the word sequence $w(1,m_1), w(m_1 + 1,m_2), \ldots, w(m_k + 1,T)$ satisfying the following equation under the condition $1 \leqq m_1 < m_2 < \cdots < m_k < T$:

$$D_T = \min_{\{m_j\},k} \{D(1,m_1) + D(m_1 + 1,m_2) + \cdots + D(m_k + 1,T)\} \tag{8.38}$$

Since this equation can be rewritten into the recursive form

$$D_0 = 0$$

$$D_n = \min_{m=1,n} \{D_{m-1} + D(m,n)\} \tag{8.39}$$

it can be efficiently solved by the DP technique.

A mean word recognition accuracy of 98.9% was obtained using this method for recognizing connected words, each of which consisted of one through four connected Japanese digits uttered by five male speakers.

2. LB (level building) method

In the level building method, the number of connected words is assumed to be one for the first condition and increased successively. Distances between input speech and connected word sequence candidates are calculated to select the optimum word sequence, namely, the best matching words, for each condition (level) of the number of connected words. Figure 8.11 illustrates the LB method (Myers and Rabiner, 1981).

For the first level, specifically, for the first word in the sequence, unconstrained endpoint DP matching is performed between input speech and each word reference template under the condition that the warping function must start from the beginning position of the input speech. For the second and later levels, unconstrained endpoint DP matching is done using the optimum accumulated distances obtained at each previous level in the end area ($m_1(1)-m_2(1)$ in Fig. 8.11) as initial values. This procedure is repeated until the allowed maximum number of words (word string length) is reached. The word sequence with the smallest accumulated distance at the end of the input speech is finally selected as being the recognition result.

The LB method is particularly beneficial in that unconstrained endpoint DP matching can be performed at every level, whereas the first level of the two-level DP matching consists of semiunconstrained endpoint matching. Consequently, since the LB method can solve the optimization problem through one-level DP matching, the amount of computation it requires is less than two-level DP matching. The LB method in the original form is

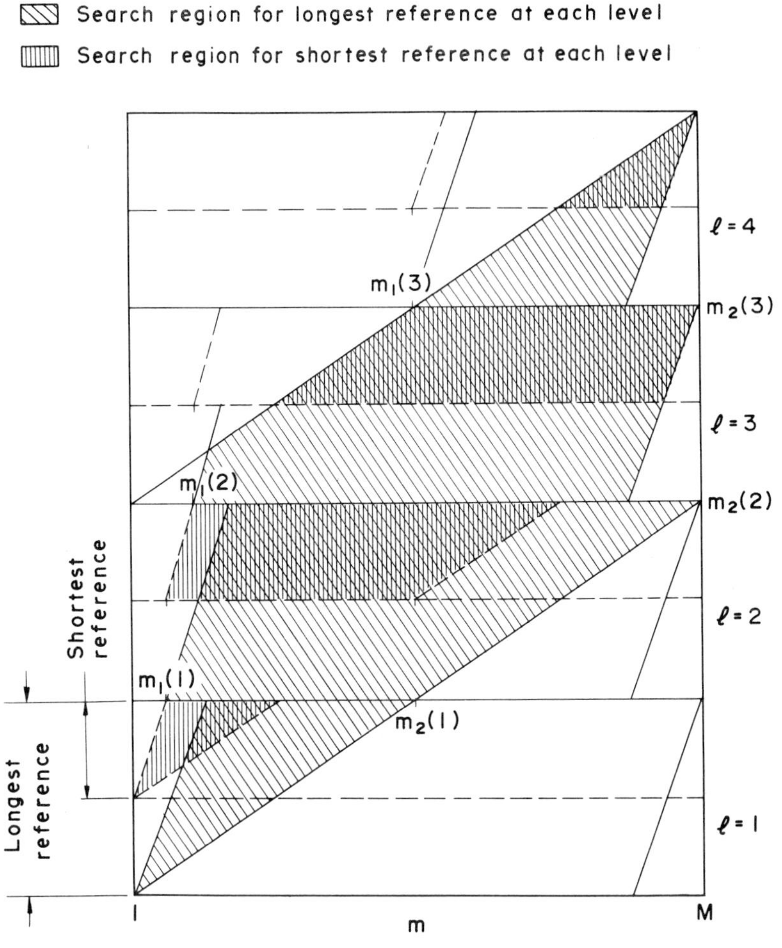


Fig. 8.11 Illustration of warping path regions in four-level DTW matching using LB method.

unsuited to frame synchronous, real-time processing, however, since scanning and matching with reference templates must be performed throughout the input string of speech at every level until the number of levels equals the allowed maximum number of words. Frame synchronous processing of the LB method has been realized by the clockwise DP method described below using an additional memory for intermediate calculation results.

Speaker-independent connected digit recognition experiments were performed using the LB method and multiple templates (see Sec. 8.11). The lengths of the strings were between two and five digits. When 12 templates were stored for each digit, an average string recognition accuracy of 95.4% was obtained. A trial was also conducted using HMM at the word level in the LB method (Rabiner et al., 1985).

3. CW (Clockwise) DP method

In contrast with the LB method in which the assumed number of connected words (level) is increased successively, and the best matching word string is selected for each level, the clockwise DP (CWDP) method performs this procedure through parallel matching synchronized to the input speech frame (Sakoe and Watari, 1981). This makes CWDP suitable for real-time processing. The number of parallel matchings corresponds to the allowable maximum number of words in the string.

In the DP matching between a certain period of input speech and each word reference template, the result of optimum matching, in particular, the optimum accumulated distance, for the speech input before this period is used as an initial condition for the recursive calculation. The repetition of the same spectral distance calculation occurring on every level of the LB method is removed in the CWDP method. Thus, CWDP requires fewer calculations than the LB method. Memory capacity increases in the CWDP method, however, since intermediate results of recursive calculations for DP matching must be stored for each figure number and for each word reference template.

4. OS (one-stage) DP method or O(n) (order n) DP method

As opposed to the two-level DP or CWDP methods, in which DP recursive calculations are performed for all the possible conditions on the number of figures at every frame, only the optimum condition is considered at every frame in the one-stage (OS) DP or order n DP method (Vintsyuk, 1971; Bridle and Brown, 1979; Nakagawa, 1983). Although investigated independently, the OSDP and O(n) DP methods are actually the same algorithm. Since this method does not involve the repetition of recursive DP calculations, it requires fewer calculations and a smaller memory.

Specifically, the number of calculations necessary to calculate the distance between input and reference frames and for distance accumulation in this method does not depend on the number of figures in the input speech. If the length of the speech input and mean length of reference templates are both constant, the number of calculations is proportional only to the size of the vocabulary, n. For this reason, this method is called the O(n) DP method.

Since the intermediate results for each stage of the figure are not maintained, it is impossible to obtain the recognition results when the number of figures is specified. For the same reason, automaton control (see Sec. 8.9.1) is also impossible with this method.

Table 8.4 compares the number of calculations and the memory size for each of the four methods described.

### 8.8.2 Continuous DP method

In addition to the methods described in the previous section, in which input speech is compared with the sequence of reference word templates, a connected word recognition method based on a word spotting technique has also been investigated (Hayamizu and Oka, 1984). Word spotting is the process of detecting words or syllables in input speech. When words are the basic units of recognition, the spectral parameter sequence of input speech is scanned from beginning to end using the reference template of each word. The reference templates are shifted frame by frame and compared with a partial period of input speech by means of DP matching. When the distance associated with a reference template as a result of DP matching falls below a predetermined threshold, the word is estimated to exist at this position. Since DP matching is continuously performed from the beginning of input speech, the method is referred to as the continuous DP method.

Matching between an arbitrary period of input speech and a reference template is done using a warping function having the slope constraint indicated in Fig. 8.12. The accumulated distance g(i,j) is defined using the distance between the ith frame of the input speech and the jth frame of the reference template, d(i,j), as

TABLE 8.4 Comparison of Number of Calculations and Memory Size for Four Kinds of Connected Word Recognition Methods

| Evaluation | Two-level DP method | LB method | CWDP method | OSDP method (O(n) DP) |
|---|---|---|---|---|
| Number of calculations | | | | |
| Local distance | JIN $\frac{3}{4}$ J (JINR) | JINX | JIN | JIN |
| Accumulated distance | JIN $\frac{3}{4}$ J (JINR) | JINX | JINX | JIN |
| Memory size | 3IX | 3IX | 3IX + 2JNX | 3I + 2JN |

I = Input speech length; J = Mean reference template length; N = Vocabulary size; X = Number of connected words in input; R = Adjustment window width

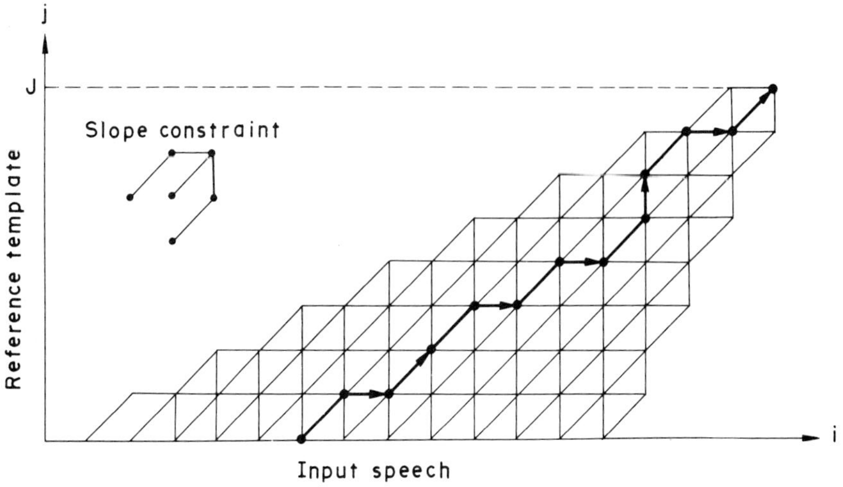


Fig. 8.12 Warping function and its slope constraint in continuous DP method.

$$g(i,j) = \min \begin{pmatrix} g(i-2,j-1) + 2d(i-1,j) + d(i,j) & \text{(a)} \\ g(i-1,j-1) + 2d(i,j) & \text{(b)} \\ g(i-1,j-2) + 2d(i,j-1) + d(i,j) & \text{(c)} \end{pmatrix} \tag{8.40}$$

The weighting factor for the DP path (warping function) is calculated at the same time according to the equation

$$c(i,j) = \begin{cases} c(i-2,j-1) + 3 & \text{if (a)} \\ c(i-1,j-1) + 2 & \text{if (b)} \\ c(i-1,j-2) + 3 & \text{if (c)} \end{cases} \tag{8.41}$$

Since g(i,J) and c(i,J), respectively, indicate the minimum accumulated distance and the optimum path length under the condition that the ith frame of the input speech and the final frame of the reference template are matched, the distance normalized by the path length can be obtained as

$$D(i) = \frac{g(i,J)}{c(i,J)} \tag{8.42}$$

If $\{D_w(i)\}$ (w is the reference word name) for all reference words are calculated in parallel for every i, $D_w(i)$ typically indicates the local minimum at the position where the utterance of the word w ends.

The number of calculations for the continuous DP is almost the same as that for the two-level DP. In continuous speech recognition using the continuous DP, spectral discrepancy at word boundaries between reference templates spoken in isolation and input speech spoken continuously can be disregarded. On the other hand, continuous DP sometimes mistakenly inserts or deletes words. To counter this problem, the duration of the input speech period assigned to each reference template as well as the accumulated distance are checked for ensuring the ability to extract an appropriate word sequence from a candidate word lattice.

## 8.9 CONVERSATIONAL SPEECH RECOGNITION

The five-year DARPA project which got under way in 1971 spurred considerable research on conversational speech recognition or speech understanding (Klatt, 1977; Reddy, 1980; Lea, 1980). In conversational speech recognition, continuous speech, which is highly complicated, is recognized using various kinds of information including a lexicon, syntax, semantics, pragmatics, context, and prosodics. The lexicon indicates the phonemic structure of words, syntax expresses the grammatical structure, semantics defines the relationship between words as well as the attributes of each word, pragmatics expresses general knowledge concerning the present topics of conversation, context concerns the contextual information obtained through human-machine conversation, and prosodics represents accent and intonation.

Various algorithms and databases used in these processes are referred to as knowledge sources for conversational speech recognition. The keys determining system performance lie with the kinds of knowledge sources used and how they are combined as quickly as possible to produce the most probable understanding. Specifically, the focus involves how best to control the process of searching through possibilities. There are three principal issues in solving these problems: the order in which these knowledge sources should be used, the direction of processes in the input speech period, and the procedures for evaluating and selecting the most probable hypothesis.

### 8.9.1 Three Principal Structural Models

There are three principal models for combining and using the knowledge sources: the hierarchy model, the blackboard model, and the network model.

1. Hierarchy model

The hierarchy model distributes knowledge sources in multiple hierarchical subsystems. Results of processes are transferred between adjacent subsystems in the bottom-up direction for task-independent processes and in the top-down direction for task-dependent processes. The fundamental structure of the hierarchy model is presented in Fig. 8.13(a).

Acoustic features are extracted in the acoustic processor from input speech and converted into a phoneme sequence by means of segmentation and phoneme recognition. At the next step, word or word-sequence candidates are produced from the phoneme sequence which usually includes recognition errors. Word dictionary as well as phonological rules representing phoneme modification rules associated with coarticulation are used for the word or word-sequence recognition. In the linguistic processor, a sentence is produced by removing incorrect candidate words according to linguistic knowledge, such as syntax, semantics, and context information.

On the other hand, restrictions on word candidates are provided in the top-down direction from the linguistic processor to the acoustic processor. Acoustic and linguistic processes are sometimes combined at a level below the word level. Actual acoustic and linguistic processors are further divided into multiple subsystems.

2. Blackboard model

In the blackboard model, as in the hierarchy model, the recognition system is divided into multiple subsystems. A special feature of this system, however, is that each subsystem gains access to a common database independently to verify various hypotheses, as shown in Fig. 8.13(b). The process in each subsystem can be performed in parallel without synchronization. The Hearsay II system is a successful example of the blackboard model (Lesser et al., 1975).

Systems based on hierarchy and blackboard models are flexible and particularly suitable for large vocabulary tasks. This is because various knowledge sources are classified and systematically combined to achieve the recognition and understanding of sentences while preserving their independence.

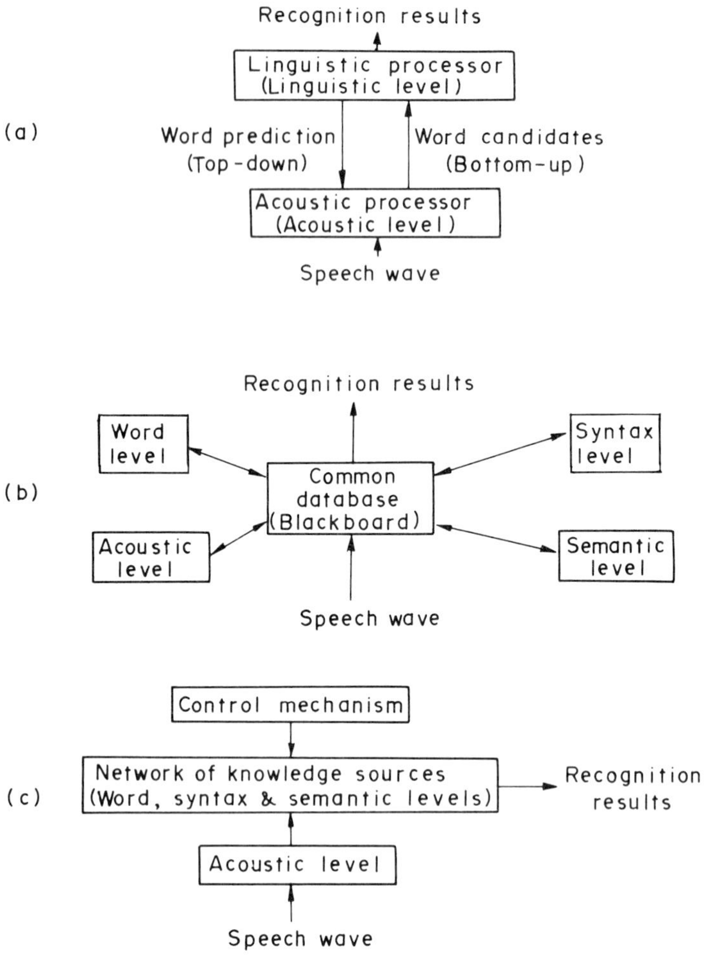


Fig. 8.13 Three principal structural models of continuous speech recognition: (a) hierarchy model; (b) blackboard model; (c) network model.

3. Network model

The network model embeds all knowledge except the system control mechanism in one network, with every process being performed in this network, as shown in Fig. 8.13(c). Sentence recognition based on this model corresponds to the process of searching for a path in the network which matches the input speech. The process is thus similar to connected word recognition. Although the number of calculations is relatively large, information loss on each level and information loss propagation can be avoided. Since all processes can be controlled homogeneously, and all knowledge sources can be handled uniformly, the network model is suitable for a relatively small recognition task. The Harpy system is a successful application of this model (Lowerre, 1976). The problem with the network model is that it is not as flexible in its application as the two previous models.

Two-stage DP matching combined with a syntax control mechanism using a finite-state automation demonstrated high-recognition performance, although the scale of the system was small, featuring a restricted syntax and only a 100-word vocabulary (Sakoe, 1981).

### 8.9.2 Other System Constructing Factors

Prevalent among the directions which processes take are exemplified by the left-to-right and island-driven methods. In the former method, input speech is successively processed from beginning to end. In the latter method, the most reliable candidate word is first detected in the input speech, which is then processed from this word to both ends. Although both methods have advantages and disadvantages, the left-to-right method is more frequently used since important words tend to be nearer the beginning of sentences.

Quantitative evaluation and selection of hypotheses are carried out by a variety of tree search algorithms. The depth-first method processes the longest word string first, and if this search fails, the system backtracks to the previous node. In the breadth-first method, all word strings of the same length are processed in parallel, with the process proceeding from short to long strings. With the best-first method, the word string having the largest evaluation value is selected at every node. Finally, the beam search method is a modification of the breadth-first method, in which word strings with relatively large evaluation values are selected and processed in parallel. These methods differ only in their search orders, exhibiting no essential difference in search capability. Reducing the search cost while maintaining the search efficiency, however, is very important for practical applications. Various other trials have also been examined including pruning until only reliable candidates remain.

Syntactic information, that is, syntactic rules and task-dependent knowledge are usually represented using context-free grammar (CFG). When more sophisticated control is required, they are represented by generation rules (rewriting rules) or by an augmented transition network (ATN) in which semantic information is embedded.

Semantic information is represented in various ways. These include being represented by

1. A combination of semantic markers which indicate fundamental concepts necessary for classifying the meaning of words
2. Embedding the restriction of semantic word classes in the syntactic description as described above
3. A semantic net which indicates the semantic relationship between word classes using a graph with nodes and branches
4. A case frame in which all words, mainly verbs, are qualified by words or phrases in a semantic class which coexist with the word

Procedural knowledge representation, predicate logic, and a production system have also been used for semantic information representation.

Three measures for representing the syntactic complexity of recognizing tasks have thus far been proposed to facilitate the evaluation of conversational speech recognition systems. The average branching factor indicates the average number of words which can be predicted, that is, the words which can follow at each position of syntactic analysis (Goodman, 1976). Equivalent vocabulary size is a modification of the average branching factor in which the acoustic similarity between words is taken into consideration (Goodman, 1976). Finally, perplexity is defined by $2^H$, where H is the entropy of a word string in sentence speech (Bahl et al., 1983). Although each measure offers its own benefits, a perfect measure has not yet been proposed.

## 8.10 EXAMPLES OF CONVERSATIONAL SPEECH RECOGNITION SYSTEMS

### 8.10.1 System Based on Hierarchy Model

As an example of a recognition system based on the hierarchy model, Fig. 8.14 outlines the structure of a continuous speech recognition system designed for spoken Japanese sentences investigated at the NTT Electrical Communications Laboratories (Matsunaga and Shikano, 1985). This system consists of four parts: feature extraction, phoneme recognition, word recognition, and syntactic analysis (sentence recognition).

Extracted for each short interval of input speech in the feature extraction part are short-time energy, the amount of spectral change, and distances between input speech and reference templates. The reference templates are prepared for five vowels and nasal sounds, each of them being automatically adapted to each speaker. The phoneme recognition part has two recognition function groups. One consists of phoneme recognition functions for detecting both vowels and consonants; the other is composed of 12 kinds of phoneme concatenation recognition functions for detecting semivowels, diphthongs (vowel concatenations), and devocalized vowels. The word recognition part incorporates a word dictionary written by a recursive transition network (RTN). In the syntactic analysis part, the word is predicted by a top-down process using the syntactic knowledge source described by the RTN.

Each processing part consists of top-down and bottom-up processors, with the results of top-down and bottom-up processes on different levels being merged and written on the particular blackboard to reduce repetition of the same processes.

One of the primary features of this system is that phoneme recognition is based on the top-down process adapted to the phoneme environment before and after the phoneme position. More precisely, syntax controls the feature measurement algorithm and thus changes the type (form) of analysis depending on the sound to be recognized. A word hypothesis is decomposed into a phoneme hypothesis string using word knowledge in the word recognition part, and each phoneme hypothesis is verified in the phoneme recognition part based on comparison with feature parameters of input speech. The word hypothesis is then verified using these results, and the sentence hypothesis is confirmed based on the results of word verification. The depth-first method is mainly used for controlling each processing part.

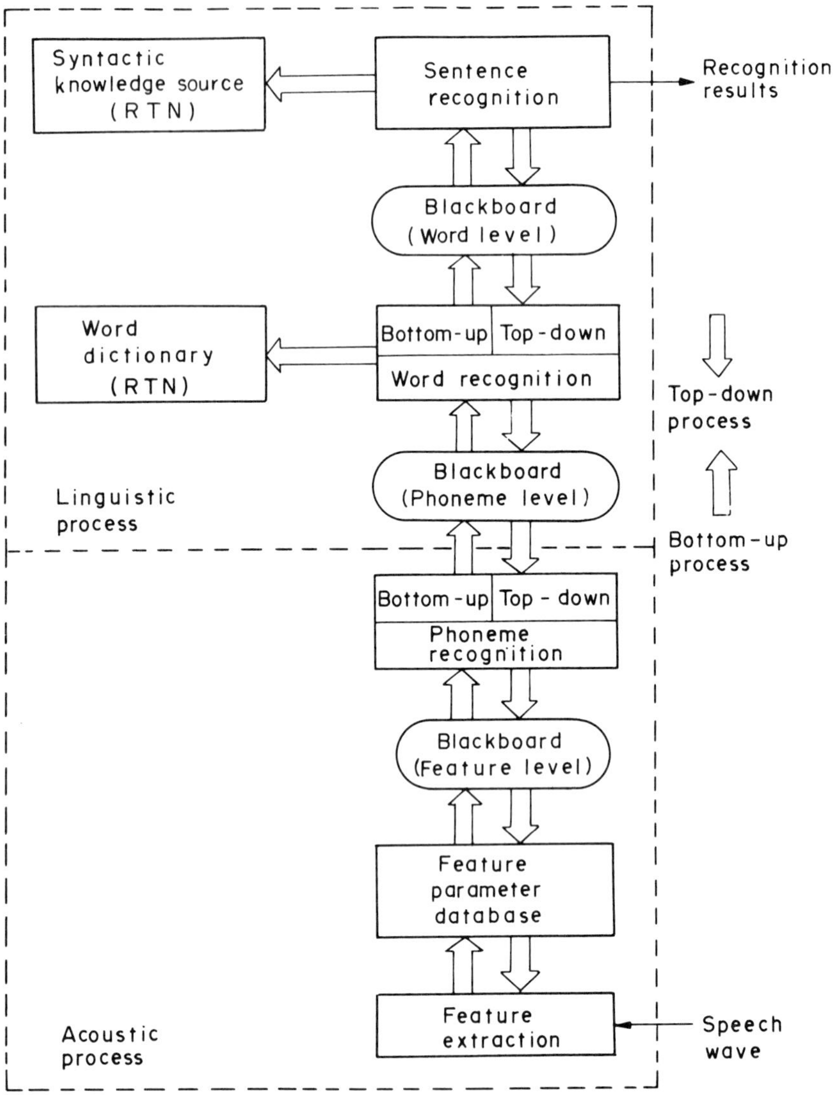


Fig. 8.14 Structure of continuous speech recognition system based on hierarchy model including top-down and bottom-up processing.

### 8.10.2 System Based on Blackboard Model

ANGELS (a new generation English language system), developed by Carnegie-Mellon University, is an example of a blackboard-based continuous speech recognition system (Adams and Bisiani, 1986). The system structure, detailed in Fig. 8.15, consists of knowledge sources and distributed blackboards. Each knowledge source works independently and in parallel, and communicates with other knowledge sources using the blackboard as a shared memory. The knowledge sources are implemented on different computers which are connected with each other by a network to build a distributed AI system called Agora (Alleva et al., 1986).

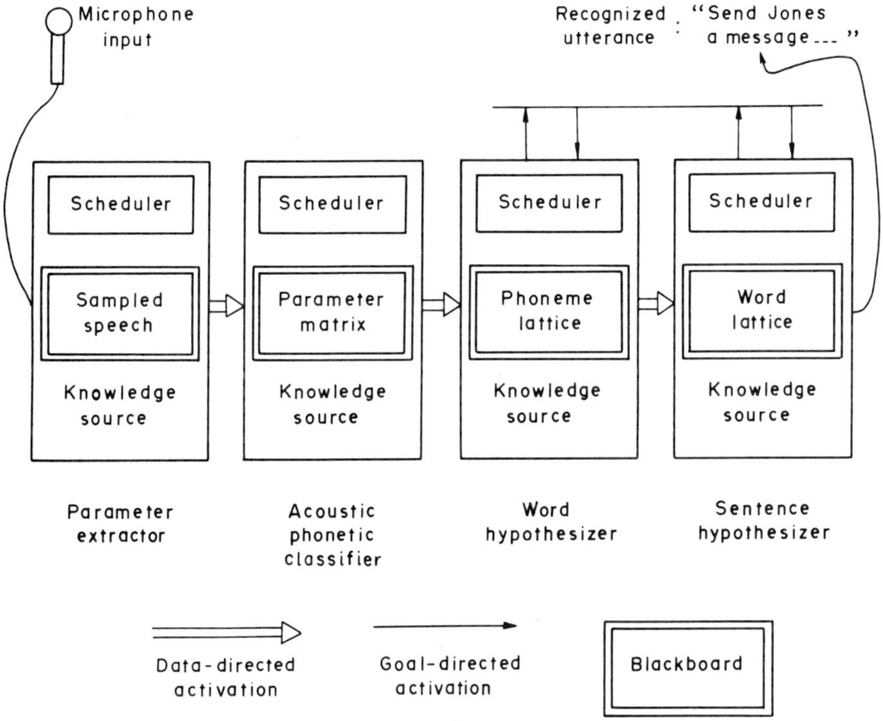


Fig. 8.15 Structure of ANGELS continuous speech recognition system based on blackboard model.

ANGELS is made up of a parameter extractor, an acoustic phonetic classifier, a word hypothesizer, and a sentence hypothesizer. The phonetic classifier consists of locators and a classifier for each class of phonemes, such as stops, fricatives, closures, and sonorants. The locator detects the approximate location of each candidate phoneme class based on various kinds of spectral information extracted by the parameter extractor. The classifier recognizes each phoneme to produce a phoneme lattice which is transmitted to the word hypothesizer along with the probability of each phoneme appearing in the lattice.

In the word hypothesizer, word spotting is performed based on the phoneme lattice and word dictionary represented by phonetic graphs which take allophones and coarticulation into consideration. Also used in word spotting are stress and syllable nuclei information. Word spotting results are transmitted to the sentence hypothesizer as a word lattice.

In the sentence hypothesizer, syntax analysis based on case frame grammar is performed using top-down processing to find the correct sentence. A trigram is employed to reduce the number of candidate word sequences. The trigram measure is derived from the conditional probability of observing the syntactic or semantic classes of three words in sequence in a set of training sequences. The measure is, in turn, used to estimate the joint probability that the syntactic or semantic structure of the sequence of three words is correct.

### 8.10.3 Systems Based on Network Model

1. IBM system

A typical example of a continuous speech recognition system based on the network model is one developed by the IBM Thomas Watson Research Center (Jelinek, 1976; Bahl et al., 1983). As shown in Fig. 8.16, conversational speech production as well as the recognition process is modeled in this system through four stages: text generation, speech production, acoustic processing, and linguistic decoding. A speaker is assumed to be a transducer that transforms into speech the text of thoughts he intends to communicate. Based on information transmission theory, the sequence of processes is compared to an information transmission system, in which a word sequence w is coded into a label sequence y through a noisy transmission channel, which is then decoded to an estimated sequence w'. A statistical model is introduced at every stage.

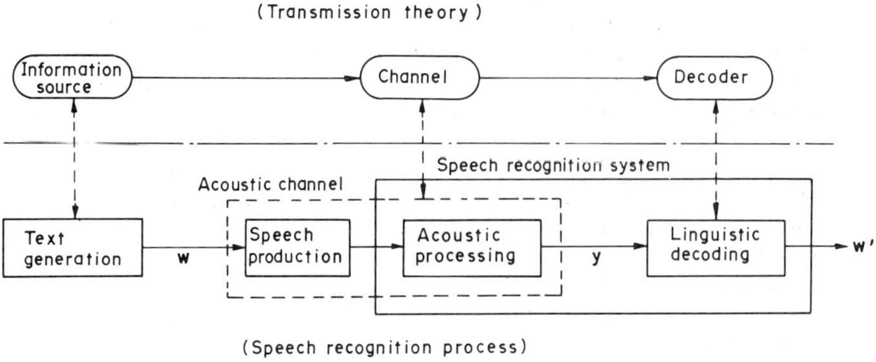


Fig. 8.16 Structure of continuous speech recognition system based on network model.

The speaker is assumed to utter a sentence w which corresponds to an information source, with his or her own modifications. The recognition system then extracts acoustic parameters y from the speech through acoustic processing, namely, analysis. The speaker and acoustic processing, which are combined and regarded as an acoustic channel, correspond to a noisy transmission channel in transmission theory.

The linguistic decoder obtains w' as an estimation of w maximizing the simultaneous chance probability $p(w,y) = p(w)p(y|w)$ based on y. Here, p(w) is the prior probability that the sentence w is generated at the sentence generator, that is, that w is internally constructed by the speaker for utterance, and $p(y|w)$ is the conditional probability that the output y is produced by the acoustic channel through speech production and analysis. The linguistic decoder part corresponds to the decoder in transmission theory, which estimates the information source using a noisy signal. p(w) is calculated using a trigram of words, and a phoneme production model for each word along with an acoustic processing model for each phoneme is represented by HMM.

Each word is modeled by a network having nodes of phonemes (45 phonemes), and each sentence is constructed by a sentence network having nodes of words. The probability that each phoneme is omitted, replaced by other phonemes, or decomposed into two phonemes in a sentence speech is calculated using phoneme production probability. The state transitional probability in the sentence network, the selection probability of each branch in the word network, and the phoneme production probability are estimated based on Markov models by self-organized training procedures using a set of laser patent-related sentences comprising some 1,500,000 words.

In the recognition phase, input speech is processed by DFT spectral analysis and converted into 80-dimensional feature vectors. Phonemes are then recognized every 10 ms, and the similarity between the phoneme sequence and each word network is calculated. The word sequence with a large similarity value and high occurrence probability is subsequently output as the recognition result. The beam search method is used to prevent the omission of indistinctly pronounced words and short functional words.

Experimental results for the speech recognition task of the laser patent-related sentences having a vocabulary of 1000 words indicate a word recognition accuracy of 91.1%. Disadvantages of this method are the extremely large size of the total network and the time-consuming training necessary to obtain state transitional probabilities which depend on each task.

2. BBN systems

Another example of the continuous speech recognition system based on the network model is the BYBLOS system developed by the BBN Laboratory (Chow et al., 1987). A block diagram of the BYBLOS system, provided in Fig. 8.17, shows the modules, knowledge sources, and their interactions comprising the complex system. These are respectively represented by rectangular boxes, ellipses, and arrows. This system integrates acoustic, phonetic, lexical, and linguistic knowledge sources into one network.

The system's basic approach centers around the extensive use of context-dependent models of phonetic coarticulation using HMM. The trainer module takes as input a dictionary and training speech and text and produces context-dependent HMMs of phonemes. The word model generator module compiles word models using the dictionary, in which phonological rules of English are used to represent each lexical item in terms of their most likely phonetic spellings. Grammatical constraints are implemented in the form of a finite-state automaton.

A top-down and linguistically driven search strategy is used to find the word sequence that best matches the input speech. The strategy is also characterized by tightly coupled knowledge

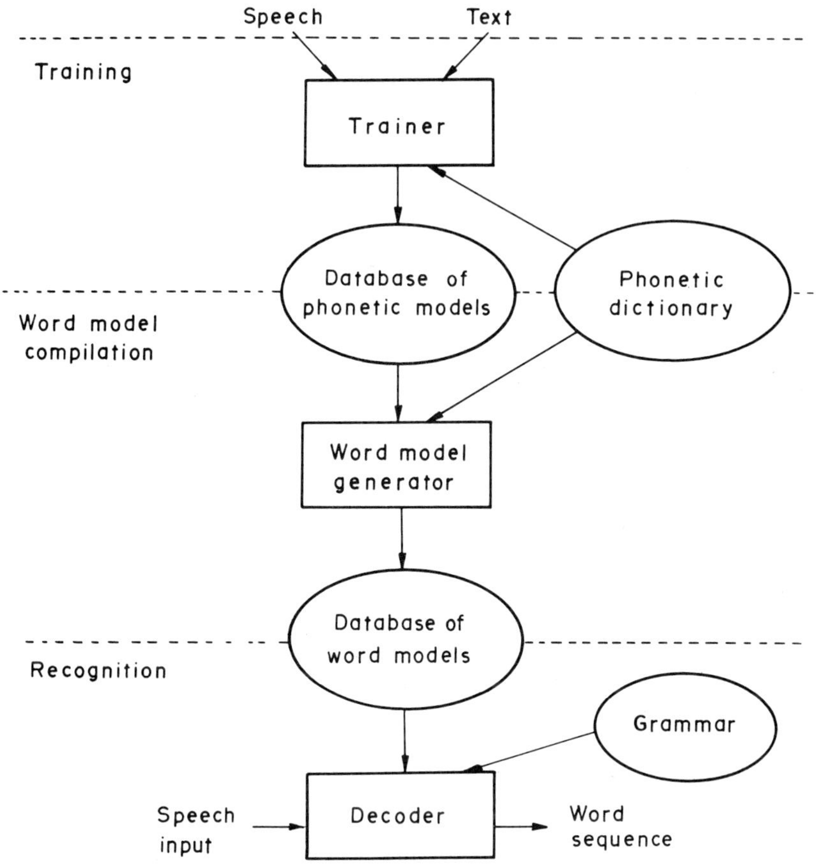


Fig. 8.17 Structure of BYBLOS continuous speech recognition system based on network model.

sources. In the speaker-dependent mode, where 15 minutes of speech is required to train the system to a particular speaker, a word recognition accuracy of 98.5% has been achieved in continuous speech for a 350-word task, using grammars with perplexity ranging from 30 to 60. In the speaker-adapted mode, HMM models for one speaker are transformed to model the speech of a second speaker by probabilistic spectral mapping. With only 15 s of training speech, a word recognition accuracy of 97% was obtained.

A modification of this system has also been tried, in which a variable-length phonetic segment represented by a sequence of feature vectors is used instead of the context-dependent HMM of each phoneme (Roucos and Dunham, 1987). These segments are produced using the MQ (matrix quantization) technique described in Sec. 6.5.6. An advantage of this method is that the spectral-temporal relationship over the duration of each phoneme can be better captured than by using a frame-by-frame method such as HMM or DTW.

## 8.11 SPEAKER-INDEPENDENT WORD RECOGNITION

Speaker-dependent variations in speech spectra are very complicated, and, as indicated in Sec. 8.1, there is no evidence that common physical features exist in the same words uttered by different speakers even if they can be clearly recognized by humans. A statistical analysis of the relationship between phonetic and individual information revealed that there is significant interaction between them (Sakai and Tabata, 1973; Furui, 1978). It is thus very difficult for a system to accurately recognize spoken words uttered by many speakers even if the vocabulary is as small as 10 digits. Only with a small vocabulary and no similar word pairs in the spectral domain can high accuracy be achieved using a reference template obtained by averaging the spectral patterns of many speakers for each word.

Although looking for phonetic invariants, principally physical features commonly existing for all speakers for each phoneme, is important as basic research, it seems too ambitious an undertaking. The present effective methods for coping with the problem of speaker variability can be classified into two types of methods. One constitutes methods in which reference templates, discrimination functions, or statistical word models are designed so that the range of individual variation is covered by them for each word, whereas the ranges of different words do not overlap. The other includes those in which the recognition system is provided with a training mechanism to automatically adapt to each new speaker. Although the former type seems easier and more straightforward, it still requires a training mechanism for speech recognizers in practical applications for variations due to telephone, microphone, background noise, room acoustics, and bandwidth limitations of transmission lines.

Leaving examples of the latter methods until Sec. 8.12, the rest of this section will focus on examples of the former type of methods. Specifically, the discussion will include (1) the multitemplate method, in which multiple templates are created for each vocabulary word by clustering individual variations; (2) the discrimination function method, in which a nonlinear discrimination function is designed to cover individual variations for each word; and (3) the HMM method, in which individual variations are represented by the statistical parameters in HMMs.

### 8.11.1 Multitemplate Method

A block diagram of a spoken word recognizer based on the multitemplate method is given in Fig. 8.18 (Rabiner et al., 1979a,b). This system clusters the speech data uttered by many speakers, and the speech sample at the center of each cluster or the mean value for the speech data associated with each cluster is stored as a reference template. Several algorithms are used in combination for clustering.

In the recognition phase, distances (or similarities) between input speech and all reference templates of all vocabulary words are calculated based on DP matching, and the word with the smallest distance is selected as the word spoken. In order to increase the reliability, the KNN (K-nearest neighbor) method is often used for the decision. Here, K reference templates with the smallest distances from the input speech are selected from the multiple-reference template set for each word, with the mean value for these K templates being calculated for each word. The word with the smallest mean value is then selected as the recognition result. It was experimentally revealed that with 12 templates for each word, the recognition accuracy for K = 2 to 3 is higher than for K = 1. Recognition accuracy for English spoken digits recorded over the telephone was 98.2%, a value almost the same as that obtained with speaker-dependent recognition.

This method is disadvantageous, however, in that when the number of reference templates for each word increases, the recognition task becomes equivalent to large-vocabulary word recognition, increasing the number of calculations and the memory size. These problems have been resolved through the investigation of two methods based on the structure shown in Fig. 8.3(b), in which phoneme templates and a word dictionary are used. In the first trial, the same word dictionary was used for all speakers, and multiple sets of phoneme templates were prepared to cover variations in individual speakers (Nakatsu et al., 1983).

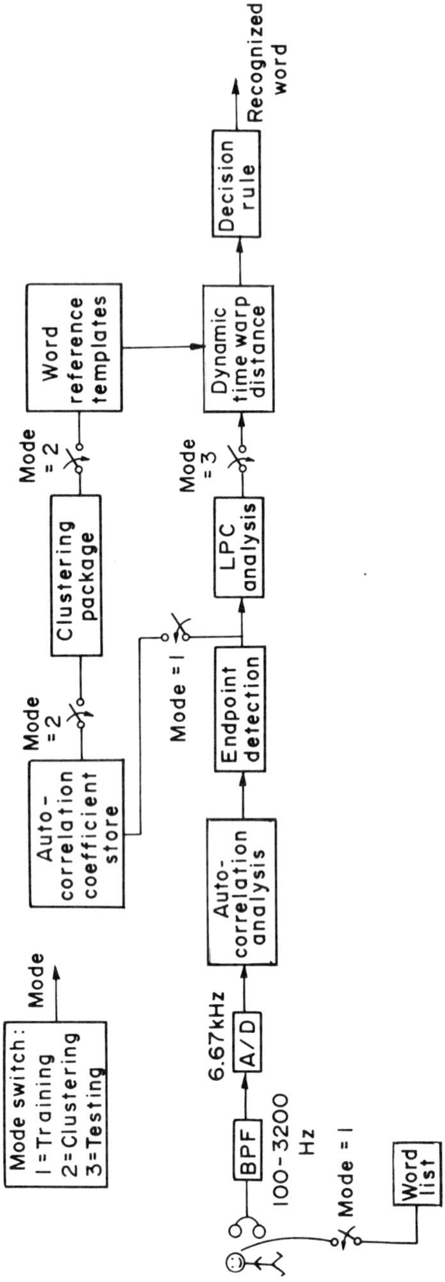


Fig. 8.18 Block diagram of speaker-independent word recognition system based on multitemplate method showing training (mode 1), clustering (mode 2), and testing (mode 3).

For the second instance, the SPLIT method was modified to use multiple-word templates (pseudophoneme sequences) for each word to cover speaker variations, whereas the set of pseudophoneme templates remain common to all speakers (Sugamura and Furui, 1984). This method was found to be able to reduce the number of calculations and memory size to roughly one-tenth of the method using word-based templates, while maintaining recognition accuracy. In this method, pseudophonemes and multiple sequences in the word dictionary are produced by the same clustering algorithm.

A VQ-based preprocessor has recently been combined with the modified SPLIT method for large-vocabulary speaker-independent isolated word recognition (Furui, 1987). Here, a speech wave is analyzed by time functions of instantaneous cepstral coefficients and short-time regression coefficients for both cepstral coefficients and logarithmic energy. Regression coefficients represent spectral dynamics in every short period, as described in Sec. 8.3.6. A universal VQ codebook for these time functions is constructed based on a multispeaker, multiword database. Next, a separate codebook is designed as a subset of the universal codebook for each word in the vocabulary. These word-specific codebooks are used for front-end processing to eliminate word candidates with large distance (distortion) scores. The SPLIT method subsequently resolves the choice among the remaining word candidates.

The effectiveness of this method was ascertained by recognition experiments using a database consisting of words from a vocabulary of 100 Japanese city names uttered by 20 male speakers. The method reduced the number of calculations to one-tenth while maintaining a recognition accuracy of 98.0%.

### 8.11.2 Discrimination Function Method

A word recognition system based on the discrimination function method consists, as shown in Fig. 8.19, of a preprocessor, which transforms speech into feature vectors, and a discriminator, which performs the recognition decision using a discrimination function (Watanabe et al., 1981). This method is based on the construction of a discrimination function in a multidimensional space spanned by feature parameters into which word utterances are projected.

In the preprocessor, a spoken word utterance is transformed into an autocorrelation function-time sequence after spectral-slope normalization using an adaptive equalization technique. The

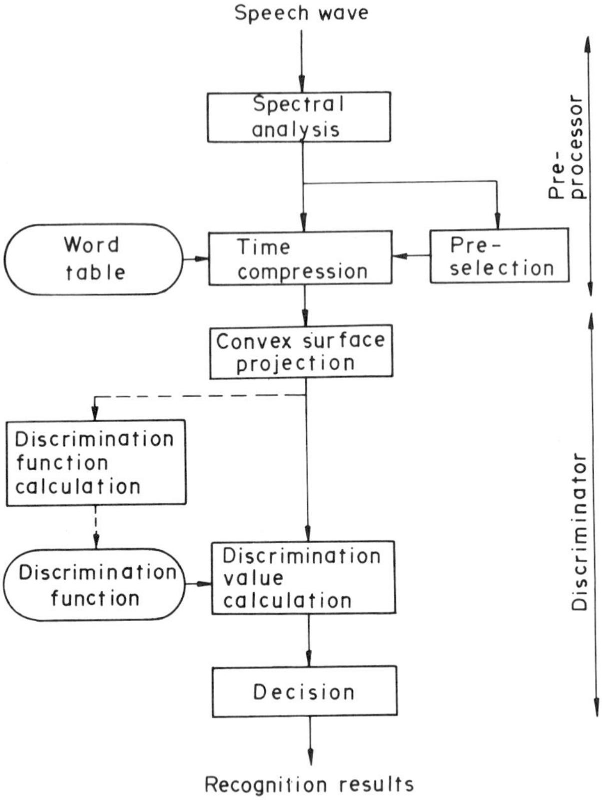


Fig. 8.19 Block diagram of speaker-independent word recognition system based on discrimination function method.

autocorrelation functions and speech amplitude are then transformed by K-L transformation (KLT) into an eight-dimensional vector. Ten cepstral coefficients (a 10-dimensional vector) were also attempted for use as an alternative to the eight-dimensional KLT vector. On the other hand, roughly 10 positions in each word representing the phonetic structure of the word and procedures for extracting these positions are assumed to be stored in advance in a table. These positions for each input utterance are detected by the top-down method by referring to the table. The 8- or 10-dimensional vectors at all of these positions are then combined to construct a roughly 100-dimensional feature vector.

Preselection of candidate words and exclusion of noise as well as words outside the vocabulary are also performed in the preprocessor in order to reduce the amount of processing in the discriminator. These processes are accomplished according to matching scores with reference templates.

The discrimination function for each word is constructed using the linear programming method employing training samples uttered by many speakers. Although the discrimination function is linear, partitioned quadratic discrimination is equivalently performed by projecting feature vectors onto a convex surface. A mean recognition accuracy of 99% was obtained in a recognition experiment for 100 words, when 80 speakers out of a total of 100 male and female speakers were used for training, leaving the remaining 20 for testing.

### 8.11.3 HMM Method

The HMM method described in Sec. 8.6.3 is capable of including spectral distribution and variation in transitional probability for many speakers in the model as a result of statistical processing. Recognition experiments using this method demonstrated that it can achieve almost the same recognition accuracy as the multitemplate method. The amount of computation required in the HMM method is much smaller than in the multitemplate method (Rabiner et al., 1983).

## 8.12 NORMALIZATION AND ADAPTATION FOR INDIVIDUALITY

The need for effectively handling individual variations in speech has resulted in two methods being tried for introducing adaptation mechanisms into a speech recognizer. Such adaptation is based on the voice characteristics of each speaker observed using training utterances of a small number of words or short sentences. In the first method, spectral variation is normalized or removed from input speech, whereas in the second method, the recognizer is adapted to each speaker. Although the recognition methods described in Sec. 8.11 can be used for a large vocabulary, adaptation mechanisms are essential for very large vocabulary speaker-independent word recognition. Since it is almost impossible to conduct training involving every word in a large vocabulary, training using a short string of speech serves as a useful and realistic way of coping with the individuality problem.

Unsupervised training has also been attempted, wherein the recognition system is automatically trained to the speaker through the repetition of the recognition process without the need for training with predetermined words or sentences. Humans have also been found to possess a similar adaptation mechanism. Specifically, although the first several words uttered by a speaker new to the listener may be unintelligible, the latter quickly becomes accustomed to the former's voice. Thus, the intelligibility of the speaker's voice increases particularly after the listener hears several words and utterances (Kato and Kawahara, 1984).

### 8.12.1 Normalization of Individuality

The nature of the speech production mechanism suggest that the vocal cord spectrum and the effects of vocal tract length cause phoneme-independent physical individuality in voiced sounds. Furthermore, the former can be observed in the averaged overall spectrum, that is, in the overall pattern of the long-time averaged spectrum, and the latter can be seen in the linear expansion or contraction coefficient along the frequency axis for the speech spectrum.

Based on this factual evidence, individuality normalization has been introduced for the phoneme-based word recognition system described in Sec. 8.6 (Furui, 1975). Experimental results show that although this method is effective, a gap exists between the recognition accuracies obtained using the method and those surfacing after training utilizing all of the vocabulary words for each speaker. This means that a more complicated model is necessary to ensure complete representation of voice individuality.

Nonlinear warping of the spectrum along the frequency axis has been attempted using the DP technique for normalizing the voice individuality (Matsumoto and Wakita, 1986). Since excessive warping causes the loss of phonetic features, an appropriate limit must be set for the warping function.

### 8.12.2 Adaptation for Voice Individuality

A procedure has been devised to adapt a phoneme-based speaker-dependent word recognition system to a new speaker using a small number of training words (Furui, 1980). Each new speaker is requested to provide utterances of only a fraction of the entire vocabulary as a training set. A set of transformation rules is then utilized to estimate phoneme templates for the entire vocabulary from phoneme templates included in the training.

The transformation rules are obtained in a pretraining procedure in which a group of speakers provides utterances of the entire vocabulary. Multiple regression analysis is employed to obtain linear estimates of the entire phoneme template set in terms of the set designated as training templates. This group of speakers generally differs from the group of training speakers. Since the transformation rules are established independently of the training speakers, the entire procedure can therefore be considered a hybrid speaker-dependent–speaker-independent system.

Results of recognition experiments using spoken digits uttered by 30 male and female speakers and 67 airport names uttered by 30 male speakers have ascertained the effectiveness of this training procedure. Importantly, a mean recognition accuracy of 98.2% was obtained for the latter utterance set after a 12-word training procedure.

A speaker-adaptation technique has also been investigated for VQ-based word recognition (Shikano et al., 1986). With this technique, the VQ codebook for a reference speaker is replaced by that for a new speaker based on the one-to-one correspondence rule of vectors. The correspondence rule is automatically determined by DP matching between training and reference utterances, both of which are represented by the sequences of codebook elements. A histogram of vector correspondence between two codebooks is obtained through DP matching and used to find the best correspondence rule. Word recognition rates of 83% and 64% were obtained with and without speaker adaptation, respectively, for a recognition experiment involving 92 words. Significantly, in a 422-word experiment, introducing the speaker adaptation technique improved the recognition accuracy from 48.1 to 80.9%.

### 8.12.3 Unsupervised Training

Figure 8.20 is a block diagram of an unsupervised training mechanism for automatically separating phonetic and individual information in speech spectra without the need for training utterances other than recognition utterances (Furui, 1974). As a preliminary stage, phonetic and individuality spaces are constructed by discriminant analysis using speech samples uttered by many speakers who are distinct from speakers taking part in the recognition tests.

Input speech is analyzed by cepstral coefficients and projected into the phonetic space. In this space, phonemes in the first five syllables in the input speech string are recognized

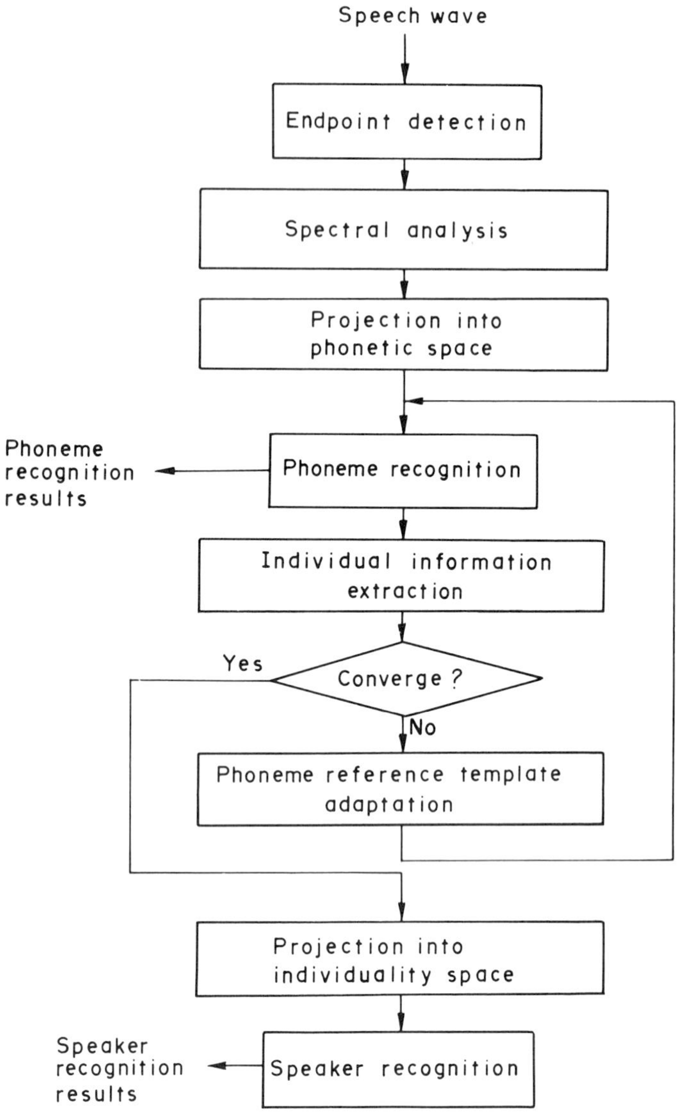


Fig. 8.20 Block diagram of system for separately extracting phonetic and individual information from speech spectrum based on unsupervised training technique.

using phoneme reference templates averaged over many speakers. Input speech is then projected into the individuality space, and individual information is extracted for each phoneme employing a phoneme-dependent analysis technique. Based on individual information for many phonemes, the phoneme reference templates are modified in the phonetic space to fit the speaker's voice. Utilizing these adapted phoneme reference templates, phoneme recognition is performed for the same test utterances again. These procedures are repeated until the extracted phoneme and individual information converge.

Based on the converged results of phoneme recognition, speaker recognition is also performed using phoneme-dependent speaker reference templates. The effectiveness of this method has been confirmed by recognition experiments.

An unsupervised training method has also been tried for a system of recognizing vowels in continuous speech (Sugiyama, 1986). In this method, many sets of vowels representing speaker variability are stored beforehand, with the most suitable set for the speaker being automatically selected in accordance with the previous recognition results. Utilizing this method has also been experimentally verified to improve recognition accuracy.

The physical characteristics of a speech wave for a word vary even if uttered by the same speaker. Although this does not influence speech recognition performance as much as it does speaker recognition performance, it cannot be ignored (Furui, 1977). Therefore, it is most desirable to automatically update reference templates at periodic intervals even for speaker-dependent speech recognition in order to maintain good recognition performance over the long term.

# 9

# Speaker Recognition

## 9.1 PRINCIPLES OF SPEAKER RECOGNITION

### 9.1.1 Human and Computer Speaker Recognition

A technology closely related to speech recognition is speaker recognition, or the automatic recognition of a speaker (talker) through measurements of the specifically individual characteristics arising in the speaker's voice signal (Atal, 1976; Rosenberg, 1976; Furui, 1978). Speaker recognition research is especially closely intertwined with the principles underlying speaker-independent speech recognition technology. In the broadest sense of the word, speaker recognition research also involves investigating clues humans use to recognize speakers either by sound spectrogram (voice print) (Kersta, 1962; Tosi et al., 1972) or by hearing.

History notes that as early as 1660 a witness was recorded as having been able to identify a defendant by his voice at one of the trial sessions summoned to determine circumstances surrounding the death of Charles I (NCR, 1976). Speaker recognition did not become a subject of scientific inquiry until over two centuries later, however, when telephony made available the possibility of speaker recognition independent of distance in conjunction with sound recording giving rise to speaker recognition independent of time. The use of sound spectrograms in the 1940s also incorporated the sensory capability of vision along with that of hearing in performing speaker recognition. It was not until 1966 that a court of law finally admitted speaker recognition testimony based on spectrograms of speech sounds.

In parallel with the aural and visual methods, automated methods of speaker recognition have continued to be developed, and are consequently yielding information strengthening the accuracy of the former methods. The automated methods have recently made remarkable progress partly owing to the influential advances in computer and information processing technologies. This chapter will focus exclusively on automatic speaker recognition technology.

The actual realization of speaker recognition systems makes use of voice as the key tool for verifying the identity of a speaker for application to an extensive array of customer-demand services. In the near future, these services will include banking transactions using the telephone network, database acquisition services including personal information accessing, and security control for protecting confidential areas of concern. Importantly, identity verification using voice is far more convenient than using cards, keys, or other artificial means for identification, and is much safer because voice can neither be lost nor stolen. In addition, voice recognition does not require the use of the hands. Accordingly, several systems are currently being planned for future applications in the rapidly accelerating information-intensive age into which we are entering.

The principal disadvantage of using voice is that its physical characteristics are variable and easily modified by transmission and microphone characteristics as well as by background noise. If a system is capable of accepting wide variation in the customer's voice, for example, it might also unfortunately accept the voice of a different speaker if sufficiently similar. It is thus extremely essential to use physical features which are stable and not easily mimicked or affected by transmission characteristics.

### 9.1.2 Individual Characteristics

Individual information includes voice quality, voice height, loudness, speed, tempo, intonation, accent, and the use of vocabulary. Various physical features interacting in a complicated manner produce these voice characterisitcs. They arise both from hereditary individual differences in articulatory organs, such as the length of the vocal tract and the vocal cord characteristics, and from acquired differences in the manner of speaking. Voice quality and height, which are the most important types of individual auditory information, are mainly related to the static and temporal characteristics of the spectral envelope and fundamental frequency (pitch).

The temporal characteristics, that is, time functions of the spectral envelope, fundamental frequency, and energy, can be used for speaker recognition in a way similar to those used for speech recognition. However, several considerations and processes designed to emphasize stable individual characteristics are necessary in order to achieve high-performance speaker recognition.

The statistical characteristics derived from the time functions of spectral features are also successfully used in speaker recognition. The use of statistical characteristics specifically reduces the dimensions of templates, and consequently cuts down the run-time computation as well as the memory size of reference templates. Similar recognition results on 40-frame words have been obtained either with standard DTW template matching or with a single distance measure involving a 20-dimensional vector employing the statistical features of fundamental frequency and LPC parameters (Furui, 1981a).

Since speaker recognition systems using temporal patterns of source characteristics only, such as pitch and energy, are not resistant to mimicked voice, they should desirably be combined with vocal tract characteristics, namely, with spectral envelope parameters, to build more robust systems (Rosenberg and Sambur, 1975).

## 9.2 SPEAKER RECOGNITION METHODS

### 9.2.1 Classification of Speaker Recognition Methods

Speaker recognition can be principally divided into speaker verification and speaker identification. Speaker verification is the process of accepting or rejecting the identity claim of a speaker by comparing a set of measurements of the speaker's utterances with a reference set of measurements of the utterance of the person whose identity is being claimed. Speaker identification is the process of determining from which of the registered speakers a given utterance comes. The speaker identification process is similar to the spoken word recognition process in that both determine which reference template is most similar to the input speech.

Speaker verification is applicable to various kinds of services which include the use of voice as the key to confirming the identity claim of a speaker. Speaker identification can be used in criminal investigations to determine which of the suspected persons produced the voice recorded at the scene of the crime.

Since the possibility always exists that the real criminal is not one of the suspects, however, the identification decision should be made through the combined processes of speaker verification and speaker identification.

Speaker recognition methods can also be divided into text-dependent and text-independent methods. The former require the speaker to issue a predetermined utterance, whereas the latter do not rely on a specific text being spoken. In general, because of the higher acoustic-phonetic variability of text-independent input, more training material is necessary to reliably characterize (model) a speaker than with text-dependent methods.

Although several text-dependent methods use features of special phonemes, such as nasals, most text-dependent systems allow words (key words, names, ID numbers, etc.) or sentences to be arbitrarily selected only if they are fixed to each speaker. In the latter case, the differences in words or sentences between the speakers improves the accuracy of speaker recognition. When evaluating experimental systems, however, common key words or sentences are usually used for every speaker.

Although key words can be fixed for each speaker in many applications of speaker verification, utterances of the same words cannot always be compared in criminal investigations. In such cases, a text-independent method is essential. Difficulty in speaker recognition varies, depending on whether or not the speakers intend for their identities to be verified. During speaker verification use, speakers are usually expected to cooperate without intentionally changing their speaking rate or manner. It is well known, however, and natural from their point of view, I suspect, that speakers are most often uncooperative in criminal investigations, consequently compounding the difficulty in correctly recognizing their voices.

### 9.2.2 Structure of Speaker Recognition Systems

The common structure of speaker recognition systems is shown in Fig. 9.1. Feature parameters extracted from a speech wave are compared with the stored reference templates for each registered speaker. The recognition decision is made according to the distance (or similarity) values. For speaker verification, input utterances with distances to the reference template smaller than the threshold are accepted as being utterances of the registered speaker (customer), while input utterances with distances larger than the threshold are rejected as being those of a different speaker (impostor). With speaker identification, the registered speaker whose reference template is nearest to the input

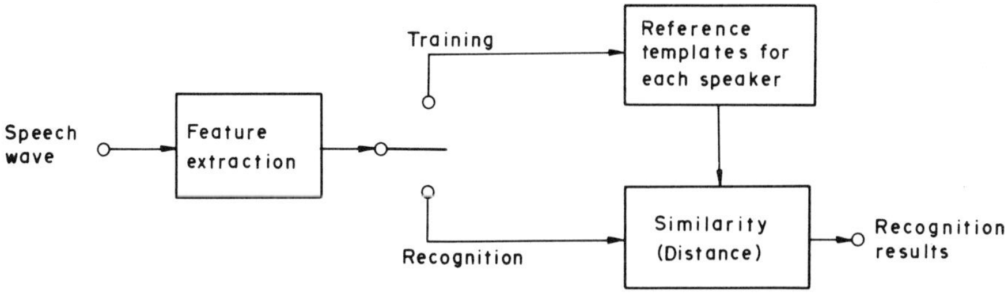


Fig. 9.1 Principal structure of speaker recognition systems.

utterance between all the registered speakers is selected as being the speaker of the input utterance.

The receiver operating characteristic (ROC) curve adopted from psychophysics is used for evaluating speaker verification systems (NRC, 1979). In speaker verification, two conditions concern the input utterance: s, or the condition that the utterance belongs to the customer, and n, the opposite condition. Two decision conditions also exist: S, the condition that the utterance is accepted as being that of the customer, and N, the condition that the utterance is rejected.

These conditions combine to make up the four conditional probabilities as designated in Table 9.1. Specifically, $P(S|s)$ is the probability of correct acceptance; $P(S|n)$ is the probability of false acceptance (FA), namely, the probability of accepting impostors, $P(N|s)$ is the probability of false rejection (FR), or the probability of mistakenly rejecting the real customer; and $P(N|n)$ is the probability of correct rejection.

Since the relationships

TABLE 9.1 Four Conditional Probabilities in Speaker Verification

| | Input utterance condition | |
|---|---|---|
| Decision condition | s (customer) | n (impostor) |
| S (accept) | $P(S\|s)$ | $P(S\|n)$ |
| N (reject) | $P(N\|s)$ | $P(N\|n)$ |

$$P(S \mid s) + P(N \mid s) = 1$$

and

$$P(S \mid n) + P(N \mid n) = 1 \tag{9.1}$$

exist for the four probabilities, speaker verification systems can be evaluated using the two probabilities $P(S|s)$ and $P(S|n)$. If these two values are assigned to the vertical and horizontal axes respectively, and if the decision criterion (threshold) of accepting the speech as being that of the customer is varied, ROC curves as indicated in Fig. 9.2 are obtained. The figure exemplifies the curves for three systems: A, B, and D. Clearly, the performance of curve B is consistently superior to that of curve A, and D corresponds to the limiting case of purely chance performance.

On the other hand, the relationship between the decision criterion and the two kinds of errors is presented in Fig. 9.3. Position a in Figs. 9.2 and 9.3 corresponds to the case in which a strict decision criterion is employed, and position b corresponds

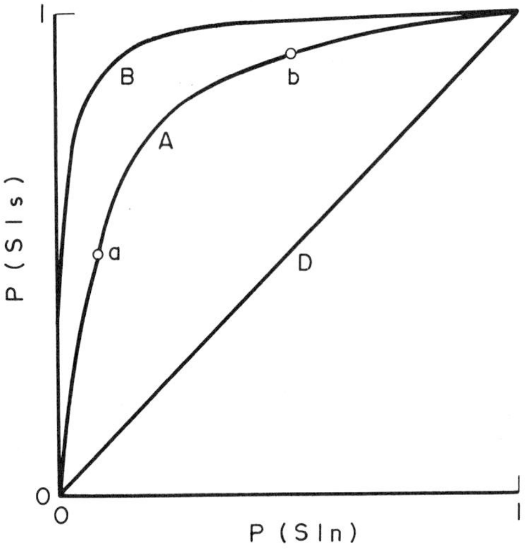


Fig. 9.2 Receiver operating characteristic (ROC) curves; performance examples of three speaker verification systems: A, B, and D.

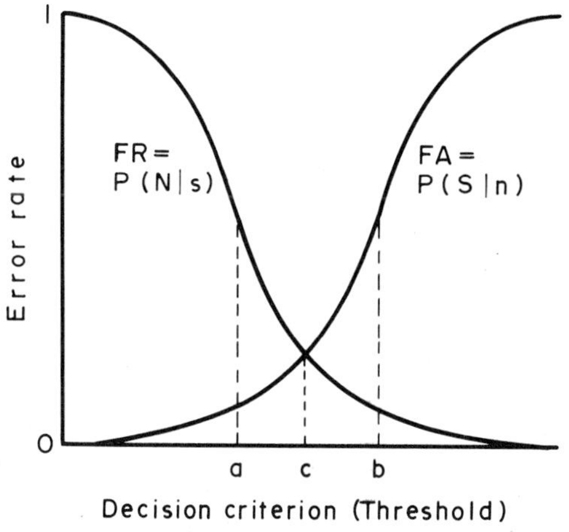


Fig. 9.3 Relationship between error rate and decision criterion (threshold) in speaker verification.

to that wherein a lax criterion is used. The decision criterion in practical applications should be determined according to the effects of decision errors. This criterion can be determined based on a priori probabilities of a match, P(s), on the cost values of the various decision results, and on the slope of the ROC curve. In experimental tests the criterion is usually set a posteriori for each individual speaker in order to match up the two kinds of error rates, FR and FA, as indicated by c in Fig. 9.3.

### 9.2.3 Relationship Between Error Rate and Number of Speakers

Let us assume that $Z_N$ represents a population of N registered speakers, that $X' = (x_1, x_2, \ldots, x_n)$ is an n-dimensional feature vector representing the speech sample, and that $P_i(X)$ is the probability density function of X for speaker i ($i \in Z_N$). The chance probability density function of X within population $Z_N$ can then be expressed as

$$P_Z(x) = \underset{i \in Z_N}{E} [P_i(X)]$$

$$= \sum_i P_i(X)\Pr[i], \qquad i \in Z_N \tag{9.2}$$

where Pr[i] is the a priori chance probability of speaker i (Doddington, 1974).

In the case of speaker verification, the region of X which should be accepted as the voice of customer i is

$$R_{Vi} = \{X \mid P_i(X) > C_i P_Z(X)\} \tag{9.3}$$

where $C_i$ is chosen to effect the desired balance between FA and FR errors. With $Z_N$ constructed using randomly selected speakers, and with the a priori probability independent of the speaker, Pr[i] = 1/N, then $P_Z(X)$ will approach a limiting density function independent of $Z_N$ as N becomes large. Thus, Pr(FA) and Pr(FR) are relatively unaffected by the size of the population, N, when it is large. From a practical perspective, $P_Z(X)$ is assumed to be constant since it is generally difficult to estimate this value precisely, and

$$R_{Vi} = \{ X \mid P_i(X) > k_i\} \tag{9.4}$$

is simply used as the acceptance region.

With speaker identification, the region of X, which should be judged as the voice of speaker i, is

$$R_{Ii} = \{X \mid P_i(X) > P_j(X), \ \forall j \neq i\} \tag{9.5}$$

The probability of error for speaker i then becomes

$$P_{Ei} = 1 - \prod_{\substack{k=1 \\ k \neq i}}^{N} \Pr(P_i(X) > P_k(X)) \tag{9.6}$$

With $Z_N$ constructed by randomly selected speakers, the equations

$$\underset{Z_N}{E}[P_{Ei}] = 1 - \underset{Z_N}{E} \left\{ \prod_{\substack{k=1 \\ k \neq i}}^{N} \Pr(P_i(X) > P_k(X)) \right\}$$

$$= 1 - \underset{i}{E} \left\{ \prod_{\substack{k=1 \\ k \neq i}}^{N} E[\Pr(P_i(X) > P_k(X))] \right\}$$

$$= -\underset{i}{E}\{P_{Ai}^{N-1}\} \qquad (9.7)$$

can be obtained, where $P_{Ai}$ is the expected probability of not confusing speaker i with another speaker. Thus, the expected probability of correctly identifying a speaker decreases exponentially with the size of the population.

This is a natural outcome of the fact that the distribution of infinite points cannot be separated in a finite parameter space. More specifically, when the population of speakers increases, the probability that the distributions of two or more speakers are very close increases. Therefore, the effectiveness of speaker identification systems must be evaluated according to their limits in population size.

Figure 9.4 indicates this relationship between the size of the population and recognition error rates for speaker identification

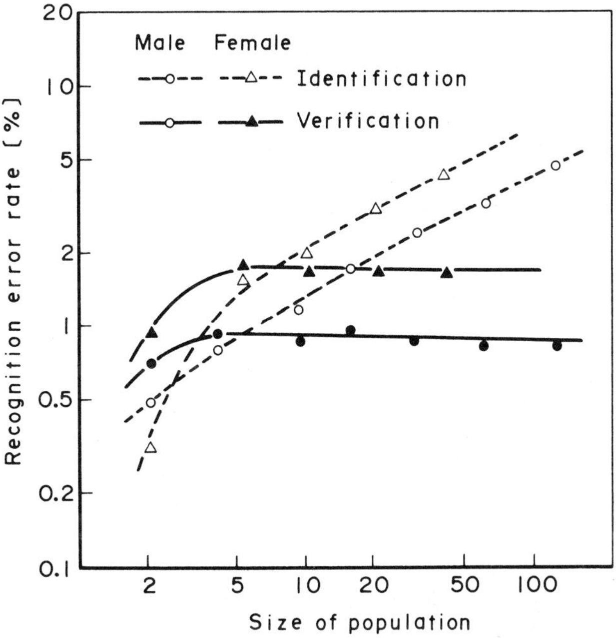


Fig. 9.4 Recognition error rates as a function of population size in speaker identification and verification.

and verification (Furui, 1978). These results were obtained for a recognition system employing the statistical features of the spectral parameters derived from spoken words (see Sec. 9.3.1).

### 9.2.4 Long-Term Variation and Evaluation of Feature Parameters

One of the most difficult problems in speaker recognition is that intersession variability (variability over time) for a given speaker significantly affects recognition accuracy. Although this does not cause extensive problems in speech recognition, it makes speaker recognition difficult for two major reasons. First, the reference template for each speaker, which is constructed using training utterances prior to the recognition, is repeatedly used later. Second, individual information in a speech wave is more detailed than phonetic information; that is, the interspeaker variation of physical parameters is much smaller than the interphoneme variation.

A number of methods have been confirmed to be effective in reducing the effects of long-term variation in feature parameters and in obtaining good recognition performance after a long interval (Furui, 1981a). These include

1. The application of spectral equalization, i.e., the passing of the speech signal through a first- or second-order critical damping inverse filter which represents the overall pattern of the time-averaged spectrum for a word or short sentence of speech
2. The selection of stable feature parameters based on statistical evaluation using speech utterances recorded over a long period
3. The combination of feature parameters extracted from a variety of different words
4. The construction of reference templates and distance measures based on training utterances recorded over a long period
5. The renewal of the reference template for each customer at the appropriate time interval

The effectiveness of the spectral equalization process was examined by means of speaker recognition experiments using statistical features extracted from a spoken word. Results with and without spectral equalization were compared for both short-term and long-term training. The short-term training set comprised utterances recorded over a period of 10 days in three or four sessions at intervals of 2 or 3 days. The long-term training set consisted of utterances recorded over a 10-month period in four sessions at intervals of 3 months. The time interval between the last training utterance and the input utterance ranged from two or three days to five years.

The speaker verification results obtained are exemplified in Fig. 9.5. Although these results clearly confirm that spectral equalization is effective in reducing errors as a function of the time interval for both short-term and long-term training, it is especially effective with short-term training. Concerning the speech production mechanism, the effectiveness of spectral

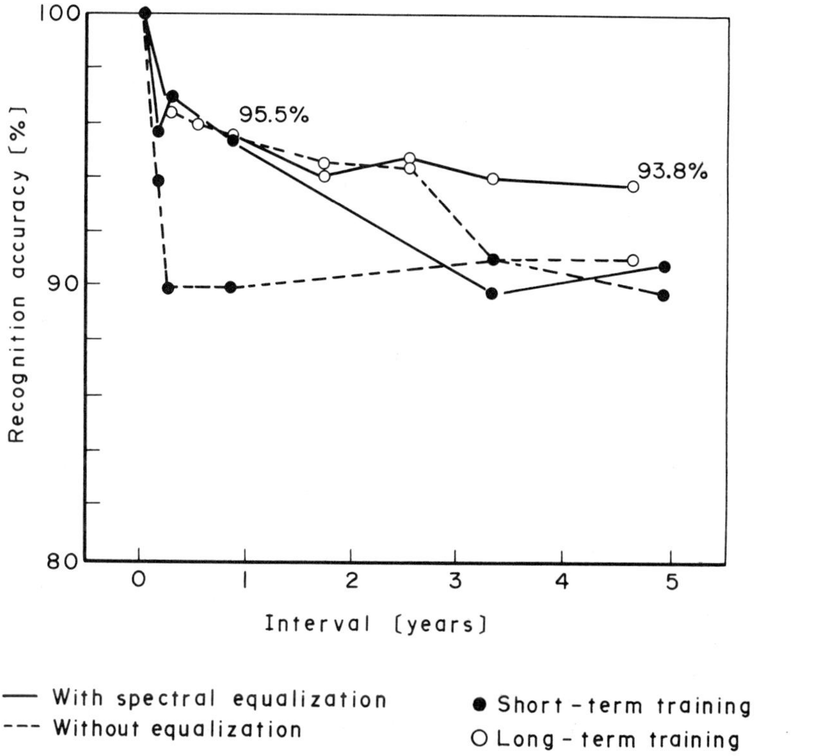


Fig. 9.5 Results of speaker verification using statistical features extracted from a spoken word with or without spectral equalization.

equalization means that vocal tract characteristics are much more stable than the overall patterns of the vocal cord spectrum.

Four methods can be used for evaluating the feature parameters:

1. Performing recognition experiments based on various combinations of parameters
2. Measuring the F-ratio (inter- to intravariance ratio) for each parameter (Furui, 1978)
3. Calculating the divergence, which is an expansion of the F-ratio into a multidimensional space (Atal, 1972)
4. Using the knockout method based on recognition error rates (Sambur, 1975)

In order to effectively reduce the amount of information, that is, the number of parameters, feature parameter sets are sometimes projected into a space constructed by discriminant analysis which maximizes the F-ratio.

## 9.3 EXAMPLES OF SPEAKER RECOGNITION SYSTEMS

### 9.3.1 Text-Dependent Speaker Recognition Systems

Large-scale experiments have been performed for some time for text-dependent speaker recognition which is more realistic than text-independent speaker recognition. They include experiments on an entry control system for a computer room at Texas Instruments in which 300 male and female speakers were used over a long period of time (Doddington, 1976), and speaker verification systems for telephone speech which were tested at Bell Laboratories using roughly 100 male and female speakers (Rosenberg, 1976b; Furui, 1981b). These methods are based on a comparison of the time functions of the spectral parameters between input speech and reference templates.

Figure 9.6 is a block diagram of the method investigated at Bell Labs (Furui, 1981b). With this method, not only is the time series brought into time registration with the stored reference functions, but a set of dynamic features (see Sec. 8.3.6) is also explicitly extracted and used for the recognition. Initially, 10 LPC cepstral coefficients are extracted every 10 ms from a short sentence of speech. These cepstral coefficients are then averaged over the duration of the entire utterance. The averaged values are next subtracted from the cepstral coefficients

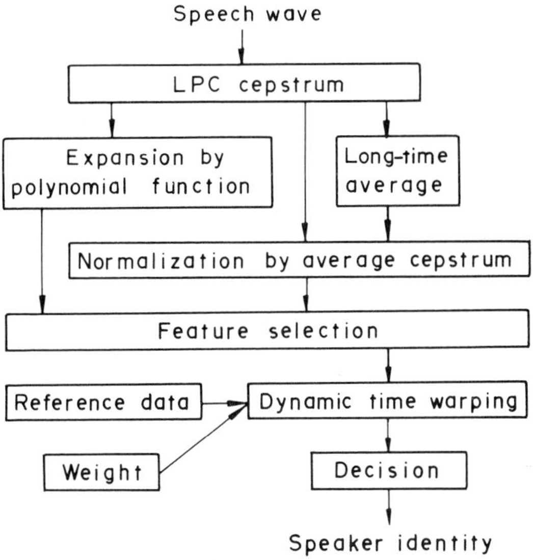


Fig. 9.6 Block diagram indicating principal operation of speaker recognition method using time series of cepstral coefficients and their orthogonal polynomial coefficients.

of every frame to compensate for the frequency-response distortion introduced by the transmission system, and to reduce long-term intraspeaker spectral variability. This procedure is similar to the spectral equalization described in the previous section.

Time functions for the cepstral coefficients are subsequently expanded by an orthogonal polynomial representation over 90-ms intervals, which are shifted every 10 ms. The first- and second-order polynomial coefficients are thus obtained as the representations of dynamic characteristics. From the normalized cepstral and polynomial coefficients, a set of 18 elements is selected which are the most effective in separating the speakers' overall distance distribution. The time function of the set is brought into time registration with the reference template in order to calculate the distance between them. The overall distance is then compared with a threshold for the verification decision. The threshold and reference template are updated every two weeks by using the distribution of interspeaker distances.

Experimental results indicate that a high degree of verification accuracy can be obtained even if the reference and input utterances are transmitted on different telephone systems, such as on those using ADPCMs and LPC vocoders. An online experiment performed over a period of six months, using dialed-up telephone speech uttered by 60 male and 60 female speakers, also supports the effectiveness of this system.

Figure 9.7 is a block diagram of the method employing statistical features of spectral parameters extracted from spoken words (Furui, 1982). Here, each speaker separately utters four kinds of words. The fundamental frequency and 10 LPC-cepstral

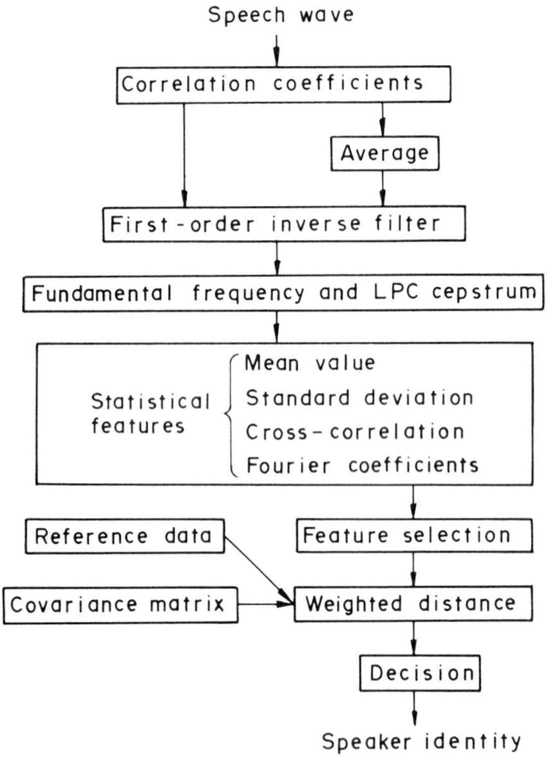


Fig. 9.7 Block diagram indicating principal operation of speaker recognition method using statistical features of spectral parameters extracted from a word utterance.

coefficients are extracted every 10 ms following spectral equalization. A set of statistical features consisting of the mean value, standard deviation, cross-correlation coefficients, and Fourier cosine expansion coefficients are measured for the time functions of fundamental frequency and cepstral coefficients in the voiced portion of each word. A fixed reduced set, which is most effective in separating the speakers, is then selected and used for speaker recognition. This selection is based on the interspeaker-to-intraspeaker variability ratio for each element, calculated through an analysis of variance over a series of training utterances.

Experimental results demonstrate that a high recognition rate can be obtained using this method for both microphone and telephone speech. An online speaker verification experiment using dialed-up telephone speech uttered by 34 male and female speakers was conducted over a six-month term. Although the recognition accuracy was not high in the initial stages of the experiment due to the unreliability of the reference templates, it rose with the increase in the number of experiments, reaching a final accuracy level of 97 to 98% in the stabilized stage.

### 9.3.2 Text-Independent Speaker Recognition Systems

Text-independent speaker recognition methods can be classified into three methods as presented in Fig. 9.8 (Furui, 1986).

The process indicated as (a) corresponds to the calculation of the long-time averaged speech spectrum (LAS). In a successful example of a speaker recognition method using LAS, that calculated for a spoken sentence roughly 10 s in length is transformed into cepstral coefficients in order to analyze and normalize its long-term intraspeaker variations (Furui et al., 1972). According to the definition of cepstrum, lower-order and higher-order elements, respectively, correspond to the global pattern and microscopic structure of the logarithmic spectrum. Therefore, both spectral features can be processed separately by the transformation into the cepstrum, and by using a weighted cepstral distance. Experimental results show that when training utterances are recorded over a long term such as up to or over 10 months, a 95% speaker verification accuracy can be obtained, even if the interval between the training and input speech is as much as three months.

Another example of the method shown in Fig. 9.8(a) is one that uses mean and variance values for the feature parameters

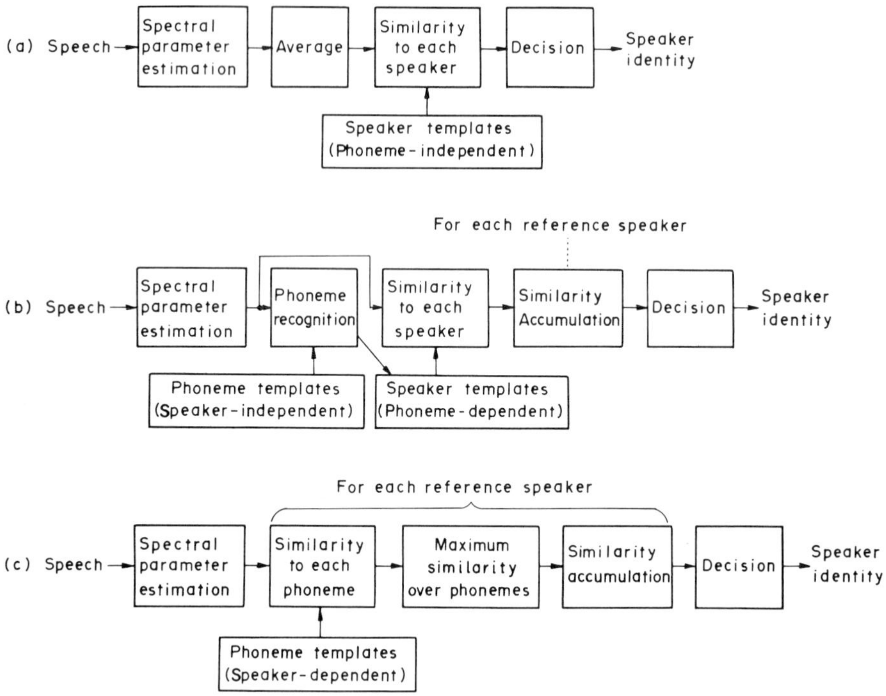


Fig. 9.8 Three kinds of text-independent speaker recognition methods: (a) method using long-time averaged characteristics; (b) method incorporating explicit phoneme decision; (c) method featuring implicit phoneme decision.

obtained by orthogonal transformation of LPC analysis parameters (Sambur, 1976). In this method, it is assumed that phonetic characteristics are emphasized by projection into a space constructed by eigenvectors having larger eigenvalues, and that individual characteristics are emphasized in the eigenvector space having smaller eigenvalues. Speaker recognition is performed in the latter space.

However, the method shown in Fig. 9.8(a) is disadvantageous in that long-period averaging is required to extract stable features, because the speaker effect in the speech spectrum is smaller than the phoneme effect and is comparable to the interaction effect (Furui, 1978). This disadvantage has been contended with through the examination of another text-independent speaker recognition method, in which individual information is extracted following the automatic recognition of phonemes. This method can be divided into two variations depending on whether phonemes are explicitly (see Fig. 9.8(b)) or implicitly (see Fig. 9.8(c)) recognized.

In the first variation, the phoneme is recognized for every short segment of the speech wave on the basis of its similarity to speaker-independent phoneme reference templates. Its similarity to the reference template of each speaker associated with the recognized phoneme is then calculated. Similarity values for all short segments are averaged across the entire speech interval to produce an overall similarity to each reference speaker. An example demonstrating the realization of this method has already been described in Sec. 8.12.3 as an unsupervised training method. Experimental results point out that the speaker identification and verification error rates are reduced to one-third of those obtained under the no-phoneme recognition condition (Furui, 1978).

The second variation, in which the phoneme is not explicitly recognized, involves the storing of a set of phoneme reference templates for each speaker. Every short segment of input speech is compared with all reference phoneme templates of each reference speaker, with a phoneme template exhibiting maximum similarity being selected. The maximum similarity values are averaged over the entire speech interval for each reference speaker. The speaker acquiring the maximum averaged value is finally selected as the speaker of the input speech (Atal, 1974).

Since phoneme recognition is not explicitly performed in this variation, the pseudophoneme templates produced by the VQ technique can be used instead of the phoneme templates. In this modification, a separate VQ codebook is designed for each reference speaker, and the distribution of VQ distortion over the entire speech interval is calculated using each codebook. Figure 9.9 presents a typical example of such distributions. Since the distortion usually acquires a small value when the speaker of the input speech and reference template are the same, speaker recognition can be performed according to the distribution.

A confirmation experiment was performed under the conditions of the speech signal being analyzed by LPC technique, a codebook size for each speaker of 40 being made up of a subset of a universal codebook with 400 elements, 11 registered speakers, and 100 s of training utterances for each speaker. The

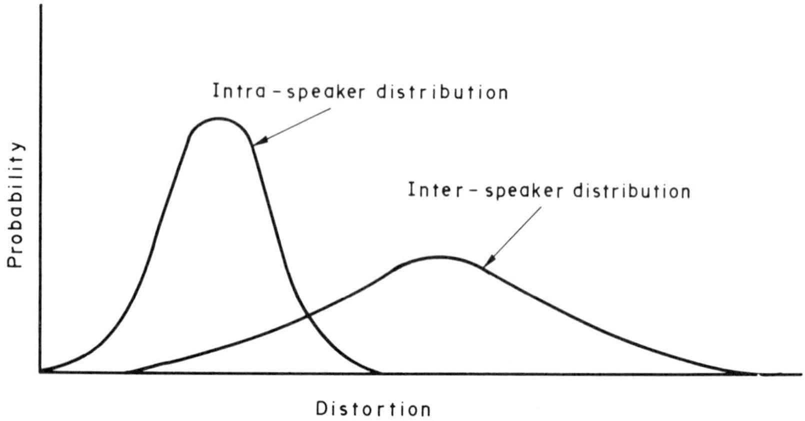


Fig. 9.9 Typical example of distribution of intra- and inter-speaker distortion for every short segment of input speech over an entire speech interval.

results show that speaker identification accuracies of 96, 87, and 79% can be obtained using 10-, 5-, and 3-s-long test utterances, respectively (Li and Wrench, 1983).

Furthermore, a recent experiment employed isolated digits (0–9) for both the training and testing of 100 speakers, with one codebook being used per speaker. In this case the speaker recognition decision was performed based on the average distortion over the entire speech interval. The recognition error was shown to decrease substantially as a function of both codebook size and test utterance duration, with errors below 2% appearing for 10-digit tests and 64-word codebooks (Fig. 9.10). Increasing codebook size increases the amount of computation but decreases the likelihood of error by reducing the standard deviations of the distortions (Soong et al., 1985).

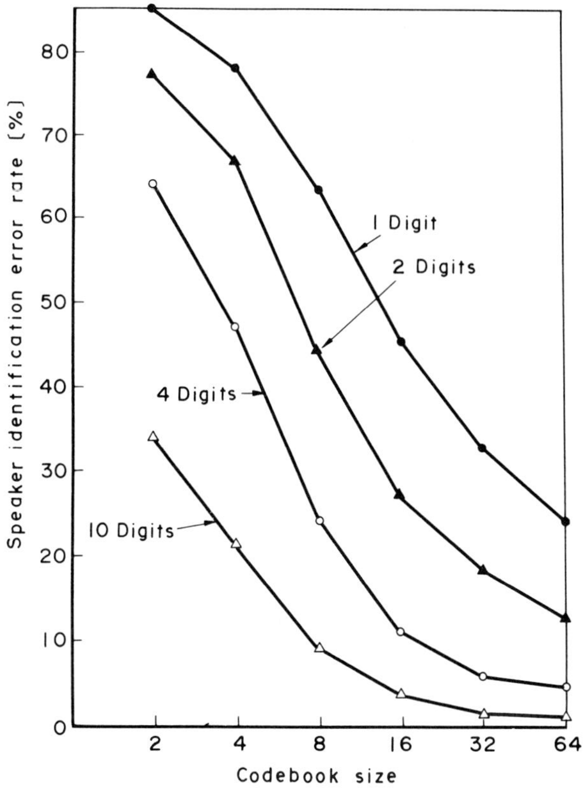


Fig. 9.10 Speaker identification error rate as a function of codebook size for test utterances of 1, 2, 4, and 10 different digits.

# 10

# Future Directions of Speech Information Processing

## 10.1 OVERVIEW

For the majority of mankind, speech understanding and production are involuntary processes quickly and effectively performed throughout our daily lives. A part of these human processes has already been synthetically realized, owing to the recent progress in speech signal processing, linguistic processing, and LSI technologies. What we are actually capable of turning into practical, beneficial tools at present using these technologies, however, can be considered very restricted at best.

Figure 10.1 attempts to simplify to a certain degree the relationships between the various types of speech recognition, understanding, synthesis, and coding technologies. Several of these remain to be investigated. It is essential to ensure that speech information processing technologies play the ever-heightening, demand-stimulated role desired in facilitating the progress of the information communications societies toward which we are aspiring. This can only be achieved by enhancing our synthetic speech technologies to the point where they approach as closely as possible our inherent human abilities. Importantly, this necessitates our competently solving the broadest possible range of interrelated problems in the near future.

In an effort to graphically clarify the relationships between the elements of engineering and human speech information processing mechanisms, Fig. 10.2 details the variations between speech information processing technologies and the scientific and technological areas serving as the foundational roots of speech

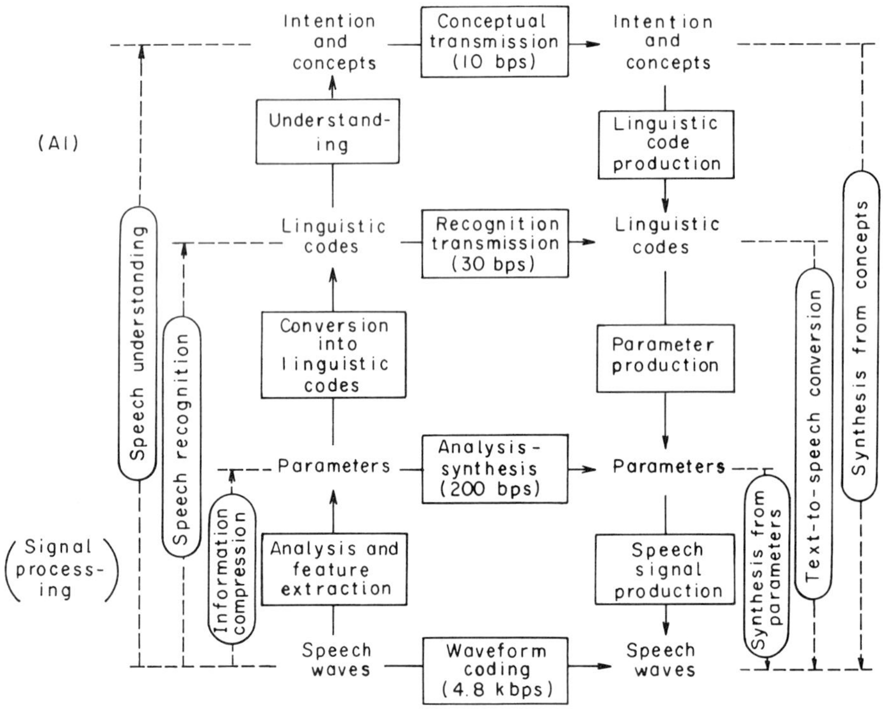


Fig. 10.1 Principal speech information processing technologies and their relationships.

research. As is evident in the figure, and as described elsewhere in this book, speech research is fundamentally and intrinsically supported by a wide range of sciences. The intensification of speech research continues to underscore an even greater interrelationship between scientific and technological interests.

Although individual aspects of speech information processing research have thus far been performed independently for the most part, they will encounter increased interaction until commonly shared problems become simultaneously investigated and solved. Only then can we expect to witness tremendous speech research progress, and hence fruition of widely applicable, beneficial techniques.

Along these lines, this chapter summarizes what are considered to be the 10 most important research topics, in particular

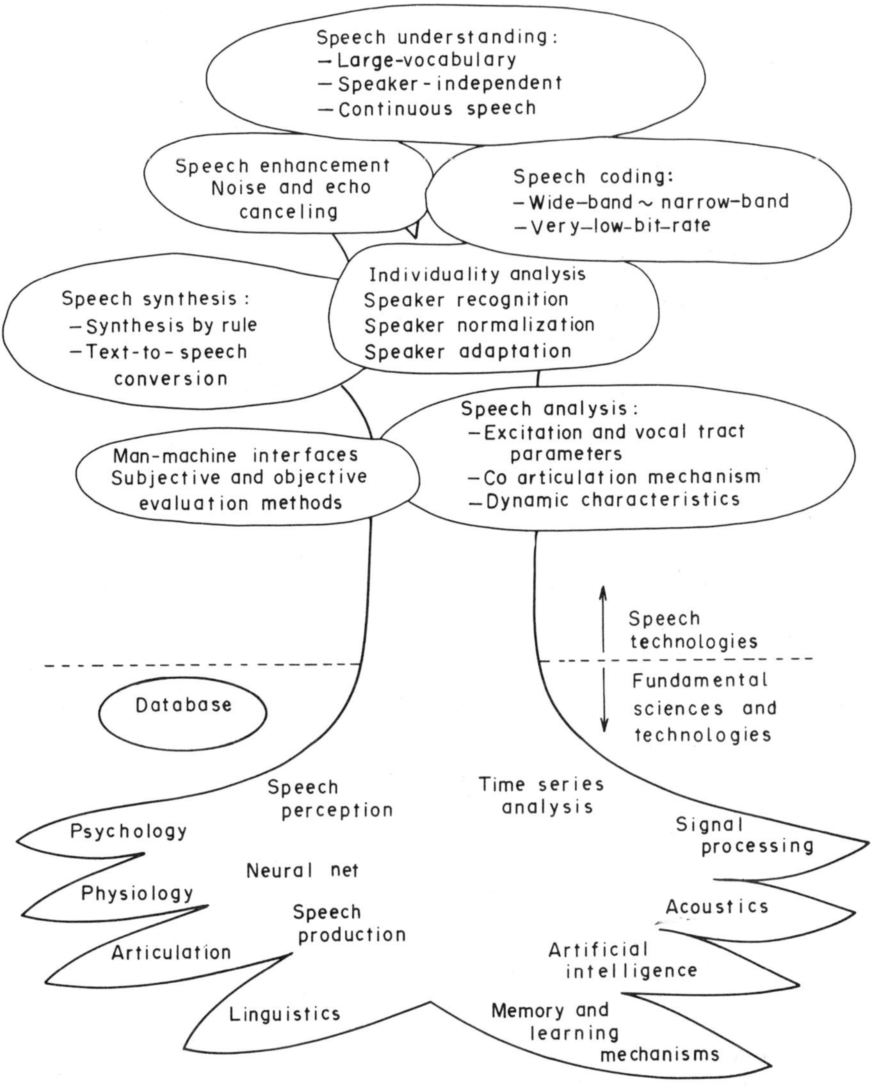


Fig. 10.2 Speech information processing "tree," consisting of present and future speech information processing technologies supported by scientific and technological areas serving as the foundations of speech research.

those which intertwine a multiplicity of speech research areas. These topics must be rigorously pursued and investigated if we are to realize our information communications societies fully incorporating enhanced speech technologies.

## 10.2 ANALYSIS AND DESCRIPTION OF DYNAMIC FEATURES

Psychological and physiological research into the human speech perception mechanisms overwhelmingly reports that the dynamic features of the speech spectrum and the speech wave over time intervals between 2 to 3 ms and 20 to 50 ms play crucially important roles in phoneme perception. This holds not only for consonants such as plosives but also for vowels in continuous speech. On the other hand, almost all speech analysis methods developed thus far, including Fourier spectral analysis and LPC analysis, assume the stationarity of the signals. Only a few methods have been investigated for representing transitional or dynamic features. Although such representation constitutes one of the most difficult problems facing the speech researcher today, the discovery of a good method is expected to produce a substantial impact on the course of speech research.

Coarticulation phenomena have usually been studied as variations or modifications of spectra resulting from the influence of adjacent phonemes or syllables. It is considered essential, however, that these phenomena be examined from the viewpoint of phonemic information existing in the dynamic characteristics.

Additionally important to these relatively "microdynamic" phonemic information-related features are the relatively "macrodynamic" features covering the interval between 200 to 300 ms and 2 to 3 s. The latter dynamic features bear prosodic features of speech such as intonation and stress. And although they seem to be easily extracted using the time functions of pitch and energy, they are actually extremely difficult to correctly extract from a speech wave by automatic methods. Even if they were to be effectively extracted, it is still very difficult to relate these features to the perceptual prosodic information. Therefore, even in the speech recognition area, in which prosodic features are expected to play a substantial role, only a few trials utilizing them have succeeded to any notable degree.

In speech synthesis, control rules for prosodic features largely affect the intelligibility and naturalness of synthesized voice. Here also, although the significance of prosodic features is clearly as great as that of phonemic features, the perception and control mechanisms of prosodic features have not yet been clarified.

## 10.3 EXTRACTION AND NORMALIZATION OF VOICE INDIVIDUALITY

Although many kinds of speech recognizers have already been commercialized, their vocabulary size is highly restricted in speaker-independent recognition. Additionally, a small fraction of people occasionally produce exceptionally low recognition rates. A similar phenomenon, which is called the "sheep and goats phenomenon," also occurs in speaker recognition.

The voice individuality problem in speech recognition has been handled to a certain extent through studies into automatic adaptation algorithms using a small number of training utterances and unsupervised training algorithms. In the unsupervised algorithms, utterances for recognition are also used for training. These algorithms are currently capable of only very restricted application, however, since the mechanism of producing voice individuality has not yet been sufficiently delineated. Accordingly, becoming increasingly more important will be research on speaker-independent speech recognition systems having an automatic speaker adaptation mechanism based on unsupervised training algorithms requiring no additional training utterances.

Speaker adaptation or normalization algorithms in speech recognition as well as speaker recognition algorithms should be investigated using a common approach. This is because they are two sides of the same problem: how best to separate the speaker's information and the phonemic information in speech waves. This approach is essential to effectively formulate the unsupervised training and text-independent speaker recognition algorithms.

In the speech synthesis area, a speech synthesizer has recently been commercialized, in which voice quality can be selected from male, female, and infant voices. No system has been constructed, however, that can precisely select or control the synthesized voice quality. Research into the mechanism underlying voice quality, inclusive of voice individuality, is thus necessary to ensure that synthetic voice is capable of imitating a desired speaker's voice or to select any voice quality such as a hard or soft voice.

Even in speech coding (analysis-synthesis and waveform coding), the dependency of the coded speech quality on the individuality of the original speech increases with the advanced, high-compression-rate methods. Put another way, in these advanced methods, only perceptual speech quality degradation of coded speech clearly depends on the original voice. It is of obvious importance then to elucidate the mechanism of voice dependency and to develop a method which increases this dependency.

## 10.4 ADAPTATION TO ENVIRONMENTAL VARIATION

For speech recognition and speaker recognition systems to bring their capabilities into full play during actual speech situations, they must be able to effectively minimize, or hopefully eliminate, the influence of overlapped stationary noise as well as unstationary noise such as other speaker's voices. Present speech recognition systems have gone a long way toward resolving these problems by using a close-talking microphone and by instituting training (registration) for each speaker's voice under the same noise characteristic environment. The environment naturally tends to vary, however, and the transmission characteristics of telephone sets and transmission lines also are not precisely controllable. Research is therefore necessary into mechanisms which facilitate automatic adaptation to these variations. Also important for practical use is the development of a method capable of accurately recognizing a voice picked up by a microphone placed at a distance from the speaker.

Since the intersession (temporal) variability of the physical properties of an individual voice decreases the recognition accuracy of speaker recognition, a set of feature parameters must be extracted that remain stable over long periods, even if, for example, the speaker should be suffering from a cold or bronchial congestion. Furthermore, these parameters must be set up in such a way that they are extremely difficult to imitate.

## 10.5 BASIC UNITS FOR SPEECH PROCESSING

Recognizing continuous speech featuring an extensive vocabulary necessitates the exploration of a recognition algorithm which utilizes basic units smaller than words. This establishment of basic speech units represents one of the principal research foci fundamental not only to speech recognition but also to speaker recognition, text-to-speech conversion, and very-low-bit-rate speech coding.

These basic speech units considered intrinsic to speech information processing should be studied from several perspectives:

1. Linguistic units (e.g., phonemes and syllables)
2. Articulatory units (e.g., positions and moving targets for the jaw and tongue)
3. Perceptual units (e.g., distinctive features, and targets and loci of formant movement)
4. Visual units (features used in spectrogram reading)
5. Physical units (e.g., centroids in VQ and MQ)

These units do not necessarily correspond. Furthermore, although conventional units have usually been produced from the linguistic point of view, future units will be established based on the combination of physical and linguistic units. This establishment will take the visual, articulatory, and perceptual viewpoints into consideration.

## 10.6 ADVANCED KNOWLEDGE PROCESSING

One of the critical problems in speech understanding and text-to-speech conversion is how best to utilize and efficiently combine various kinds of knowledge sources including our common sense concerning language usage. Typical characteristics of large-vocabulary continuous speech recognition are that the number of similar words increases and that the pronunciation becomes less clear or garbled. Clearly, then, a variety of information, such as shared knowledge between listeners and speakers, the present topic of conversation, semantic relationships among words, and grammatical constraints, contributes vitally to understanding the speaker's intention during conversation.

The technological realization of these processes encompasses the use of the fruits of artificial intelligence, particularly expert systems, which provide methods capable of representing knowledge sources, including syntax and semantics, parallel and distributed processing methods for managing the knowledge sources, and tree search methods. A key factor in actualizing high-performance speech understanding concerns the most potent way to combine the obscurely quantified acoustical information with the different types of symbolized knowledge sources.

The use of phrase-structured grammar for English and case-structured grammar for Japanese is especially convenient in the linguistic processing stage in speech understanding. The methods produced from the results garnered from natural language processing research are not always useful in speech processing, however, since there is a vast difference between written and spoken language. An entirely new linguistic science must therefore be invented for speech processing based on the presently available technologies for natural language processing. Clearly, this novel science must also take the specific characteristics of conversational speech into consideration.

## 10.7 CLARIFICATION OF SPEECH PRODUCTION MECHANISM

A careful look into the dynamics of the diverse articulatory organs functioning during speech production, coupled with trials for elucidating the relationship between the articulatory mechanism and the acoustic characteristics of speech waves, exhibits considerable potential for producing key ideas fundamental to developing the new speech information processing technologies needed.

Recent investigation has shown that the actual sound source of speech production is neither a simple pulse train nor white noise, nor is it necessarily linearly separable from the vocal tract articulatory filter. This finding runs contrary to the production model now widely used. Furthermore, it is quite possible that simplification of the model is one of the primary factors causing the degradation of synthesized voice. Therefore, development of a new sound source model that precisely represents the actual source characteristics, as well as research on the mutual interaction between the sound source and the articulatory filter, would seem to be necessary to enhance the progress of speech synthesis.

Well-suited formulation of the rules governing movement of the articulatory organs holds the promise of producing a clear representation of the coarticulation phenomena which are very difficult to properly delineate at the acoustic level. Consequently, a dynamic model of coarticulation is in the process of being established based on these rules. This research is also expected to lead to a solution of the problem of not being able to clearly discern voice individuality, and to produce techniques for segmenting the acoustic feature sequence into basic speech units.

The actual direction this research is assuming is divided into a physiological approach and an engineering approach. The former approach involves the direct observation of the speech production processes. For example, vocal cord movement is observed using a fiberscope, an ultrasonic pulse method, or an optoelectronic method. On the other hand, articulatory movement in the vocal tract can be observed by scanning-type x-ray microbeam device, ultrasonic tomography, dynamic palatography, or electromyography (EMG). Although each of these methods have their own specially applicable features, none of them is capable of precisely observing the dynamics of the vocal organs. Accordingly, there will be a continuous need to improve on such devices and observation methods.

The engineering approach concerns the estimation of source and vocal tract information from the acoustic features based on speech production models. This approach, founded on the results of the physiological approach, is expected to produce key ideas for developing new speech processing technologies.

## 10.8 CLARIFICATION OF SPEECH PERCEPTION MECHANISM

As is well known, a mutual relationship exists between the speech production and speech perception mechanisms. Psychological and physiological research into human speech perception is anticipated to give rise to new principles for guiding more broad-ranging progress in speech information processing. As described earlier, one of the most significant factors toward which speech perception research is being directed is the mechanism involved in perceiving dynamic signals.

Application of the neural net to speech recognition and speech synthesis has recently attracted a great deal of attention. The neural net is a parallel processing network having multiple layers that are capable of imitating the human nerve network. Constituent elements of the neural net function similar to neurons. The neural net approach is formulated to replicate the human auditory system and its learning function. Although a wide variety of structures have been proposed, the input-output characteristics for all of these networks are nonlinear, making theoretical analysis of these functions very difficult.

Among these structures, a multilayer perceptron-type neural net, which incorporates a learning mechanism for adjusting the network structure, has been applied to speech recognition with good results being produced. The back-propagation method is used for the learning process. Although the future prospects for this method remain unclear, it does exhibit considerable possibility for realizing new functions which cannot be performed by conventional methods. The structures and operation of the neural net are precisely explained in Appendix E.

## 10.9 EVALUATION METHODS FOR SPEECH PROCESSING TECHNOLOGIES

Objective evaluation methods ensuring quantitative comparison between a broad range of techniques are essential to technological developments in the speech processing field. Establishing methods for evaluating the multifarious processes and systems employed here is, however, very difficult for a number of important reasons. One is that natural speech varies considerably in its linguistic properties, voice qualities, and other aspects as well. Another is that efficiency of speech processing techniques often depends to a large extent on the characteristics of the input speech.

Therefore, the following three principal problems must be solved before effectual evaluation methods can be established:

1. Task evaluation: creating a measure fully capable of evaluating the complexity and difficulty of the task (synthesis, recognition, or coding task) being processed
2. Technique evaluation: formulating a method for evaluating the techniques both subjectively and objectively
3. Database for evaluation: preparing a large-scale universal database for evaluating an extensive array of systems

Evaluation factors for speech coding systems include bit rate (amount of information in coded speech), coded speech quality, including robustness against noise and coding errors, complexity of coder and decoder (usually a coder is more complex than a decoder), and coding delay. The cost of coding hardware generally increases with its complexity. Coding delays can be objectionable in two-way telephone conversations, especially when they are added to the existing delays in the transmission network and combined with uncanceled echoes.

Table 10.1 compares the trade-offs incurred in using representative types of speech coding algorithms. The algorithms must be evaluated based on the total measure, which is constructed from an appropriately weighted combination of these factors. A broader range of coding methods from high-quality coding to very-low-bit-rate coding are now being investigated in order to meet the expected demands. High-quality coding transmits not only speech but also wideband signals such as

TABLE 10.1 Trade-offs between Four Evaluation Factors for Representative Types of Speech Coding Algorithms

| Coding algorithms | Coding techniques | Bit rate (kbps) | Complexity (MIPS) | Coding delay (ms) | Speech quality |
|---|---|---|---|---|---|
| PCM | Nonlinear quant. | 64 | 0.01 | 0 | High |
| ADPCM | Adaptive quant.<br>Predictive quant. | 32 | 0.1 | 0 | High |
| APC-AB | Adaptive quant.<br>Predictive quant.<br>Time-freq. split. | 16 | 1 | 25 | High |
| MPC | Multipulse for LPC residual | 8 | 10 | 35 | Mid. |
| CELP | Noise-VQ for LPC residual | 4 | 100 | 35 | Mid. |
| LPC vocoder | Analysis-synthesis | 2 | 1 | 35 | Low |

PCM = pulse code modulation
ADPCM = adaptive differential PCM
APC-AB = adaptive predictive coding with adaptive bit allocation
MPC = multipulse LPC
CELP = code-excited LPC

music at a rate of 64 kbps. Very-low-bit-rate coding fully utilizes the speech characteristics to transmit speech signals at 200 to 300 bps.

The evaluation methods for these coding techniques, specifically, the weighting factors for combining evaluation factors, must be determined, depending on their bit rates and application purposes. A crucial future problem is how best to measure the individuality and naturalness of coded and synthesized speech.

## 10.10 DEVELOPMENT OF NEW STATISTICAL ANALYSIS METHODS

Establishing and evaluating methods for processing a vast array of speech signals necessitates excellent use of statistical analysis methods that can efficiently and effectively process large-scale databases. Currently in wide employ are a number of multivariate analysis methods, such as discriminant analysis, principal component analysis, factor analysis, canonical correlation analysis, multiple regression analysis, multivariate analysis of variance, and cluster analysis. When utilizing any of these methods, it is very important to have a clear understanding of their fundamental applicability. Complementary to these, it is also desirable that an assortment of new statistical analysis methods be created to meet the present and foreseeable speech processing goals.

## 10.11 LSI FOR SPEECH PROCESSING USE

Development and utilization of LSIs are indispensable to the actualization of diverse, well-suited speech processing devices and systems. LSI technology has, on occasion, had considerable impact on the speech technology trend. Those algorithms that are easily packaged in LSIs, for example, tend to become mainstream tools even if they require a relatively large number of elements and computation.

Speech processing algorithms can be realized through special-purpose LSIs and digital signal processors (DSPs). Although both avenues have advantages and disadvantages, the DSP approach generally seems to be more beneficial, because speech processing algorithms are becoming substantially more diversified and continue to incorporate rapid advancements. The actual production of fully functioning speech processing hardware necessitates the fabrication of DSP-LSIs, which include high-speed circuits and large memories capable of processing and storing sufficiently long-word-length data in their design. Furthermore, the provision of appropriate developmental tools for constructing DSP-based systems using high-level computer languages is essential. It would be particularly beneficial if speech researchers were to assist in proposing the design policies behind the production of these LSIs and developmental devices.

# Appendix A

# Convolution and z-Transform

## A.1 CONVOLUTION

The convolution of x(n) and h(n), usually written x(n)*h(n), is defined as

$$\sum_{k=-\infty}^{\infty} x(k)h(n - k)$$

If h(n) and x(n) are the impulse response of a linear system and its input, respectively, the system response can be expressed by the convolution

$$y(n) = \sum_{k=-\infty}^{\infty} x(k)h(n - k) \tag{A.1}$$

The convolution operation features the following properties:

1. Commutativity: For any h and x,

$$x(n)*h(n) = h(n)*x(n) \tag{A.2}$$

2. Associativity: For any $h_1$, $h_2$, and $h_3$,

$$[h_1(n)*h_2(n)]*h_3(n) = h_1(n)*[h_2(n)*h_3(n)] \tag{A.3}$$

3. Linearity: If parameters a and b are constants, then

$$h(n)*[ax_1(n) + bx_2(n)] = a[h(n)*x_1(n)] + b[h(n)*x_2(n)] \tag{A.4}$$

Generally,

$$h(n)* \sum_i x_1(n) = \sum_i h(n)*x_i(n) \tag{A.5}$$

which means that the convolution and summing operations are interchangeable.

4. Time reversal: If $y(n) = x(n)*h(n)$, then

$$y(-n) = x(-n)*h(-n) \tag{A.6}$$

5. Cascade: If two systems, $h_1$ and $h_2$, are cascaded, then the overall impulse response of the combined system is the convolution of the individual impulse responses,

$$h(t) = h_1(t)*h_2(t) \tag{A.7}$$

and the overall impulse response is independent of the order in which the systems are connected.

## A.2 z-TRANSFORM

The direct z-transform of a time sequence x(n) is defined as

$$X(z) = \sum_{n=-\infty}^{\infty} x(n)z^{-n} \tag{A.8}$$

where z is a complex variable and X(z) is a complex function. The inverse transform is given by

$$x(n) = \frac{1}{j2\pi} \oint_C X(z)z^{n-1}\, dz \tag{A.9}$$

where the contour C must be in the convergence region of X(z).

The z-transform has the following elementary properties, in which Z[x(n)] represents the z-transform of x(n):

1. Linearity: Let x(n) and y(n) be any two functions and let X(z) and Y(z) be their respective z-transforms. Then for any constants, a and b,

$$Z[ax(n) + by(n)] = aX(z) + bY(z) \tag{A.10}$$

2. Convolution: If w(n) = x(n)*y(n), then

$$W(z) = X(z)Y(z) \tag{A.11}$$

3. Shifting:

$$Z[x(n - k)] = z^{-k}X(z) \tag{A.12}$$

4. Differences:

$$Z[x(n - 1) - x(n)] = (z - 1)X(z) \tag{A.13}$$

$$Z[x(n) - x(n - 1)] = (1 - z^{-1})X(z) \tag{A.14}$$

5. Exponential weighting:

$$Z[a^n x(n)] = X(a^{-1}z) \tag{A.15}$$

6. Linear weighting:

$$Z[nx(n)] = -z\,\frac{dX(z)}{dz} \tag{A.16}$$

7. Time reversal:

$$Z[x(-n)] = X(z^{-1}) \tag{A.17}$$

The z-transforms for elementary functions are as follows.

1. Unit impulse: The unit impulse is defined as

$$\delta(n) = \begin{cases} 1, & n = 0 \\ 0, & \text{otherwise} \end{cases} \tag{A.18}$$

If x(n) = δ(n), then

$$X(z) = \sum_{n=-\infty}^{\infty} \delta(n)z^{-n} = 1 \tag{A.19}$$

2. Delayed unit impulse: If $x(n) = \delta(n - k)$,

$$X(z) = \sum_{n=-\infty}^{\infty} \delta(n - k)z^{-n}$$

$$= z^{-k} \tag{A.20}$$

3. Unit step: The unit step function is defined as

$$u(n) = \begin{cases} 1, & n \geq 0 \\ 0, & \text{otherwise} \end{cases} \tag{A.21}$$

If $x(n) = u(n)$, then

$$X(z) = \sum_{n=-\infty}^{\infty} z^{-n} = 1 + z^{-1} + z^{-2} + z^{-3} + \cdots$$

$$= \frac{1}{1 - z^{-1}} \tag{A.22}$$

4. Exponential: If $x(n) = a^n u(n)$,

$$X(z) = \sum_{n=0}^{\infty} a^n z^{-n}$$

$$= \frac{1}{1 - az^{-1}} \tag{A.23}$$

## A.3 STABILITY

A system is stable if a bounded (finite-amplitude) input $x(n)$ always produces a bounded output $y(n)$. That is, if

$$|x(n)| < M \quad \text{for all } n \tag{A.24}$$

and if

$$|y(n)| < M \sum_{k=-\infty}^{\infty} |h(k)| \tag{A.25}$$

where M is a finite constant, the system is stable. Hence, the necessary and sufficient condition for the stability of the system can be written as

$$\sum_{k} |h(k)| < \infty \tag{A.26}$$

An equivalent requirement is that all poles of H(z) lie within the unit circle.

# Appendix B

# Vector Quantization Algorithm

## B.1 VQ (VECTOR QUANTIZATION) TECHNIQUE FORMULATION

The VQ technique, which is one of the most important and widely used methods in speech processing, is formulated as follows (Gray, 1984; Makhoul et al., 1985). It is assumed that x is a k-dimensional vector whose components are real-valued random variables. In vector quantization, a vector x is mapped onto another k-dimensional vector y. x is thus quantized as y and is written as

$$y = q(x) \tag{B.1}$$

y takes on one of a finite set of values, $Y = \{y_i\}$ $(1 \leqq i \leqq K)$. The set Y is referred to as the codebook, and $\{y_i\}$ are code vectors or templates. The size K of the codebook is referred to as the number of levels.

To design such a codebook, the k-dimensional space of vector x is partitioned into K regions $\{C_i\}$ $(1 \leqq i \leqq K)$ with a vector $y_i$ being associated with each region $C_i$. The quantizer then assigns the code vector $y_i$ if x is in $C_i$. This is represented by

$$q(x) = y_i \tag{B.2}$$

When x is quantized as y, a quantization distortion measure or distance measure d(x,y) can be defined between x and y. The overall average distortion is then represented by

$$D = \lim_{M \to \infty} \frac{1}{M} \sum_{n=1}^{M} d[x(n),\ y(n)] \tag{B.3}$$

A quantizer is said to be an optimal (minimum-distortion) quantizer if the overall distortion is minimized over all K-level quantizers.

Two conditions are necessary for optimality. The first is that the quantizer be realized by using a minimum-distortion or nearest-neighbor selection rule,

$$q(x) = y_i \quad \text{iff} \quad d(x,y_i) \leq d(x,y_j), \qquad j \neq i, \quad 1 \leq j \leq K \tag{B.4}$$

The second is that each code vector $y_i$ be chosen to minimize the average distortion in region $C_i$. Such a vector is called the centroid of region $C_i$. The centroid for a particular region depends on the definition of the distortion measure.

## B.2 LLOYD'S ALGORITHM (K-MEANS ALGORITHM)

Lloyd's algorithm or the K-means algorithm is an iterative clustering (refining) algorithm for codebook design. The algorithm divides the set of training vectors $\{x(n)\}$ into K clusters $\{c_i\}$ in such a way that the two previously described conditions necessary for optimality are satisfied. The four steps of the algorithm are as follows.

Step 1: Initialization
Set $m = 0$ (m: iterative index). Choose a set of initial code vectors, $\{y_i(0)\}$ $(1 \leq i \leq K)$, using an adequate method.

Step 2: Classification
Classify the set of training vectors $\{x(n)\}$ $(1 \leq n \leq M)$ into clusters $\{C_i(m)\}$ based on the nearest-neighbor rule,

$$x \in C_i(m) \quad \text{iff} \quad d[x,y_i(m)] \leq d[x,y_j(m)] \qquad \text{all } j \neq i \tag{B.5}$$

Step 3: Code vector updating
Set $m \leftarrow m + 1$. Update the code vector of every cluster by computing the centroid of the training vectors in each cluster as

$$y_i(m) = \text{centroid } (C_i(m)), \qquad 1 \leq i \leq K \tag{B.6}$$

Calculate the overall distortion D(m) for all training vectors.

Step 4: Termination
If the decrease in the overall distortion D(m) at iteration m relative to D(m − 1) is below a certain threshold, stop; otherwise, go to step 2. (Any other reasonable termination criteria may be substituted.)

This algorithm systematically decreases the overall distortion by updating the codebook. The distortion sometimes converges, however, to a local optimum which may be significantly worse than the global optimum. Specifically, the algorithm tends to gravitate towards the local optimum nearest the initial codebook. A global optimum may be approximately achieved by repeating this algorithm for several types of initializations, and choosing the codebook having the minimum overall distortion results.

## B.3 LBG ALGORITHM

Lloyd's algorithm assumes that the codebook has a fixed size. A codebook can begin small and be gradually expanded, however, until it reaches its final size. One alternative is to split an existing cluster into two smaller clusters and assign a codebook entry to each. The following steps describe this method for building an entire codebook (Gray, 1984; Parsons, 1986).

Step 1: Create an initial cluster consisting of the entire training set. the initial codebook thus contains a single entry corresponding to the centroid of the entire set, as is depicted in Fig. B.1(a) for a two-dimensional input.

Step 2: Split this cluster into two subclusters, resulting in a codebook of twice the size (Fig. B.1(b),(c)).

Step 3: Repeat this cluster-splitting process until the codebook reaches the desired size (Fig. B.1(d),(e)).

Splitting can be done in a number of ways. Ideally, each cluster should be divided by a hyperplane which is normal (rectangular) to the direction of maximum distortion. This ensures that the maximum distortions of the two new clusters will be smaller than that of the original. As the number of codebook entries increases, however, the computational expense rapidly becomes prohibitive.

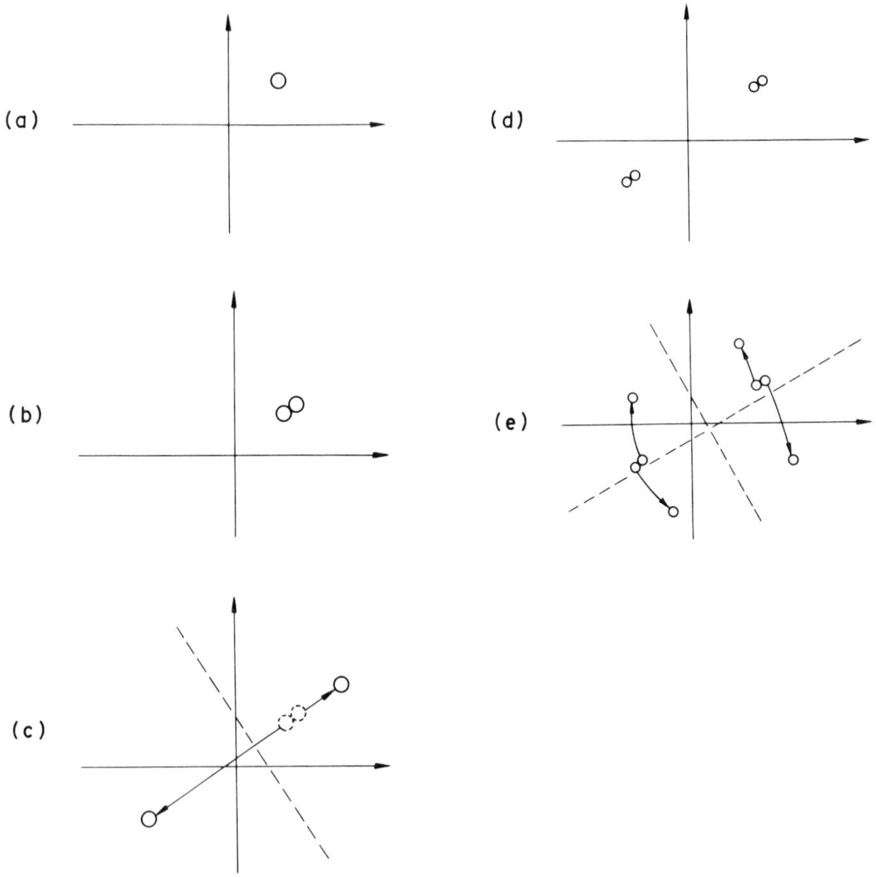


Fig. B.1 Splitting procedure. (a) Rate 0: The centroid of the entire training sequence. (b) Initial Rate 1: The single codeword is split to form an initial estimate of a two-word code. (c) Final Rate 1: The algorithm produces a good code with two words. The dotted line indicates the cluster boundary. (d) Initial Rate 2: The two words are split to form an initial estimate of a four-word code. (e) Final Rate 2: The algorithm is run to produce a final four-word code.

Some authors perturb the centroid to generate two different points. If the centroid is x, then an initial estimate of two new codes can be created by forming $x + \Delta$ and $x - \Delta$, where $\Delta$ is a small perturbation vector. The algorithm will then produce good codes (centroids).

# Appendix C

# Phonocode (Matrix Quantization) Algorithm

## C.1 MATRIX QUANTIZATION

The phonocode method uses spectral segments representing multiple frames of spectral parameters as quantization units (Shiraki and Honda, 1988). Denoting the segment by matrix $X_j$, which has $n_j$ column vectors consisting of spectral parameters, the original spectral sequence is represented as the sequence of segments $X_1,..,X_j,..,X_J$. Here, $X_1$ is the first segment and $X_J$ the last segment in a given interval, for example, a voice interval having silence segments at both sides. Each segment length $n_j$, namely, the column number of the matrix, is variable. The segments $\{X_j\}$ are generated from a set of fixed-length segments stored in a segment codebook, $C = \{Y_i\}_{i=1}^{N}$.

Therefore, both the sequence of code segments and their length must be determined in the coding process. Such a joint segmentation and quantization procedure is represented in Fig. C.1. The entire spectral sequence is generated by concatenating the code segments after converting from fixed to variable length. This is followed by comparing it with the original spectral sequence in the voice interval. The optimum segment-sequence which minimizes the overall distortion is

$$\{X_j\}_{j=1}^{J} = \underset{\substack{n_j \\ 1 \leqq j \leqq J}}{\operatorname{argmin}} \left[ \min_{Y_{i(j)} \in C} \sum_{j=1}^{J} d(X_j, Y_{i(j)}) \right] \tag{C.1}$$

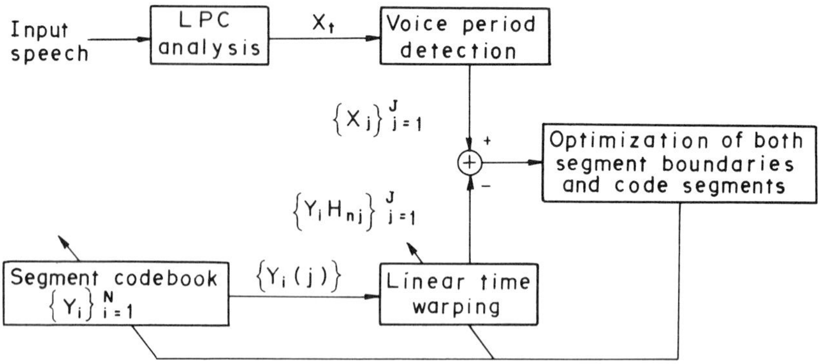


Fig. C.1 Block diagram of variable-length segment vocoder based on joint segmentation and quantization.

where $d(X_j, Y_i)$ represents the distance measured between the original and code segments. The sum of the segment lengths $\{n_j\}$ is constrained to be equal to the voice interval length.

The weighted Euclidean distance associated with the LSP parameters and speech power is used as the spectral distance measure for computational simplicity. Weighting factors for the LSP parameters are determined so that the weighted distance appoximates, by the least mean square error criterion, the Euclidean distance between the power-normalized LPC spectra in dB. The weighting factor for speech power is determined to maximize the intelligibility of the coded speech.

The code segment having the fixed length n is linearly interpolated and resampled at equal intervals to produce the segment having length $n_j$. This conversion can be written in a matrix form as $YH_{nj}$, using the $n \times n_j$ interpolation or time warping matrix $H_{nj}$. The distance measured between the original and code segments is then defined as the sum of the distances between the original and interpolated code vectors over the number of frames in the original segment. This can be shown as

$$d(X,Y) = \mathrm{tr}(X_j - YH_{nj})^t W(X_j - YH_{nj}) \qquad (C.2)$$

where tr(A) denotes the trace of matrix A and is defined as $\mathrm{tr}(A) = \Sigma a_{ii}$.

The optimum solution for the minimum distortion rule (Eq. (C.1)) is efficiently selected as follows using a dynamic programming procedure.

First, parameter notations are defined:

T = number of frames in the voice interval
J = number of segments in the voice interval
$t_j$ = segment boundary
$t_j^0$ = initial (provisional) segment boundary
$t_j^*$ = optimum (final) segment boundary
$\Delta$ = search range of segment boundaries
$X(t_{j-1}, t_j)$ = segment having boundary positions, $t_{j-1}$ and $t_j$
$q(X, Y)$ = minimum distortion when quantizing X using a segment codebook $C = \{Y_i\}_{i=1}^N$

Accumulated distortion $\sigma(t_j)$ and optimum boundary positions $s(t_j)$ from the beginning to boundary position $t_j$ $(j = 1, 2, \ldots, J)$ are obtained using the forward recursions

$$\sigma(t_j) = \min_{t_{j-1} \in R_{j-1}} [\sigma(t_{j-1}) + q(X(t_{j-1}, t_j), Y)] \qquad (C.3)$$

and

$$s(t_j) = \operatorname*{argmin}_{t_{j-1} \in R_{j-1}} [\sigma(t_{j-1}) + q(X(t_{j-1}, t_j), Y)] \qquad (C.4)$$

where

$$t_j^0 - \Delta \leqq t_j \leqq t_j^0 + \Delta$$

$$\sigma(t_0) = 0, \quad t_0 = 1, \quad t_J = T$$

$$q(X, Y) = \min_{Y_i \in C} d(X, Y_i)$$

$$R_{j-1} = \{t \mid t_{j-1}^0 - \Delta \leqq t \leqq \min(t_{j-1}^0 + \Delta, t_j)\}$$

When the final accumulated distortion $\sigma(t_J)$ is obtained, the optimum boundary positions are derived using the backward recursion

$$t_{j-1}^* = s(t_j) \qquad (j = J, J-1, \ldots, 2) \qquad (C.5)$$

Experimental results show that nearly optimum performance can be obtained with moderate computation by using the initial estimates of the segment boundaries based on detecting spectral changes and by setting the search range to greater than 160 ms.

## C.2 CODEBOOK DESIGN

Using the training data of spectral parameter sequences, the phonocode codebook is designed by determining both the segment boundaries and the code segments which minimize

$$D = \sum_{j=1}^{J} \min_{Y_i \in C} d(X(t_{j-1}, t_j), Y_i) \tag{C.6}$$

An actual codebook design algorithm (Fig. C.2) composed of training segment-sequence updating and MQ codebook updating has five steps.

Step 1: Initialization
Training vector sequence $\{x_t\}_{t=1}^{T}$, total number of training segment data J, codebook segment length n, and thresholds $\varepsilon_1$ and $\varepsilon_2$ are given. Choose by an adequate method an initial codebook $C_0 = \{Y_i\}_{i=1}^{N}$ and initiate segment boundaries $\{t_j^0\}_{j=1}^{J}$. Set k = 0 and initial distortion $D_0 = \infty$.

Step 2: Training segment-sequence updating
Set $k \leftarrow k + 1$. Update the training segment-sequence to $\{X_j(k) = X(t_{j-1}^*, t_j^*)\}_{j=1}^{J}$ by using codebook $C_{k-1}$, and by applying the joint segmentation and quantization algorithm to

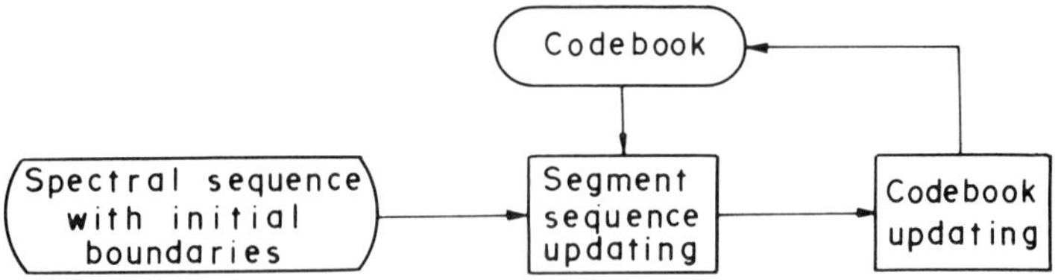


Fig. C.2 Iterative algorithm for designing a variable-length segment quantizer.

the training vector sequence. Update the segment boundaries to $\{t_j^0(k) = t_j^*\}_{j=1}^J$. Compute the minimum distortion for the training segment sequence as

$$D_k(0) = \sum_{j=1}^{J} \min_{Y_i \in C_{k-1}} d(X_j, Y_i) \tag{C.7}$$

Step 3: Initialization for codebook updating
Set $m = 0$ and $C_k(0) = C_{k-1}$.

Step 4: Codebook updating
Set $m \leftarrow m + 1$. Encode the training segment sequence using the minimum distortion rule

$$S_i = \{j;\ X_j = Y_i\} \tag{C.8}$$

where

$$X_j = \operatorname*{argmin}_{Y_i \in C_k(m-1)} d(X_j, Y_i)$$

For each cluster, compute the centroid as

$$Y_i = \left( \sum_{j \in S_i} X_j H_{nj}^t \right) \left( \sum_{j \in S_i} H_{nj} H_{nj}^t \right)^+ \tag{C.9}$$

using the training sequence data. Here $A^+$ is a generalized inverse matrix of A.

Update the codebook to $C_k(m) = \{Y_i\}_{i=1}^N$ and compute the distortion decrease by

$$\delta = \frac{D_k(m-1) - D_k(m)}{D_k(m)} \tag{C.10}$$

where

$$D_k(m) = \sum_{j=1}^{J} \min_{Y_i \in C_k(m)} d(X_j, Y_i) \tag{C.11}$$

Step 5: Termination

Go to step 4 unless $\delta \leqq \varepsilon_2$. Set $C_k = C_k(m)$ and $D_k = D_k(m)$, and go to step 2 unless $(D_{k-1} - D_k)/D_k \leqq \varepsilon_1$.

This algorithm ensures a nonincreasing sequence of distortions

$$D_0 \geqq D_1 \geqq \cdots \geqq D_k \geqq D_{k+1} \geqq \cdots \tag{C.12}$$

Convergence of this algorithm is also guaranteed.

# Appendix D

# HMM Procedures

## D.1 HMM ELEMENTS

The model notations for a discrete observation HMM are defined as follows (Rabiner and Juang, 1986).

$O = \{O_1, O_2, \ldots, O_T\}$ = observation sequence (input utterance)
$T$ = length (duration) of observation sequence
$Q = \{q_1, q_2, \ldots, q_N\}$ = (hidden) states in the model
$N$ = number of states
$V = \{v_1, v_2, \ldots, v_M\}$ = discrete set of possible symbol observations (VQ) codebook)
$M$ = number of observation symbols (VQ codebook size)
$A = \{a_{ij}\}$, $a_{ij} = \text{Prob}(q_j \text{ at } t + 1 \mid q_i \text{ at } t)$ = state transition probability distribution
$B = \{b_j(k)\}$, $b_j(k) = \text{Prob}(v_k \text{ at } t \mid q_j \text{ at } t)$ = observation symbol probability distribution in state j
$\pi = \{\pi_i\}$, $\pi_i = \text{Prob}(q_i \text{ at } t = 1)$ = initial state distribution

An observation sequence O is generated as follows.

Step 1: Set $t = 1$.
Step 2: Choose an initial state I according to the initial state distribution $\pi$.
Step 3: Choose $O_t$ according to $b_i(k)$, the symbol probability distribution in state i.

Step 4: Choose j according to $\{a_{ij}\}$ $(j = 1,2,\ldots,N)$, the state transition probability distribution for state j.

Step 5: Set $t \leftarrow t + 1$. Return to step 3 if $t < T$; otherwise terminate the procedure.

The compact notation $\lambda = (A,B,\pi)$ is used to represent an HMM. Specifying an HMM involves choosing the number of states, N, as well as the number of discrete symbols, M, and specifying the three probability densities, A, B, and $\pi$.

## D.2 THREE HMM PROBLEMS

There are three key problems that must be solved when utilizing the HMM model.

### Problem 1: Evaluation Problem

Given the observation sequence $O = \{O_1,O_2,\ldots O_T\}$ and the model $\lambda = (A,B,\pi)$, how can the observation sequence probability $\text{Prob}(O \mid \lambda)$ be computed?

### Problem 2: Hidden State Sequence Uncovering Problem

Given the observation sequence $O = \{O_1,O_2,\ldots,O_T\}$, how can a state sequence $I = \{i_1,i_2,\ldots,i_T\}$, which is optimal in some meaningful sense, be chosen?

### Problem 3: Training Problem

How can the model parameters $\lambda = (A,B,\pi)$ be adjusted to maximize $\text{Prob}(O \mid \lambda)$?

The principal structure of spoken word recognition systems based on the HMM was detailed in Fig. 8.8 in Sec. 8.6.3. This structure requires the derivation of solutions to these three problems for particular use. The solution to Problem 1 is utilized to score each word model based on the given test observation sequence for recognizing an unknown word. The solution to Problem 2 is used to develop an understanding of the physical meaning of the model states. The solution to Problem 3 is employed to optimally obtain model parameters for each word model using training utterances.

## D.3 SOLUTIONS TO THREE HMM PROBLEMS

Problem 1: Prob(O | λ) can be represented as

$$\text{Prob}(O\,|\,\lambda) = \sum_{i_1, i_2, \ldots, i_T} \pi_{i_1} b_{i_1}(O_1) a_{i_1 i_2} \cdots a_{i_{T-1} i_T} b_{i_T}(O_T) \tag{D.1}$$

The summation in this equation is efficiently computed by the forward-backward procedure. Consider the forward variable $\alpha_t(i)$ as

$$\alpha_t(i) = \text{Prob}(O_1, O_2, \ldots, O_t, i_t = q_i \mid \lambda) \tag{D.2}$$

This indicates the probability of the partial observation sequence (until time t) and state $q_i$ at time t, given model λ. We can solve for $\alpha_t(i)$ recursively as follows.

Step 1: $\alpha_1(i) = \pi_i b_i(O_1) \qquad (1 \leq i \leq N)$ (D.3)

Step 2: For $t = 1, 2, \ldots, T - 1 \qquad (1 \leq j \leq N)$,

$$\alpha_{t+1}(j) = \left[\sum_{i=1}^{N} \alpha_t(i) a_{ij}\right] b_j(O_{t+1}) \tag{D.4}$$

Step 3: Then,

$$\text{Prob}(O\,|\,\lambda) = \sum_{i=1}^{N} \alpha_T(i) \tag{D.5}$$

This algorithm can be easily derived by transforming the HMM into a trellis or lattice diagram as shown in Fig. D.1.

In a similar manner, a backward variable $\beta_t(i)$ is defined as

$$\beta_t(i) = \text{Prob}(O_{t+1}, O_{t+2}, \ldots, O_T \,|\, i_t = q_i, \lambda) \tag{D.6}$$

This demonstrates the probability of the partial observation sequence from t + 1 to the end, given state $q_i$ at time t and model λ. Again we can solve for $\beta_t(i)$ recursively as follows.

Step 1: $\beta_T(i) = 1 \qquad (1 \leq i \leq N)$ (D.7)

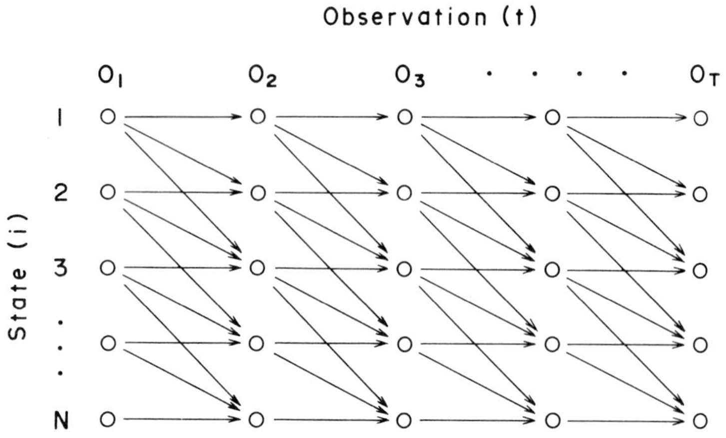


Fig. D.1 Trellis or lattice diagram representing an HMM.

Step 2: For t = T − 1, T − 2, ..., 1 $(1 \leqq i \leqq N)$

$$\beta_t(i) = \sum_{j=1}^{N} \beta_{t+1}(j) a_{ij} b_j(O_{t+1}) \tag{D.8}$$

Step 3: Then

$$\text{Prob}(O \mid \lambda) = \sum_{i=1}^{N} \pi_i b_i(O_1) \beta_1(i) \tag{D.9}$$

Problem 2: Problem 2 can be solved using the Viterbi algorithm. This algorithm is similar to the forward-backward procedure, except that a maximization over previous states is used in place of the summing procedure. The Viterbi algorithm is a follows.

Step 1: Initialization

$$\delta_1(i) = \pi_i b_i(O_1) \qquad (1 \leqq i \leqq N) \tag{D.10}$$

$$\Psi_1(i) = 0 \tag{D.11}$$

Step 2: Recursion. For $2 \leq t \leq T$, $1 \leq j \leq N$,

$$\delta_t(j) = \max_{1 \leq i \leq N} [\delta_{t-i}(i)a_{ij}]b_j(O_t) \tag{D.12}$$

$$\Psi_t(j) = \operatorname*{argmax}_{1 \leq i \leq N} [\delta_{t-1}(i)a_{ij}] \tag{D.13}$$

Step 3: Termination

$$P^* = \max_{1 \leq i \leq N} [\delta_T(i)] \tag{D.14}$$

$$i_t^* = \operatorname*{argmax}_{1 \leq i \leq N} [\delta_T(i)] \tag{D.15}$$

Step 4: State sequence backtracking. For $t = T - 1, T - 2, \ldots, 1$,

$$i_t^* = \Psi_{t+1}(i_{t+1}^*) \tag{D.16}$$

Here, $P^*$ is the maximum likelihood, and $\Psi$ indicates the maximum likelihood state sequence. If one only wishes to compute $P^*$, $\Psi$ values need not be maintained. The Viterbi algorithm is a form of the well-known dynamic programming method.

Problem 3: An iterative procedure, such as the Baum-Welch method, or a gradient technique for optimization is used for solving this problem. With the Baum-Welch algorithm, $\xi_t(i,j)$ is first defined as

$$\xi_t(i,j) = \text{Prob}(i_t = q_i, i_{t+1} = q_j \mid O, \lambda) \tag{D.17}$$

This denotes the probability of a path being in state $q_i$ at time $t$ and making a transition to state $q_j$ at time $t + 1$, given observation sequence O, and model $\lambda$. $\xi_t(i,j)$ can be written as

$$\xi_t(i,j) = \frac{\alpha_t(i)a_{ij}b_j(O_{t+1})\,\beta_{t+1}(j)}{\text{Prob}(O \mid \lambda)} \tag{D.18}$$

In the above equation, $\alpha_t(i)$ accounts for the first t observations, ending in state $q_i$ at time t. The term $a_{ij}b_j(O_{t+1})$ accounts for the transition to state $q_j$ at time $t + 1$ with the occurrence of symbol $O_{t+1}$. The term $\beta_{t+1}(j)$ accounts for the remainder of the observation sequence. $\text{Prob}(O \mid \lambda)$ is the normalization factor.

Next, $\gamma_t(i)$ is defined as

$$\gamma_t(i) = \text{Prob}(i_t = q_i \mid O, \gamma) \tag{D.19}$$

This represents the probability of being in state $q_i$ at time t, given observation sequence O, and model $\lambda$. $\gamma_t(i)$ can be expressed as

$$\gamma_t(i) = \frac{\alpha_t(i)\ \beta_t(i)}{\text{Prob}(O \mid \lambda)} \tag{D.20}$$

$\gamma_t(i)$ can be related to $\xi_t(i,j)$ by summing $\xi_t(i,j)$ over j, giving

$$\gamma_t(i) = \sum_{j=1}^{N} \xi_t(i,j) \tag{D.21}$$

If $\gamma_t(i)$ and $\xi_t(i,j)$ are each summed over the time index t (from t = 1 to t = T − 1), quantities are obtained which can be interpreted as

$$\sum_{t=1}^{T-1} \gamma_t(i) = \text{expected number of transitions made from } q_i$$

and

$$\sum_{t=1}^{T-1} \xi_t(i,j) = \text{expected number of transitions from state } q_i \text{ to state } q_j$$

Using these quantities, the HMM parameter values can be reestimated such that

$$\tilde{\pi}_i = \gamma_1(i) \qquad (1 \leq i \leq N), \tag{D.22}$$

$$\tilde{a}_{ij} = \frac{\sum_{t=1}^{T-1} \xi_t(i,j)}{\sum_{t=1}^{T-1} \gamma_t(i)} \tag{D.23}$$

$$\tilde{b}_j(k) = \frac{\sum_{t=1, O_t=k}^{T} \gamma_t(j)}{\sum_{t=1}^{T} \gamma_t(j)} \qquad (D.24)$$

The reestimation formula for $\pi_i$ corresponds to the probability estimation of being in state $q_i$ at $t = 1$. The reestimation formula for $a_{ij}$ represents the ratio of the expected number of transitions from state $q_i$ to $q_j$ divided by the expected number of transitions out of state $q_i$. Finally, the reestimation formula for $b_j(k)$ is equal to the ratio of the expected number of times of being in state j and observing symbol k divided by the expected number of times of being in state j.

It can be verified that $\text{Prob}(O|\tilde{\lambda}) \geq \text{Prob}(O|\lambda)$ $(\tilde{\lambda} = (\tilde{\pi}, \tilde{A}, \tilde{B}))$. Therefore, if $\tilde{\lambda}$ is iteratively used in place of $\lambda$ and the above reestimation calculation is repeated, the probability of O being observed from the model can be improved until some limiting point is reached.

# Appendix E

# Neural Nets

Neural net models are composed of many simple nonlinear computational nodes (elements) operating in parallel and arranged in patterns simulating biological neural nets (Lippman, 1987). The node sums N-weighted inputs and passes the result through a nonlinearity as shown in Fig. E.1. The node is characterized by an internal threshold or offset $\theta$ and by the type of nonlinearity (nonlinear transformation). Shown in Fig. E.1 are three types of nonlinearities: hard limiters, threshold logic elements, and sigmoidal nonlinearities.

Among various kinds of neural nets, multilayer perceptrons have been proven successful in dealing with many types of problems. The multilayer perceptrons are feedforward nets with one or more layers of nodes between the input and output nodes. These additional layers contain hidden nodes that are not directly connected to either the input or output nodes. A three-layer perceptron with two layers of hidden nodes is shown in Fig. E.2. The nonlinearity can be any of the three types shown in Fig. E.1. The decision rule involves selection of the class which corresponds to the output node having the largest output. In the formulas, $x'_j$ and $x''_k$ are the outputs of nodes in the first and second hidden layers, $\theta'_k$ and $\theta''_\ell$ are internal thresholds in those nodes, and $w_{ij}$ is the connection strength from the input to the first hidden layer. $w'_{ij}$ is the connection strength between the first and the second layers, and $w''_{ij}$ is the connection strength between the second and output layers.

The capabilities of multilayer perceptrons stem from the nonlinearities used within nodes. By way of example, the capabilities of perceptrons having one, two, and three layers that use hard-

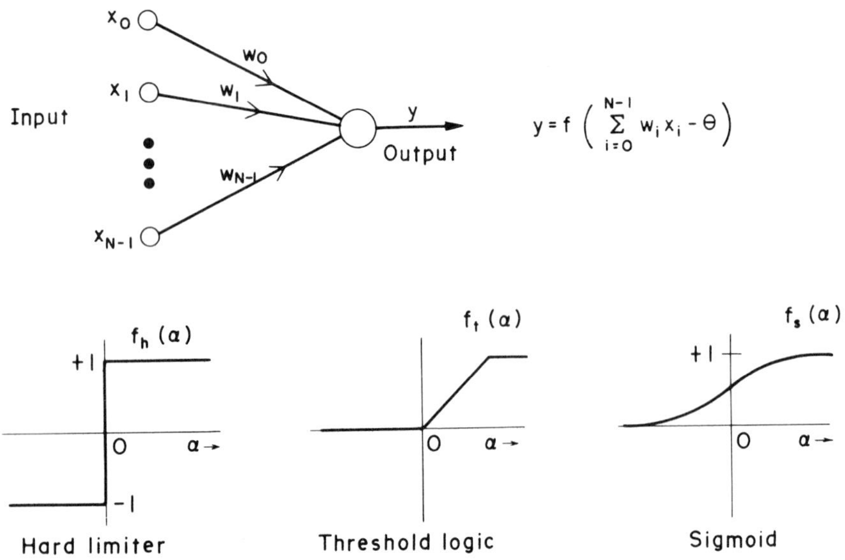


Fig. E.1 Computational element or node which forms a weighted sum of N inputs and passes the result through a nonlinearity. Three representative nonlinearities are shown below.

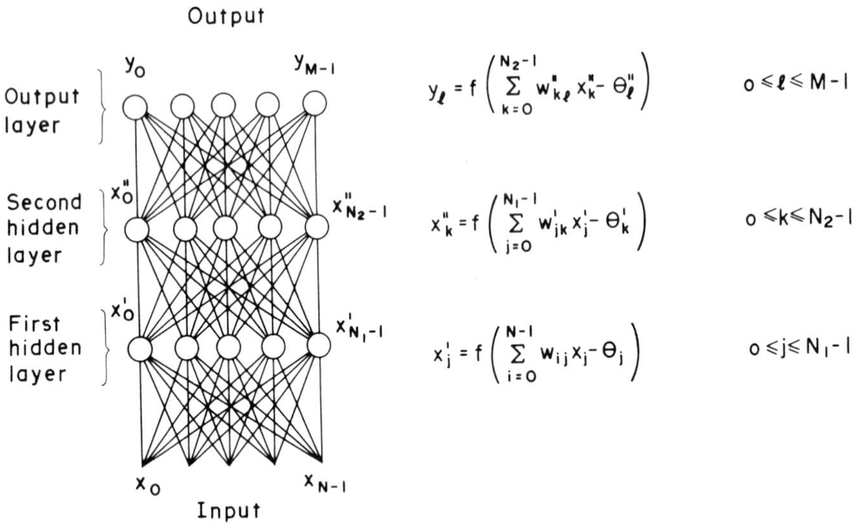


Fig. E.2 A three-layer perceptron with N continuous valued inputs, M outputs, and two layers of hidden units.

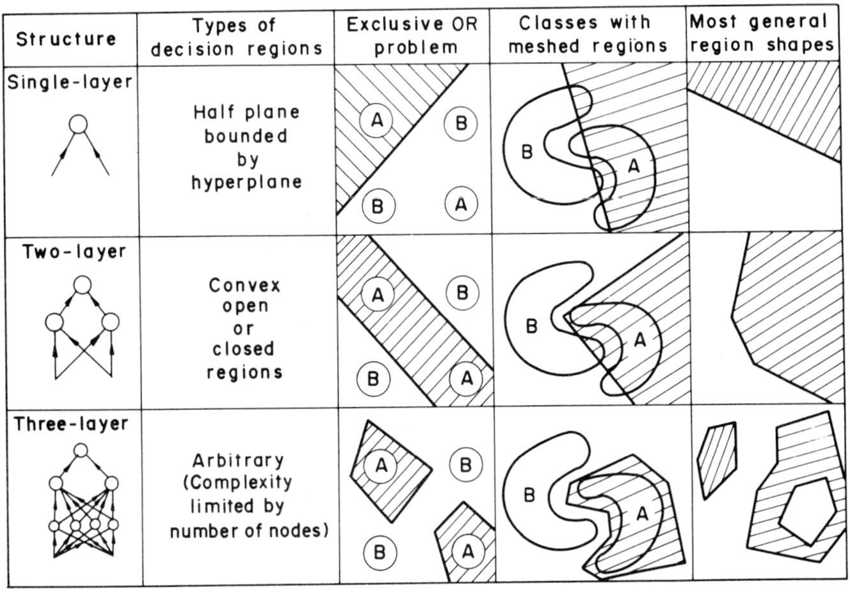


Fig. E.3 Types of decision regions that can be formed by single- and multilayer perceptrons with one and two layers of hidden units and two inputs. Shading indicates decision regions for class A. Smooth, closed contours bound input distributions for classes A and B. Nodes in all nets use hard-limiting nonlinearities.

limiting nonlinearities are illustrated in Fig. E.3. A three-layer perceptron can form arbitrarily complex decision regions, and can separate the meshed classes as shown in the bottom of Fig. E.3. Generally, decision regions required by any classification algorithm can be generated by three-layer feedforward nets.

The multilayer feedforward perceptrons can be automatically trained to improve classification performance with the back-propagation training algorithm. This algorithm is an iterative gradient algorithm designed to minimize the mean square error between the actual output of the net and the desired output. If the net is used as a classifier, all desired outputs are set to zero except for the one corresponding to the class from which the output originates. That desired output is 1. The algorithm propagates error terms required to adapt weights backward from nodes in the output layer to nodes in lower layers.

The following outlines a back-propagation training algorithm which assumes a sigmoidal logistic nonlinearity for the function $f(\alpha)$ in Fig. E.1.

$$f(\alpha) = \frac{1}{1 + \exp[-(\alpha - \theta)]} \tag{E.1}$$

Step 1: Weight and threshold initialization
Set all weights and node thresholds to small random values.

Step 2: Input and desired output presentation
Present an input vector $x_0, x_1, \ldots, x_{N-1}$ (continuous values) and specify the desired outputs $d_0, d_1, \ldots, d_{M-1}$. Present samples from a training set cyclically until weights stabilize.

Step 3: Actual output calculation
Use the sigmoidal nonlinearity and formulas as in Fig. E.2 to calculate the outputs $y_0, y_1, \ldots, y_{M-1}$.

Step 4: Weight adaption
Use a recursive algorithm starting at the output nodes and working back to the first hidden layer. Adjust weights using

$$w_{ij}(t + 1) = w_{ij}(t) + \mu\varepsilon_j x_i' \tag{E.2}$$

where $w_{ij}(t)$ is the weight from hidden node i or from an input to node j at time t, $x_i'$ is the output of node i or an input, $\mu$ is the gain term, and $\varepsilon_j$ is an error term for node j. If node j is an output node,

$$\varepsilon_j = y_j(1 - y_j)(d_j - y_j) \tag{E.3}$$

If node j is an internal hidden node,

$$\varepsilon_j = x_j'(1 - x_j') \sum_k \varepsilon_k w_{jk} \tag{E.4}$$

where k indicates all nodes in the layers above node j. Adapt internal node thresholds in a similar manner by assuming they are connection weights on links from imaginary inputs having a value of 1. Convergence is sometimes faster and weight changes are smoothed if a momentum term is added to Eq. (E.2) as

$$w_{ij}(t + 1) = w_{ij}(t) + \mu\varepsilon_j x_j' + \gamma(w_{ij}(t) - w_{ij}(t - 1)) \tag{E.5}$$

where $0 < \gamma < 1$.

Step 5: Repetition by returning to step 2

Repeat steps 2 to 4 until the weights and thresholds converge.

Neural nets typically provide a greater degree of robustness or fault tolerance than do conventional sequential computers. One difficulty noted with the back-propagation algorithm is that in many cases the number of training data presentations required for convergence is large (more than 100 passes through all the training data).

# Bibliography

## CHAPTER 1

Fagen, M. D. Ed. (1975) A History of Engineering and Science in the Bell System, Bell Telephone Laboratories, Inc., New Jersey, p. 6.

Flanagan, J. L. (1972) Speech Analysis Synthesis and Perception, 2nd Ed., Springer-Verlag, New York.

Markel, J. D. and Gray, Jr., A. H. (1976) Linear Prediction of Speech, Springer-Verlag, New York.

Rabiner, L. R. and Schafer, R. W. (1978) Digital Processing of Speech Signals, Prentice-Hall, New Jersey.

Saito, S. and Nakata, K. (1985) Fundamentals of Speech Signal Processing, Academic Press Japan, Tokyo.

## CHAPTER 2

Denes, P. B. and Pinson, E. N. (1963) The Speech Chain, Bell Telephone Laboratories, Inc., New Jersey.

Furui, S., Itakura, F., and Saito, S. (1972) "Talker recognition by the longtime averaged speech spectrum," Trans. IECEJ, 55-A, 10, pp. 549–556.

Furui, S. (1986) "On the role of spectral transition for speech perception," J. Acoust. Soc. Amer., 80, 4, pp. 1016–1025.

Irii, H., Itoh, K., and Kitawaki, N. (1987) "Multi-lingual speech database for speech quality measurements and its statistic characteristics," Trans. Committee on Speech Research, Acoust. Soc. Jap., S87–69.

Jakobson, R., Fant, G., and Halle, M. (1963) Preliminaries to Speech Analysis: The Distinctive Features and Their Correlates, MIT Press, Boston.

Peterson, G. E. and Barney, H. L. (1952) "Control methods used in a study of the vowels," J. Acoust. Soc. Amer., 24, 2, pp. 175–184.

Saito, S., Kato, K., and Teranishi, N. (1958) "Statistical properties of fundamental frequencies of Japanese speech voices," J. Acoust. Soc. Jap., 14, 2, pp. 111–116.

Saito, S. (1961) Fundamental Research on Transmission Quality of Japanese Phonemes, Ph.D Thesis, Nagoya Univ.

Sato, H. (1975) "Acoustic cues of male and female voice quality," Elec. Commun. Labs Tech. J., 24, 5, pp. 977–993.

Stevens, K. N., Keyser, S. J., and Kawasaki, H. (1986) "Toward a phonetic and phonological theory of redundant features," in Invariance and Variability in Speech Processes (eds. J. S. Perkel and D. H. Klatt), Lawrence Erlbaum Associates, New Jersey, pp. 426–449.

## CHAPTER 3

Fant, G. (1959) "The acoustics of speech," Proc. 3rd Int. Cong. Acoust., Sec. 3, pp. 188–201.

Fant, G. (1960) Acoustic Theory of Speech Production, Mouton's Co., Hague.

Flanagan, J. L. (1972) Speech Analysis Synthesis and Perception, 2nd Ed., Springer-Verlang, New York.

Flanagan, J. L., Ishizaka, K., and Shipley, K. L. (1975) "Synthesis of speech from a dynamic model of the vocal cords and vocal tract," Bell Systems Tech. J., 54, 3, pp. 485–506.

Flanagan, J. L., Ishizaka, K., and Shipley, K. L. (1980) "Signal models for low bit-rate coding of speech," J. Acoust. Soc. Amer., 68, 3, pp. 780–791.

Ishizaka, K. and Flanagan, J. L. (1972) "Synthesis of voiced sounds from a two-mass model of the vocal cords," Bell Systems Tech. J., 51, 6, pp. 1233–1268.

Kelly, Jr., J. L. and Lochbaum, C. (1962) "Speech synthesis," Proc. 4th Int. Cong. Acoust., G42, pp. 1–4.

Rabiner, L. R. and Schafer, R. W. (1978) Digital Processing of Speech Signals, Prentice-Hall, New Jersey.

Shirai, K. and Honda, M. (1980) "Estimation of articulatory motion from speech waves and its application for automatic recognition," in Spoken Language Generation and Understanding (ed. J. C. Simon), Reidel, Dordrecht, Holland, pp. 87–99.

Stevens K. N. (1971) "Airflow and turbulence noise for fricative and stop consonants: static considerations," J. Acoust. Soc. Amer., 50, 4(Part 2), pp. 1180–1192.

Stevens, K. N. (1977) "Physics of laryngeal behavior and larynx models," Phonetica, 34, pp. 264–279.

## CHAPTER 4

Atal, B. S. (1974) "Effectiveness of linear prediction characteristics of the speech wave for automatic speaker identification and verification," J. Acoust. Soc. Amer., 55, 6, pp. 1304–1312.

Atal, B. S. and Rabiner, L. R. (1976) "A pattern recognition approach to voice-unvoiced-silence classification with applications to speech recognition," IEEE Trans. Acoust., Speech, Signal Processing, ASSP-24, 3, pp. 201–212.

Bell, C. G., Fujisaki, H., Heinz, J. M., Stevens, K. N., and House, A. S. (1961) "Reduction of speech spectra by analysis-by-synthesis techniques," J. Acoust. Soc. Amer., 33, 12, pp. 1725–1736.

Bogert, B. P., Healy, M. J. R., and Tukey, J. W. (1963) "The frequency analysis of time-series for echoes," Proc. Symp. Time Series Analysis, Chap. 15, pp. 209–243.

Crochiere, R. E. and Flanagan, J. L. (1983) "Current perspectives in digital speech," IEEE Commun. Magazine, January, pp. 32–40.

Dudley, H. (1939) "The vocoder," Bell Labs Record, 18, 4, pp. 122–126.

Furui, S. (1981) "Cepstral analysis technique for automatic speaker verification," IEEE Trans. Acoust., Speech, Signal Processing, ASSP-29, 2, pp. 254–272.

Gold, B. and Rader, C. M. (1967) "The channel vocoder," IEEE Trans. Audio, Electroacoust., AU-15, 4, pp. 148–161.

Imai, S. and Kitamura, T. (1978) "Speech analysis synthesis system using the log magnitude approximation filter," Trans. IECEJ, J61-A, 6, pp. 527–534.

Itakura, F. and Tohkura, Y. (1978) "Feature extraction of speech signal and its application to data compression," Joho-shori, 19, 7, pp. 644–656.

Itakura, F. (1981) "Speech analysis-synthesis based on spectrum encoding," J. Acoust. Soc. Jap., 37, 5, pp. 197–203.

Markel, J. D. (1972) "The SIFT algorithm for fundamental frequency estimation," IEEE Trans. Audio. Electroacoust., AU-20, 5, pp. 367–377.

Noll, A.M. (1964) "Short-time spectrum and 'cepstrum' techniques for vocal-pitch detection," J. Acoust. Soc. Amer., 36, 2, pp. 296–302.

Noll, A. M. (1967) "Cepstrum pitch determination," J. Acoust. Soc. Amer., 41, 2, pp. 293–309.

Oppenheim, A. V. and Schafer, R. W. (1968) "Homomorphic analysis of speech," IEEE Trans. Audio, Electroacoust., AU-16,2, pp. 221–226.

Oppenheim, A. V. (1969) "Speech analysis-synthesis system based on homomorphic filtering," J. Acoust. Soc. Amer., 45, 2, pp. 458–465.

Oppenheim, A. V. and Schafer, R. W. (1975) Digital Signal Processing, Prentice-Hall, New Jersey.

Rabiner, L. R. and Schafer, R. W. (1975) Digital Processing of Speech Signals, Prentice-Hall, New Jersey.

Schroeder, M. R. (1966) "Vocoders: analysis and synthesis of speech," Proc. IEEE, 54, 5, pp. 720–734.

Shannon, C. E. and Weaver, W. (1949) The Mathematical Theory of Communication, University of Illinois Press.

Smith, C. P. (1969) "Perception of vocoder speech processed by pattern matching," J. Acoust. Soc. Amer., 46, 6(Part 2), pp. 1562–1571.

## CHAPTER 5


Atal, B. S. and Schroeder, M. R. (1968) "Predictive coding of speech signals," Proc. 6th Int. Cong. Acoust., C-5-4.

Atal, B. S. (1970) "Determination of the vocal-tract shape directly from the speech wave," J. Acoust. Soc. Amer., 47, 1(Part 1), 4K1, p. 64.

Atal, B. S. and Hanauer, S. L. (1971) "Speech analysis and synthesis by linear prediction of the speech wave," J. Acoust. Soc. Amer., 50, 2(Part 2), pp. 637–655.

Fukabayashi, T., and Suzuki, H. (1975) "Speech analysis by linear pole-zero model," Trans. IECEJ, J58-A, 5, pp. 270–277.

Ishizaki, S. (1977) "Pole-zero model order identification in speech analysis," Trans. IECEJ, J60-A, 4, pp. 423–424.

Itakura, F. and S. Saito (1968) "Analysis synthesis telephony based on the maximum likelihood method," Proc. 6th Int. Cong. Acoust., C-5-5.

Itakura, F. and Saito, S. (1971) "Digital filter techniques for speech analysis and synthesis," Proc. 7th Int. Cong. Acoust., Budapest, 25-C-1.

Itakura, F. (1975) "Line spectrum representation of linear predictor coefficients of speech signal," Trans. Committee on Speech Research, Acoust. Soc. Jap., S75–34.

Itakura, F. and Sugamura, N. (1979) "LSP speech synthesizer, its principle and implementation," Trans. Committee on Speech Research, Acoust. Soc. Jap., S79–46.

Itakura, F. (1981) "Speech analysis-synthesis based on spectrum encoding," J. Acoust. Soc. Jap., 37, 5, pp. 197–203.

Kitawaki, N., Itakura, F., and Saito, S. (1978) "Optimum coding of transmission parameters in PARCOR speech analysis synthesis system," Trans. IECEJ, 61-A, 2, pp. 119–126.

Markel, J. D. (1972) "Digital inverse filtering-A new tool for formant trajectory estimation," IEEE Trans. Audio, Electroacoust., AU-20, 2, pp. 129–137.

Markel, J. D. and Gray, Jr., A. H. (1976) Linear Prediction of Speech, Springer-Verlag, New York.

Matsuda, R. (1966) "Effects of the fluctuation characteristics of input signal on the tonal differential limen of speech transmission system containing single dip in frequency-response," Trans. IECEJ, 49, 10, pp. 1865–1871.

Morikawa, H. and Fujisaki, H. (1984) "System identification of the speech production process based on a state-space representation," IEEE Trans. Acoust., Speech, Signal Processing, ASSP-32, 2, pp. 252–262.

Nakajima, T., Suzuki, T., Ohmura, H., Ishizaki, S., and Tanaka, K. (1978) "Estimation of vocal tract area function by adaptive deconvolution and adaptive speech analysis system," J. Acoust. Soc. Jap., 34, 3, pp. 157–166.

Oppenheim, A. V., Kopec, G. E., and Tribolet, J. M. (1976) "Speech analysis by homomorphic prediction," IEEE Trans. Acoust., Speech, Signal Processing, ASSP-24, 4, pp. 327–332.

Sagayama, S. and Furui, S. (1977) "Maximum likelihood estimation of speech spectrum by pole-zero modeling," Trans. Committee on Speech Research, Acoust. Soc. Jap., S76–56.

Sagayama, S. and Itakura, F. (1981) "Composite sinusoidal modeling applied to spectral analysis of speech," Trans. IECEJ, J64–A, 2, pp. 105–112.

Sugamura, N. and Itakura, F. (1981) "Speech data compression by LSP speech analysis-synthesis technique," Trans. IECEJ, J64–A, 8, pp. 599–606.

Tohkura, Y. and Itakura, F. (1979) "Spectral sensitivity analysis of PARCOR parameters for speech data compression," IEEE Trans. Acoust., Speech, Signal Processing, ASSP-27, 3, pp. 273–280.

Tohkura, Y. (1980) Speech Quality Improvement in PARCOR Speech Analysis-Synthesis Systems, Ph.D Thesis, Tokyo Univ.

Wakita, H. (1973) "Direct estimation of the vocal tract shape by inverse filtering of acoustic speech waveforms," IEEE Trans. Audio, Electroacoust., AU-21, 5, pp. 417–427.

Wiener, N. (1966) Extrapolation Interpolation and Smoothing of Stationary Time Series, MIT Press, Cambridge, Massachusetts.

## CHAPTER 6

Abut, H., Gray, R. M., and Rebolledo, G. (1982) "Vector quantization of speech and speech-like waveforms," IEEE Trans. Acoust., Speech, Signal Processing, ASSP-30, 3, pp. 423–435.

Anderson, J. B. and Bodie, J. B. (1975) "Tree encoding of speech," IEEE Trans. Information Theory, IT-21, 4, pp. 379–387.

Atal, B. S. and Schroeder, M. R. (1970) "Adaptive predictive coding of speech signals," Bell Systems Tech. J., 49, 8, pp. 1973–1986.

Atal, B. S. and Schroeder, M. R. (1979) "Predictive coding of speech signals and subjective error criteria," IEEE Trans. Acoust., Speech, Signal Processing, ASSP-27, 3, pp. 247–254.

Atal, B. S. and Remde, J. R. (1982) "A new model of LPC excitation for producing natural-sounding speech at low bit rates," Proc. IEEE Int. Conf. Acoust., Speech, Signal Processing, Paris, France, pp. 614–617.

Atal, B. S. and Schroeder, M. R. (1984) "Stochastic coding of speech signals at very low bit rates," Proc. Int. Conf. Commun., Pt. 2, pp. 1610–1613.

Atal, B. S. and Rabiner, L. R. (1986) "Speech research directions," AT&T Tech. J. 65, 5, pp. 75–88.

Buzo, A., Gray, Jr., A. H., Gray, R. M., and Markel, J. D. (1980) "Speech coding based upon vector quantization," IEEE Trans. Acoust., Speech, Signal Processing, ASSP-28, 5, pp. 562–574.

Crochiere, R. E., Webber, S. A., and Flanagan, J. L. (1976) "Digital coding of speech in sub-bands," Bell Systems Tech. J., 55, 8, pp. 1069–1085.

Crochiere, R. E., Cox, R. V., and Johnston, J. D. (1982) "Real-time speech coding," IEEE Trans. Commun., COM-30, 4, pp. 621–634.

Cummiskey, P., Jayant, N. S., and Flanagan, J. L. (1973) "Adaptive quantization in differential PCM coding of speech," Bell Systems Tech. J., 52, 7, pp. 1105–1118.

Cuperman, V. and Gersho, A. (1982) "Adaptive differential vector coding of speech," Conf. Rec., 1982 IEEE Global Commun. Conf., Miami, FL, pp. E6.6.1–E6.6.5.

David, Jr., E. E., Schroeder, M. R., Logan, B. F., and Prestigiacomo, A. J. (1962) "Voice-excited vocoders for practical speech bandwidth reduction," IRE Trans. Information Theory, IT-8, 5, pp. S101–S105.

Esteban, D. and Galand, C. (1977) "Application of quadrature mirror filters to split band voice schemes," Proc. IEEE Int. Conf. Acoust., Speech, Signal Processing, Hartford, CT, pp. 191–195.

Farges, E. P. and Clements, M. A. (1986) "Hidden Markov models applied to very low bit rate speech coding," Proc. IEEE Int. Conf. Acoust., Speech, Signal Processing, Tokyo, Japan, pp. 433–436.

Fehn, H. G. and Noll, P. (1982) "Multipath search coding of stationary signals with applications to speech," IEEE Trans. Commun., COM-30, 4, pp. 687–701.

Flanagan, J. L., Schroeder, M. R., Atal, B. S., Crochiere, R. E., Jayant, N. S., and Tribolet, J. M. (1979) "Speech coding," IEEE Trans. Commun., COM-27, 4, pp. 710–737.

Foster, J., Gray, R. M., and Dunham, M. O. (1985) "Finite-state vector quantization for waveform coding," IEEE Trans. Information Theory, IT-31, 3, pp. 348–359.

Gersho, A. and Cuperman, V. (1983) "Vector quantization: A pattern-matching technique for speech coding," IEEE Commun. Magazine, December, pp. 15–21.

Honda, M. and Itakura, F. (1984) "Bit allocation in time and frequency domains for predictive coding of speech," IEEE Trans. Acoust., Speech, Signal Processing, ASSP-32, 3, pp. 465–473.

Jayant, N. S. (1970) "Adaptive delta modulation with a one-bit memory," Bell systems Tech. J., 49, 3, pp. 321–342.

Jayant, N. S. (1973) "Adaptive quantization with a one-word memory," Bell Systems Tech. J., 52, 7, pp. 1119–1144.

Jayant, N. S. (1974) "Digital coding of speech waveforms: PCM, DPCM, and DM quantizers," Proc. IEEE, 62, 5, pp. 611–632.

Jayant, N. S. and Noll, P. (1984) Digital Coding of Waveforms, Prentice-Hall, New Jersey.

Jayant, N. S. and Ramamoorthy, V. (1986). "Adaptive Postfiltering of 16 kb/s-ADPCM Speech," Proc. IEEE Int. Conf. Acoust., Speech, Signal Processing, Tokyo, Japan, 16.4, pp. 829–832.

Jelinek, F. and Anderson, J. B. (1971) "Instrumentable tree encoding of information sources," IEEE Trans. Information Theory, IT-17, 1, pp. 118–119.

Juang, B. H. and Gray, Jr., A. H. (1982) "Multiple stage vector quantization for speech coding," Proc. IEEE Int. Conf. Acoust., Speech, Signal Processing, Paris, France, pp. 597–600.

Juang, B. H. (1986) "Design and performance of trellis vector quantizers for speech signals," Proc. IEEE Int. Conf. Acoust., Speech, Signal Processing, Tokyo, Japan, pp. 437–440.

Kitawaki, N., Itoh, K., Honda, M., and Kakeki, K. (1982) "Comparison of objective speech quality measures for voiceband codecs," Proc. IEEE Int. Conf. Acoust., Speech, Signal Processing, Paris, France, pp. 1000–1003.

Krasner, M. A. (1979) "Digital encoding of speech and audio signals based on the perceptual requirement of the auditory system," Lincoln Lab. Tech. Rep., 535.

Linde, Y., Buzo, A., and Gray, R. M. (1980) "An algorithm for vector quantizer design," IEEE Trans. Commun., COM-28, 1, pp. 84–95.

Lloyd, S. P. (1957) "Least squares quantization in PCM," Institute of Mathematical Statistics Meeting, Atlantic City, NJ, September; also (1982) IEEE Trans. Information Theory, IT-28, 2(Part I), pp. 129–136.

Makhoul, J. and Berouti, M. (1979) "Adaptive noise spectral shaping and entropy coding in predictive coding of speech," IEEE Trans. Acoust., Speech, Signal Processing, ASSP-27, 1, pp. 63–73.

Malah, D., Crochiere, R. E., and Cox, R. V. (1981) "Performance of transform and subband coding systems combined with harmonic scaling of speech," IEEE Trans. Acoust., Speech, Signal Processing, ASSP-29, 2, pp. 273–283.

Max, J. (1960) "Quantizing for minimum distortion," IRE Trans. Information Theory, IT-6, 1, 3, pp. 7–12.

Moriya, T. and Honda, M. (1986) "Speech coder using phase

equalization and vector quantization," Proc. IEEE Int. Conf. Acoust., Speech, Signal Processing, Tokyo, Japan, pp. 1701–1704.

Noll, P. (1975) "A comparative study of various schemes for speech encoding," Bell Systems Tech. J., 54, 9, pp. 1597–1614.

Ozawa, K., Araseki, T., and Ono, S. (1982) "Speech coding based on multi-pulse excitation method," Trans. Committee on Communication Systems, IECEJ, CS82–161.

Ozawa, K. and Araseki, T. (1986) "High quality multi-pulse speech coder with pitch prediction," Proc. IEEE Int. Conf. Acoust., Speech, Signal Processing, Tokyo, Japan, pp. 1689–1692.

Rabiner, L. R. and Schafer, R. W. (1978) Digital Processing of Speech Signals, Prentice-Hall, New Jersey.

Richards, D. L. (1973) Telecommunication by Speech, Butterworths, London.

Roucos, S., Schwartz, R., and Makhoul, J. (1982a) "Vector quantization for very-low-rate coding of speech," Conf. Rec. 1982 IEEE Global Commun. Conf., Miami, FL, pp. E6.2.1–E6.2.5.

Roucos, S., Schwartz, R., and Makhoul, J. (1982b) "Segment quantization for very-low-rate speech coding," Proc. IEEE Int. Conf. Acoust., Speech, Signal Processing, Paris, France pp. 1565–1568.

Schafer, R. W. and Rabiner, L. R. (1975) "Digital representation of speech signals," Proc. IEEE, 63, 1, pp. 662–677.

Schroeder, M. R. and Atal, B. S. (1982) "Speech coding using efficient block codes," Proc. IEEE Int. Conf. Acoust., Speech Signal Processing, Paris, France, pp. 1668–1671.

Schroeder, M. R. and Atal, B. S. (1985) "Code-excided linear prediction (CELP): high-quality speech at very low bit rates," Proc. IEEE Int. Conf. Acoust., Speech, Signal Processing, Tampa, FL, pp. 937–940.

Shiraki, Y. and Honda, M. (1986) "Very low bit rate speech coding based on joint segmentation and variable length segment quantizer," Proc. Acoust. Soc. Amer. Meeting, J. Acoust. Soc. Amer., Supple. 1, 79, p. S94.

Smith, C. D. (1969) "Perception of vocoder speech processed by pattern matching," J. Acoust. Soc. Amer., 46, 6(Part 2), pp. 1562–1571.

Stewart, L. C., Gray, R. M., and Linde, Y. (1982) "The design of trellis waveform coders," IEEE Trans. Commun., COM-30, 4, pp. 702–710.

Tribolet, J. M. and Crochiere, R. E. (1978) "A vocoder-driven adaptation strategy for low bit-rate adaptive transform coding of speech," Proc. Int. Conf. Digital Signal Processing, Florence, Italy, pp. 638–642.

Tribolet, J. M. and Crochiere, R. E. (1979) "Frequency domain coding of speech," IEEE Trans. Acoust., Speech, Signal Processing, ASSP-27, 5, pp. 512–530.

Tribolet, J. M. and Crochiere, R. E. (1980) "A modified adaptive transform coding scheme with post-processing-enchancement," Proc. IEEE Int. Conf. Acoust., Speech, Signal Processing, Denver, Colorado, pp. 336–339.

Watanabe, T., Itoh, K., and Kitawaki, N. (1982) "Comparison of performance on voiceband codecs by several speech quality measures," Trans. Committee on Speech Research, Acoust. Soc. Jap., S82–48.

Wong, D. Y., Juang, B. H., and Gray, Jr., A. H. (1982) "An 800 bit/s vector quantization LPC vocoder," IEEE Trans. Acoust., Speech, Signal Processing, ASSP-30, 5, pp. 770–780.

Wong, D. Y., Juang, B. H., and Cheng, D. Y. (1983) "Very low data rate speech compression with LPC vector and matrix quantization," Proc. IEEE Int. Conf. Acoust., Speech, Signal Processing, pp. 65–68.

Zelinski, R. and Noll, P. (1977) "Adaptive transform coding of speech signals," IEEE Trans. Acoust., Speech, Signal Processing, ASSP-25, 4, pp. 299–309.

## CHAPTER 7

Allen, J., Carlson, R., Granstrom, B., Hunnicutt, S., Klatt, D., and Pisoni, D. (1979) MITalk-79: Conversion of Unrestricted English Text to Speech, MIT.

Coker, C. H., Umeda, N., and Browman, C. P. (1978) "Automatic synthesis from ordinary English text," IEEE Trans. Audio, Electroacoust., AU-21, 3, pp. 293–298.

Crochiere, R. E. and Flanagan, J. L. (1986) "Speech processing: An evolving technology," AT&T Tech. J., 65, 5, pp. 2–11.

Dixon, N. R. and Maxey, H. D. (1968) "Terminal analog synthesis of continuous speech using the diphone method of segment assembly," IEEE Trans. Audio, Electroacoust., AU-16, 1, pp. 40–50.

Flanagan, J. L. (1972) "Voices of men and machines,: J. Acoust. Soc. Amer., 51, 5(Part 1), pp. 1375–1387.

Hirose, K., Fujisaki, H., and Kawai, H. (1986) "Generation of prosodic symbols for rule-synthesis of connected speech of Japanese," Proc. IEEE Int. Conf. Acoust., Speech, Signal Processing, Tokyo, 45.4, pp. 2415–2418.

Klatt, D. H. (1980) "Software for a cascade/parallel formant synthesizer," J. Acoust. Soc. Amer., 67, 3, pp. 971–995.

Klatt, D. H. (1987) "Review of text-to-speech conversion for English," J. Acoust. Soc. Amer., 82, 3, pp. 737–793.

Lovins, J. B., Macchi, M. J., and Fujimura, O. (1979) "A demisyllable inventory for speech synthesis," 97th Meeting of Acoust. Soc. Amer., YY4.

Sagisaka, Y. and Tohkura, Y. (1984) "Phoneme duration control for speech synthesis by rule," Trans. IECEJ, J67-A, 7, pp. 629–636.

Sagisaka, Y. and Sato, H. (1986) "Some accentual characteristics in Japanese phrases and long compounds," J. Acoust. Soc. Jap., 7, 1, pp. 65–74.

Sato, H. (1978) "Speech synthesis on the basis of PARCOR-VCV concatenation units," Trans. IECEJ, J61-D, 11, pp. 858–865.

Sato, H. (1984a) "Speech synthesis using CVC concatenation units and excitation waveforms elements," Trans. Committee on Speech Research, Acoust. Soc. Jap., S83–69.

Sato, H. (1984b) "Japanese text-to-speech conversion system," Rev. of the Elec. Commun. Labs., 32, 2, pp. 179–187.

## CHAPTER 8

Adams, D. A. and Bisiani, R. (1986) "The Carnegie-Mellon University distributed speech recognition system," Speech Technology, March/April, pp. 14–23.

Aldefeld, B., Rabiner, L. R., Rosenberg, A. E., and Wilpon, J. G. (1980) "Automated directory listing retrieval system based on isolated word recognition," Proc. IEEE, 68, 11, pp. 1364–1379.

Alleva, F., Bisiani, R., Forin, S., and Lerner, R. (1986) "A distributed system architecture for speech recognition," Proc. IEEE Int Conf. Acoust., Speech, Signal Processing, Tokyo, Japan, 30.4, pp. 1573–1576.

Bahl, L. R. and Jelinek, F. (1975) "Decoding for channels with insertions, deletions, and substitutions, with applications to speech recognition," IEEE Trans. Information Theory, IT-21, pp. 404–411.

Bahl, L. R., Jelinek, F., and Mercer, R. L. (1983) "A maximum likelihood approach to continuous speech recognition," IEEE Trans. Pattern Analysis, Machine Intelligence, PAMI-5, 2, pp. 179–190.

Baker, J. K. (1975) "Stochastic modeling for automatic speech understanding," in Speech Recognition (ed. D. R. Reddy), pp. 521–542.

Baum, L. E. (1972) "An inequality and associated maximization technique in statistical estimation for probabilistic functions of a Markov process," Inequalities, 3, pp. 1–8.

Bellman, R. (1957) Dynamic Programming, Princeton Univ. Press, New Jersey.

Bridle, J. S. and Brown, M. D. (1979) "Connected word recognition using whole word templates," Proc. Inst. Acoust. Autumn Conf., pp. 25–28.

Chow, Y. L., Dunham, M. O., Kimball, O. A., Krasner, M. A., Kubala, G. F., Makhoul, J., Price, P. J., and Roucos, S. (1987) "BYBLOS: the BBN continuous speech recognition system," Proc. IEEE Int. Conf. Acoust., Speech, Signal Processing, Dallas, TX, 3.7, pp. 89–92.

Davis, K. H., Biddulph, R., and Balashek, S. (1952) "Automatic recognition of spoken digits," J. Acoust. Soc. Amer., 24, 6, pp. 637–642.

Fujisaki, H., Takamura, F., and Sato, Y. (1977) "Non-uniform sampling of features and its application to spoken word recognition," Trans. Committee on Speech Research, Acoust. Soc. Jap., S77–12.

Furui, S. (1974) "On the method of separating the personal and phonemic information in speech wave," Trans. Committee on Speech Research, Acoust. Soc. Jap., S74–17.

Furui, S. (1975) "Learning and normalization of the talker differences in the recognition of spoken words," Trans. Committee on Speech Research, Acoust. Soc. Jap., S75–25.

Furui, S. (1976) "Effect of intersession variability of speech spectrum on spoken word recognition," Proc. Fall Meeting of Acoust. Soc. Jap., 2-4-2.

Furui, S. (1978) Research on Individual Information in Speech Waves, Ph.D Thesis, Tokyo University.

Furui, S. (1980) "A training procedure for isolated word recognition systems," IEEE Trans. Acoust., Speech, Signal Processing, ASSP-28, 2, pp. 129–136.

Furui, S. (1982) "A new technique for spoken Japanese syllable recognition and its application to large vocabulary word recognition," Trans. IECEJ, J65-A, 2, pp. 175–182.

Furui, S. (1986a) "Speaker-independent isolated word recognition using dynamic features of speech spectrum," IEEE Trans. Acoust., Speech, Signal Processing, ASSP-34, 1, pp. 52–59.

Furui, S. (1986b) "On the role of spectral transition for speech perception," J. Acoust. Soc. Amer., 80, 4, pp. 1016–1025.

Furui, S. (1987) "A VQ-based preprocessor using cepstral dynamic features for large vocabulary word recognition," Proc. IEEE Int. Conf. Acoust., Speech, Signal Processing, Dallas, TX, 27.2, pp. 1127–1130.

Goodman, R. G. (1976) Analysis of Languages for Man-Machine Voice Communication, Ph.D Thesis, Carnegie-Mellon University.

Gray, Jr., A. H. and Markel, J. D. (1976) "Distance measures for speech processing," IEEE Trans. Acoust., Speech, Signal Processing, ASSP-24, 5, pp. 380–391.

Hayamizu, S. and Oka, R. (1984) "Experimental studies on the connected words recognition using continuous dynamic programming," Trans. IECEJ, J67-D, 6, pp. 677–684.

Itakura, F. (1975) "Minimum prediction residual principle applied to speech recognition," IEEE Trans. Acoust., Speech, Signal Processing, ASSP-23, 1, pp. 67–72.

Jelinek, F. (1976) "Continuous speech recognition by statistical methods," Proc. IEEE, 64, 4, pp. 532–556.

Juang, B. H., Rabiner, L. R., Levinson, S. E., and Sondhi, M. M. (1985) "Recent developments in the application of hidden Markov models to speaker-independent isolated word recognition," Proc. IEEE Int. Conf. Acoust., Speech, Signal Processing, Tampa, FL, 1.3, pp. 9–12.

Kato, K. and Kawahara, H. (1984) "Adaptability to individual talkers in monosyllabic speech perception," Trans. Committee on Hearing Research, Acoust. Soc. Jap., H84-3.

Klatt, D. H. (1982) "Prediction of perceived phonetic distance from critical-band spectra: A first step," Proc. IEEE Int. Conf. Acoust., Speech, Signal Processing, Paris, France, S11.1, pp. 1278–1281.

Klatt, D. H. (1977) "Review of the ARPA speech understanding project," J. Acoust. Soc. Amer., 62, 6, pp. 1345–1366.

Kohda, M., Hashimoto, S., and Saito, S. (1972) "Spoken digit mechanical recognition system," Trans. IECEJ, 55-D, 3, pp. 186–193.

Lea, W. A. (Ed.) (1980) Trends in Speech Recognition, Prentice-Hall, New Jersey.

Lesser, V. R., Fennell, R. D., Erman, L. D., and Reddy, D. R. (1975) "Organization of the Hearsay II speech understanding system," IEEE Trans. Acoust., Speech, Signal Processing, ASSP-23, 1, pp. 11–24.

Lowerre, B. T. (1976) The Harpy Speech Recognition System, Ph.D Thesis, Computer Science Department, Carnegie-Mellon University.

Matsumoto, H. and Wakita, H. (1986) "Vowel normalization by frequency warped spectral matching," Speech Communication, 5, 2, pp. 239–251.

Matsunaga, S. and Shikano, K. (1985) "Speech recognition based on top-down and bottom-up phoneme recognition," Trans. IECEJ, J68-D, 9, pp. 1641–1648.

Myers, C. S. and Rabiner, L. R. (1981) "Connected digit recognition using a level-building DTW algorithm," IEEE Trans. Acoust., Speech, Signal Processing, ASSP-29, 3, pp. 351–363.

Nakagawa, S. (1983) "A connected spoken word or syllable recognition algorithm by pattern matching," Trans. IECEJ, J66-D, 6, pp. 637–644.

Nakatsu, R., Nagashima, H., Kojima, J., and Ishii, N. (1983) "A speech recognition method for telephone voice," Trans. IECEJ, J66-D, 4, pp. 377–384.

Nocerino, N., Soong, F. K., Rabiner, L. R., and Klatt, D. H. (1985) "Comparative study of several distortion measures for speech recognition," Speech Communication, 4, 4, pp. 317–331.

Paliwal, K. K. (1982) "On the performance of the quefrency-weighted cepstral coefficients in vowel recognition," Speech Communication, 1, 2, pp. 151–154.

Rabiner, L. R., Levinson, S. E., Rosenberg, A. E., and Wilpon, J. G. (1979a) "Speaker-independent recognition of isolated words using clustering techniques," IEEE Trans. Acoust., Speech, Signal Processing, ASSP-27, 4, pp. 336–349.

Rabiner, L. R. and Wilpon, J. G. (1979b) "Speaker-independent isolated word recognition for a moderate size (54 word) vocabulary," IEEE Trans. Acoust., Speech, Signal Processing, ASSP-27, 6, pp. 583–587.

Rabiner, L. R., Levinson, S. E., and Sondhi, M. M. (1983) "On the application of vector quantization and hidden Markov models to speaker-independent, isolated word recognition," Bell Systems Tech. J., 62, 4, pp. 1075–1105.

Rabiner, L. R. and Levinson, S. L. (1985) "A speaker-independent, syntax-directed, connected word recognition system based on hidden Markov models and level building," IEEE Trans. Acoust., Speech, Signal Processing, ASSP-33, 3, pp. 561–573.

Rabiner, L. R. and Juang, B. H. (1986) "An introduction to hidden Markov models," IEEE ASSP Magazine, 3, 1, pp. 4–16.

Reddy, D. R. (1980) "Machine models of speech perception," in

Perception and Production of Fluent Speech (ed. R. A. Cole), Lawrence Erlbaum Associates, New Jersey, pp. 215–242.

Rosenberg, A. E., Rabiner, L. R., and Wilpon, J. G. (1980) "Recognition of spoken spelled names for directory assistance using speaker-independent templates," Bell Systems Tech. J., 59, 4, pp. 571–592.

Roucos, S. and Dunham, M. O. (1987) "A stochastic segment model for phoneme-based continuous speech recognition," Proc. IEEE Int. Conf. Acoust., Speech, Signal Processing, Dallas, TX, 3.3, pp. 73–76.

Sakai, T. and Tabata, K. (1973) "Multivariate statistical analysis of VCV Syllables," Trans. IECEJ, 56-D, 1, pp. 63–70.

Sakoe, H. and Chiba, S. (1971) "Recognition of continuously spoken words based on time-normalization by dynamic programming," J. Acoust. Soc. Jap., 27, 9, pp. 483–500.

Sakoe, H. and Chiba, S. (1978) "Dynamic programming algorithm optimization for spoken word recognition," IEEE Trans. Acoust., Speech, Signal Processing, ASSP-26, 1, pp. 43–49.

Sakoe, H. (1979) "Two-level DP-matching—A dynamic programming-based pattern matching algorithm for connected word recognition," IEEE Trans. Acoust., Speech, Signal Processing, ASSP-27, 6, pp. 588–595.

Sakoe, H. and Watari, M. (1981) "Clockwise propagating DP-matching algorithm for word recognition," Trans. Committee on Speech Research, Acoust. Soc. Jap., S81–65.

Sakoe, H. (1981) "Computation and memory improvements of automaton controlled two-level DP-matching continuous speech recognition algorithm," Trans. Committee on Pattern Recognition and Language, IECEJ, PRL81–25.

Shikano, K. (1982) "Spoken word recognition based upon vector quantization of input speech," Trans. Committee on Speech Research, Acoust. Soc. Jap., S82–60.

Shikano, K. and Aikawa, K. (1982) "Staggered array DP matching," Trans. Committee on Speech Research, Acoust. Soc. Jap., S82-15.

Shikano, K., Lee, K.-F, and Reddy, R. (1986) "Speaker adaptation through vector quantization," Proc. IEEE Int. Conf. Acoust., Speech, Signal Processing, Tokyo, Japan, 49.5, pp. 2643–2646.

Slutsker, G. (1968) "Non-linear method of analysis of speech signal," Trudy N. I. I. R.

Soong, F. K. and Rosenberg, A. E. (1986) "On the use of instantaneous and transitional spectral information in speaker recognition," Proc. IEEE Int. Conf. Acoust., Speech, Signal Processing, Tokyo, Japan, 17.5, pp. 877–880.

Sugamura, N. and Furui, S. (1982) "Large vocabulary word recognition using pseudo-phoneme templates," Trans. IECEJ, J65-D, 8, pp. 1041–1048.

Sugamura, N., Shikano, K., and Furui, S. (1983) "Isolated word recognition using phoneme-like templates," Proc. IEEE Int. Conf. Acoust., Speech, Signal Processing, Boston, MA, 16.3, pp. 723–726.

Sugamura, N. and Furui, S. (1984) "Isolated word recognition using strings of phoneme-like templates (SPLIT)," J. Acoust. Soc. Japan, (E)5, 4, pp. 243–252.

Sugiyama, M. and Shikano, K. (1981) "LPC peak weighted spectral matching measures," Trans. IECEJ, J64-A, 5, pp. 409–416.

Sugiyama, M. and Shikano, K. (1982) "Frequency weighted LPC spectral matching measures," Trans. IECEJ, J65-A, 9, pp. 965–972.

Sugiyama, M. and Shikano, K. (1983) "WLR measure applied to word recognition," Trans. IECEJ, J66-D, 4, pp. 385–391.

Sugiyama, M. (1986) "Unsupervised speaker adaptation methods for vowel templates," Proc. IEEE Int. Conf. Acoust., Speech, Signal Processing, Tokyo, Japan, 49.4, pp. 2639–2642.

Tohkura, Y. (1986) "A weighted cepstral distance measure for speech recognition," Proc. IEEE Int. Conf. Acoust., Speech, Signal Processing, Tokyo, Japan, 14.17, pp. 761–764.

Velichko, V. and Zagoruyko, N. (1970) "Automatic recognition of 200 words," Int. J. Man-Machine Studies, 2, pp. 223–234.

Vintsyuk, T. K. (1968) "Speech recognition by dynamic programming," Kybernetika, 4, 1, pp. 81–88.

Vintsyuk, T. K. (1971) "Element-wise recognition of continuous speech composed of words from a specified dictionary," Kibernetika, 2, pp. 133–143.

Viterbi, A. J. (1967) "Error bounds for convolutional codes and an asymptotically optimal decoding algorithm," IEEE Trans. Information Theory, IT-13, pp. 260—269.

Watanabe, T., Watari, M., Chiba, S., Takahashi, T., Ohfuchi, T., Uenoyama, T., Hoyano, A., and Saki, K. (1981) "Speaker independent speech recognizer SR-1000 series," Proc. Spring Meeting of Acoust. Soc. Jap., 3-1-24.

## CHAPTER 9

Atal, B. S. (1972) "Automatic speaker recognition based on pitch contours," J. Acoust. Soc. Amer., 52, 6(Part 2), pp. 1687—1697.

Atal, B. S. (1974) "Effectiveness of linear prediction characteristics of the speech wave for automatic speaker identification and verification," J. Acoust. Soc. Amer., 55, 6, pp. 1304—1312.

Atal, B. S. (1976) "Automatic recognition of speakers from their voices," Proc. IEEE, 64, 4, pp. 460—475.

Doddington, G. R. (1974) "Speaker verification," Rome Air Development Center, Tech Rep., RADC 74—179.

Doddington, G. R. (1976) "Personal identity verification using voice," Proc. ELECTRO-76, 22-4, pp. 1—5.

Furui, S., Itakura, F., and Saito, S. (1972) "Talker recognition by longtime averaged speech spectrum," Trans. IECEJ, 55-A, 10, pp. 549—556.

Furui, S. (1978) Research on Individuality Information in Speech Waves, Ph.D Thesis, Tokyo University.

Furui, S. (1981a) "Comparison of speaker recognition methods using statistical features and dynamic features," IEEE Trans. Acoust., Speech, Signal Processing, ASSP-29, 3, pp. 342—350.

Furui, S. (1981b) "Cepstral analysis technique for automatic speaker verification," IEEE Trans. Acoust., Speech, Signal Processing, ASSP-29, 2, pp. 254—272.

Furui, S. (1982) "Speaker recognition by statistical features of cepstral parameters," Trans. IECEJ, J65-A, 2, pp. 183—190.

Furui, S. (1986) "Research on individuality features in speech waves and automatic speaker recognition techniques," Speech Communication, 5, 2, pp. 183–197.

Kersta, L. G. (1962) "Voiceprint identification," Nature, 196, pp. 1253–1257.

Li, K. P. and Wrench, Jr., E. H. (1983) "An approach to text-independent speaker recognition with short utterances," Proc. IEEE Int. Conf. Acoust., Speech, Signal Processing, Boston, MA, 12.9, pp. 555–558.

National Research Council (1979) On the Theory and Practice of Voice Identification, Washington, D.C.

Rosenberg, A. E. and Sambur, M. R. (1975) "New techniques for automatic speaker verification," IEEE Trans. Acoust., Speech, Signal Processing, ASSP-23, 2, pp. 169–176.

Rosenberg, A. E. (1976a) "Automatic speaker verification: a review," Proc. IEEE, 64, 4, pp. 475–487.

Rosenberg, A. E. (1976b) "Evaluation of an automatic speaker-verification system over telephone lines," Bell Systems Tech. J., 55, 6, pp. 723–744.

Sambur, M. R. (1975) "Selection of acoustic features for speaker identification," IEEE Trans. Acoust., Speech, Signal Processing, ASSP-23, 2, pp. 176–182.

Sambur, M. R. (1976) "Speaker recognition using orthogonal linear prediction," IEEE Trans. Acoust., Speech, Signal Processing, ASSP-24, 4, pp. 283–289.

Soong, F. K., Rosenberg, A. E., Rabiner, L. R., and Juang, B. H. (1985) "A vector quantization approach to speaker recognition," Proc. IEEE Int. Conf. Acoust., Speech, Signal Processing, Tampa, FL, 11.4, pp. 387–390.

Tosi, O., Oyer, H., Lashbrook, W., Pedrey, C., Nicol, J., and Nash, E. (1972) "Experiment on voice identification," J. Acoust. Soc. Amer., 51, 6(Part 2), pp. 2030–2043.


## APPENDICES


Gray, R. M. (1984) "Vector quantization," IEEE ASSP Magazine, 1, 2, pp. 4–29.

Lippmann, R. P. (1987) "An introduction to computing with neural nets," IEEE ASSP Magazine, 4, 2, pp. 4–22.

Makhoul, J., Roucos, S., and Gish, H. (1985) "Vector quantization," Proc. IEEE, 73, 11, pp. 1551–1588.

Parsons, T. W. (1986) Voice and Speech Processing, McGraw-Hill, New York, pp. 274–275.

Rabiner, L. R. and Juang, B. H. (1986) "An introduction to hidden Markov models," IEEE ASSP Magazine, 3, 1, pp. 4–16.

Shiraki, Y. and Honda, M. (1988) "LPC speech coding based on variable-length segment quantization," IEEE Trans. Acoust., Speech, Signal Processing, ASSP-36, 9, pp. 1437–1444.

# Index

J



K



L

## Q



## R



## S